Anti-Black Racism in America

SERIES IN POLITICAL PSYCHOLOGY

Series Editor
John T. Jost

Editorial Board
Mahzarin Banaji, Gian Vittorio Caprara, Aleksandra Cichocka, Christopher Federico, Donald P. Green, John Hibbing, Jon Krosnick, Arie Kruglanski, Jaime L. Napier, David P. Redlawsk, David Sears, Phil Tetlock, Tom Tyler

Image Bite Politics: News and the Visual Framing of Elections
Maria Elizabeth Grabe and Erik Page Bucy

Social and Psychological Bases of Ideology and System Justification
John T. Jost, Aaron C. Kay, and Hulda Thorisdottir

The Political Psychology of Democratic Citizenship
Eugene Borgida, Christopher M. Federico, and John L. Sullivan

On Behalf of Others: The Psychology of Care in a Global World
Sarah Scuzzarello, Catarina Kinnvall, and Kristen R. Monroe

The Obamas and a (Post) Racial America?
Gregory S. Parks and Matthew W. Hughey

Ideology, Psychology, and Law
Jon Hanson

Representing Red and Blue: How the Culture Wars Change the Way Citizens Speak and Politicians Listen
David C. Barker and Christopher Jan Carman

On Voter Competence
Paul Goren

The Ambivalent Partisan: How Critical Loyalty Promotes Democracy
Howard G. Lavine, Christopher D. Johnston, and Marco R. Steenbergen

The Impacts of Lasting Occupation: Lessons from Israeli Society
Daniel Bar-Tal and Izhak Schnell

Competing Motives in the Partisan Mind: How Loyalty and Responsiveness Shape Party Identification and Democracy
Eric W. Groenendyk

Personalizing Politics and Realizing Democracy
Gian Vittorio Caprara and Michele Vecchione

Disenchantment with Democracy: A Psychological Perspective
Janusz Reykowski

Hot Contention, Cool Abstention: Positive Emotions and Protest Behavior during the Arab Spring
Stephanie Dornschneider

Divided: Open-Mindedness and Dogmatism in a Polarized World
Victor Ottati and Chadly Stern

Hope amidst Conflict: Philosophical and Psychological Explorations
Oded Adomi Leshem

Ideology and the Microfoundations of Conflict: From Human Needs to Intergroup Violence
Veronika Müller and Thomas Gries

Political Persuasion: The Use of Values in Communication
Thomas E. Nelson

Anti-Black Racism in America: Is It Declining?
Thomas F. Pettigrew

Anti-Black Racism in America

Is It Declining?

Thomas F. Pettigrew

OXFORD
UNIVERSITY PRESS

Oxford University Press is a department of the University of Oxford.
It furthers the University's objective of excellence in research, scholarship,
and education by publishing worldwide. Oxford is a registered trade mark of
Oxford University Press in the UK and in certain other countries.

Published in the United States of America by Oxford University Press
198 Madison Avenue, New York, NY 10016, United States of America.

© Oxford University Press 2025

All rights reserved. No part of this publication may be reproduced, stored in a retrieval system, transmitted, used for text and data mining, or used for training artificial intelligence, in any form or by any means, without the prior permission in writing of Oxford University Press, or as expressly permitted by law, by license or under terms agreed with the appropriate reprographics rights organization. Inquiries concerning reproduction outside the scope of the above should be sent to the Rights Department, Oxford University Press, at the address above.

You must not circulate this work in any other form
and you must impose this same condition on any acquirer.

Library of Congress Cataloging-in-Publication Data
Names: Pettigrew, Thomas F., 1931- author.
Title: Anti-Black racism in America : is it declining? / Thomas F. Pettigrew.
Description: New York, NY : Oxford University Press, [2025] |
Series: Series in political psychology |
Includes bibliographical references and index.
Identifiers: LCCN 2024044916 (print) | LCCN 2024044917 (ebook) |
ISBN 9780197803103 (hardback) | ISBN 9780197803127 (epub) |
ISBN 9780197803134
Subjects: LCSH: Racism against Black people—United States. |
African Americans—Social conditions. |
Social change—United States. | United States—Race relations.
Classification: LCC E185.61 .P478 2025 (print) | LCC E185.61 (ebook) |
DDC 305.896/073—dc23/eng/20250122
LC record available at https://lccn.loc.gov/2024044916
LC ebook record available at https://lccn.loc.gov/2024044917

DOI: 10.1093/9780197803134.001.0001

Printed by Integrated Books International, United States of America

The manufacturer's authorised representative in the EU for product safety is Oxford University Press España S.A. of El Parque Empresarial San Fernando de Henares, Avenida de Castilla, 2 – 28830 Madrid (www.oup.es/en or product.safety@oup.com). OUP España S.A. also acts as importer into Spain of products made by the manufacturer.

I wish to dedicate this book to my son, Dr. Mark Fraser Pettigrew, and my two grandchildren, Aysha Ann Pettigrew and Yousif Ian Pettigrew. I am very proud of them. And without their help and encouragement, this book would never have been completed. I also benefited from the advice of the series editor, Professor John Jost, and the review comments from former doctoral students. I also wish to thank Desiree Anne Ryan for her help with references, and the four anonymous reviewers for Oxford University Press for their helpful suggestions.

Contents

Introduction: Is It Declining?	1
1. Prejudice: Implicit and Explicit Racial Mindsets	11
2. Racial Discrimination	33
3. The Power of Racial Norms	43
4. Race and Economics	49
5. Race and Education	69
6. Race, Crime, and Justice	89
7. Race and Health	105
8. Race and Politics	122
9. Interracial Contact	143
10. Race and Housing	155
11. So, Has American Racism Declined?	172
12. The Need for Reparations	179
Bibliography	194
Index	228

Introduction

Is It Declining?

One brisk winter day, Katherine Brown set out from Washington, D.C., to cross the Potomac River and visit Alexandria, Virginia. Little did she realize that her 25-cent round-trip rail ticket entitled her to fire an opening shot in the long, post-slavery struggle for racial desegregation. For this was 1868, Brown was a Black American, and her trip was to prove historic (*U.S. Supreme Court Reports*, 1873).

She enjoyed a quiet and pleasant ride over to Virginia, but her attempt to return the same day was neither quiet nor pleasant. No segregation was practiced on the trains leaving Washington, but trains leaving Virginia had a special car for all passengers "of color." This "Jim Crow" car, as might be expected, was placed closest to the steam locomotive, where noise and cinders had to be endured. Brown, however, did not take her seat in the Jim Crow car. Instead, she made herself comfortable in a rear coach reserved for White people.

A depot attendant spotted her and told her she must leave the "white car" and go to the Jim Crow car. She refused to leave, "whereupon the man attempted to put her out by great force and violence, with insults and indignities." According to her lawyers, Brown "was compelled to employ a physician and remain under treatment."

For redress, Brown turned to the courts. She sued the railroad for $20,000 in the District of Columbia's Supreme Court. The Reconstruction jury ruled in her favor and awarded her $1,500 (about $35,000 in 2024 dollars). The railroad's motion for a new trial was denied, so the defendant carried the case to the U.S. Supreme Court on a writ of error. The 1873 arguments before the High Court have a modern ring.

The case revolved largely around the meaning of the 1863 and 1866 congressional charters to the railroad. Both contained the provision that "no person should be excluded from the cars on account of color." The railroad's lawyers held that this provision had been met by the separate Jim Crow car that ensured no Black passengers would be totally excluded from the train. The Supreme Court saw through that thin claim and ruled in favor of Brown.

On another cold day 87 years later, the Brown scene was repeated in Montgomery, Alabama (King, 1958; Morsell, 1958). Rosa Parks, a middle-aged Black seamstress, started for home one evening, weary from her day's work at a department store. After boarding a city bus and walking past the reserved White section, she slumped into the first open seat of the back section. Soon the bus filled with passengers, and the

Anti-Black Racism in America. Thomas F. Pettigrew, Oxford University Press. © Oxford University Press (2025).
DOI: 10.1093/9780197803134.003.0001

2 Anti-Black Racism in America

White driver ordered her and three other Black riders to surrender their seats for the White men who had just boarded. The three others complied, but Parks, like Brown before her, quietly refused. She was arrested at once.

There had been previous arrests following similar bus incidents in Montgomery and other southern cities. Yet this one of a widely admired woman ignited the Black community. Parks had trained in protest tactics at the Highlander Folk School in Monteagle, Tennessee—a central institution in the fight to end racial segregation in the 1950s.[1] Her protest had to some extent been partly formulated in advance.

Soon the boycott of the city's buses was initiated as planned, and leaflets describing the arrest and calling for a boycott were distributed. Four days later the trial was held and the boycott began in earnest. Usually in such cases, southern courts typically either dismissed the charges or found the defendants guilty of such evasive charges as disorderly conduct or not obeying an officer. But Parks was tried directly for disobeying the city's segregation ordinance, found guilty, and fined $10 plus court costs of $4 (worth $160 in 2024 dollars). Thus, her case, when immediately appealed, made a prime test of the legality of segregation. Meanwhile, the Black community's boycott of the city's buses was virtually complete.

Six months later, Alabama federal judges ruled Montgomery's segregation ordinance to be a violation of the 14th Amendment of the U.S. Constitution. Five months later, the U.S. Supreme Court upheld the lower court ruling.

More important than the legal victory, however, was the impetus and form the bus boycott gave to Black protest in America. Non-violent protest was again added to the Black arsenal for effective protest. Soon it would be fashioned into the sit-in and freedom ride protests. And a new leader, Dr. Martin Luther King Jr., rose to become the chief symbol and spokesman of this form of protest (Pettigrew, 2018b; see Sidebar I.1). The bus boycott idea spread quickly to other southern cities and even to two cities in the Union of South Africa: Johannesburg and Port Elizabeth. In 1960, the non-violence technique was applied effectively to widespread lunch-counter sit-ins by students (See Sidebar I.1). The movement triggered by the quiet seamstress had become a turning point in American race relations as well as having worldwide implications for racial change.[2]

The striking similarities of these two episodes 87 years apart raises questions about the pace of racial change in America: Has it been as static as this comparison implies? Or has the United States been making slow progress? This book addresses this question directly: *Has Black racism declined in America?*

---

[1] Martin Luther King, Jr. also attended Highlander. In 1961 the state of Tennessee closed the school and seized its property, ostensibly because it engaged in commercial activities in violation of its charter.

[2] However, Parks's personal problems only intensified. Her financial and health problems mounted as she lost her $30-a-week job as a department store seamstress (Poinsett, 1960). By 1960, she was living in Detroit, where she remained until her death in 2005 at the age of 92. Late in life, she began to receive widespread recognition for her brave act, including the Congressional Gold Medal, the Presidential Medal of Freedom, and a posthumous statue in the U.S. Capitol's National Statue Hall. Troy State University in Montgomery established the Rosa Parks Library and Museum on the site where Parks was arrested on December 1, 1955. It opened on the 45th anniversary of her arrest.

Introduction **3**

Four Different Perspectives

Without question massive social change has taken place throughout the United States and, indeed, the world in the past century. Yet change alone does not ensure any decline in American racism. It could even increase racism. Four different perspectives shape how you judge whether racism is receding: (1) your age; (2) your politics; (3) which Black Americans you are focusing on—by age and social class; and (4) the particular societal domain under review. Consider each of these in turn.

Age

As a nonagenarian, I have witnessed truly remarkable changes in American race relations. Some of them were so sweeping—such as Barack Obama's two presidential victories—that I never thought I would live to see them. Nor did I expect to witness a Black American winning the vice presidency, Virginia's governorship, a Senate seat from Georgia, and two seats on the Supreme Court. Nor did I ever think I would live to see Richmond's imposing statue of Confederate general Robert E. Lee on Monument Avenue taken down and put in a museum. I lived near it and passed it hundreds of times in my childhood. But I never dared think White Richmonders would ever allow this reminder of White supremacy to come down.[3]

In 1996, all of Monument Avenue's statues of Confederate leaders were ordered by the mayor to be taken down. Only one statue was left on the broad avenue. Just one block from my childhood home, a statue of the Black tennis great Arthur Ashe was erected after some controversy. Ashe was a Richmond native, but when growing up the future champion was not allowed to play on the vast public tennis courts in the city's all-White Byrd Park that I had enjoyed playing on for years. He left the city in search of a more accommodating location.

Even more striking is the large number of Blacks who have become presidents of predominantly White universities. These include Brown, Smith, Rutgers, Maryland, College of the Holy Cross, Simmons, George Mason, DePauw, Louisiana State, Old Dominion, Ohio State, and the University of California system. Who would have thought this was possible even a generation ago?

Without doubt, my lifetime has witnessed *major changes* in both race and gender. However, these many changes do not necessarily translate into an overall decline in the nation's racism. Look at it from the perspective of much younger Americans. Those under 35 years old never experienced the intense racial barriers of the past, as I did. They typically focus on the recent blatant police murders of George Floyd, Trayvon Martin, Daunte Wright, Breonna Taylor, Eric Garner, Michael Brown,

---

[3] No White contractor was willing to take on the task. So a Black American contractor, Devon Henry, did so and became an expert at taking down Confederate statues throughout the South—23 of them by 2023.

4 Anti-Black Racism in America

Daniel Prude, Tyre Nichols, and all too many others. Having never witnessed the even worse routine racism of the past, young Americans of all races are unlikely to perceive racism as waning.

Political Position

Conservatives typically perceive massive racial change, while liberals are more circumspect. Consider the now established cliché in the mass media that America is in a stage of *post-racism* after the 2008 election. When Obama first won the presidency, America's hunger for racial optimism overflowed with self-congratulation. The code word for this phenomenon became "post-racism." The claim was that we were entering a new era in America in which race has substantially lost its special significance.

As the *Wall Street Journal* phrased it, "[A] long-suppressed people have raised up a president. It is moving and beautiful and speaks to the unending magic and sense of justice of our country" (Nonnan, 2009). To be sure, Obama's election represented a major step forward. But, unfortunately, America's "unending magic and sense of justice" are still being tested—as later police shootings, the Black Lives Matter movement, and Trump's election and actions soon made clear.

We will look at this phenomenon in detail in Chapter 1. We will find that a majority of White Americans in 2000 believed that the nation's race problems were fundamentally solved by the civil rights movement in the 1960s. A third believed racial equality had already been achieved; others believed that it would soon be achieved.

With Obama's victory, the urge to erase the nation's four-century-long racist slate became even more irresistible. Consider a column in the *New York Times* three days after the presidential election titled "Where Have All the Bigots Gone?" (Tierney, 2008) The writer lacked advanced scientific training but, oddly enough, was a science editor for the *Times*. Obama's triumph proved to his satisfaction that racism was rapidly disappearing from America, that the social science "crowd" whose intensive research reveals that racial bigotry was still widespread throughout America is simply biased and wrong. The science editor made this claim despite literally thousands of studies documenting the ongoing presence of conscious and unconscious racism in the minds of White Americans and the incontrovertible evidence of the direct and indirect effects of such prejudice on discriminatory treatment in housing, job selection, medical treatment, and judicial fairness. I will describe this research throughout this book.

To support his position, Tierney misreported survey data. He claimed that decades of surveys showed that racism was in "steep decline." Chapter 1 shows there has been some general reduction in prejudice but no "steep decline." The assumption that Obama's election indicates American racism has vanished is tantamount to saying that Benjamin Disraeli, Margaret Thatcher, and Rishi Sunak becoming prime ministers essentially ended anti-Semitism, sexism, and racism in the United Kingdom.

Which Black Americans?

Social outcomes vary considerably according to which segment of Black America is the focus of analysis—the young or the old, the poor, the growing middle-class, or the small wealthy group.

Which Social Domain?

How to assess the nation's racism also strongly depends on the particular domain under review. Some domains show positive trends overall, but others show the opposite. We shall look at the trends in nine key areas: attitudes, discrimination, politics, economics, education, health, criminal justice, housing, and interracial contact. In each of these domains, we will find both positive and negative trends that make a simple yes-or-no overall evaluation impossible.

On top of these three trends, Mitchell and Tetlock (2022) claim that there is a general tendency to see societal matters getting worse than they actually are. This tendency may act to obscure genuine racial progress that is occurring. That said, we will note that political conservatives counter this trend repeatedly by perceiving far more racial progress than there is in order to claim that remedies are not needed.

So, is America's racism declining? I ask you to review carefully the conflicting evidence presented throughout this volume. There has been considerable change, but reaching an overarching conclusion remains difficult. Nonetheless, we will attempt one in the closing chapters.

Black Americans Have Also Been Changing

Before analyzing data on White racism, we need to check on the changes that have been occurring for Black Americans as an evolving group in the 21st century (Lopez and Moszimani, 2023).

Greater Diversity

By 2023, about 50 million Americans regarded themselves as Black—roughly one in every seven Americans. The U.S. Census recognizes three distinct groups within this large group. (1) There are those who identify as Black who are of full African heritage. (2) A second group identify as Black who are of mixed Black-White heritage. This group comprises about three-quarters of Black Americans, but it tends not to identify as a separate group. (3) Finally, a third group identify as Black and also report a Hispanic background. The Census now often provides their data separately. Seven percent of those who regard themselves as Hispanic also describe themselves as Black.

6 Anti-Black Racism in America

For the purposes of this book, the term "Black Americans" will signify only the first two groups. Mixed-race Blacks are generally considered Black in American society by both Whites and Blacks as well as by the mixed-race group itself. The Black-Hispanic third group have specific concerns, such as language, that must be considered separately.

Black American diversity goes further. By 2019, 4.6 million (10%) of those who identify as Black were born outside the United States—up from 7% in 2000. There are an increasing number of African-born Americans as well as numerous immigrants and their offspring from Haiti and throughout the West Indies. Increasingly, professional basketball players are coming from Africa, among them Hakeem Olajuwon, Dikembe Mutombo, and now Joel Embiid and Jonathan Kuminga. Many West Indians have become prominent figures in the United States, such as Eric Holder (1951–), Claude McKay (1889–1948), Sidney Poitier (1927–2022), General Colin Powell (1937–2021), and Cicely Tyson (1924–2021), to name just a few.

Young

Black Americans constitute a relatively young group. Their median age in 2019 was 32—six years younger than the nation's average. About a third were below the age of 20 in 2019, while only 11% were older than 64.

Live in the South and Large Cities

With some Black Americans returning in recent years, the South remains the principal region of the Black population: 56% in 2019. Only 10% live in the West, 17% in the Midwest, and 17% in the Northeast. And most of those who reside outside the South live in large metropolitan areas. In 2019, they constituted 8% of the area covering New York City, Newark, and Jersey City (3.8 million people), and 4% each for the Washington, D.C., and Chicago areas (1.7 million each).

Christians

Black Americans are more formally religious than White Americans, and two-thirds are Protestants. Only 6% are Roman Catholics, and these are centered in New Orleans. Just 1% are Muslims, yet they still accounted for about 20% of all American Muslims in 2020. A growing number, about a fifth, are religiously unaffiliated.

The Concept of Racism

The term "racism" is widely used quite loosely. Since it is the key concept of this book, it is imperative that it be explicitly defined in this introduction.

Formal dictionary definitions typically read like the following two from the Merriam-Webster dictionary: "Racism is a belief that race is a fundamental determinant of human traits and capacities and that racial differences produce an inherent superiority of a particular race" and "racism is a belief that race is a fundamental determinant of human traits and capacities and that racial differences produce an inherent superiority of a particular race."

Note how these definitions apply only at the level of individuals.

Yet racism operates at all three basic levels of analysis: individual, interpersonal, and structural. The social sciences generally and this volume consider all three levels to obtain a complete picture of the phenomenon. So, three different levels of racism require definitions.

To start, we can define individual racism as the dictionary does. Chapter 1 focuses on the much studied phenomenon of individual racial prejudice. Next, Chapters 2 and 3 cover racial discrimination and the power of social norms to shape racial behavior in face-to-face encounters between Black and White people. Here *racism can be defined as discriminatory behavior between interacting social groups based on perceived race.*

Finally, we consider the broad structural level of social institutions. Here *racism can be defined as deeply established operations of institutions that serve to benefit the advancement of particular racial groups and deter the advancement of other racial groups.* These racist operations are described in Chapters 4–8 that focus on the economic, educational, criminal, medical, and political domains.

Other minority groups also face racism, such as Asian Americans, Hispanic Americans, and Native Americans. But this book focuses on the experiences of African Americans. Data on the other groups are provided throughout the book only as comparisons for African American data bearing on anti-Black racism.

A central theme of the book is how these three levels of racism interact and reinforce one another. In sociology, this phenomenon is known by the term "intersectionality." The tight ties between the three racist levels are what make combatting racism so difficult.

The Focus of This Book

There are dozens of excellent books on American race relations. We shall draw on them and recommend especially notable ones following each chapter. These books typically inspect in great depth one specific aspect of racism, such as attitudes, housing, crime, or some other single slice of the broader phenomenon.

8   Anti-Black Racism in America

This volume is a *comprehensive assessment* of racism, employing not one but virtually all the major aspects of the phenomenon. The reader who wishes to take a deeper dive into any particular area can start with the books that are recommended at the end of each chapter. The ambitious reader who wishes to take an even deeper dive into American race relations can use the more than 700-item bibliography which is provided to support the book's contentions.

A Final Word

Throughout the book, charts are provided to emphasize key trends together with sidebars that focus in more detail on the people and circumstances of central events and theories. The sidebars often describe racial events I experienced or witnessed over my seven decades of studying intergroup relations and my nine decades of life.

Sidebar I.1   Martin Luther King Speaks to the American Psychological Association

Elected president of the Society for the Psychological Study of Social Issues in 1967, I had the opportunity to name a speaker for the 1968 meeting of the American Psychological Association in Washington. I chose Dr. King. And my social psychological colleague Kenneth Clark, who knew him well, got his acceptance.

Many of the APA establishment were less than enthusiastic about the idea. Some thought it "too political," that it had nothing to do with psychology, and few psychologists would be interested. They could not have been more mistaken.

The APA first assigned us only a small room. Clark and I objected strenuously, and the location was belatedly moved to one of the largest meeting rooms in the hotel. At the appointed time, however, it became clear that even this room would not accommodate the enormous swell of psychologists who arrived for the talk. Hastily, another large room with a video feed was opened. Psychologists of all specialties *were* interested in hearing the address.

Given the threats to his life, King arrived at a hidden back entrance to the hotel's basement. Clark and I greeted him. We walked through the basement to the private elevator, where all the workers were Black Americans. King persisted in warmly shaking hands with each worker. I cannot forget their faces as they personally met their hero. Only then could I fully appreciate just how much he meant to African Americans.

It was several hours before the speech, so we had time to talk. Having given hundreds of speeches, King was relaxed and interested in the news blaring forth from the room's television set. The news centered on the arrest of Father James Groppi, a Catholic priest leading demonstrations for open housing in Milwaukee. King and Groppi had marched together at Selma. As he watched, King exclaimed, "They had better arrest that wild man—he is really dangerous!" Everyone laughed.

Introduction   9

King implored psychologists to convey more effectively to the American White public the enormous burden that racism thrusts on Black Americans. And when he cited his favorite quotation—"Let justice roll down like waters and righteousness like a mighty stream"—listeners could visualize Niagara's waters pouring down.

Sidebar I.2 An Eventful Trip South

My sociological mentor at Harvard was Samuel Stouffer, the famed survey specialist (Pettigrew, 2015b). He strongly believed in "getting there when it is still hot"—that is, studying a phenomenon as soon as possible, before later events cloud memories. So when the lunch-counter sit-ins began in Greensboro, North Carolina, I scurried to obtain a small foundation grant and set out with my wife, Ann, on an eventful trip south. Stouffer kindly agreed to teach one of my classes so that I could make the trip.

On February 1, 1960, four brave male students from historically Black North Carolina Agricultural and Technical College in Greensboro sat down at the lunch counter of a Woolworth store. Given the store's racial segregation policy, they were refused service. They left when the store closed, but returned in greater numbers the next day. Similar sit-ins had been conducted years earlier, but this one captured the headlines internationally and sparked a sit-in movement throughout southern cities that had nearby historically Black colleges.

The immediate and predictable response of many White southern leaders was that radicals, maybe even Communists, were coming down from the North and stirring up their otherwise contented Black populations. I realized this put us in jeopardy. We were a young White couple driving an old Chevrolet with Massachusetts license plates, mysteriously showing up regularly just before a sit-in protest occurred. I had learned from Black colleagues that the movement was being spread by the North Carolina A&T basketball team. As they went to other historically Black colleges for games, they systematically spread how to plan and execute the sit-ins.

Indeed, when we arrived in Charlotte, North Carolina, to visit Johnson C. Smith University, a city police car began following us. We were never pulled over, but the officers went out of their way to make themselves conspicuous to let us know they were watching us.

Among other schools, we also visited South Carolina State University in Orangeburg. Here we witnessed one of the most moving events of my long life. The student protesters marched through the city waving American flags while singing the national anthem and "We Shall Overcome." A large White crowd—definitely not a mob—watched in total silence. It was clear that the national symbols struck a sensitive chord. The spectators seemed to grasp that racial matters in Orangeburg were never going to be the same again.

As we left Orangeburg, a South Carolina State Police car roared up behind us and signaled that we should pull to the side and stop. My wife and I looked at each other and braced ourselves, anticipating that we were about to be hassled. But then we got the biggest surprise of our lives. After I rolled down the car window, the officer politely asked

10 Anti-Black Racism in America

my wife if she were Ann Hallman Pettigrew. A bit taken back, she said she was. With a broad smile the officer said, "I have good news for you. Your father knew you were in Orangeburg and called us to find you and tell you that you have just been accepted by the Medical School of the University of Virginia!"

To say the least, we were absolutely astonished and relieved on two counts: we experienced no hassle whatsoever and learned that my wife's start on her distinguished six-decade career in medicine was about to begin. To this day, I have no idea what possessed my father-in-law to call the state police. He had never lived in the South and had no understanding that calling the state police for a favor was not what you normally do anywhere, and especially not in the South.

The sit-in movement soon spread to Woolworth stores throughout the nation. While its stores in the North did not discriminate racially, the hope was that a nationwide movement would cause the chain to change its southern policies. And it did. So when I returned to Cambridge many of my Harvard students were planning a demonstration in front of the Woolworth store near Harvard Square. I joined them. But as I was walking with the students, carrying my boycott sign, an elderly White lady rushed up close to me and shouted in my face, "AND YOU—YOU ARE OLD ENOUGH TO KNOW BETTER!"

Clearly, my attempt to look like a 19-year-old student had failed. The students and I burst out laughing.

Chapter 1
Prejudice

Implicit and Explicit Racial Mindsets

For more than a dozen years, I have benefited from the expert services of one of the many doctors I must, at my advanced age, see regularly. I liked his cool efficiency and limited chatter. But one day this abruptly changed. He asked me perfunctorily what I was doing in my retirement. I made the mistake of telling him that I was writing this book on race relations.

His demeanor changed at once and his face turned red. He was not angry with me; it was just the word "race" that set him off. "Yes," he commented with disgust in his voice, "Isn't race relations in this country *completely crazy*? I had a Black friend in college who applied to all the same medical schools that I did back in the eighties. I had better grades than he had, still he was accepted by *all* of the schools, and I was accepted by only one - *absolutely crazy!*"

Let us assume that this is an accurate portrayal of my doctor's experience—although such accounts often involve gross exaggerations and embellishments. But note his implied contention that grades should be the lone gauge for admission to medical school.

First, realize that he was actually accepted by and trained at a prestigious Ivy League medical school. He has a booming practice with a large staff and is regarded as one of the best doctors in his specialty in central California. He is a multimillionaire with a beautiful home overlooking the Pacific Ocean in California's lovely Santa Cruz County. By any standard, America has treated him well. Yet he remains upset over his brush with affirmative action more than three decades ago.

We need also to consider the societal perspective underlying the incident that still haunts him. Black Americans, like Native Americans and Latino Americans, are grossly underserved medically throughout the nation. By 2012, Black Americans made up 14% of the nation's "working age population" but only 5% of active physicians, 3% of dentists, and 10% of nurses (Noonan, Velasco-Mondragon, and Wagner, 2016). And Blacks tend to prefer Black doctors (Smedley, Butler, and Bristow, 2004). Moreover, there is growing evidence that Black patients fare better under the care of Black physicians (e.g., Greenwood et al., 2020).

By the 1980s, medical schools, concerned about this situation, were aware that minority doctors were far more likely than White doctors to treat minorities. Serving minorities typically pays less and conveys less status. Apart from affirmative

Anti-Black Racism in America. Thomas F. Pettigrew, Oxford University Press. © Oxford University Press (2025).
DOI: 10.1093/9780197803134.003.0002

action, that concern influenced the schools' eagerness to enroll a well-qualified Black candidate more than White applicants who were unlikely to serve minorities. And they were right. In my many years as his patient, I have never seen a single minority patient in his office.

Although I have long studied racial prejudice (Pettigrew, 1964b, 2021), I confess that this sudden burst of deep racial resentment took me by surprise. This highly educated professional is no stereotypical bigot. He could with some justification stoutly deny being a "racist." Yet here he is, completely oblivious to the nation's racial needs and problems even though he did not himself suffer from affirmative action. This personal experience illustrates how the racial attitudes of White Americans are undeniably complex and often self-contradictory—as we shall learn in this chapter.

Attitudes are important. Some structural social scientists argue that attitudes are of little or no importance when considering such large-scale phenomena as societal racism. Social psychologists strongly disagree. Consider the widespread misuse by American police of disproportionate traffic stops of Black drivers. Some localities have many such stops of Black drivers; some have very few. What differentiates these areas? Two extensive studies arrived at the same conclusion (Stelter et al., 2022; Ekstrom, Le Forestier, and Lai, 2022). At the county level, those localities where anti-Black prejudice was highest among its residents had significantly more police stops of Black drivers. The basic level of prejudice in the various communities shaped local racial norms that in turn influenced the behavior of the county's police. In effect, the individual prejudices of the communities sanctioned the racist behavior of their police. It is also the case that dramatic events, such as school desegregation, can shape relevant attitudes of individuals (Riley & Pettigrew, 1976).

Two Common Types of Racial Mindsets

We will consider two different types of racial stances: implicit and explicit. Social psychology has only recently learned how to measure implicit racial bias, and how it differs from upfront explicit attitudes. This breakthrough is a result of the discipline's emphasis on cognition.

Implicit Racial Bias. Implicit bias refers to automatically evoked mental associations about social groups. They are unconscious biases that occur automatically and unintentionally but nevertheless influence our judgments and behavior. They can be measured in several ways.

Payne and his colleagues (2005) used the well-established phenomenon of affect misattribution. Subjects are asked to make evaluative judgments in an ambiguous situation. For each judgment, subjects are exposed first to a positive or negative prime (e.g., furry kitten or poisonous snake). Then they are asked to ignore the influence of the prime while evaluating a third object. Typically, the prime does indeed influence the judgment. And this misattribution is used as the measure of positive or negative influence of the prime. When the prime is racial this implicit bias is then considered to be "reflecting racism" (Payne and Hannay, 2021).

Most work on implicit bias has used the Implicit Association Test (IAT). Like the misattribution method, the IAT digs deeper than measures of explicit attitudes. It has attracted considerable attention as well as controversy since its introduction in 1998 (Greenwald, McGhee, and Schwartz, 1998). Widely used in social psychology, it has spawned extensive applications. Beyond psychology the technique is now commonly employed, and often misused, in business, law, criminal justice, medicine, education, and political science (Greenwald and Lai, 2020).

The IAT grew out of an earlier paper that held that the differentiation of explicit and implicit memory should also apply to social constructs (Greenwald and Banaji, 1995). The IAT requires subjects using a computer to classify exemplars of two concept categories (e.g., flowers and insects) and two attributed categories (pleasant and unpleasant), each represented by words or pictures. When the same key must be used to identify two associated categories (e.g., flowers and pleasant), response is faster than when the two categories are not associated (e.g., insects and pleasant). The difference in speed between "the combined task" pairings measures the strength of the associations of the concepts to the attributes.

The underlying idea of the IAT is that traces of past experience will mediate the positive or negative feeling, thought, or action toward the social objects (race, gender, etc.). The reader is encouraged to take the test in order to appreciate how it operates. It is available at https://implicit.harvard.ed/implicit/take-test.html.

There are now many forms of the IAT for various social categories, such as race, gender, obesity, suicide risk, and political preferences. The test's popularity derives from the promise that it can avoid the social-desirability bias that bedevils widely used explicit measures of attitudes—particularly those involving attitudes toward stigmatized groups. Consequently, the IAT has become the dominant measure of implicit views.

There is some disagreement as to just what these implicit measures are. In this book, we shall think of them as primarily a *trait* of individuals—albeit an unstable one. Others hold them to be a feature of social contexts (Payne, Vuletich, and Lundberg, 2017).

Critics of the method also challenge just what the IAT is actually measuring. Some argue that it is merely taping familiarity, cultural knowledge, or attribute salience independent of any personal preferences or attitudes. Some of these criticisms, such as the measurement of cultural knowledge and attribute salience, could be valid yet still not disrupt the focus of the IAT assessment.

Numerous misreadings of the IAT and popular claims by non-psychologists have also led to specious criticisms. For the reader who wishes to understand better the debate between those who defend and those who attack the method, Jost (2019) provides an excellent starting point. Gawronski (2019) combines the criticisms of implicit bias measures and tests them with the available evidence.

14   Anti-Black Racism in America

Despite attacks by doubting critics (Oswald, et al., 2013, 2015), implicit tests have proven invaluable in a variety of areas. For instance, a racial prejudice implicit measure predicted voting choice for 1,057 registered voters in the 2008 presidential election. High scorers tended to vote against Obama. It also predicted voting choice independent of explicit prejudice measures, political conservatism, and a symbolic racism measure (Greenwald et al., 2009).

Indeed, implicit measures have proven useful in a wide range of areas. Thus, an implicit measure had a 43% larger effect size than an explicit prejudice measure in predicting less willingness to adopt Black children (Bell et al., 2021). And in Sweden, the IAT predicted greater employment discrimination against Arab men (Rooth, 2010). Even in medicine, the IAT correctly predicted which physicians chose not to employ the more efficacious thrombolysis treatment for Black patients with acute coronary syndromes (Green et al., 2007). Those scoring high on the racial IAT also significantly more often regarded Black patients as "less cooperative."

How well does the IAT predict prejudice? The results of an initial study of internet-administered attitude and stereotype measures with more than 2.5 million subjects were promising (Nosek et al., 2007). It uncovered a marked difference between the IAT and parallel self-report measures. The IAT scores tended to be more extreme, and they revealed a much larger degree of White preference (i.e., implicit prejudice) than the explicit scores.

Later, three meta-analyses tested the IAT. The first meta-analysis reviewed 122 research reports boasting 184 samples with 14,900 subjects. The meta-analytic estimates of the positive correlations between the IAT or self-report measures predicted various criterion measures. This first study found an IAT average of +.27 for all types of psychological measures (Greenwald et al., 2009). For the 32 samples involving just Black-White interracial behavior, the IAT significantly outperformed the self-report measures, +.24 to +.12, when compared against criterion measures of intergroup behavior. Thus, as predicted, the IAT measure did better than the usual type of self-report measure when attitudes of a stigmatized group are involved.

Using the IAT and self-report measures together rendered the strongest prediction of all. And the more the IAT and self-report measures were intercorrelated, the greater the predictive validity of each. For all samples, the two types of measures correlated +.214; for just the 30 racial samples, they correlated +.114.

A larger meta-analysis improved on the earlier attempts; it had 36,999 subjects from 217 research reports and employed structural equation modeling (SEM) (Kurdi et al., 2019). The SEM revealed modest but significantly unique contributions of both implicit and explicit measures. The IAT data varied sharply as a function of purely methodological factors. When stronger IAT methods were used, the IAT's relationships with criterion measures of intergroup behavior improved.

A summary conclusion can be broached (Greenwald and Lai, 2020). Both implicit-explicit and implicit-criterion correlations with prejudice are consistently small to moderate and are lower when the target is as socially sensitive as racial views.

We conclude that the IAT offers an additional measure of prejudice (and other phenomena) to social psychology's methodological arsenal. IAT studies are cited throughout the book.

Trends in Implicit Racial Bias. Charlesworth and Banaji (2019, 2021, 2022) have followed trends in both implicit and explicit reactions toward a range of groups from 2007 to 2020. They analyzed more than 7.1 million tests from Americans drawn from their Project Implicit website. All the explicit bias measures declined slowly and continuously over these years; attitudes about old age, sexuality, disability, skin tone, and race improved. Implicit attitudes also declined for sexuality, skin tone, and race, but not for age, disability, or body weight. As expected from the social desirability bias, more prejudice was generally indicated by the implicit than the explicit measures. These general findings typically held for both females and males.

The difficulty in interpreting these encouraging results is that these implicit data are from a convenience sample. They do not comprise a probability sample of the American population. Indeed, it seems likely that more educated, politically liberal people would be especially interested in trying out the IAT on their computers. However, the researchers found ways to suggest that such biases may not be as large as you might expect. For instance, they showed that during Trump's first presidency (2017–2020) there was a temporary increase in implicit racial attitudes consistent with Trump's racist words and actions. And this increase was concentrated among political conservatives and in predominantly Republican states.

Thus, we have a trade-off between (1) more sensitive measures of prejudice (IAT) with nonrepresentative data and (2) less sensitive measures with probability samples. Used together, however, these two data sources provide us with a wider perspective by which to judge whether Americans' racist attitudes have declined.

Trends in Explicit White American Racial Attitudes

We are fortunate to have five first-rate summaries of trends in explicit racial attitudes tapped by rigorous national surveys. First, Schuman, Steeh, and Bobo (1985) published a summary of the relevant survey data through 1984. A later volume updated the trends to 1995 (Schuman et al., 1996). Next, Larry Bobo and his colleagues provided an overview of racial attitude trends up to 2008 using data from the General Social Survey of the National Opinion Research Center (NORC) at the University of Chicago (Bobo et al., 2012). Later analyses updated the data to 2021 (Gallup Polls, 2021; Krysan and Moberg, 2021).

These summaries concur in delineating several major trends. First, *blatant biological racism has diminished but has by no means disappeared entirely.* While 56% of White respondents believed that Whites were "more intelligent" than Black Americans in 1990, this figure declined to 25% by 2008. Figure 1.1 combines beliefs of White Americans about racial inequalities over three decades (Bobo et al., 2012). Only 9% of White respondents by 2008 believed that racial inequality was due to "less inborn ability" of Black Americans (the darkest bars)—down from 20% two decades earlier. Also in 2008, 30% believed that the inequality was due to discrimination, and 43% thought it due to a "lack of the chance for education." This shift is important; biological claims of racial inferiority have long been the spurious bedrock belief of racism (Pettigrew, 1964b, 2020). And clear evidence to the contrary is typically discounted (see Sidebar 1.1).

But also note in Figure 1.1 how many Whites think "lack of motivation" remains a major explanation (the lightest bars) for African American behavior. Another NORC poll question showed that almost half of White Americans believed that White people were more "hard-working" than Black people. Viewed realistically, it is odd that this stereotype still persists when Black workers today are conspicuously overrepresented in lower-status occupations that often require difficult manual labor.

Second, there have also been *increasing percentages of White respondents who agree with the principles of racial equality*. Only 32% of White Americans supported interracial schools in 1941, compared with 96% in 1995. Yet, while desegregated schools now receive wide support, the busing necessary to achieve desegregation is still sternly resisted.

Figure 1.2 shows this general acceptance in two other areas (Bobo et al., 2012). In 1973, 64% of White Americans favored their supposed "right" to maintain racial segregation in housing. By 1990, this has declined to 45%, then by 2002 only 14% did so. In 1973, 37% of White respondents supported laws against racial intermarriage, but only 16% did so in 1996.

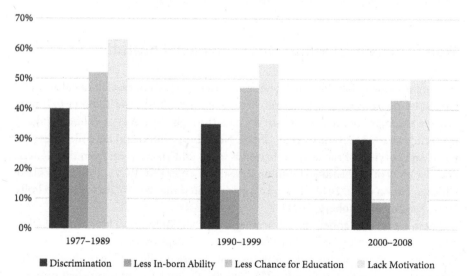

Figure 1.1 White Americans' explanations for racial inequality.
Source: Bobo et al., 2012

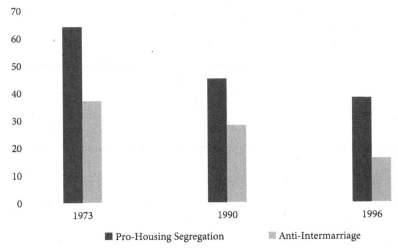

Figure 1.2 White Americans' attitudes toward racial discrimination.
Source: Bobo et al., 2012

These steady changes importantly reflect *generational replacement*: old, more bigoted White cohorts are dying and being replaced by more tolerate young White cohorts. This process also helps to explain the steady decreases in implicit prejudice noted earlier. A 2021 Pew Research Center poll found 70% of teenagers of all races supported the Black Lives Matter movement (BLM) compared with 56% of adults and only half of those 65 years and over. Among White teens, 57% favored BLM (Hurst, 2022).

One reflection of this cohort-replacement process is White attendance at BLM rallies. In the 1960s, save for the 1963 March on Washington, there was negligible White participation in public racial protests. I recall in the 1960s being almost the lone White in repeated racial demonstrations in the South. In recent years, there is typically a sizable presence of young Whites. According to a *New York Times* article that analyzed the BLM movement, about 95% of counties that held rallies were composed of a majority of White residents (Buchanan, Bui, and Patel, 2020). In my town of Santa Cruz, California, the White police chief himself participated enthusiastically in the local, majority-White BLM march. As those who have marched in a protest know well, such participation establishes public commitment and deepens one's dedication to the cause.

The BLM movement burst out throughout the world, and it encouraged 56% of Black American adults to believe it would "lead to changes that will improve Black people's lives." But a year later, this statistic fell back to 35% (Cox and Edwards, 2022). Yet a Pew poll in 2022 found that Black American adults see the BLM movement as helping Black people (39%) more than the NAACP (11%), religious organizations (13%), or the National Urban League (3%). And young Blacks (70%) support the BLM more than Black adults do (57%) (Gramlich and Edwards, 2022).

Right-wing commentators proclaimed the non-violent movement to be an intense threat to the nation—even though, in Kenosha, Wisconsin, and other locales, it was White racists who damaged property and shot and killed protesters. Incredibly, in Kenosha, 17-year-old Kyle Rittenhouse was found innocent of killing two White men and seriously injuring a third with his illegal automatic rifle. Hundreds of White sympathizers sent Rittenhouse almost a million dollars for his bail and defense costs. He was allowed to keep the crowd-funded money. Thus, with an AK-15 automatic rifle, he became wealthy by shooting three White men who were not even near him. Imagine how different the outcome would have been had Rittenhouse been a Black American.

But the positive trends in White attitudes are severely mitigated by the persistence of opposition to governmental action to combat racial inequality. In both 1975 and 2008, 58% of White respondents favored "no special treatment" when asked about government aid for Black Americans. Thus, there was no change whatsoever on this crucial item over a third of a century—otherwise, a period of considerable social change.

Consistently in surveys from 1994 to 2008, most Whites believed "Blacks should overcome prejudice without special favors." In 2002, 81% of Whites opposed making "cash payments to Black Americans who are descendants of slaves." In both 1994 and 2008 surveys, 90% of White respondents opposed preference in hiring or promotion for Blacks. This declined to 80% by 2018. That year only 20% of White Americans believed that "the government has a special obligation to help improve Black people's living standards."

Underlying these beliefs is a strong sense of denial. For example, a 2023 Pew poll found 45% of White American adults believe that "people seeing racial discrimination where it doesn't exist" is a "bigger problem" than "people not seeing racial discrimination where it really does exist." From their own experience, Black Americans overwhelmingly disagree: 88% believe people do not perceive the racial discrimination that exists (Pew Research Center, 2023).

More than half of White participants in polls spanning 1990 to 2008 think it is at least somewhat likely that affirmative action for Black Americans "hurts" White Americans. These consistent results over the years opposing governmental efforts to counter racist effects do not support the conclusion that American racism is markedly declining.

This substantial White opposition to the federal government directly intervening to aid Black citizens relates directly to those White people who tend to see race relations as a zero-sum game -that if Black Americans get more, then White Americans must necessarily get less. This finding came from data from the 1950s and into the 21st century (Norton and Summers, 2011). Later research replicated this finding and also found that political ideology is involved. Only White conservatives thought that "Whites" were "losing" this perceived zero-sum tug-of-war. Moderate and liberal Whites disagreed that Whites were somehow losing out (Rasmussen et al., 2022).

In her popular book, *The Sum of Us*, Heather McGhee (2021) probes deeper into this zero-sum thinking of many White Americans. She maintains that such thinking is encouraged by White elites; in reality, it actually costs Whites as well as minorities. The clearest illustration of her point involved free public swimming pools in many American towns and cities in the 1930s and 1940s. Later, once courts required them to be open to Blacks as well as Whites, many towns either closed down the pools completely or set up private clubs that required membership fees. What had been free to White swimmers was now either non-existent or costly. Racism had harmed Whites as well as non-Whites.

McGhee's contention is that "racism costs everyone." She obviously wants White Americans to realize this fact and thus, hopefully, question their racism out of self-interest. Her book proceeds to demonstrate how racism costs White Americans in multiple domains throughout the nation.

While the financial crisis of the early 2000s hurt Black people first and the most, given their greater numbers, a majority of those hurt were White people, In Chapter 7, we will discuss a striking example of McGhee's point. Black Americans have less health insurance, although the 2010 passage of Obama's Affordable Care Act (ACA) significantly narrowed this racial gap (Sommers et al., 2015).

Twelve states, however, rejected Medicaid expansion under ACA, even though it did not require state funds. Eight of these states are in the South—Alabama, Florida, Georgia, Mississippi, North Carolina, South Carolina, Tennessee, and Texas—about 40% of the Black American population live in these states (Artiga, Damico, and Garfield, 2015). But low-income White residents of these states are also hurt by their state's refusal to accept federal Medicaid funds. Because the ACA was a liberal act advanced by a Black president, it got rejected by racist politicians. Now *all* the indigent in these states receive poorer healthcare.

McGhee cites other examples of how racism ends up hurting White citizens as much as or more than it hurts Black citizens. Often, she points out, the predatory practices of banks and the real estate industry begin and are shaped in Black communities. Pushing subprime mortgages on those families who could afford lower-interest prime loans offer one example. These practices are found to be so profitable that they are then employed against White families. Since White Americans outnumber Black Americans, the total cost of such malpractice ends up being far greater for the White community than the Black community.

Social Distance Preferences Remain—Especially When White People Are in the Minority. By 2008, 40% of White respondents still opposed a "close family member marrying a Black American." The same percentage objected "to sending their children to a school where more than half of the children are African American." And 25% opposed "living in a neighborhood where half of the residents are of another race." Thus, while there is greater White American willingness to interact with Black people, their willingness rapidly dissipates when they are in the minority (Bobo et al., 2012).

20 Anti-Black Racism in America

Gross Misperceptions of Black Americans Endure. Given racial segregation, most White Americans do not know well a single Black American—a critical point that will be expanded on in Chapter 9. This widespread lack of interracial contact helps to explain why one in five White Americans in 2008 held such erroneous beliefs as that Black Americans were as wealthy as or even wealthier than White Americans (Bobo et al., 2012). It also helps to explain why a national survey conducted in 2000 revealed that a majority of White Americans believed that racial discrimination of the past had largely been eliminated (Bobo, Dawson, and Johnson, 2001).

Such beliefs underlie the widespread White view that Black people themselves are responsible for ending whatever racial disparities remain—a modern form of "blaming the victim" (Ryan, 1971). In fact, ever since the 1960s, many White Americans have believed that the nation's race problems were basically solved by the civil rights movement. Note, too, how America in 2004 "celebrated" the 50th anniversary of the *Brown v. Board of Education* school desegregation decision while it ignored the failure to implement the historic ruling (Pettigrew, 2004).

In addition, only 6% of White respondents in 1994 rarely if ever felt both "admiration" and "sympathy" for Black Americans.[1] Withholding *positive* emotions toward Blacks has partly replaced the active expression of *negative* emotions. Does this constitute progress? Or is it simply an example of American racism becoming more subtle?

Whites' misconceptions of Black life also explain why they are either unaware of or oblivious to the routine mistreatment and everyday racial experience of Black Americans. By 2021, only about 30% of White respondents thought Black people were treated unfairly in shops and restaurants compared with twice that percentage or more of Black respondents. In 2021, Gallup found 60% of White people even believed that qualified Blacks had as good a chance as Whites of getting "any kind of job" as Whites (Gallup Polls, 2021). An exception, not surprisingly, involves the police. Following widespread publicity of gross police misconduct, 50% of White respondents in 2021 recognized the unfair treatment of Blacks by police—compared with 80% of Black respondents (Gallup Polls, 2021).

Interracial Contact Is a Major Predictor of Racial Attitudes

These crude misconceptions that White Americans have of their Black fellow citizens are importantly shaped by the widespread lack of interracial contact. Literally thousands of studies conducted around the world have demonstrated how intergroup contact and intergroup prejudice are intertwined. Indeed, intergroup contact theory has become one of the best-supported theories in social psychology (Allport, 1954,

---

[1] These items test "emotional prejudice." They form two items of a Subtle Prejudice Scale that has been successfully employed throughout Europe and South America (Pettigrew and Meertens, 1995).

1958; Pettigrew, 2022a; Pettigrew and Tropp, 2006, 2008, 2011). We shall return to this theme in Chapter 9.

Political Identification Is Also a Key Predictor of Explicit Racial Attitudes. Pew Research Center (2021) polls conducted in 2021 found that Republicans are far more likely than Democrats to think a "lot of progress on race" has been made in the United States in the past half-century (71% to 29%). And they are far less likely to think that "increased attention to U.S. history of slavery and racism is good for society" (25% to 78%). Hence the nationwide attempt by Republicans to ban the accurate teaching of American racial history. Republicans are also far less likely than Democrats to admit that "White people benefit a great deal from advantages that Black people do not have" (6% to 53%).[2] As expected, racial attitudes are entwined with the nation's intense partisan split that heightened during the first Trump presidency (Pettigrew, 2017).

Avoiding Dissonance. One might think that the growing number of White Americans who simultaneously reject racial discrimination and oppose governmental actions to reduce this discrimination would experience cognitive dissonance (Stone and Fernandez, 2008). If you think racial discrimination is wrong, should you not also wish to see the government combat the problem? At the societal level, Myrdal (1944) called this "the American dilemma." However, there is little evidence that such dissonance is actually felt and recognized among many White Americans. Why not?

A major stratagem is simply to claim that racial progress has been so extensive that there is little racism remaining (see Sidebar 1.1). Other means of denying dissonance have just been mentioned. The specious belief that Black Americans are as wealthy as White Americans helps believers to deny the issue. So does the widespread ignorance of the daily forms of racial discrimination faced by Black Americans. The introduction noted how Obama's presidential victory in 2008 was immediately interpreted by some White analysts as proof that racism no longer existed in America.

This belief that racial prejudice and discrimination are in the distant past is a critical part of White denial. The insistence that one is "color-blind" - almost an impossibility in modern America - is another common example of this protective phenomenon. Indeed, laboratory research in social psychology has demonstrated that Black Americans are likely to distrust White people who claim to be color-blind and believe that great racial progress has been made in the United States (Rosenblum, Jacoby-Senghor, and Brown, 2022). Two other social psychological studies show that Black people are correct in this perception. Those White subjects who claimed to be color-blind were on average *more* prejudiced than those who made no such claims (Awad, Cokley, and Ravitch, 2005). And they significantly support the "All Lives Matter" movement more than the Black-led Black Lives Matter movement (West et al., 2021).

Another way to ignore the racial issue is to employ euphonious language (Rothstein, 2017). The term "ghetto" for Black areas is largely used by social scientists. The

---

[2] These differences are slightly heightened by the fact that the Pew data included Blacks in the totals of both Republicans and Democrats.

preferred polite term is the neutral "inner city." Have you ever heard of "inner-city Whites"? "*De facto* segregation" is preferred to the usually correct term—"*de jure* segregation"—to imply that the racial separation happened naturally. And problems unique to Black Americans are submerged within the expansive term "people of color."

Different Levels of Prejudice

Research has uncovered multiple layers of prejudice: from bias, indifference, and resentment to hatred, fanaticism, and dehumanization.

Bias. All of us are susceptible to *bias*. Growing up in America, we naturally absorb our culture's major racial themes and stereotypes that have accumulated over the centuries. Eberhardt (2019) outlines in her insightful book *Biased* how a host of cognitive factors make this absorption of stereotypes and intergroup biases inevitable. In effect, White Americans are taught to interpret the world racially. She has worked specifically on the unprovoked murders of Black men by White police. And she shows how centrally involved these biases are in these murders.

It has long been thought that many biased behaviors are so accepted by racist norms that they are not even recognized as prejudicial acts by the perpetrators. But ingenious research involving films of 3.5 million pitches in Major League Baseball games calls this assumption into question (Parsons et al., 2011). This study found that White umpires tended to call pitches at the edge of the strike zone differentially according to the race of the pitcher, more often calling a *strike* if the pitcher were White, and a *ball* if the pitcher were Black. Yet in ballparks where every pitch was filmed for careful review, this racial differential disappeared. Apparently, the umpires were at least partially aware of their racial bias and fully capable of correcting it,

Some bias derives from provincialism (Pettigrew, 2010) and mindlessness (see Sidebar 1.2). Measures of these variables predict prejudice over and above that of the prior major predictors. Social psychologists have long emphasized the importance of authoritarianism and social dominance orientation (SDO) to predict group prejudices of many types at the individual level of analysis (Adorno et al., 1950; Sidanius and Pratto, 1999). Together these two factors are such strong and persistent correlates of prejudice that they have become known as the "lethal duo" in the dual process model of Duckitt and Sibley (2009).

In an Italian study of anti-immigrant prejudice with 758 subjects, the authoritarian and SDO variables accounted for 52% of the variance of prejudice. When a nine-item measure of deprovincialization was added to the equation, this percentage rose to 58%. This significant difference ($p < .001$) demonstrates that the deprovincialization measure, even though it is strongly related to the two personality correlates, contributes further to a broader understanding of the complexity of prejudice. Similarly, mindfulness is an additional correlate of prejudice beyond authoritarianism and SDO (Fuochi et al., 2023) (see Sidebar 1.2).

Prejudice **23**

Indifference. Many White Americans who are prejudiced against Black Americans are simply *indifferent* to racial issues generally. Martin Luther King Jr. understood this distinction: "Nothing in this world is more dangerous than sincere ignorance and conscientious stupidity."

Indifferent White Americans routinely explain away clear indications of racial discrimination with various explanations that focus upon blaming Blacks—the blaming the victim technique (Ryan, 1971) —examples of which we have repeatedly noted throughout this volume (See Sidebar 1.3).

Resentment. Political scientists have promoted the concept of White resentment as a major factor in modern American racism (Riley and Peterson, 2020; Davis and Wilson, 2022).[3] Like McGhee (2021), they stress the White perception of a racial zero-sum game. Today's White Americans often claim they oppose racist discrimination, yet they perceive Black American progress as coming at their expense. Trump's "Make America great again" (MAGA) cry fits neatly within this sense of perceived loss. They resent this situation, constantly fed to them by Fox "News," even if it means supporting anti-democratic measures that hurt themselves as well as Black people. The important special feature of resentment is that it stems from a strong sense of injustice.

Hatred. Many people equate prejudice with hatred, but this is mistaken. Hatred is generally the product of the adoption of an anti-minority ideology—such as advanced by Trump's MAGA movement (Martinez, Prooijen, and Van Lange, 2022). Only a minority of those White Americans who can be correctly called prejudiced actually hate Black Americans. That said, those who do hate are dangerous and potentially violent - as when Payton Gendron shot Black shoppers at a Buffalo, New York, grocery store in 2022.

Hate can lead to irrational racist rants, as shown in the outburst by Scott Adams, the creator of the *Dilbert* cartoon. He responded to a poorly conducted survey by Rasmussen Reports, which claimed to find that 26% of Black respondents thought it *not* "OK to be White"—a key phrase popular among racist groups. "If nearly half of all Blacks are not OK with White people," Adams claimed, "that's a hate group." And he no longer would "help" Black Americans. He further urged White people "to get the hell away" from Black people. Of course, 26% is not "nearly half," and there is no evidence that Adams ever helped Blacks. He also evoked the victimhood stance popular among political reactionaries by stressing the money he had lost because of his views (del Barco, 2023).[4]

The worse example of racist hatred that I ever personally experienced occurred on April 4, 1968. That was the day Martin Luther King Jr. was shot and killed in Memphis. I spent the night of the 4th talking to Kenneth Clark and other close Black

---

[3] Davis and Wilson (2022) do not regard resentment as a form of prejudice. But I regard it as one important facet of prejudice which differs in some respects from the other facets described here.

[4] The immediate cancelation of his *Dilbert* cartoon by newspapers throughout the world as well as a canceled book contract were striking developments. Twenty-five years earlier, Adams's remarks might have invited public criticism at most, but not such a widespread rejection. One could argue that this is evidence for the recent decline in the acceptance of blatant racism.

friends—grieving and commiserating together. But in the midst of the evening, a call came in from an old acquaintance, a woman I had grown up with as a neighbor in Richmond, just two houses down from mine. She had married wealth and lived now in Albemarle County, Virginia.

I could hear the murmur of widespread conversation and the clanking of glasses in the background. "I just called to invite you to come down to our party," she said. "We are having a great time celebrating the death of King." Nothing had prepared me for such an outburst of racial hatred from her.

Fanaticism. Taking one step beyond hatred, some Whites can be accurately described as *fanatically* anti-Black. Research has found that fanaticism in general arises when people are absolutely certain of their beliefs and perceive that these beliefs are thought to be completely wrong by a majority of other people (Gollwitzer et al., 2022). The thoroughly disproven idea that the 2020 presidential election was "stolen" that is still believed by many Americans is a prime example of political fanaticism. So are many anti-Black beliefs, such as that the BLM movement supports violence against White people.

Dehumanization. This is the most extreme of the various depths of prejudice. Leyens and his colleagues (2000) experimentally demonstrated the phenomenon with the differential attribution of emotions to out-groups and in-groups. Racists view their in-group as more "human" than out-groups. This European research distinguished "primary emotions" (e.g., joy, guilt) from "secondary emotions" (e.g., hostility, jealousy). Primary emotions are instinctive responses; for example, if threatened, we feel fear. Secondary emotions are experienced in response to other emotions. Primary emotions are shared with animals, while secondary emotions are thought to be uniquely "human." This research shows how these particularly "human" emotions are less often ascribed to out-groups than to in-groups—precisely what those in the slave trade did.

The most compelling—and distressing—experimental evidence for dehumanization is supplied by Eberhardt (2019) and her Stanford University co-workers (Goff et al., 2008; Rattan and Eberhardt, 2010). They found in many White subjects a persistent cognitive link between Black people and African animals: gorillas, baboons, and chimpanzees. This is an old racist association, one found throughout the long history of racist thought in Western culture (Kendi, 2016). Its origins extend back to Europe's first encounters with Black Africans. Even Shakespeare engaged in this raw racism in both *The Tragedy of Othello* and *The Tempest* (Kendi, 2016, pp. 34, 37).

Sometimes the link is just blurted out. The television actress Roseanne Barr likened President Obama's Black advisor Valerie Jarrett to an ape in a late-night tweet and was summarily dismissed by the American Broadcasting Corporation. Realizing the slur had damaged her career, Barr blamed it on her taking the sedative Ambien. The pharmaceutical company that makes Ambien responded tartly that "racism is not a known side effect" of the drug.

President Trump described Alvin Bragg, the Black Manhatten district attorney who won a dramatic case against him, as "an animal." Later Trump, like Hitler, described all his enemies as "vermin." Trump took these occasions to strengthen the tie uncovered by Eberhardt's research.

Moreover, this dangerous dehumanizing link has been found in other largely White nations, including Poland, Portugal, Italy, Spain, Belgium, England, and Australia (Eberhardt, 2019, p. 148). Throwing bananas and other fruit at Black people is the disgusting behavioral actualization of this extreme phenomenon. In America, this utmost racist behavior has occurred at baseball and basketball games. At American University in Washington, D.C., bananas hanging on nooses were found around the campus in 2017 (McLaughlin and Burnside, 2017). In Italy, the nation's first Black governmental minister, Cécile Kyenge, was the target of tossed bananas (Yan, Russell, and Milanover, 2013). Kendi (2016, pp. 333–334) reminds us that this deeply racist association was furthered in the 1930s by such popular movies as *King Kong* and the *Tarzan* series.

This link serves to associate Black males with violence and danger. This connection can even have life-or-death consequences when the defendant is Black and a murder victim is White (Eberhardt et al., 2006). After controlling for multiple factors, the likelihood the accused Black person will be sentenced to death is significantly greater if the defendant is perceived to be more stereotypically Black. Thus, meeting White conceptions of what looks like a Black person can actually shape a verdict. Think about that for a moment. The color of your skin, under these circumstances, can actually lead to your death.

Horrific occurrences can arise from this link between blackness and danger in the minds of some Whites. Ralph Yarl was a teenager in Kansas City, Missouri, in 2023 (Hatzipanagos and Bella, 2023). All of five-feet-eight-inches tall and 140 pounds in weight, he was hardly a threatening figure. Yet when he mistakenly rang the doorbell of an 84-year-old White man, he seemed to be "six feet tall" to Andrew Lester. He shot the teenager because he "was scared to death due to the male's size."

Like most racial phenomena, American dehumanization has its roots in slavery. Charles Dew (2016), a prominent Williams College historian of the American South, provides stark evidence of dehumanization during slavery. He studied the letters between slave traders in Richmond and the slave owners who were interested in selling or buying slaves. One after another, the letters coldly reveal the purely monetary interests of the writers. Routinely, families were broken up, the youngest of the children sold apart from their parents, even the most loyal servants sold and sent to the Deep South for "a good price." Dew searched in vain for some expression - no matter how meager - of humanity, some sense that the owners and traders understood that they were dealing with human beings. The writers of these letters had clearly desensitized themselves from the results of their inhuman actions. It provides a classic case of dehumanization.

Haslam (2006) notes two different types of dehumanization, both of which seem to be operating in Dew's slave letters. He provides a systematic review of the recent proliferation of research studies on dehumanization. He distinguishes between *"animalistic" dehumanization* that denies the rejected out-group human attributes and *"mechanistic" dehumanization* that views the out-group as mere objects. Among racists, dehumanization becomes an everyday social phenomenon that is rooted in ordinary cognitive processes.

Harris and Fiske (2006) go further to show differential neuroimaging responses to extreme out-groups. Using the stereotype content model (Fiske et al., 2002), they show that the low-competence, low-warmth type is especially disparaged. And most slaves were viewed as fitting this lowly caricature. The disgust elicited by this type of out-group activates the left insula (related to disgust) and the amygdala (related to fear). It is this out-group category that is most likely to endure dehumanization.

Some may view the dehumanization process as too extreme an indictment of the intensely prejudiced. However, *The Making of a Racist* (Dew, 2016) makes a strong historical case that such a process is necessary to understand the responses to slavery before the Civil War and the continued unrelenting discrimination against Black Americans after the Civil War—as depicted in later chapters.

Avoiding Today's Racial Inequities. Jennifer Richeson (2020) has expanded on these trends by proposing the existence of *"a mythology of racial progress."* She maintains that there is a dominant narrative in White America of almost continuous improvement in race relations. This book's analyses support her contention. The mythology makes supposed "color blindness" the preferred method of dealing with racial matters. In each realm we will analyze, there has been some improvement together with continuing inequality. The mythology accentuates the advances and ignores the counter-trends and the vast remaining inequality. Its willful ignorance thus justifies inaction and continued discrimination. It reduces the personal problem of cognitive dissonance. "Racial discrimination is, of course, wrong; but there is much less of it now, and it is rapidly disappearing from American society" goes the popular reasoning.

How Black Americans Cope with Racism

Twenty-six studies in psychology have explored how Black Americans respond to racism in the United States and Canada. A review of this research uncovers a wide range of coping mechanisms (Jacob et al., 2022). Most cope through social support from family and friends; some simply avoid stressful situations. Many, like the BLM participants, confront racism directly. And many others, especially the Black elderly, depend heavily on religion. The power of religion throughout Black American history is hard to overestimate. True, the influence of Black religion has waned in recent years, particularly among Black youth outside of the South. Yet throughout its long history it has played a central role in Black life.

African slaves initially had their own religions. And White Americans were in conflict over whether they should try to convert them to Christianity (Kendi, 2016).

Many prominent White leaders believed strongly that it was essential the slaves be encouraged to adopt the White faith. But slave owners objected; they had two concerns. They feared abolitionists would use religion as an argument for ending slavery—that Christians should never be held as slaves. And they worried, with good reason, that Black church gatherings outside of White surveillance could lead to slave uprisings. Nonetheless, in time Black slaves and freedmen alike became overwhelmingly Christian.

Black Americans modified Christianity in significant ways, emphasizing the New Testament and employing the Old Testament only selectively. The Sermon on the Mount offered hope. Religion became the foundation for Black aspirations and freedom. It provided a "Black space" apart from White scrutiny, a place where Black worshipers could be temporally free. Little wonder that so many Black leaders have been Christian ministers—not just King but Ralph Abernathy, John Lewis, Adam Clayton Powell Jr., Jessie Jackson, and many others. Taylor (2006) suggests this phenomenon is a direct legacy of West African culture that featured leaders who occupied both sacred and secular roles.

Black Americans in Social Psychology

As their educational level has risen, Blacks are now entering many new areas of American life where they were previously absent. They have enhanced many fields by contributing their own distinctive and needed perspectives. Social psychology is no exception.

Earlier, the most famous Black social psychologist was my friend and colleague Kenneth Clark (1914–2005). His research and activism sparked the legal cases that led directly to the *Brown* school desegregation Supreme Court ruling (Jones and Pettigrew, 2005). Many have now followed Clark. Eight in particular have influenced me and the discipline generally. James Jones (1972, 1997) of the University of Delaware wrote two editions of *Prejudice and Racism* that have served as widely adopted texts. James Jackson (1944–2020) of the University of Michigan established the first national probability surveys of Black Americans (Jackson, 1991). Claude Steele (1997, 2020) at Stanford University advanced the concept of stereotype threat and its application to minority student test performance.

Larry Bobo at Harvard University helped to supply the valuable survey data used throughout this chapter. The late Jim Sidanius (1945–2021) trained in Sweden and later taught at UCLA and Harvard University. With Felicia Pratto, he introduced social dominance theory and its measures that have proven highly useful (Sidanius et al., 2008; Sidanius and Pratto, 1999). And John Jemmott III at the University of Pennsylvania has worked in southern Africa as well as in the United States to develop new methods to combat such diseases as AIDS (Jemmott, Jemmott, and Fong, 1998).

Now a new and larger cohort of Black social psychologists are introducing innovative ideas to the discipline, such as Richeson's (2020) mythology of racial progress. Jennifer Eberhardt (2019) at Stanford University summed up her work in the acclaimed volume *Biased: Uncovering the Hidden Prejudice That Shapes What*

28   Anti-Black Racism in America

We See, Think, and Do. Both Richeson and Eberhardt obtained their doctorates at Harvard University and are the first social psychologists to receive MacArthur "Genius" Awards.

Bringing new ideas and experiences to the discipline, these Black Americans have reinvigorated social psychology.

A Final Assessment

Has American racism at the level of attitudes declined? We have noted marked improvements in both implicit and explicit racial attitudes. In general, we can conclude that racist attitudes have declined to some degree. Yet there are also strong counter-trends. And the political polarization of the country during the Trump years has led to a solid minority of White Americans being more open in their expression of their racist views.

The following chapters will document how racial counter-trends operate throughout major American institutions. In education, Black Americans have attained more years of training, but school segregation remains widespread for Black children. In politics, the 1965 Civil Rights Act promised a major breakthrough for Black voting, yet it has been constantly narrowed ever since. In economics, dire Black poverty has been reduced, but many Blacks remain on the brink of privation. In the health domain, some diagnoses have improved for Black Americans, while their death rates from heart, cancer, and other key diagnoses remain higher than those of Whites.

Justice still eludes Black America. Not only does blatant racial discrimination exist throughout the nation's criminal justice system, but mass Black incarceration now replaces slavery and Jim Crow as a major means of maintaining White supremacy. Finally, racial segregation in housing has slowly declined in the past 60 years; however, major cities with the largest Black populations show the smallest declines. So the perpetuation of racial discrimination and separation holds firm as long as massive housing segregation is maintained—a major theme of this book.

Highly recommended additional reading on this subject:

> Kendi, I. X. (2016). *Stamped from the beginning: The definitive history of racist ideas in America*. New York: Bold Type Books.

Sidebar 1.1 Discounting Black Accomplishments

White America can simply ignore Black accomplishments, and it can restrict Blacks from roles that would counter negative stereotypes. Consider two examples of these processes—one relatively unknown, the other widely publicized.

Have you ever heard of Garrett Morgan—the Black Thomas Watson (DeLuca, 2021)? He was the son of a Confederate general father and a slave mother. Among other achievements, two of Morgan's inventions have saved countless lives. He invented an early version of a gas mask, which he called a "safety hood." He used it in an emergency in 1916 to save the lives of eight men trapped in an underground pipe in Cleveland, Ohio.

The saved men were awarded generous cash bonuses and medals, while Morgan went unrecognized. Indeed, the *New York Times*, the *Chicago Tribune*, and other newspapers carried the story but failed to mention Morgan.

Five years later, Morgan witnessed a horrific crash between a horse-drawn cart and an early automobile at an intersection. He reasoned that the accident was the result of the then widely used two-light traffic signal: red for stop, green for go. Morgan patented a three-light traffic signal in 1923, adding a yellow light in between the red and green signals. Thanks to his patent, Morgan was recognized this time. Watson's General Electric Corporation paid him $40,000 (roughly $739,000 in 2025 dollars). He spent much of the money to establish a country club for Black Americans outside of Cleveland.

A second example has been widely publicized: the long-held belief that Black athletes were not smart enough to be effective quarterbacks in professional football (Brewer, 2023). This stereotype caused some astoundingly racist (and stupid) decisions throughout the 20th century. Charlie Ward, a star Black quarterback at Florida State University, won the 1993 Heisman Trophy as the nation's best collegiate football player of the year. Yet, based on the long-term racist stereotype, not a single team in the National Football League would hire him. A gifted athlete, Ward went on to play in the National Basketball Association League for 11 years.

By 2023, 11 NFL teams had Black quarterbacks, and for the first time the Superbowl featured two Black quarterbacks: Patrick Mahomes of the Kansas City Chiefs and Jalen Hurts of the Philadelphia Eagles. Much was made by the mass media of this belated occurrence. And as if to end the negative stereotype forever, the two put on an amazing display of talent. Hurts set a record for Superbowl quarterbacks by personally scoring three touchdowns. Mahomes, playing on an injured ankle, won the game, 38–35, with a dazzling passing exhibition.

Such publicized accounts of stereotype-defying performances are strongly welcomed by Black America. Black observers are not surprised by them and hope that White Americans recognize their significance. Witness the reaction of many Black people when Deion Sanders, the vibrant star pro-athlete, left his highly successful football coaching position at Mississippi's Jackson State University, a predominantly Black institution, and moved to the predominantly White University of Colorado.

While Colorado football previously had endured a season of 1 win and 11 losses, Sanders, his own sons, and other new recruits astounded the sports world by upsetting several major football powers. Sanders became a highly publicized folk hero. And Black celebrities began cheering on the Colorado team although they had no attachment to the university. He had punctured another racist myth for all to see.

Sidebar 1.2 Two Newly Uncovered Correlates of Prejudice

Two important correlates of prejudice have been recently uncovered: provincialism (Pettigrew, 2010) and mindlessness (Fuochi et al., 2023). Provincialism describes being unsophisticated and centered in one's own small world. The term developed to describe one who lives in the provinces and is oblivious to the ways of the broader, outside world. Provincial people are more easily threatened by new and strange experiences. Provincialism develops from group separation, from insular life in highly segregated

30   Anti-Black Racism in America

communities. Thus, breaking out from the in-group cocoon is a major means of weakening provincialism.

Many forms of diverse experiences can erode the phenomenon, from changing your job to moving your residence. All of them, however, involve being thrust out of old patterns of thought and life into new patterns. When these new experiences involve other groups and cultures, we can be aroused out of our narrow provincialism—a process of *deprovincialization* (Pettigrew, 1997, 2010; Lucarini et al., 2023; Verkuyten, Thijs, and Bekhuis, 2010; Verkuyten, Voci, and Pettigrew, 2022).

Both popular writers and psychologists have suggested that diversity of experience leads to a host of positive outcomes. Heightened creativity in the arts is often cited: German-born Handel composed his celebrated works in England; Spanish-born Picasso painted his greatest works in France; and American-born T. S. Eliot wrote his famous poetry in England.

Mark Twain is perhaps the leading advocate of travel and wide experience to broaden one's perspective. He benefited from wide travel combined with extended stays in Sweden, Hawaii, Germany, and the United Kingdom. This led him to write in *The Innocents Abroad*, "Travel is fatal to prejudice, bigotry, and narrow-mindedness. . . . It liberates the mind to travel—you never saw a bigoted, opinionated, stubborn, narrow-minded, self-concerned man in your life but he had stuck in one place since he was born."

Beyond these anecdotal examples, corroborating research findings include the results of MacKinnon's (1962) study of the world's most creative architects. Compared with lesser-known architects, these men as children had more often moved with their families, leading to a greater diversity of experience. This diversity enhanced their ability to adopt multiple perspectives.

Experiments show that diversifying experiences enhance cognitive flexibility (Ritter et al., 2012). At broader levels, living abroad (not just traveling abroad) consistently relates to greater creativity (Leung et al., 2008; Maddux, Adam, and Galinsky, 2010; Maddux and Galinsky, 2009). And at the macro level, periods of immigration in Japan have been followed by sharp rises in cultural achievement (Simonton, 1997).

Thus, deprovincialization entails diminished provincialism and removing provincial blinders. It indicates a growing acceptance of other peoples and cultures. Deprovincialized individuals are more experienced in the wider world. They learn their group's norms, customs, and lifestyles are not the only ways to manage the social world successfully. This new perspective individualizes out-group members and serves to provide a fresh perspective on your own in-group and culture (Pettigrew, 2011). This reappraisal need not cause you to view your own group and culture less positively—just differently.

Deprovincialization allows one to respect, even admire other peoples and cultures while looking at your own group in a new and more complex way. The late U.S. Supreme Court's associate justice Ruth Bader Ginsburg provides a pertinent example. While a law student, she became especially interested in civil procedure—which, among other functions, determines the cases that get heard in court. Then she had the opportunity to study in Sweden and learn about its civil procedure. "Reading and observing another

Prejudice **31**

system," she later commented, "made me understand my own system so much better" (quoted in Biskupic, 2020).

Research has shown that Ginsburg's experience is widely shared. As noted, research has repeatedly found that living abroad is positively related to creativity generally. Other studies show personality traits are involved in this process. Multicultural experience effects on reducing stereotypes and prejudice can be fully mediated by a reduction in *the need for cognitive closure*—so-called "epistemic unfreezing" (Tadmore et al., 2012). These effects can also be fully mediated by increases in *openness to new experiences* (Sparkman, Eidelman, and Blanchar, 2017). A primary, though not the only, means of attaining deprovincialism is though *intergroup contact* (Pettigrew, 2021). We explore this link in detail in Chapter 9.

Deprovincialism has two intercorrelated facets (+.65): (1) *a nuanced perspective on your in-group* and (2) *greater acceptance of out-groups*. Short scales of both have been employed in the Netherlands, Germany, and Italy (Martinovic and Verkuyten, 2013; Boin, Fuochi, and Voci, 2020). A sample item from the first facet, called the Cultural Deprovincialization Scale, is "How we perceive the world in our country is just one of many possibilities." A sample item for the second facet, called the Group Deprovincialization Scale, is "Getting to know individuals from different cultures makes me feel more open toward other people."

The two facets have similar correlates, including significantly more positive attitudes toward immigrants. The total scale has *positive* correlations with cognitive flexibility, multilingualism, openness to new experience,[5] more second-language usage, greater open-mindedness, higher educational level, and left-wing political attitudes. It also relates positively with time spent living in foreign countries. Further construct validity is also shown by its *negative* associations with social dominance orientation, authoritarianism, and right-wing nationalism.[6]

Lucarini and her colleagues (2023), using 770 Italian subjects, provide a network analysis of the two facets with seven predictors. The two sub-scales have the strongest link of all paths in the network—further support that they belong together in a single deprovincialization scale. Both facets link strongly and negatively with prejudice.

Overall, these associations confirm the construct validity of the full scale, showing that deprovincialization is an individual orientation strongly related to openness toward other individuals and new experiences and to a flexible, open, and tolerant mindset.

Similarly, mindfulness is also associated with a tolerant mindset. It is both a mental state and a dispositional, non-judgmental attitude. Using a five-item Italian-language version of a scale that operationalizes dispositional mindfulness (Bishop et al., 2006),

---

[5] Genetic research on 3,177 twins and their siblings suggests an intriguing possibility (Nacke and Riemann, 2023). Social dominance orientation and authoritarianism seem to share a common genetic background with later environmental factors dividing them. Openness to new experience could be part of this genetic commonality. Since it relates strongly to all three of these variables, deprovincialization could also be partly shaped by this genetic factor. Yet, since it is also heavily determined by experience, one can speculate that its genetic etiology is less than that of the other three factors.

[6] Brewer (2008) discusses another concept close to deprovincialization: *social identity complexity*. Though measured differently, it, too, correlates highly and negatively with prejudice.

32 Anti-Black Racism in America

Fuochi et al. (2023) found that it relates positively with deprovincialization and positive intergroup contact and negatively with prejudice against immigrants. The dispositional curiosity and reflection facets of the measure mediate most of these effects.

Sidebar 1.3 The Significance of "BUT"

Focusing on one major characteristic of White American indifference, Whitney Young, Jr., former head of the National Urban League, often in his speeches highlighted the significance of the conjunction, *BUT*, in White America's discourse on Black-White relations.[7] "I support better race relations," goes a common refrain, "*BUT* you cannot expect things to change overnight." "*BUT* Blacks themselves will first have to reform their own communities before we can have real progress." "I favor racially integrated schools, *BUT* I oppose all the bussing of children that it requires." "I am ashamed that our nation tolerated the institution of slavery, *BUT* I oppose compensatory funds going to Black Americans a century-and-a-half later." In 2003, President George Bush celebrated Dr. Martin Luther King's birthday in a nationally televised statement; *BUT* he simultaneously announced his strident opposition to affirmative action programs at the University of Michigan.

So Young lamented, "It's the *BUTS* that kill me!"

This volume follows up in detail on Whitney Young's incisive point. Seven decades after *Brown v. Board of Education*, we can note the truly significant improvements in African-American life in many areas of life that have occurred over these years. *But* in every domain, we still have a long way to go in America before racial equality is even approached in America. We should recognize the progress; *but* we cannot as yet celebrate the demise of American racism as long as there remains so much to achieve. And it is these many continuing barriers to full equality for African Americans that are the particular focus of this volume.

---

[7] Young was especially effective at opening up jobs for Blacks in major corporations. His charming manner helped, and he could hold his own when faced with racial naivety. Once in my presence, a corporate head said to him: "Whit, if all Negroes were like you, there would be no racial problem." Young snapped back, "If all *White* people were like me, there would no racial problem!".

Chapter 2
Racial Discrimination

Racial discrimination must be carefully distinguished from prejudice (Pettigrew, 2015a). The two concepts and phenomena are intricately interrelated, but they are distinctly different. One can occur without the other, depending on the norms involved (see Chapter 3). Racial discrimination involves the unfair denial of resources and opportunities to a group on the grounds of race. A comprehensive review of racism requires careful attention to both phenomena.

The causal order of the two phenomena is commonly thought to be that prejudice leads to discrimination. But the racial historian Ibram Kendi (2016) provides convincing evidence that at the level of American society the causal order is often reversed. That is, racial discrimination (e.g., slavery, disenfranchisement, the Black codes, segregated housing and schools) has often come first, followed by racial prejudice that attempts to explain and justify the discrimination.

Discrimination exists in straightforward actions as well as in complex systems of social relations that produce racial inequities. Some analysts view *all* racial disparities as the result of discrimination; others restrict the concept to those acts *intended* to limit an out-group's resources. The first view is too broad, the second too restrictive (Pettigrew and Taylor, 1992).

Social scientists make an important distinction between direct and indirect discrimination. The direct form occurs at points where inequality is generated—often intentionally, though not always. The indirect form develops when the inequitable results of direct discrimination shapes later decisions; it perpetuates and magnifies the original injury.

Discrimination Is Normative

The structural web of discrimination outlives its initiators and may not reflect current attitudes. Indeed, we will note throughout later chapters how discriminatory practices that took shape during slavery and into the 1930s still influence modern racism even though they are not generally supported by current generations of White Americans.

Moreover, discrimination feeds upon itself; it is cumulative and self-perpetuating. Effective remedies must intervene and reverse this "vicious circle." Such action is not simply a matter of reducing the prejudice of individuals. Altering the social structure and its supporting norms is much more difficult to achieve than changing attitudes.

Anti-Black Racism in America. Thomas F. Pettigrew, Oxford University Press. © Oxford University Press (2025).
DOI: 10.1093/9780197803134.003.0003

34 Anti-Black Racism in America

Discriminatory structures often remain long after racial attitudes have markedly improved.

Racial discrimination is not, as popularly thought, simply the accumulation of individual acts of unfairness between members of different groups. It consists as well of an elaborate web of institutional arrangements that produces group inequalities, a web that becomes *racial* discrimination when the groups perceive each other as separate "races." We will note throughout the following chapters that these inequalities, which are studied by most of the social sciences, can involve political power, economic resources, cultural and educational access, and where people can live.

Conceptual Complexities

Viewing racial discrimination as an institutional web casts a wide net but leaves considerable room for ambiguity. Disagreement about what constitutes discrimination stems from two sources—one ideological and political, the other empirical. First, because discrimination typically violates law and America's professed values, the judgment that unequal outcomes reflect discrimination is a call for unpopular change and costly remedies.

This is especially true in today's America, when the right-left political split is so intense. Conservatives are quick to deny racial inequities as discrimination, while liberals are quick to argue that discrimination is involved. Complicating interpretations further, deficiencies in analysis and evidence limit the ability of social science to trace precisely the dynamic system of effects triggered by discrimination.

Consider First the Political Issue. The broadest definitions of discrimination assume that racial minorities have no inherent characteristics that warrant inferior social outcomes—a complete reversal of racist thinking. Thus, *all* inequality becomes a legacy of discrimination and a social injustice to be remedied. Favored by the political left, this view is simply too sweeping.

By contrast, political conservatives favor a narrow definition that limits the concept's scope by including only actions directly *intended* to restrict a group's opportunities. Social science specialists resist this reformulation for several reasons. An intentionality criterion returns the concept to the realm of psychology and deflects attention from the restraining social structure. Moreover, the invisibility of intentions creates formidable obstacles for proving discrimination. Last, the effects of discrimination are the same whether or not the causal institutional mechanisms were intended to produce group inequalities.

Direct and Indirect Discrimination

This rejection of the intentionality criterion leads to the distinction between direct and indirect discrimination (Pettigrew, 1985). Direct racial discrimination occurs at points where inequality is generated, often intentionally. When decisions are based explicitly on race, discrimination is direct. Indirect discrimination occurs when the inequitable results of direct discrimination serve as the basis for later decisions. Hence, discrimination is indirect when an ostensibly nonracial criterion becomes a proxy for race in determining social outcomes. Indirect discrimination perpetuates and magnifies the original injury. And it is more difficult to detect. We will uncover numerous examples of this indirect form of racial discrimination in later chapters.

Wage discrimination illustrates this direct versus indirect distinction. Direct racial discrimination exists when employers pay equally qualified members of two races different rates for the same work. Indirect discrimination exists when employers pay the two groups unequally because prior discrimination in employment, education, or housing created apparent differences in qualifications or channeled the groups into better- or worse-paying jobs.

This distinction between direct and indirect discrimination resembles the distinction made by legal systems between *disparate treatment* and *disparate impact*. While intentional direct discrimination may have triggered the causal chain, the original injury is often perpetuated and magnified by largely unwitting accomplices. To be sure, these accomplices typically benefit from the discriminatory arrangements and have little incentive to alter them. Still, the critical point is that these beneficiaries of the discriminatory practices did not initiate them and may not even be aware of their existence.

This conceptual complexity carries over to impede the empirical study of discrimination. Apparently rigorous quantitative analyses often camouflage the crucial issues, as an examination of wage decomposition research reveals. Assessments of discrimination produced by decomposing gross racial differences in social outcomes are common in sociology and economics. This approach first assigns one segment of the gross racial differential to "qualifications" and other factors deemed legitimate determinants of social rewards, such as years of education. The residual segment not demonstrably linked to these "legitimate" determinants of the outcomes is then presented as the estimate of discrimination. However, without better information than is usually available and closer agreement about what constitutes discrimination, no unique estimate of discrimination is possible. The particular choice of control variables to index "legitimate" determinants of social outcomes directly shapes the answers. Any appearance of scientific certitude is an illusion. Not surprisingly, discrimination estimates from this approach vary widely.

Empirical research on group discrimination must mirror the phenomenon in its variety and complexity. The regression decomposition approach is useful but limited. Regression analyses could provide more pertinent information if based on structural equation models that test reciprocal causation. If the aim is to guide policy, a framework far more complex than the dichotomous discrimination-or-not approach is required. Research that traces the actual processes of institutional discrimination is essential. Also needed is more attention to victims' perceptions of discrimination and to the changes generated by anti-discrimination efforts.

36 Anti-Black Racism in America

American Labor Unions and Racial Discrimination

By the mid-20th century, the United States had developed into the world's leading industrial nation. Europe was still recovering from the devastation of World War II, and China had not begun its industrial rise. It was a rare time in the American economy when the nation's working class actually made gains that narrowed the financial gap with wealthier citizens. Indeed, today's middle class can be largely traced back to these prosperous years (1950–1970).

Black Americans, however, were typically left out of this middle-class growth. Unions played a major role in the racial discrimination that typically locked Black workers out of the improving job market. Craft unions in particular successfully and vigorously opposed their entry. These unions tended to view it as *a zero-sum game*: assuming there was no expansion in jobs, the more jobs Black workers obtained, the fewer such jobs would be open to White workers. This was the basic stance of the American Federation of Labor (AFL). Founded in 1886 when several unions joined together, it was a politically conservative organization that focused on bread-and-butter issues for its almost entirely White membership. At its height in the 1920s and 1930s, the AFL combined about 100 skill unions, a loose confederation of local organizations that maintained their independence.

In the 1930s, tensions began to rise between the craft unions (e.g., plumbers, pipefitters, carpenters, shoemakers, nurses) and the industrial unions (e.g., automobile workers, miners, teamsters, longshoremen). The AFL had largely ignored unskilled and semi-skilled workers, many of whom were African Americans in large industrial corporations. This led to a breakup of the old AFL and the formation of the Congress of Industrial Organizations (CIO) in 1935. Its membership was open to Black Americans (see Sidebar 2.1).

The CIO's Sharply Different Tack on Race

Led by Walter Reuther, the CIO argued for unity between Black and White workers. This meant giving up the old AFL conception of a zero-sum game of finite resources. With the races together, Reuther maintained union power was much stronger. As long as the races were divided, corporate power was enhanced by the constant threat to replace White strikers with desperate Black workers—a tactic that for decades had been successively used against AFL unions. Slowly yet steadily, the interracial view became widely adopted by organized labor.

The AFL and CIO organizations joined together in 1955, but the tension between the two remained. Two years later, the more militant Teamsters Union was expelled on corruption charges. It was not until 1987 that the Teamsters rejoined the larger AFL-CIO. However, tensions accumulated as the ranks of union members declined sharply. The percentage of Black union members has declined faster than that of White members, but it remains somewhat greater than that of Whites.

In 2005, the Teamsters together with the Service Employees International Union (SEIU) and two smaller unions bolted from the AFL-CIO, taking with them a third of the larger union's 13 million members. While the Teamsters have been open to Black membership, its White members have been reluctant to elect Black members to leadership roles. Still, the Teamsters have continued their success at unionizing many previously unorganized groups—even graduate student teaching assistants in the University of California.

The SEIU's two million members includes police unions, yet the group still condemned police violence and supported the Black Lives Matter movement. The SEIU is one of the few unions actually gaining members, many of them Black Americans. Indeed, the loss of members is now a severe problem for other unions. The percentage of wage and salaried workers who belong to unions was only 10.1% in 2022, down from 20.1% in 1983 (U.S. Bureau of Labor Statistics, 2023). McGhee (2021, pp. 115–116) maintains that the steep decline in union membership occurred partly as a result of the United Auto Workers' becoming more racially liberal. This is yet another example of racism hurting White as well as Black Americans.

Attempts to regain union members at Starbucks and Amazon have been met with fierce opposition by the companies. According to the National Labor Relations Board, these nationwide companies have employed "old-school union busting" with their anti-union tactics that are both illegal and effective (Greenhouse, 2023).

Union Effects on Racial Attitudes. Discrimination at the societal level increases prejudice at the individual level. In reverse, the reduction in discrimination lessens prejudice. In a groundbreaking study, Frymer and Grumbach (2020) found that union membership reduces racial prejudice and resentment. Cross-sectional analyses between 2010 and 2016 showed that White union members express less racial resentment than non-members and offer greater support for policies that benefit Black Americans. Overtime panel analyses also found that Black workers gaining union membership during these years reduced racial resentment among White workers.

Racial Discrimination in the United States and Western Europe

Both direct and indirect forms of racial discrimination can be found throughout the world. Most of the available research, however, focuses on America's long-festering racial problems (Pager and Shepherd, 2008). In such long-term situations, injuries of indirect discrimination are often more extensive than those of direct discrimination.

This conclusion does not imply that direct discrimination no longer exists. Employment complaint records reveal the continued operation of highly direct forms of discrimination. U.S. women and minorities have filed more than 2 million job discrimination complaints since 1965. Not all such complaints reflect genuine discrimination. That said, analysts believe that false complaints are minimal in

38 Anti-Black Racism in America

comparison with the amount of actual discrimination that goes unreported and undetected (Tomaskovic-Devey and Stainback, 2007).

Many major corporations have been hit with racial discrimination suites by the U.S. Equal Employment Opportunity Commission - such as Lockheed Martin, A & P grocers, a Toyota dealership, and Jackson National Life Insurance Company. And employment audits using paired, equally qualified applicants reveal widespread direct discrimination. Employers admit to interviewers that their stereotypes of minorities, particularly of inner-city Black men, lead them to avoid minority hiring (Eberhardt, 2019; Reskin, 1998).

Along with direct employment discrimination, indirect discrimination is also pervasive. Many employers rely on word-of-mouth recruiting of new employees, especially for unskilled jobs. Thus, the current workforce, often disproportionately White, reproduces existing racial inequalities in employment by bringing in White friends and relatives as the next generation of workers. This is just one aspect of "business as usual" that represents indirect discrimination. Although word-of-mouth recruiting appears to be color-blind, it actually serves to perpetuate racial inequalities (Greenwald and Pettigrew, 2014; Reskin, 1998).

Analogous dynamics afflict the minorities of other nations. Research on the subject has emerged in Western Europe. Discrimination against the region's new immigrant racial minorities is pervasive (Pettigrew, 1998b). Thirty-three percent of all minority respondents in an EU-wide survey reported they had been personally discriminated against, and 12% felt they had been a victim of a racially motivated crime in the past 12 months (European Union Fundamental Rights Agency, 2010). Romas and Black Africans are particular targets. Survey results in France, where Black people are only 4% of the population, show an even sharper degree of perceived discrimination. Sixty-one percent of French minority respondents in 2007 believed that they had personally experienced discrimination in the past year (BBC News, 2007).

Both direct and indirect discrimination are involved, though the indirect forms often go unrecognized in Europe. Investigators have repeatedly uncovered direct discrimination. Controlled tests reveal the full litany of discriminatory forms involving employment, housing, public accommodation, the courts, police, insurance, and banks. Data on police stops and searches in England and Wales, for example, indicated that Black drivers were nine times more likely to be stopped and searched by police than were White drivers (Dodd, 2020).

Employment discrimination poses the most serious problem. In every European Union nation, minorities have markedly higher unemployment rates than natives. As in the United States, there are many reasons for minority unemployment disparities. The "last-hired, first-fired" principle and seniority rights selectively affect younger minority workers. Typically less skilled, they are more affected by job upgrading. Minorities also are more likely to be in older, declining industries.

Planners put minorities into these industries for cheaper labor precisely because of their decline. Yet these multiple factors offer insufficient explanations for the greater unemployment of minorities. Veenman and Roelandt (1990) found that education, age, sex, region, and employment level explained only a small portion of the differential group unemployment rates in the Netherlands.

Indirect discrimination arises when a person is denied citizenship, restricting immigrants' opportunities for suitable housing, employment, and schooling. In short, the lives of Europe's non-citizens are severely circumscribed. Castles (1984) contends that the guest-worker system that brought many immigrants to Europe in the 1950s and 1960s was itself a state-controlled system of institutional discrimination. It established the newcomers as a stigmatized out-group suitable for low-status jobs but not citizenship. Racial prejudice adds to this stigma. Widespread indirect discrimination, then, was inevitable for these victims of direct discrimination.

Psychological Effects of Racial Discrimination

Social psychologists have examined extensively the effects of discrimination upon its victims. Multiple studies show that when people perceive themselves to be the target of systematic discrimination, their physical and psychological health suffers. I keenly recall when my wife, Ann, accidentally learned that she was being paid substantially less then male medical interns in the same service with the same duties. She was more hurt and depressed than angry that her employer, whom she liked, would do this behind her back.

Moreover, perceived discrimination both increases the likelihood of engaging in dangerous and unhealthy behaviors and decreases the likelihood of performing healthy behaviors (Pacoe and Richman, 2009). These effects are largely mediated by increased stress, and they have been found for a variety of groups, including White people. Greater drug use among those perceiving discrimination is part of this process (Gibbons et al., 2004). Chapter 7 explores this process in detail.

Discrimination also heightens victims' awareness of any cultural stigmatization of their group. Such *"stereotype threat"* can be stressful and hinder performance. It is triggered by situations that contain cues that make a negative stereotype salient. This situation raises the strong possibility that one's own performance will conform to the stereotype and confirm it. Thus, African Americans tend to score higher on intelligence tests when they take the test apart from White Americans. Stereotype threat is not unique to racial minorities. Women tend to score higher on tests of mathematics when there are no men in the room, and Whites score higher on such tests when there are no Asians present (Steele, 1997, 2010).

Remedies for Racial Discrimination

The most elaborate array of remedial measures for racial discrimination is found in North America. Both Canada and the United States have instituted a battery of laws against many types of racial and other forms of discrimination. Court rulings in the

40 Anti-Black Racism in America

two nations have also proven helpful. The effects of these legal actions are magnified by *class action suits*, the ability of single litigants to sue for remedy for their entire "class" or group. Further remedies have involved various forms of "affirmative action" in which special efforts are made to close group disparities caused by discrimination. These approaches have led to narrowing racial disparities in social outcomes. However, sharp racial inequities remain in both countries, and majority resistance has hardened against the most successful remedies.

It is informative to compare the North American experience with that of European nations facing similar workplace problems. Anti-discrimination remedies have been largely ineffective in Europe. Germany guarantees basic rights only to citizens, so the disadvantages of non-citizenship include the inability to combat discrimination. There is extensive German legislation to combat anti-Semitism and Nazi ideology, but these laws have proven ineffective in protecting non-citizens. The German Constitution explicitly forbids discrimination on the basis of origin, race, language, beliefs, or religion—but not citizenship. The Federal Constitutional Court has ruled that differential treatment based on citizenship is constitutional only if there is a reasonable basis for it and if it is not wholly arbitrary.

In 2006, under pressure from the European Union, Germany passed the General Equal Treatment Act (*Allgemeines Gleichbehandlungsgesetz - AGG*). It prohibits discrimination in the labor market, in access to public services such as social welfare benefits, and in the housing market based on race, ethnic origin, sex, religion, disability, age, or sexual orientation (Wikipedia, 2024). This is especially critical in getting a work permit. Refugees usually need this permit to get a job. However, since the Russian invasion of the Ukraine in 2022, Ukrainian refugees have had immediate access to the job market. German unions, in fields where they are strong, have a reputation for accepting non-German workers, yet there are still problems in the application procedures.

Even though Germany's AGG does not place the burden of proof on them, plaintiffs must submit the initial evidence to support their claim that discrimination has occurred. Then the accused party must prove otherwise. Yet it remains difficult for plaintiffs to claim their rights. Often the victims of discrimination do not know their full rights, and consultancy services are rarely available. Not surprisingly, few cases have been brought under the law, and fewer still have been successful.

Effective means of combating discrimination are also rare in France. Commentators often view discrimination as "natural" and universally triggered when a "threshold of tolerance" (*seuil de tolerance*) is surpassed. Without supporting evidence, this rationalization supports quotas and dispersal policies that restrict minority access to suitable housing and employment. Precise data are difficult to obtain since French law prohibits the collection of religious and ethnic data (Wikipedia, 2023).

The Netherlands, the United Kingdom, and Sweden have enacted anti-discrimination legislation that specifically applies to new immigrant minorities. And the Dutch have instituted modest affirmative action programs for women and minorities (De Vries and Pettigrew, 1994). Yet this legislation has been largely ineffective for two interrelated reasons. First, European legal systems do not allow class action suits—a forceful North American weapon to combat discrimination. Second, European efforts rely heavily on individual complaints rather than systemic remedies. The United Kingdom's 1976 Act gave the Commission for Racial Equality power to cast a broader net, but individual complaints remain the chief tool (MacEwen, 1995). These weaknesses underline the importance of class action suits and federal enforcement in North American attempts to combat employment discrimination.

A Major Benefit of Immigration

When new immigrants get their chance, Germany, like the United States, has often benefited markedly. Consider the married couple Ugur Sahin and Ozlem Tureci, who developed one of the most successful vaccines against the COVID-19 virus. Sahin was born in Turkey and immigrated to Germany at the age of four. Tureci was born in Germany of recent Turkish immigrants. Both trained in Germany. Their firm, BioN-Tech, joined with America's Pfizer Pharmaceutical Corporation to make the vaccine internationally available. In turn, Pfizer was founded by two German immigrants to the United States in 1849.

Opponents of immigration rarely consider this clear benefit of immigration. It brings in fresh talent, although it has the negative effect of depriving the sending nations of talent. The president of the National Academy of Science, Marcia McNutt (2023), provides Nobel Prize data to reveal the enormous value of immigration to American science. Since the first Nobel Prizes were awarded in 1901, the United States has garnered 368—far more than any other nation. Immigrants are a critical part of this achievement: 33% of Nobel Prizes in Physics, 21% of Nobel Prizes in Economics, and 28% of all Nobel Prizes awarded to Americans.

Overall Assessment

Given the belated acceptance of Black workers into America's major unions, there has been some reduction in racial discrimination in working-class employment. Yet this advance is limited by the fact that unions now comprise an ever smaller share of the country's workforce. Further efforts to upgrade Black employment will be hampered by numerous factors. Individual efforts are unlikely to alter discrimination because they are non-strategic. Minorities bring few charges against the worst discriminatory firms because they avoid applying to these firms in the first place. Complaints about job promotion are common, but they are made largely against employers that hire minorities. Effective anti-discrimination laws must provide broad powers

42 Anti-Black Racism in America

to an enforcement agency to initiate strategic, institution-wide actions that uproot the structural foundations of discrimination. You cannot depend on individual complaints. Such strategic laws are yet to be enacted.

Sidebar 2.1 Sneaking Past Racial Job Barriers

As a teenager in the 1940s, I witnessed firsthand how employment discrimination operated and what it took to sneak past it. My father was a mechanical engineer who owned a small heating and plumbing company in Richmond, Virginia. He grew up in the Alleghany Mountains of Virginia, where there were no Black residents and consequently no racial norms.

He thus escaped being raised in racism and was quite non-political. He had three engineering degrees, and his life revolved around his family and his work. He tended to accept society as it was, although he never objected to my anti-racism activities—just gently warning me occasionally to be "careful." He served with others as a model for my doctoral thesis contention that conformity was the primary force behind racism in the southern United States rather than enhanced authoritarianism (Pettigrew, 1959). He largely conformed to Virginia's racial norms but was the very opposite of an authoritarian. I labeled such Southerners "latent liberals" on the expectation that they would shift their conformist views once southern racial norms changed.

I went on jobs with him in the 1940s and got to know personally the company's small staff. Business was booming because of war contracts to heat the newly built factories of Reynolds Metal Company south of the city. On the staff were two Black workers who had become highly skilled. They worked hard and had made themselves indispensable to the company and its White workers. Contact theory had worked (Chapter 9).

Problems arose around pay. The involved craft union, like many such White unions throughout the nation at that time, sternly forbade equal pay and promotions for Black workers. My father did not see this in racial terms particularly; he just saw it as patently unfair. In quiet defiance of both the union and Virginia's discriminatory state regulations, he paid the Black workers their rightful full wage equal to that of White workers doing comparable jobs—wages that looked big following the lean years of the Great Depression.

What fascinated me at the time was that everyone in the small company knew that my father was breaking union rules and state law—the bookkeeper, the secretary, and even White workers who had grown up in the most racist parts of southern Virginia. They liked the Black workers, admired their willingness to work hard and skillfully, and never once reported my father's violation of union regulations and state law. It helped, too, that there was a scarcity of such skilled workers during World War II. It was also important that the company was a small one that ensured close contact among the entire staff.

Still, this situation was a rare case. Nationally, union resistance to Black workers being hired and receiving equal pay was intense, save where there was a shortage of White workers for work directly involved with war orders (Rothstein, 2017).

Chapter 3
The Power of Racial Norms

In many interracial situations, highly prejudiced people *do not* discriminate. And in many other situations, quite tolerant people *do* discriminate. These exceptions are shaped by the racial norms that govern in these situations. Strong norms, supported by punishment, against discrimination persuade many bigots to avoid discriminatory behavior. Wide acceptance of discrimination in other situations can cause even the tolerant to exhibit discriminatory behavior. Thus, marked changes in racial norms can have major effects on individual behavior. These normative effects are contingent on how strong the norms are and how firmly they are enforced (Pettigrew, 1991).

In rough outline, normative theory holds that most group interaction—at both the interpersonal and intergroup levels—is shaped by the existence of widely shared expectations regarding how the groups should and will interact. The *formal norms* comprise these shared expectations of what will happen in intergroup contact.

The *informal norms* are reflected in the consistency of the actual intergroup behavior that does occur. When most members of both groups share similar expectations and conform to the same behavioral consistencies, intergroup norms in a given situation can be said to be strong, stable, and controlling. *Intergroup norms, then, are widely accepted and legitimated standards that shape intergroup interaction.*

The Importance of Norms

Most direct and convincing evidence for the importance of norms in intergroup interaction is provided by an array of American research studies that focused on the question in the 1940s and 1950s, when racial norms were starting to shift (Allport, 1954; Pettigrew, 1961, 1991). These studies used field observation of interactions between Black and White Americans in a wide variety of interracial situations. They sought to answer four questions: (1) What happens when racial norms are strong, consistent, and sanctioned with rewards and punishments? (2) What happens when racial norms are strong but in conflict across different institutions? (3) What happens when racial norms are changing? (4) What happens when there are no operating racial norms?

Strong racial norms, whether racist or equalitarian in character, were repeatedly shown to lead to consistent behavior by most Black and White Americans. This massive conformity in the mid-20th century was importantly shaped by sanctions.

Anti-Black Racism in America. Thomas F. Pettigrew, Oxford University Press. © Oxford University Press (2025).
DOI: 10.1093/9780197803134.003.0004

44 Anti-Black Racism in America

In the racially segregated South, harsh punishments were swift for both Black and White Southerners who broke the status quo. Thus, when equalitarian racial norms were developing in some institutions of American society during this same period, most Black and White people managed to conform to these norms, too, when these norms were also sanctioned with rewards and punishments. But such equalitarian racial norms in American society were rare at the time.

When they did exist in particular institutions, such norms necessarily clashed with those of most surrounding institutions. How, then, did the same Black and White Americans behave with each other when faced with *equalitarian norms in one sector of their lives and racist norms in other sectors*? A series of field studies aimed at answering this question provides powerful evidence for the importance of inter-group norms. All-pervasive norms were often not involved. Most people proved fully capable of immediate behavioral change as they moved from one set of institutional norms to another. Thus, in a coal-mining area, the majority of Black and White miners followed a traditional pattern of racial integration below the ground and racial segregation above the ground (Minard, 1952).

The research literature abounds with similar examples. In years past, when the United States still controlled the Panama Canal, there was a divided street, racially segregated on the Canal side and racially desegregated on the Panamanian side (Biesanz and Smith, 1951). Both Panamanians and Americans had no trouble shopping on one side of the street and then on the other while obeying the contrasting norms. Similarly, southern White migrants readily adjusted to racially desegregated situations on Chicago's West Side (Killian, 1949).

Another striking example came from a Chicago suburb where there was a large steel mill. Inside the mill, Black and White workers were fully integrated in a multiracial labor union. Pay, jobs, promotions, and even elected positions within the union were distributed about equally across the two racial groups. Yet these same workers went home each evening to almost totally segregated residential areas. Indeed, many of the same White workers who believed strongly in an interracial union also belonged to a neighborhood organization that worked to keep Black people from living in their area (Reitzes, 1953).

What appears to outside observers as inconsistent, illogical behavior does not appear that way to the people in these actual situations. In each of the different situations, most people simply conform to the prevailing racial norms as they understood them. The normative demands made upon them were inconsistent, not their norm-following behavior.

Such widespread conformity to intergroup norms does not imply that generalized, prejudiced attitudes are never invoked. Some of Minard's White coal miners were either equalitarian or racist both below and above the ground. Likewise, a small minority of the White steel workers either accepted or rejected Black Americans in both their work and home situations. These were people whose racial attitudes were so salient that they defied the prevailing racial norms in one or the other of the conflicting normative situations. The critical point, however, is that the majority

The Power of Racial Norms **45**

of people followed the norms of whatever institutions they were in at the moment, even when these norms conflicted with those of other critical institutions in their daily lives.

Firmly established norms are necessary for smooth social interaction of all types. Shared expectations guide the behavioral flow as well as provide a context that allows the interactants to interpret their contact in similar ways. Thus, norms shape social interaction and provide the interaction with a common meaning. But when norms are shifting, smooth interaction becomes difficult. The old norms have not completely disappeared, yet the new norms have not yet won full acceptance. Intergroup interactions become awkward, even tense. Each side does not quite know how to act, nor what to expect from the other group.

Often members of the more powerful group voice a yearning for the "good old days" when the traditional norms were firmly in place and unequal interaction was unproblematic. Indeed, intergroup interaction can be so uncomfortable for members of each group during such transition periods that patterns of avoidance develop. Tension is reduced simply by avoiding contact with members of the other group.

The civil rights movement began the process of eliminating traditional racist norms in the 1960s. New equalitarian norms of interracial interaction have slowly emerged throughout most of the United States since the 1960s. It has been a painfully gradual process in many sectors of American life, and in many areas of the nation these new norms are only now starting to emerge - especially among the young. Products of integrated schools evince it most; products of segregated schools show it least.

Both Black and White Americans realize that the old patterns of imperious, dominant behavior by White supremacists and subservient behavior by Black people are diminishing and slowly becoming counter-normative. Yet new patterns of equality have to be learned by members of both races. The awkwardness and discomfort, as well as resistance, that results from this major normative shift have at times led to patterns of interracial avoidance by both groups over the past half-century.

The establishment of the new normative structure is also deterred by another social psychological process. Blatant racism, a reflection of the older, traditional norms, is now somewhat disparaged in both North America and Western Europe. The new equalitarian norms are widely complied with, though not necessarily internalized, by White and Black people alike. In other words, most dominant group members publicly follow what they understand to be the new expectations in their intergroup behavior, but many of them have not yet fully accepted these new norms of equality. This disparity between compliance with and internalizing the new norms has led to the development of a more subtle racism. This phenomenon has been widely studied and documented in social psychology (Pettigrew, 1989).

When *no norms for intergroup interaction exist*, their absence reveals the strong need for such norms. Cornell University investigators demonstrated this issue in rural New York State, where few Black people lived (Kohn and Williams, 1956). Consequently, the bars in the area had never established racial norms for service.

46 Anti-Black Racism in America

Teams of Black and White graduate students in sociology sought service in these bars. When the Black student entered these all-White establishments, confusion among the patrons and staff was the typical response. Without racial norms to guide them, the White waitresses did not know whether or not to serve the Black customer. Often the slightest cue from other staff members or customers, even a mere facial gesture, decided the issue. If the bartender and White customers paid no attention, the waitresses usually served the Black customer. But if there was any apparently negative attention paid to the novel appearance of the Black customer, waitresses often refused to serve the Black student—even though this violated the state's anti-discrimination law. In short, pointed reactions to strong racial norms, to conflicting or changing norms, and to the absence of relevant norms lay bare the crucial significance of norms in intergroup interaction.

Personality variables remain important for understanding individual differences in anti-Black prejudice. Yet these variables cannot account for the racist practices of the American South or those of South Africa. Thus, normative theory has both applied and theoretical importance. Pessimists in the 1950s claimed that the only way positive changes could be introduced in either region was to conduct mass psychoanalytic therapy for millions of White Southerners and South Africans. This naive misuse of personality explanations was actually a not so subtle way of claiming that racial change in these areas was essentially impossible.

From the normative perspective, I argued quite the opposite sequence for remedy, and events support this alternative perspective (Pettigrew, 1961, 1991). Instead of viewing personality change as the initial causal variable which must trigger social change, direct structural change to which individuals (even authoritarian personalities) must accommodate is both more practical and more effective. Indeed, this example of the greater effectiveness of the top-down approach rather than the bottom-up approach to social change has generally proven to be one of the more successful practical applications of social psychology (Pettigrew, 1988).

This contention does not mean that personality considerations are of no importance. Individual personality and attitude changes remain significant for the successful completion of the change cycle. But they are usually not initially causal. Such changes in individuals are most easily triggered not by the one-on-one medical model of individual therapy but by altering the racial norms of social institutions in which both Black and White individuals lead their daily lives.

The perception of the inevitability of the institutional changes is critical. Public opinion favoring the changes is not necessary. The perception of their inevitability and permanence is sufficient. However, if such perceptions are not forthcoming, resistance can be strengthened by the perception that strong, even violent protest can turn back the clock. This possibility is particularly acute in nations where conflicting intergroup policies have come and gone frequently in the past.

The Importance of Laws in Changing Perceptions of Racial Norms. New racial laws, when enforced, are a major way racial norms shift. Such laws can modify and create norms in many ways. They can change material payoffs; they provide information on societal values; and they can change the perception of social norms by providing information on what is acceptable behavior. Gradual enforcement of new laws appears to enhance their power to modify norms (Acemoglu and Jackson, 2017). But pluralistic ignorance—the mistaken belief that other group members believe differently from oneself - can limit these changes (Eisner, Spini, and Sommet, 2020).

In addition to changing norms directly, new laws influence the perceptions that people have of the social norms. Many people may have been unaware of the operating norms, but now the new law makes them salient (Galbiati et al., 2021). Witnessing prominent people modeling the new norms also augments the normative change. When two Black American members of the U.S. Supreme Court both have White marriage partners, the relatively recent new norm of interracial marriage is further entrenched and accepted.

Behavioral Change Typically Leads to Attitude Change

Conventional wisdom also holds that people must be persuaded to engage in new behavior, that attitude change must precede behavioral change. But literally hundreds of social psychological studies have demonstrated the efficacy of the opposite causal sequence: behavior change is generally the precursor of attitude change.

This sequence seems particularly important for intergroup relations. Institutional alterations that require new intergroup behavior become powerful attitude change mechanisms. Chapter 9 will discuss how intergroup contact under optimal conditions can reduce intergroup conflict and improve intergroup attitudes (see also Sidebar 3.1). When these positive conditions do not hold, intergroup contact can lead to increased intergroup distrust and conflict.

The disconfirmation of intergroup fears can reduce both prejudice and discrimination even without intergroup contact. Intergroup contact can be extremely helpful, but it is not essential for positive change. Just having your worst fears and expectations about the outgroup convincingly shown to be unjustified has positive effects. This process is especially important in tense situations, where such fears are often so extreme that their disconfirmation is made easier. But the problem in such situations often involves overcoming resistance to perceiving and accepting the disconfirming evidence.

Note that, like the other processes, this process is a two-edged sword. The reversal of the process - the confirmation of intergroup fears - will lead to further entrenchment of intergroup fears and conflict. This backward thrust is illustrated on a national scale by Trump's MAGA movement. The Trump-led MAGA movement illustrates how fears enhanced by the perception of changing norms can act to increase prejudice. Fox "News" constantly drums up fears of changing racial norms that enhance racial fears and prejudice. Repeatedly, Fox and the MAGA movement refer back to the 1950s. Why?

48 Anti-Black Racism in America

The 1950s decade was the last time MAGA's major thrusts were clearly dominant in American society. The movement represents a brash reactionary call to an earlier time when America's position in the world was unchallenged; when America's presidents, vice presidents, and Supreme Court justices were all White men; when abortion was outlawed; when American workers saw their real wages rising; when immigration was severely restricted; when homosexuality was not discussed "in polite company"; and when the government's affirmative action programs largely helped White men (the G.I. Bill of Rights, federal housing loans, etc.). The MAGA movement embraces this "nostalgic politics" (Gest, Reny, and Mayer, 2018), and its followers are deeply upset by the sweeping normative shifts of the past 75 years.

What was previously taken for granted as intrinsic components of America are now disappearing. As racial norms gradually shift throughout most (but not all) of America, old norms clash with new ones. Those perceived as responsible for these normative shifts increasingly become targets of abuse, prejudice, and even death threats. In other words, we are witnessing how extensive normative changes can provoke extreme prejudice.

Sidebar 3.1 Military Norms Achieve Attitude Change

Gathering data for my doctoral thesis (Pettigrew, 1958, 1959), I encountered a remarkable example of how norms can radically change racial attitudes. It was a scorchingly hot day in a small town in southern Georgia. My randomly selected interviewee was a lone, young White worker in a cola bottling plant. He kindly granted me the interview and surprised me by answering almost all of my racial prejudice questions in the non-prejudiced direction. Then he told me his story.

He had been in an infantry company in the Korean War. Thanks to orders by President Harry Truman, the battalion had both Black and White soldiers. "One of the Black guys and I were the only Southern guys in the company, and we were constantly teased for our accents and everything else," he volunteered. "So we became good friends, and we have kept up the friendship even though he lives now in Alabama." The change in military norms had led to profound attitude change in this young man.

We shall return to discuss in detail the operation of such contact effects on racial attitudes and behavior in Chapter 9.

Chapter 4
Race and Economics

Pessimists who believe that American racism has not declined in recent years need only point to trends in wealth. The most extensive study ever conducted of American wealth by race reveals that in 2020 the White-to-Black per capita wealth ratio was six to one (Derenoncourt et al., 2022). Phrased differently, for every dollar individual White Americans had in 2020, individual Black Americans had only 17 cents.

In recent years, this huge gap has only slightly declined. In fact, many Black families actually have a negative net worth—more debt than wealth (Hamilton et al., 2015). In stark contrast, 96% of the nation's wealth is held by White households, compared with 2% by Black households (Moore, 2015).

Researchers have looked back at racial wealth trends since 1860. The biggest convergence of racial wealth came during the first half-century after emancipation. Slaves owned little or nothing, while free Black Americans began to earn and save a modicum of funds. However, these post–Civil War earnings were greatly constrained by the many slavery-like mechanisms adopted widely throughout the South (Blackmon, 2008). As shown in Figure 4.1, the racial difference in wealth was still 10-to-1 in 1900. It slowly narrowed until about 1980, when gradual improvement basically stopped.

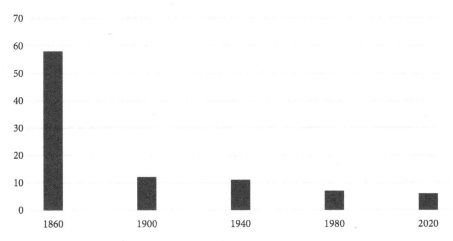

Figure 4.1 White-Black per Capita Wealth Ratio, 1860–2020
Source: Derencourt et al., 2002.

Anti-Black Racism in America. Thomas F. Pettigrew, Oxford University Press. © Oxford University Press (2025).
DOI: 10.1093/9780197803134.003.0005

50 Anti-Black Racism in America

Indeed, the racial difference in wealth actually increased after the 2008 recession that hit Black Americans especially hard and involved a major loss in Black home-ownership. Between 2006 and 2016, ownership dropped a dramatic 5.6% for Black householders compared with 2.6% for White and 3.7% for Hispanic householders (Goodman, McCargo, and Zhu, 2018).

This structural process of indirect discrimination can operate without explicit racial prejudice being involved. Racial discrimination is often viewed as a psychological rather than structural phenomenon. Prejudiced members of the dominant race are thought to cause the racial unfairness intentionally. However, White American workers nominating White friends for job openings can simply reflect society's widespread racial segregation (Greenwald and Pettigrew, 2014). African Americans are rarely in White friendship networks (Chapter 9). Here housing segregation plays a major role (Chapter 10). White nominators need not possess hostile views of Black Americans to engage in this common form of indirect discrimination.

Important analyses of indirect discrimination in America focus on wealth. Racial inequalities in assets dwarf disparities in other social outcomes. Although the magnitude of inequality in home equity is severe, racial inequality in liquid assets is even more marked. This racial difference in assets results from a history of direct and indirect discrimination. Prohibitions against Black self-employment and landownership in the American South were an early part of the picture. Occupations to which African Americans were confined (agricultural and domestic work) were initially excluded from Social Security provisions. Direct and indirect discrimination by federal housing agencies, banks, realtors, and White homeowners have limited the opportunity of Black Americans to accrue wealth through homeownership (Chapter 10) (Conley, 1999; Rank, 2009; Shapiro, 2004).

The sharp economic recession that began in 2008 and centered on housing made matters worse. Black and Hispanic Americans were the hardest hit in home foreclosures and other asset-reducing events.

The accumulation of disadvantage is particularly acute when the focus is on assets. Since wealth can reproduce itself exponentially, the racial gap in assets in the United States has continued to grow rapidly. And assets have important implications for such other social outcomes as education and labor market success. When parents do not have the means to live in higher-status neighborhoods, children do not have access to the best public schools. And for most students, attendance at the best colleges and universities increasingly depends on their parents' ability to provide thousands of dollars per year to cover rising tuition costs and expenses.

Labor market outcomes reflect educational disadvantage, but restricted assets have other indirect effects as well. Access to networks of information crucial to job-seekers, proximity to lucrative employment, automobile transportation to work—all these are a function of assets which place Black Americans at a pronounced disadvantage (Conley, 1999). Innovative intervention must be devised to break into the spiraling disadvantage produced by these wealth deficits of Black Americans.

There are two wealth sources that play major roles in this wide racial discrepancy. Homeownership is an important source of White wealth which Black people cannot fully emulate given the extreme racial discrimination in housing (Chapter 10). Black Americans necessarily rent housing (58%) twice as much as White Americans (28%) (Desilver, 2021). Not owning a home is one reason Black wealth is far below that of Whites since more than half of White wealth reflects homeownership.

Even more important in the racial gap is the central role of capital gains—the increase in value of such assets as stocks, bonds, and property relative to their original prices. Far fewer Black Americans (36%) than White Americans (60%) have money in the stock market—another major source of White wealth. And "the great recession" of 2007–2013 hurt Black family median net worth harder than it did White family median net worth (44% to 26%) (Hanson, 2020).

Extreme Discrimination Kept Black Americans Poor, 1865–1941

Immediately following the close of the Civil War, many southern states adopted *the Black Codes*. These Codes severely limited the freedom of the 4 million Black citizens then remaining in the South. They were largely designed to replace slavery and guarantee the availability of a cheap labor force. In many states, Black people were required to sign yearly labor contracts; refusal to sign risked arrest and fines. The Black Codes infuriated many in the North and soon led to the 1867 Civil Rights Act and the 1870 15th Amendment giving Black men the right to vote. Yet widespread racial discrimination continued.

In his no-holds-barred volume on the subject, *Slavery by Another Name*, Douglas Blackmon (2008) traces in detail the history of how White America systematically excluded Black Americans from economic opportunities of all types from 1865 to 1941. The book won a Pulitzer for general non-fiction in 2009, became a *New York Times* best-seller, and in 2012 was adapted into a documentary film for the Public Broadcasting System.

Blackmon's book was followed a few years later by Talitha LeFlouria's (2016) *Chained in Silence*. Like Blackmon, she uses publicly available but long-ignored data. Her work supports and enlarges Blackmon's thesis by focusing on the horrors that Black women suffered in Georgia during 1865–2041. A Black American historian at the University of Virginia, LeFlouria also received numerous awards for her book. Together, these two volumes sharply overturn the traditional views about race relations after the Civil War.

Blackmon focuses on how following the Civil War, slavery-like control was maintained in order to keep labor costs low. In the South, Black men were often arrested on such vague and false charges as vagrancy or even no charges at all. Open corruption involved bogus fees and penalties that lined the pockets of judges and other officials. This in turn forced the victims to work for Whites at low wages in order to pay off their phony debt. In other words, so-called convict labor replaced slave labor.

Blackmon, a classic southern White liberal,[1] does not spare the reader the gory details of this corrupt, illegal and heartless process of involuntary servitude. The early death of workers in the mines and forests, the inhuman conditions in which these essentially re-enslaved Black workers lived—with inadequate clothing, routine lashings, limited and disgusting food—it all rivals the worst of Joseph Stalin's Gulag prisons. LeFlouria shows how Black women endured many of these same hardships with sexual exploitation added on.

Blackmon concentrates his analysis on several counties in Alabama where he uncovered the best documentation of this process. He also shows that the "convict labor" technique was employed throughout Alabama as well as in Florida, Georgia, and much of the Deep South during this period. And LeFlouria enhances his argument for Georgia.

The major benefactors of this convict labor technique were the "old families," the former slave-owning Whites. They had endured an enormous loss of wealth with the ending of slavery. Still, they remained socially dominant, and many soon turned to convict labor to recoup their losses.

A remarkable study by the National Bureau of Economic Research uncovers the success of this effort (Ager, Boustan, and Eriksson, 2019). It shows how the sons of former slaveholders recovered their losses relative to comparable sons of non-slave-owners. Their grandsons surpassed their counterparts in occupational and educational attainment by 1940. The study's authors attributed this rise to the maintenance of social networks involving sons marrying into other former slaveholding families. This is undoubtedly true. However, Blackmon's analysis strongly suggests that the economic recovery of these former slaveholding families was also due in large part to their greater ability to engage in the illegal use of convict labor.

Convict labor can still be found in such institutions as Louisiana's Angola Prison, where "convict leasing" is prevalent (Benns, 2015). The prisoners at Angola receive no pay for their work. In 2022, four states approved changes in their constitutions to remove all language that enables such involuntary servitude of convicts. In Louisiana, however, a vote to end the practice was opposed by the state's Republican Party and soundly defeated (McGoogan, 2023).[2] In Texas in 2023, death-row inmates sued the state over their "brutal" solitary confinement in breach of the 8th Amendment to the U.S. Constitution. In some cases, prisoners have been kept in solitary for 23 years without a single break—torture by any standard (Pilkington, 2023).

---

[1] Like others of this small and hearty band, Blackmon grew up in the South—in tiny Leland in the Mississippi delta—and early in his life rejected the racism he witnessed up close.

[2] When an Angola convict spoke about the practice to a *Washington Post* reporter and said he was often told he was "a slave," he was immediately punished - placed on "lockdown" and isolated, his privileges taken away (McGoogan, 2023).

Mississippi's Parchman Prison shares the same sordid reputation as Angola Prison.[3] Started in 1901 on a vast 3,800-acre plot and operated like a pre–Civil War plantation, it has used largely Black convict labor to enrich the state—by 2005 the equivalent of about 5 million 2020 dollars. The prison received national attention when the Freedom Riders were imprisoned and mistreated there in the 1960s.

Blackmon and LeFlouria both demonstrate that these peonage techniques effectively re-enslaved Black Southerners through the Great Depression and until World War II. According to LeFlouria (2016), African Americans comprised the majority of the South's prison population from 1860 to 1930. Their number began to decline at the start of World War II in part because the federal government became concerned that the phenomenon would make for damaging publicity for the Axis powers in Africa and elsewhere (Kendi, 2016).

The widespread use of convict labor challenges the common assumption long maintained in popular history books that African Americans were truly freed after the Civil War. The full extent of injustice over these critical 64 years wrought upon former slaves and their descendants has largely been denied. There was also a persistent myth I recall from my childhood education in Virginia that the newly freed Blacks were violent upon being freed and that this required harsh measures to control them.

We will see throughout this volume that Black citizens have been treated as inferior to White citizens in every major realm of American society. This is true despite the fact that Black Americans were granted citizenship in the 14th and 15th Amendments to the Constitution a century and a half ago.

In addition, such racist organizations as the Ku Klux Klan (KKK) have openly suppressed Black life. The racism was so extensive that virtually all Black Southerners lived under constant fear and oppression. They could not move freely or demand better pay for their work because of this oppressive environment that included violence and threats from such racists as the KKK's "night riders." Many of these racist practices have been maintained by the election of White male sheriffs and prosecutors throughout the nation. Thus, 90% of the nation's sheriffs even today are White males, although they constitute only 30% of the American population (Fatherree, 2023).

The Blackmon and LeFlouria books reveal how African Americans were treated in America after slavery. Their findings answer two central questions. First, how were the norms and traditions of slavery carried over into the 20th century? Second, what kept Black Americans from accumulating wealth in the first eight decades after the abolition of slavery?

These two authors challenge those who view racist treatment as simply an inevitable result of the Civil War. They demonstrate that such treatment was basically

---

[3] A third example is the Ferguson Unit Prison in Midway, Texas. It, too, was fashioned out of an old slavery plantation and uses mostly Black convict labor to maintain a wealth-producing farm for the state.

54 Anti-Black Racism in America

caused by racist beliefs and financial greed—even the U.S. Steel Corporation and other private businesses in the North were deeply involved. For instance, Lehman Brothers, a global financial firm prior to its collapse in 2008, had its start in 1847 in Alabama. It bought cotton at low prices made possible by slave labor that planted and picked the crop. Then the company shipped it to Europe and sold it at much higher prices. So slavery was an essential part of the company's beginnings (McGhee, 2021, pp. 97–98).

The infamous 1876 "compromise" between the North and South had two effects. It allowed the Republican Party to steal the presidency for Rutherford Hayes, and it freed the White southern leadership to handle race relations as they wished. Jim Crow laws were passed throughout the South that closely resembled the old Black Codes. The compromise marked the end of the North's reconstruction efforts to remedy the economic and other negative effects of slavery. At odds with the popular and cleansed version of this inglorious era of American history, Blackmon, LeFlouria, and Kendi all show that it was the 1876–1920 period when 20th-century racism took shape.

If anyone should mistakenly think that this convict-labor scheme has completely ended, the White sheriff of Louisiana's Caddo Parish makes it abundantly clear that the practice continues. He boasted that instead of prison reform he would rather extend jail time for Black convicts. The "good ones," he explained, "we use every day to wash cars, to change oil in the cars, to cook in the kitchen, to do all that where we save money" (quoted in Fatherree, 2023).

The Key Role of Racial Lynching

Something similar to lynching has occurred throughout the world. But in one of the darkest pages of American history, it developed into a national tradition. More than 4,400 of these extrajudicial killings were recorded from 1882 to 1941, and many more went unrecorded. Georgia alone has had more than 450 documented lynchings. Lynchings typically occurred in the Deep South as the key symbol of White supremacy. As such, it was a major means of maintaining cheap labor and thus wealth creation and perpetuation for upper-status White Southerners.

Black females were among the victims, as were more than a thousand White males and females. At least 99 Black females were victims, as were more than another 100 non-Black minority victims (71 of Mexican origin, 38 Native Americans, 11 Asian Americans). Moreover, lynchings have occurred throughout the nation. A 1909 lynching of Will James, a Black American, in Cairo, Illinois, and the 1920 lynching of three Black men in Duluth, Minnesota, among others in the North and West, received media attention at the time. Often large White crowds, including children, would gather to witness these gruesome "proletariat lynchings" and have their pictures taken.

Race and Economics   55

There was also a lesser-known type, called "bourbon lynchings." These often went unrecorded as they were quietly committed by upper-status Whites who were protecting their lucrative economic situation described by Blackmon. Because of the prevalence of this type, it is certain that the total number of lynchings is much larger than the 4,400 known and counted.

In 2018, the National Memorial for Peace and Justice was opened in Montgomery, Alabama, to remember the many victims of lynching as well as other victims of American racism down through the years. Inspired by the open-air Berlin memorial to the victims of the Holocaust, it contains a victim-inscribed stone for each county in which one or more recorded lynchings occurred.

Lynching had direct economic consequences. Blackmon notes that lynching was often used to perpetuate the lucrative convict-labor scheme he describes in detail. It also became the very symbol of White supremacy. It was the constant and imminent threat that racial discrimination in the South relied upon. It is so central to American racism that I analyzed lynching at the start of all 35 of my university race courses I taught from 1957 to 2000 as well as my 1967 *Epitaph for Jim Crow* series for the Public Broadcasting System (Pettigrew, 1962, 1964a). It served well to open up the audience's perspective on the depth of American racism over the centuries.

Two lynchings are especially remembered—one because the victim was a Jewish American, the other because it occurred as late as 1957. Mary Phagan was a 13-year-old White worker at a pencil factory in Atlanta, Georgia. Two days after her dead body was found in the basement of the factory, Leo Frank, an Atlanta businessman, was arrested and charged with the murder, found guilty, and sentenced to hang. Frank appealed up to the U.S. Supreme Court, which supported the verdict by a seven-to-two vote. Four months later, residents of Phagan's hometown, Marietta, Georgia, somehow managed to kidnap Frank from the state prison and hanged him. This lynching of a White victim garnered more national publicity than the thousands of Black lynchings that preceded it.

In 1955, Emmett Till, a 14-year-old African-American boy from Chicago, was visiting relatives in Money, Mississippi. Carolyn Bryant, a local White woman, accused Till of whistling at her. This set off a trail of events that led to the seizure, torture, and murder of Till. The tragedy might not have attracted national attention had not Till's mother agreed to leave his casket open so that pictures could be taken to show what unspeakable cruelty her son had endured. All-White local juries refused to indict Bryant and the accused lynchers.

The blatancy and butchery of this lynching captured the nation's attention as no other had. Till was so battered, his body could be identified only by a ring he wore. Several motion pictures have now been made about this horror. It drew renewed attention when Bryant (at 88 years old) was located living quietly in North Carolina. She was never charged by Mississippi authorities, although she later admitted that she had lied.

Later Economic Trends

The Black gains in education and politics described in other chapters translated into some modest gains in Black economics in the second half of the 21st century. Indeed, the U.S. definition of "austere poverty" shows that the Black level declined from 40% in 1965 to 19% in 2019.

Yet the overall picture is far less encouraging. Many Black families still live on the *brink* of poverty. Any emergency puts these families in extreme distress. When the COVID-19 pandemic struck, 31% of Black families reported they were unable to pay for such basic necessities as food, heat, and rent, and 38% said they had used up all or most of their savings (Getachew et al., 2020). A national study found that Blacks had significantly more financial problems from the COVID-19 epidemic than either Hispanic Americans or White Americans (Admon et al., 2023).

Like racial wealth statistics, data on unemployment and income also show just how precarious the economic situation is for many Black Americans. Black unemployment rates over recent decades have remained at roughly twice that of Whites through good and bad economic times. Racial differences in employment have shown scant change over past decades, in contradiction to earlier claims of "the declining significance of race" (Wilson, 1978) (see Figure 4.1). To his credit, Wilson (2011a, 2011b) later revised his thesis to include the importance of class and wealth.

A meta-analysis of 28 field experiments reveals that there has been essentially no change in hiring discrimination against Black Americans since 1989 (Quillian et al., 2017). The 28 studies involved 55,842 applications submitted for 26,326 positions and employed two types of tests. One involved in-person audits in which racially dissimilar but otherwise matched pairs of trained testers applied for the same job. The other method used fictionalized résumés with distinct racial names sent online or by mail.

The meta-analysis controlled for important rival explanations: the applicant's education and gender, the study's methodology, and local labor market conditions. However, these controls had little effect on the primary finding: across 25 years (1989–2014), hiring discrimination at the point of hire had *not* improved for Blacks and had improved only slightly for Latinos. White applicants on average received 36% more callbacks than Black applicants and 24% more callbacks than Latino applicants.

Other research uncovered just how extreme racial discrimination can be. One study found that White job applicants with a criminal record were more likely to receive a job offer than a Black applicant with an identical résumé who had no criminal record (Pager, 2003).

Further job vulnerability for Black males is their concentration in both state and federal employment. Back in 1913, Woodrow Wilson fired virtually all Black federal workers as one of his first acts as president. He was a lifelong, unadulterated racist. As president of Princeton University, he had refused to accept Black students. In the 1960s, I met an elderly Black South Carolinian who was still anguished over having been fired by Wilson a half-century earlier. It was the first time I had heard about Wilson's racist actions as president.

Federal employment of Blacks did not improve until Franklin Roosevelt came to power. In the 1940s, I recall that almost all mail carriers in Richmond, Virginia, were African American males. It was a prime job for them. This concentration in public-sector jobs has been a critical component of upward mobility and the development of the expanding Black middle class. By 2022, 18% of the federal government workforce was Black (USA Facts, 2022b). Thus, when there are pronounced reductions in these jobs, Black workers are differentially affected.

Unemployment rates for Black males are typically higher than for Black females. Yet Black females have had their own special problems, with sexist discrimination combining with racist discrimination. In 1935, the Social Security Act was enacted, but southern senators forced President Roosevelt to exclude domestic workers.[4] Not corrected until years later, this exclusion hurt the incomes of Black females in particular. Indeed, 65% of Black workers, compared with 27% of White workers, were totally excluded from this invaluable legislation. Black women have long had the highest levels of labor force participation regardless of age, marital status, or presence of children at home. They are paid about 63 cents for every dollar paid to non-Hispanic White men. Yet, according to the U.S. Census, 80% of Black mothers are the sole, primary, or co-provider for their households.

By 2016, a survey by the Federal Reserve found that the total median Black *family wealth* was only $17,000 compared to the median White *family wealth* of $171,000 (Ray and Perry, 2020). In 2021, the U.S. Census recorded the median White family income to be $78,000 compared to the median Black family income of $48,000 - 38% less. And this reduced Black income is reflected in numerous domains (National Urban League, 2022a). For example, a sixth of Black American households were without a computer in 2021 (National Urban League, 2022b).

Roughly a third of Blacks with student loans in 2021 were "not sure when or if ever they will be able to pay them off." Making this a greater hardship is a provision in the Student Loan Act that makes it virtually impossible to discharge this debt through bankruptcy—unlike most other forms of debt. And when President Biden moved in 2022 to lessen this student debt for 560,000 borrowers, extensive right-wing opposition arose in part because his efforts would differentially benefit minorities. Many of the same members of the U.S. Congress who voted against student debt relie, allegedly because its cost of $5.8 billion was "too great," had not hesitated to vote in 2017 for President Trump's tax reduction bill for the super-wealthy and major corporations that cost the U.S. Treasury an estimated $1.9 *trillion* over 10 years—an amount more than 327 times greater (Center for Budget and Policy Priorities, 2019). The politically-charged Supreme Court then ruled against the debt relief.

---

[4] Teachers, nurses, librarians, social workers, and hospital workers—largely female occupations—were also initially excluded. The sexist rationale at the time was that female workers had their husband's salaries to live on—an impossibility for single women and far more available for White than Black married women.

With little opportunity in past years to gain business-ownership acumen, less than 3% of small businesses with fewer than 500 employees were owned by Blacks in 2019. Then COVID-19 hit small Black businesses especially hard (Saraiva, 2022). These sparce Black-owned firms had their earnings decrease 28% in 2020 compared to a White-owned business decrease of 15%. Already fragile, many Black firms were pushed completely out of business by such a large cut.

In 2020, the U.S. Census reported there remained 141,000 Black-owned businesses with 1.3 million employees, an annual payroll of $42 billion and $141 billion in annual receipts. More than a quarter of these businesses were in healthcare. Compare these data to those of Asian Americans, who in 2020 comprised only half the population size of Black Americans yet their businesses had $841 billion in annual receipts—six times as much as Black-owned businesses.

Fifteen percent of Black adults in 2021 held more than one job; 50 percent said that the second job was "essential for meeting . . . basic needs." Only 36% of Blacks reported that they had at least "a three-month emergency fund," compared with 54% of Whites (Edwards, 2022). While the poor of all groups often live a paycheck-to-paycheck existence, Black employees are overrepresented in the deprived cluster of workers who earn less than $15 an hour, lack basic benefits, and endure erratic work schedules. Fast-food workers are prominent in this cluster. We shall return to this situation in the medical Chapter 7, as these work situations heighten bad health.

A New and Positive Employment Trend for Black Americans

In 2022, an unforeseen trend emerged that holds promise of major improvements for minority employment in general (Long, 2023). White baby boomers began to retire in large numbers. At first, careless observers claimed that "Americans did not want to work anymore."

This was not true. The nation's minorities and immigrants were eager to get jobs and advance in the job market. At the same time, the tight job market made it more difficult for firms to discriminate against them.

This new situation has had a marked positive effect on Black American employment generally and Black females in particular. Whereas in 1980, non-Whites comprised only 19% of the nation's workforce, by 2020 they were 41% of workers. Mexican and Asian Americans are an important part of this swift change. So, too, are immigrants, who make up more than half of the new workers[5] (Long, 2023). The special benefits of this sudden demographic shift for Blacks are clearly revealed in income data from the U.S. Census: 2022 witnessed a record low official poverty

---

[5] This important fact provides a strong argument for continued immigration to the United States. Many European countries, Japan, and even aging China are experiencing crucial labor shortages and the need for more immigrants.

rate for Black individuals (Shrider and Creamer, 2023). The historic low in 2022 was 17.1%—still high, to be sure, but one in six Blacks suffering extreme poverty was the lowest ever recorded. Compare it to the 1959 rate of 55%. All Black age groups revealed this improvement, but it was especially strong for those under 18 years old (U.S. Census, 2023).

The Pipeline of Privilege

Despite the difficulties posed by racism, a select few Black Americans have somehow managed to rise to major leadership roles. Who they are and how they did it reveals how racism operates and how it can sometimes be overcome. One theory focuses on the "pipeline of privilege" (Pettigrew, 2021b). Informational flows and institutional access have long benefited Whites and shut out Blacks. In short, life chances in America still largely flow through White-dominated institutions. Black Americans who have risen to key positions in society have managed to break through this White monopoly. And once in the pipeline, access to additional previously all-White institutions becomes far easier.

The later success of Blacks who had integrated education, we will note in Chapter 5, enables them to break into this pipeline (Braddock and Dawkins, 1984). Jomills Braddock (1980) focused on this phenomenon and named it *perpetuation theory*. He showed that Black students in interracial high schools were significantly more likely later to attend interracial colleges than those in segregated high schools. Later studies supported perpetuation theory by finding that school segregation even shapes later housing choices (Goldsmith, 2016; Stearns, 2010).

Here we extend perpetuation theory by maintaining that interracial education can lead to Black Americans gaining the ability and status to pry open the domain of special privilege. Products of interracial schools are viewed more positively by White gatekeepers, and this in turn allows further advancement up the ladder. In short, the pipeline of privilege enjoyed by many prosperous White Americans is cumulative. Entry at an early stage greatly enhances the probability of advancing to the next stage.

Popular parlance speaks loosely of "White privilege." However, the pipeline of privilege emphasized here is more complex. It involves the interaction of race, social class, and gender; its beneficiaries have traditionally been not only White but also wealthy and male. It would be a great surprise to the White residents of Kenova, West Virginia, one of the poorest towns in the entire nation, to learn that they are "privileged."

Lower-status White Americans are generally not able to enter this pipeline. So when they perceive that a growing number of African Americans are gaining access, it ignites two types of threat. Black progress not only invokes envy and resentment; it also provides evidence against deeply held racist theories of White superiority. Have these lower-status White people ever been labeled "gifted" or headed a major corporation? This leads some White Americans to turn to extreme right-wing politics.

60   Anti-Black Racism in America

Indeed, racial prejudice as well as a sense of relative deprivation proved to be major correlates of the Trump vote in 2016 (Pettigrew, 2021a).[6]

In support of these contentions, we review the educational experiences of those Black Americans who in recent years have risen to elite positions in business that were not open to them in the past (see Sidebar 4.1).

Closing the Racial Wealth Gap

We have noted the enormous wealth gap that exists between Black and White Americans. Indeed, wealth is far more unequally distributed than income. The Duke University economist, William Darity Jr., has spent his career on this subject. With his Cook Center colleagues, Darity has shown how difficult closing the gap will be and how many popular views of the subject are basically wrong (Darity et al., 2018). We can learn a lot about Black American economics by reviewing these misconceptions about the racial wealth gap.

Myth 1: *If only Black Americans would get more education and work harder, the racial wealth gap would close.*

This myth is widely believed by White Americans. Blacks and Whites of similar levels of education do not have similar levels of wealth. Figure 4.2 shows the racial differences in median household net worth by education and race (drawn from Darity et al., 2018, p. 6).

Note that Black households whose heads have graduated from college have less average annual income ($70,219) than White households whose head is a high school dropout ($82,968). Nor can such differences be attributed to Black indifference to education. As we have noted, Blacks actually value education more than comparable Whites. Controlling for parental educational attainment and occupational status as well as household income, Black youth attain more years of education than comparable White youth (Mason, 1997; Mangino, 2010).

The vast differentials shown in Figure 4.2 are not the result of different employment statuses. In 2014 the median household net worth of full-time-employed White workers was 13 times more than full-time Black workers ($144,220 compared with $11,000). In fact, the median household net worth of *unemployed* White Americans ($55,710) is five times greater than that of full-time-employed Black Americans.

Myth 2: *Differential homeownership is the primary reason for America's racial wealth gap. Racial differences in homeownership contribute to the wealth gap.*

Racial differences in homeownership do indeed contribute to the wealth gap but do not begin to explain the yawning disparity. White homeowners in 2014 possessed a median net worth of $239,300, compared with Black homeowners' $99,840.

---

[6] This same phenomenon involving immigrants can be found operating in the pro-Brexit vote in the United Kingdom and in right-wing voting throughout Europe (Van Assche, Dhont, and Pettigrew, 2019; Pettigrew, 2022a).

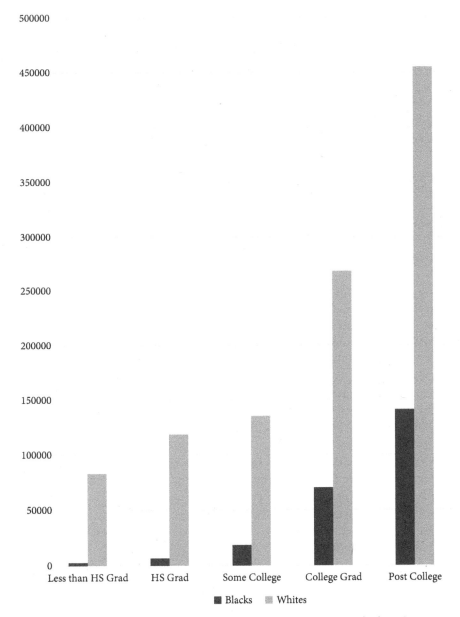

Figure 4.2 Black and White average household income by race and education
Source: Darity et al., 2018, p. 6.

Chapter 10 details the many ways discriminatory housing actions of the federal government, together with the real estate and banking industries, brought about this situation. It should also be noted that the greater share of Blacks who rent are not accumulating equity, while homeowners with mortgages are enhancing their wealth.

Myth 3: *Buying and banking with Black-owned businesses will close the racial wealth gap.*

Many Black leaders through the years, from Marcus Garvey to Martin Luther King, Jr., have advocated "buying Black." Even Richard Nixon extoled "Black capitalism." But Black businesses are simply too small in scale to strongly influence the racial wealth differential.

Darity points out that the total assets of the five largest Black-owned banks ($2.3 billion) in 2016 are minuscule compared with the worth of just one New York Bank, J. P. Morgan, with more than *$2 trillion* in assets. Similarly, in 2016 the giant Walmart chain grossed more than 20 times as much in revenue and employed 2.2 million more workers than all Black-owned businesses combined. Black business owners would, undoubtedly, be delighted to see Black Americans "buy Black" more often. However, to erode the racial wealth disparity significantly, this is not a viable strategy.

Myth 4: *If Black Americans would just save more, they would close the racial wealth gap.*

Wrong again. Once income is controlled, Black families have a slightly greater savings rate than their White equivalents (Gittleman and Wolff, 2004). Spending studies reveal the same result: Whites spend 1.3 times more than comparable Blacks (Traub et al., 2017). Still, if you are poor, there is a severe limit to how much you can save.

Myth 5: *If only Black Americans would acquire greater financial literacy, they would close the racial wealth gap.*

It is true that Black people make more use of such sub-optimal financial services as check cashing and payday loan shops. They also engage far less in the stock market than Whites. However, as Darity's work makes clear, these racial differences do not reflect financial illiteracy so much as austere economic circumstances. Black Americans often turn to predatory financial stores as a last resort after other possibilities, such as borrowing from friends, are exhausted. They may well know better yet have no choice. In any event, less use of such predatory services could hardly close the wide racial difference in wealth. And when basic controls are applied, there is no statistically significant racial difference in the value of Black and White family unsecured debt (Hamilton and Darity, 2017).

Myth 6: *Like Myth 3, this myth views Black-owned businesses as the primary means to eradicate the racial wealth gap.*

This, too, is an insufficient prognosis. Large-scale entrepreneurship can lead to local income *inequality* (Darity et al., 2018). And the primary examples of huge and successful businesses, the size needed to influence sufficiently the racial gap in wealth, were typically begun with family wealth passed down through the generations. Jeff Bezos and Mark Zuckerberg both started their famous businesses with hefty sums of money from their parents. This generational transfer of large financial amounts safely through family trusts has not been available to aspiring Black entrepreneurs. So far, Black business in America has consisted overwhelmingly of tiny, mom-and-pop enterprises. The U.S. Census finds that more than 90% of Black firms in 2020 have no employees other than their owners. Despite talk about "Black capitalism," there has been no significant federal support to develop larger-scale Black businesses. Any future reparations must include aid to Black-owned business (Chapter 12).

This point has wider importance for Black wealth beyond that of starting businesses. One in three American workers obtain a job with a parental employer, and those who do tend to earn more; 29% of individuals work for a parent's employer at least once by age 30. Staiger (2022) estimates that working for a parental employer increases initial earnings by 19%. This major economic benefit, called "the nepotism baby effect," is strongest among high-income White families. Consequently, getting a job with a parental employer reduces the probability of obtaining only an unskilled service sector job by 31%.

In short, wealth makes for more wealth. This economic inheritance from which many White Americans benefit is rare among Black Americans. It constitutes yet another reason why Blacks have difficulty developing wealth.

Myth 7: *Blacks should emulate the nation's successful minorities in order to close the racial wealth gap.*

This is one of many tropes that put the blame for the wealth gap on Blacks themselves. It must be something about Black people themselves that is holding them back, goes the argument. It cannot be discrimination—look at the business success of Asian Americans.[7]

Immigrant success in America derives in large part from two interacting factors that do not apply to Black Americans. First, Darity, Dietrich, and Guilkey (2001) offer a "lateral mobility" hypothesis that holds that the social position held by adult immigrants in their nation of origin will be typically obtained by their children in America. For instance, middle-class immigrants from China often have business skills that enable their children to secure a similar status in the United States.

Second, except when emigrating out of desperation from poverty and war, those who manage to surmount the formidable American immigration system are selectively more persistent strivers. Immigrants to the United States from the West Indies, for example, have done better economically than those who went to Great Britain, where it was far easier for them to become citizens (Foner, 1979).

Myth 8: *Black family disorganization is the principal reason for the racial wealth gap.*

This is yet another trope that blames the wealth disparity on Blacks themselves. If only they would "straighten up and live right," they could overcome the disparity. Such an argument became especially popular in the 1960s and 1970s with the emphasis on the "culture of poverty" by the anthropologist Oscar Lewis (1959). He argued, on the basis of his study of just five deprived families in Mexico, that the poor live within a self-perpetuating culture. Through behaviors and beliefs acquired in this culture, they make their destitute situation worse. This is why, Lewis claimed, the racial wealth gap is so enormous.

---

[7] Those making this argument typically overlook the pockets of poverty among Asian Americans that do exist. High 2020 poverty rates exist for Burmese (19%), Hmong (17%), Mongolian (16%) Americans and other Asian groups (Tien and Ruiz, 2024).

On its face, the theory has a causal-order problem. Poverty causes the development of such a culture more plausibly than the hypothesized culture of poverty causes poverty. Lewis's argument also ignores the structural factors that largely shape poverty and are out of the control of the poor.

Although the theory was widely criticized throughout the social sciences, it gained notoriety when Undersecretary of Labor Daniel Patrick Moynihan picked it up and applied it to poor Black families. Moynihan was not a social scientist; his degrees from Tufts University were in naval studies and history. But he was adept at using social science to support his shifting political positions, from the Democratic administration of President Johnson to the Republican administration of President Nixon. He became prominent in both administrations, and his colorful quotes made him a mass media favorite—especially after he later became a senator from New York. But it was his proclivity for extreme terms that made Moynihan a controversial public figure.

The Negro Family: The Case for National Action (Moynihan, 1965),[8] popularly known as "the Moynihan Report," was attacked even before it was released. Read now, one might wonder why it stirred such a passionate negative response. Expanding on Lewis's thesis, Moynihan held that the decline of the Black American nuclear family was impeding all racial progress. A half-century later, the Urban Institute (Acs, 2013) brought the report's analyses up to date.[9] It found most of the racial family trends uncovered by Moynihan had continued. And now the family trends for White America closely resemble those of Black America back in the 1960s, including increased female-headed households, father absence, and illegitimate births. These trends strongly suggest that these indicators of the breakdown of patrimonial family structure is society-wide, not just a Black American phenomenon.

The "culture of poverty" reasoning became popular because it bolstered the White tendency to blame Black people for their situation. Black family problems were now held to be the basic reason for the racial wealth gap. This let White Americans off the hook. It soon became a popular explanation for Black poverty among White conservatives.

Slavery Effects Live On

White Americans tend to regard slavery as a horrible, long-ago phenomenon of no direct significance to the nation a century and a half later. Yet throughout the counties of the border and southern states, the prevalence of slavery in 1860 predicts gun ownership today (Buttrick and Mazen, 2022).[10] Also consider two research papers that tie

---

[8] The complete report is available on the web.
[9] This report is also available on the web.
[10] The authors ascribe this effect as a result of the tumultuous post–Civil War period. Yet it could also reflect the earlier acquiring of arms by slaveholders following such slave uprisings as Nat Turner's rebellion in Southampton, Virginia in 1831.

the past to today's implicit racial views (see Sidebar 4.1). The first paper compared across counties and states the average levels of implicit racial bias with the 1860 number of slaves in the area (Payne, Vuletich, and Brown-Iannuzzi, 2019). It found that in those areas with more slavery in 1860, Whites today display a greater pro-White implicit bias. Moreover, Blacks in these old slavery areas also show less pro-White bias.

Nor are such long-term effects limited to the South. In a second paper, a significant link was found between those counties in the North with the highest proportion of Blacks during the years of the "Great Migration" (1900–1950) and significantly greater White American implicit bias toward Black Americans today (Vuletich, Sommet, and Payne, 2023). These longitudinal effects are mediated by such structural inequalities as current Black poverty and racial housing segregation. In other words, areas in the North that received large numbers of southern Black migrants tended to segregate housing by race and increase Black poverty. In turn, these conditions molded more anti-Black implicit bias within their White populations. In effect, racial discrimination creates conditions that lead to greater racial prejudice.

We will note in Chapter 10 that housing segregation is routinely a major factor in modern American racism.

A Final Assessment

As Chapter 1 noted, White Americans routinely read about multimillion-dollar contracts signed by Black American athletes and entertainers and conclude that Black people must be doing well economically. Our review shows that such unrepresentative cases seriously distort the economic reality for Black America generally. Educational gains in recent years have led to the growth of the Black middle class and modest income gains for the group as a whole. Nevertheless, the economic situation for many Blacks has improved only from dire deprivation to living on the brink.

None of the common beliefs in how to close the wide wealth gap stands up to scrutiny. If these popular explanations do not begin to account for the wealth gap, what does? The answer to this question is described throughout this book in the multitude of discriminatory practices that have systematically restrained Blacks Americans from accumulating wealth: slavery, penury labor, biased federal housing practices and veterans' benefits, segregated schools, and all the other racial biases throughout society.

The slightest turndown in the American economy can and has thrown many Blacks back into extreme poverty. Consequently, we can say racism in the economic realm has only modestly declined over the years—although we note that this may be changing to some degree as the White population ages. Furthermore, this analysis leads to the conclusion that the major way to begin to close the

66 Anti-Black Racism in America

enormous racial gap in wealth, besides a widespread reduction in racial discrimination of all types, is through targeted reparations—a topic discussed in the final chapter.

Highly recommended additional reading on this subject:

> Blackmon, D. A. (2008). *Slavery by another name: The re-enslavement of Black Americans from the Civil War to World War II*. New York: Anchor.
>
> Cha-Jua, S. K. (2010). The new nadir: The contemporary Black racial formation. *The Black Scholar*, 40(1), 38–58.
>
> Darity, W., Jr., Hamilton, D., Paul, M., Aja, A., Price, A., Moore, A., and Chiopris, C. (April 1, 2018). What we get wrong about closing the racial wealth gap. S. B. Cook Center for Social Equity. Retrieved December 11, 2022. https://insightcced.org/what-we-get-wrong.
>
> LeFlouria, T. L. (2016). *Chained in silence: Black women and convict labor in the new South*. Chapel Hill: University of North Carolina Press.

Sidebar 4.1 Eight Black-American Business Leaders

Consider the details of eight highly successful Black Americans who became business leaders. They each achieved their success by dint of effort and talent to secure a place in the privileged pipeline that had long been the exclusive preserve of White Americans.

Ursula Burns. Raised with siblings in a New York City housing project by a single mother who was a Panamanian immigrant, Burns became the first Black woman to head a company (Xerox) in the Fortune 500 (2009–2016).

Her entry into the privileged pipeline started with enrollment at the all-girls, then-highly diverse Cathedral High School in Manhattan. She next obtained a B.S. degree in mechanical engineering from Brooklyn Polytechnic Institute - now part of New York University. Then she earned an M.S. in mechanical engineering from Columbia. This extensive background led to a summer internship at Xerox that began her four-decade career with the company. Burns (2021) describes her extraordinary journey in which she overcame both sexism and racism in her pointed memoir, *Where You Are Is Not Who You Are*.

Rosalind "Roz" Brewer. Like Michelle Obama, Brewer attended an interracial public magnet school for the gifted - Cass Technical High School—when growing up in Detroit. She and her four siblings were the first of their family to attend college. Brewer graduated from historically Black Spelman College in Atlanta. From there, she was able to enter into the pipeline of privilege by graduating from the University of Chicago's Booth School of Business and then Stanford University's Law School. Her business career has been extensive and has included leadership positions at Kimberly-Clark, Starbucks, and Sam's Club. In 2021, Brewer became the CEO of the Walmart-Boots Alliance and the only Black woman then head of a Fortune 500 company.

Kenneth Chenault served with success as the CEO of American Express from 2001 to 2018. Son of a dentist and a dental hygienist, he grew up on Long Island and attended the highly diverse Alternative Waldorf School. There he was elected senior class president and captained sports teams. This promising and diverse start enabled Chenault to flow into the privileged pipeline - first as a history major at Bowdoin College and then at Harvard Law School.

Thasunda Brown Duckett. Born in Rochester, New York, Duckett moved with her parents to Texas and attended Sam Houston High School in Arlington. This school is diverse, with a majority of Hispanic students, but it receives low ratings in improving student test scores. Duckett started her climb into the privileged pipeline when she enrolled in the University of Houston. A timely college scholarship from the Federal National Mortgage Association made it possible for her to continue her education. This allowed her to obtain a degree in finance and marketing and later to receive an MBA degree at Baylor University's School of Business.

Duckett's business career took root at the J. P. Morgan Chase Bank. From work on mortgages, she rose to become the head of Chase auto finance and then CEO of Chase Consumer Banking. In 2021, she became the CEO of the Teachers Insurance and Annuity Association of America and joined Rosalind Brewer as the second Black female CEO of a Fortune 500 company.

Kenneth Frazier, a Philadelphia native and son of a janitor and former sharecropper, was the CEO of Merck Pharmaceuticals from 2011 to 2021. Though he grew up in a poor neighborhood of North Philadelphia, his outstanding grades got him enrolled in the city's Masterman Laboratory and Demonstration School. This institution prides itself as a highly diverse international and multicultural school. He then attended Philadelphia's Northeast High School—another highly diverse school. These institutions, together with his strong grades, got him into Pennsylvania State University. Now within the privilege pipeline, Frazier was next accepted by Harvard Law School.

Roger Ferguson Jr. became the CEO of the Teachers Insurance and Annuity Association in 2008. Earlier he had served as the vice-chair of the Federal Reserve Board of Governors (1999–2006). He grew up in a middle-class family and won a scholarship to attend Washington's desegregated private Sidwell Friends School.

That put him early in the privilege stream, and he went on to Harvard University and majored in economics. He graduated in 1973 with magna cum laude honors. He then won a scholarship for a year of study at Pembroke College at Cambridge University. Next, he entered Harvard Law School and received his J.D. with cum laude honors in 1979. Then he earned his Harvard doctorate in economics. Years later, in 2016, Harvard's Graduate School of Arts and Sciences presented Ferguson with its Centennial Gold Medal for his "contributions to society." He has also received honorary doctorates from 19 colleges and universities.

Ferguson's achievements at Harvard are especially noteworthy. Despite undergraduate grade inflation in recent decades, Harvard jealously safeguards its standards for special honors. To receive magna cum laude honors as an undergraduate and then cum laude honors with his law degree is a rare occurrence. It was later equaled at Harvard by Associate Justice Ketanji Brown Jackson, who joined the U.S. Supreme Court as its second Black member in 2022.

68 Anti-Black Racism in America

Jide Zeitlin was briefly the CEO of Tapestry, Inc., a purveyor of luxury accessories. He boasts the most diverse background of all the CEOs. Born in Lagos, Nigeria, he was adopted at the age of five by the Zeitlins, a White-American, world-traveling journalistic family. He attended school in Nigeria with the Zeitlins' daughter. As he grew up, he lived for extended periods in Pakistan and the Philippines with his adopted parents. After studying at New England private preparatory schools, he majored in economics and English at Amherst College. Ensconced on the privilege track, he next got his MBA at Harvard Business School.

René Jones is the CEO of M & T Bank, headquartered in Buffalo, New York. Son of a Black American father and a White Belgian mother who met in the midst of World War II, Jones grew up in Ayer, Massachusetts, near Fort Devens, where he attended interracial schools. He earned his B.A. from Boston College and his MBA from the University of Rochester. Like Barack Obama, he not only experienced interracial schooling all his life, but grew up in an interracial family.

Marvin Ellison, former CEO of J.C. Penny department stores, became the CEO of Lowe's Home Improvement stores. He just half-fits the recurrent theme of gaining access to the pipeline of privilege early in life. He was one of seven children born on an impoverished farm outside the hamlet of Brownsville, near Memphis in the southwestern delta region of Tennessee. His early education was racially segregated. He later enrolled in Memphis University, a majority-White school with a substantial African-American presence. This marked his late entry onto the privilege track. Once in it, Ellison made the most of his opportunities. After obtaining his marketing degree from Memphis University, he earned his MBA from Emory University in Atlanta.

Note how many of these talented people, like both Obamas, got their final push into elite circles via the Ivy League—many of them at Harvard University. This is not a coincidence. Harvard was one of the first major universities to seek out highly talented Black Americans—as it had done earlier with W. E. B. Du Bois (B.A., 1890; M.A., 1891; Ph.D., 1895). Harvard College officials have tended to seek Black talent from predominantly White institutions where they had trusted contacts and were accustomed to looking for White talent—such as Long Island's Waldorf School and Washington's Sidwell Friends School. Likewise, Harvard's Law School routinely looks for promising talent at other Ivy League universities. That is how the access network - the privileged pipeline - operates from stage to stage.

Chapter 5
Race and Education

In 1950, the Reverend Oliver Brown, a lifelong resident of Topeka, Kansas, tried in vain to enroll his seven-year-old daughter, Linda, in the all-White Sumner Elementary School just three blocks from their home. Instead, she was assigned and bused to the all-Black Monroe Elementary School 21 blocks from their home.[1] Rev. Brown sued the Topeka Board of Education. A three-judge federal court ruled against him by holding that the "separate-but-equal" doctrine of *Plessy v. Ferguson* in 1896 still held sway. Brown appealed to the U.S. Supreme Court, where his case was combined with other school segregation cases. The rest is history.

The story of Rev. Brown and his daughter did not end with the Supreme Court ruling of May 17, 1954, that found racial segregation in public schools to be unconstitutional. The determined father died of a heart attack seven years later. Linda Brown lived on in Topeka, worked as a keypunch operator, then attended Washburn University in Topeka and Kansas State University in Manhattan. Her two children attended racially desegregated schools. In later life, she successfully brought another school desegregation case against the Topeka School Board and became a public speaker on race relations. In 2018, she died in her hometown at the age of 76.

The Browns' belief in the importance of education is widely shared among Black Americans. Indeed, they have long highly valued education as a way up and out of their suppressed status. Right after federal troops entered Richmond in 1865, the Richmond Theological Institute was established to offer literacy to ex-slaves. It later became Virginia Union University. In the mid-20th century the demands of Black parents for integrated schools caused the NAACP Legal Defense and Education Fund to alter its plans for what to litigate (Greenberg, 1959). The Fund's lawyers had been focusing on opening up state-funded professional schools. But Black parents demanded cases be brought against segregation in primary and secondary education as well. The *Brown* decision of 1954 was a direct result of this shift in emphasis (see Sidebar 2.1).

---

[1] Note that busing to school was widely used and accepted when it was employed to maintain racial segregation of public schools. It became a national and controversial issue only later, when it was employed to achieve racial desegregation of public schools.

Anti-Black Racism in America. Thomas F. Pettigrew, Oxford University Press. © Oxford University Press (2025).
DOI: 10.1093/9780197803134.003.0006

Post-*Brown* Retrenchment

White supremacists over the past seven decades have managed to roll back the historic 1954 *Brown* ruling outlawing racially segregated schools. By 2020 Black American children in the nation's public schools were virtually as segregated as they were prior to *Brown*.[2] In 1955, the High Court undercut its historic desegregation ruling with a vague "all deliberate speed" order. The White South, quite deliberate but rarely speedy, viewed this order as a sign of weakness. This second decision had the unfortunate, if unintended, consequence of heightening opposition to the original decision. Resistance groups called White Citizens' Councils—basically middle-class Ku Klux Klans - sprang up in small towns throughout the South.[3]

In addition, the segregationist White South responded by establishing numerous "segregationist academies." Ostensibly private schools, they were allowed to counter desegregation orders from the federal courts. The Internal Revenue Service even granted tax exemptions for these blatantly racist institutions until 1970, when civil right groups secured a court injunction. Segregated private schools have continued to exist throughout the South with token Black enrollment. Thus, Clarksdale, Mississippi, in 2010 had a "private" Lee Academy with 92% White students, and the public Clarksdale High School with 92% Black students. In 2024, a check of the two schools' student pictures on the web show little has changed at either school.

Consequently, scant progress was made for a decade. In response to this delay, three strong federal court rulings emerged. In 1968, *Green v. County School Board of New Kent County, Virginia* struck down a "freedom of choice" attempt to avoid desegregation. In 1971, *Swann v. Charlotte-Mecklenburg Board of Education* established that desegregation required affirmative action—including the busing of students throughout Charlotte's metropolitan area. In 1973, *Keyes v. School District No. 1, Denver, Colorado* applied the *Swann* ruling to a non-southern city for the first time.

In reaction to this progress, deep resistance to school integration developed. It was encouraged by President Richard Nixon, who strongly opposed the busing needed to achieve it. This opposition gathered strength as it seized on the claim of massive "White flight" from cities to avoid desegregation. Bolstered by the publicized assertions of the sociologist James Coleman, conservative judges began to use it as an excuse to roll back desegregation orders (Orfield and Eaton, 1996).

The "White flight" argument ignored two key points. First, the Coleman analysis was seriously flawed. While more White families did move to the suburbs and private schools during the first year of a city's integration, it was largely a "hastening up"

---

[2] This is true, although desegregation involving Latino American children has markedly increased (Meckler and Rabinowitz, 2019). Paradoxically, this means that millions more American children are attending ethnically diverse schools, while Black children remain almost as segregated as before 1954. This point is often obscured by some writers who claim massive interracial schooling is now the national norm.

[3] Even Atticus Finch, the fictitious name Harper Lee (1960) gave her father as the hero of her famed novel *To Kill a Mockingbird*, was a member of the White Citizens' Council of Monroeville. Alabama—as revealed in Lee's (2015) *Go Set a Watchman*.

effect. That is, large urban districts that started school desegregation did not lose significantly more White students over the critical 1967–1976 period than did districts that remained racially segregated. This was true because desegregating districts were already losing White families before the process, and after a few years would have lost just as many White families without any desegregation whatsoever (Farley, Richards, and Wurdock, 1980).

Second, the "White flight" phenomenon was especially acute in large cities such as Detroit, where the High Court flatly rejected metropolitan plans for school desegregation in *Milliken v. Bradley* (Pettigrew, 2004). However, in smaller cities, such as Richmond, Virginia,[4] Lexington, Kentucky, and Wilmington, Delaware, metropolitan plans are far more feasible.

Court-ordered school desegregation plans were generally effective in reducing racial segregation. As soon as continued court oversight was removed, however, desegregation began to fade (Reardon et al., 2012). Adding to the problem is that right-wing judges, even on the U.S. Supreme Court, have been openly dismissive of relevant social science evidence when it does not support their personal beliefs and prejudices (Tropp, Smith, and Crosby, 2007).

Thus, it is not surprising that when the U.S. Supreme Court reversed the historic *Brown* decision it did so without admitting it. A five-judge majority, all Republican appointments, held narrowly tailored desegregation plans of two school districts—Seattle, Washington, and Jefferson County, Kentucky—to be in violation of the Equal Protection Clause of the 14th Amendment (Tropp, Smith, and Crosby, 2007). They so ruled because a few White children had been denied access to the schools of their choice in order to further racial desegregation, and because prior state de jure segregation was not directly involved.

This sweeping ruling prohibited assigning students to public schools solely for the purpose of achieving racial desegregation and declined to recognize racial balancing as a compelling state interest. These decisions directly affected hundreds of other desegregated school districts. Earlier, four lower federal courts had consistently upheld the modest Seattle and Jefferson County plans to be constitutional. Now these rulings were abruptly overturned.

Ironically, just two years before, the nation had celebrated the 50th anniversary of *Brown* as a great step forward for American democracy. Accordingly, the Seattle and Jefferson County cases that essentially ended *Brown* can be seen as great steps *backward* for American democracy. They made *race* alone an unacceptable constraint for limiting school choice, while such restrictions have never been explicitly applied to the categories of gender, religion, social class, and disabilities (Minow, 2010). These two decisions, together with Detroit's *Milliken* anti-metropolitan decision, marked the 21st century's partial return to the 19th century's infamous *Plessey v. Ferguson* pro-segregation case.

---

[4] I served as an expert witness in the case in Richmond, where a metropolitan desegregation plan actually had the potential for *reducing* busing because of extensive suburban busing to maintain racial segregation.

The Role of Property Tax Support for Public Schools

State aid is the primary source of public school funding. Close behind is the support that public schools receive from property taxes in their district. This tax-funding arrangement has a deleterious effect on schools in poor districts. Children in rich districts get well-supported schools; children in poor districts get poorly supported schools. While this class discrepancy in resources affects both Black and White children, given the economic differences between the races it affects Black schools far more.

Recurring Problems with School Desegregation

Black Americans have endured two types of burden for their desegregation efforts. First, many hundreds of qualified Black educators were vindictively fired in the last third of the century - especially in the Deep South. White supremacists vainly hoped that this would deter Black efforts.[5] Research shows this was a major setback for public school education for both White and Black children. High-minority schools with children from poor families suffer from high teacher turnover. However, minority teachers are less likely to flee these situations than others (Achinstein et al., 2010). White students with a Black teacher can potentially break the racist cycle that develops early in life (Quiocho and Rios, 2000). Most important of all, Black teachers typically have higher expectations for their Black students than White teachers do— a major predictor of enhanced Black student performance (Gershenson, Holt, and Papageorge, 2016).

Second, desegregation often requires Black students to give up their own schools to attend as minorities in predominantly White institutions. As a Black Virginian succinctly phrased it, "It felt like being a visitor, but in many ways an unwanted visitor in somebody else's house" (quoted in Schneider, 2021).

Two books look closely at the later effects of *Brown*. The first, by Martha Minow (2010), concentrates on the worldwide significance of this landmark decision. A Harvard law professor who clerked for Associate Justice Thurgood Marshall, she shows how the *Brown* decision has shaped cases involving immigrants, gender, religion, other minorities, and the disabled. Indeed, the decision has even influenced foreign litigation in the Republic of South Africa and the Czech Republic. It seems as if *Brown* has had a greater effect for other groups than it has had for Black Americans.

The second book surveys the ensuing lives of 268 Black and White graduates in 1980 of six racially desegregated high schools located throughout the nation

---

[5] Now there is a serious teacher shortage—especially of minority teachers. The Pew Research Center found that in 2017–2018, 79% of elementary and secondary public school teachers were White, while 47% of their students were Black (Schaeffer, 2021).

(Wells et al., 2009). The researchers chose 1980 as desegregation's high point prior to the pro-segregation Reagan era. Their results reinforced several important earlier findings—namely, that color-blind strategies in these schools did not work well (Schofield, 1997) and that competition from private schools leads to the use of public school resources being heavily spent to keep White parents content (Clotfelter, 2004).

Nevertheless, these products of interracial schools had more positive attitudes toward each other than products of segregated schools. Yet they have not been able to exercise their beliefs in later life. Both the Black and White respondents reported how difficult it had been for them to stay in touch with their other-race friends and to live in interracial neighborhoods. They had changed, while American society had not changed enough to accommodate their altered racial views.

Educational Trends beyond Desegregation

Black educational gains in recent years are substantial on numerous indicators: reduced high school dropout, increased high school graduation, and increased college attendance and graduation. By 2017, 94% of 18-to-24 year-old Black Americans had graduated from high school - equivalent for the first time to that of White Americans (McFarland, et al., 2020).

Black American rates of college enrollment and graduation rose sharply from 1968 to 2018. And many predominantly White colleges changed their structure to better accommodate the incoming Black students. From 1967 to 1970, almost 1,000 colleges and universities initiated Black studies departments, programs, and courses (Kendi, 2016, p. 407). This sweeping change had multiple positive effects for largely White institutions. It helped to make the Black students on these campuses feel they were included in the institution's intellectual life. Black studies also gave training and jobs to those who wished to specialize in the subject. And, not incidentally, these programs often attracted White students who could learn a whole new perspective on the nation's race relations.

As more Black students attend predominantly White institutions, the ratio of Black college graduates finishing at one of the historically Black colleges and universities (HBCU) is declining—from 35% of Black graduates in 1976–1977 to 16% in 2010–2011 (Noonan, Velasco-Mondragon, 2016). The HBCU institutions have produced 80% of Black judges, 25% of Black scientists, 70% of Black dentists and physicians, and 40% of the Black members of Congress. Yet they receive only a tiny portion of federal funding for higher education. For example, Johns Hopkins University alone has received about seven times the amount of federal funds as *all* 101 of the HBCUs combined (Allen and Glover, 2022).

These educational advances made possible the growth of the Black American middle class over the past half-century. Black parents correctly saw that better lives for their children were achievable primarily through greater educational opportunities.

74   Anti-Black Racism in America

Indeed, research has shown that there have been many positive effects for Black products of interracial schools (Pettigrew, 2021). With social class controlled, early research indicated that Black children from desegregated schools, when compared with equivalent Black children from segregated schools, were found to be more likely later (1) to attend and finish majority-White colleges; (2) to work with White colleagues; (3) to live in interracial neighborhoods; (4) to have somewhat higher incomes; and (5) to have more White friends and contacts and more positive attitudes toward Whites. Moreover, White products of desegregation were found to have more positive attitudes toward Black people than comparable Whites from segregated schools.

More rigorous research on the long-term impacts of interracial schools was needed. In 2011, the National Bureau of Economic Research analyzed data on more than 4,000 children born between 1950 and 1975 (Johnson, 2011, 2019). This research found that previous studies had actually *underestimated* the positive effects of interracial education for Black children.

While court-ordered school desegregation did not harm White outcomes, it significantly improved such Black outcomes as graduation rates, later annual earnings, and adult health. For Black men, each additional year in desegregated schools increased their annual earnings by about 5%. And interracial education as a child even reduced by 15% the probability of Black males being in jail by age 30.

Johnson (2012, 2019) furthered this research with a check on the outcomes of interracial education for the children of the desegregated Black students—aptly named "the grandchildren of *Brown*." For cohorts born since 1980, the positive effects of educational desegregation had significantly extended into this next generation: enhanced math and reading test scores plus greater likelihood of high school graduation and college attendance. These grandchildren of *Brown* were also more likely to choose more selective colleges with greater racial diversity. Part of these effects can be traced to school quality. Thus, desegregated parental education proved to be a causal determinant of generational mobility. This groundbreaking research reveals how educational opportunities have both cumulative and lasting effects.[6]

The most important gain was not mere increases in test scores. The critical advance was that integrated education pried open the *pipeline of privilege* through which only White people had benefited previously. The pipeline, once entered, allows you to attend better schools and obtain better employment. Note the paths taken by today's leading Black Americans in business and politics, described in Chapters 4 and 8. Almost all of them had early entrance into privileged, high-status educational settings (Pettigrew, 2021).

---

[6] Interestingly, the econometrician and chief author of these studies, Rucker Johnson, is himself a Black product of integrated education in his youth. He later studied what he had lived. He became the Chancellors Professor of Public Policy at the University of California, Berkeley. Many of the best ideas in social science arise from personal experience.

Political Restrictions on the Content of Public Education

Far-right White politicians wish to restrict severely what is taught about race in public schools. They would reduce dissonance over race with a variety of heavy-handed, undemocratic methods. They would ban all textbooks and teaching that dare to discuss slavery and other key topics in the complex history of American racism. More than 1,600 books—including even *To Kill a Mockingbird* (Lee, 1960) - were banned during the 2021–2022 school year somewhere in the United State (Feldman, 2022). Imagine accurately describing the Civil War without mentioning its basic cause: slavery.

One Republican legislator in Tennessee called for Nazi-style racial book burning. Georgia's legislature moved to restrict the discussion of race in the state's classrooms. Florida even began proscribing "suspicious" mathematics textbooks. And Governor Glenn Youngkin of Virginia frightened White parents by claiming that their children were being "indoctrinated" in public schools by the teaching of critical race theory (CRT) (see Sidebar 5.1). His electoral success with this baseless claim led Republicans to employ it throughout the nation. But CRT is grossly mischaracterized. It focuses on structural barriers baked into American law, not the racial attitudes of individuals. Moreover, no public school in Virginia taught the theory, and Youngkin sent his own sons to a racially desegregated private school in Washington that proudly advertises that it teaches CRT (Milbank, 2022).

Not all of White America has opposed educational desegregation. Local groups in such places as Shaker Heights, Ohio, vigorously fought for interracial schools. And the Civil Rights Project at the University of California in Los Angeles has focused on the subject for decades. Indeed, many social scientists have contributed research on the subject and supported the process (see Sidebar 5.2).

Solid Black Gains in Amount of Education

In spite of the stiff resistance to interracial education, Black Americans have managed to make significant gains in the amount of education they obtain. Drawn from the U.S. Census Bureau (2022a), Figure 5.1 and Figure 5.2 reveal these advances.

Rates of Black youth who have completed four years of high school education have impressively climbed from less than half that of White youth in 1962 to almost equal by 2021. Note in Figure 5.1 that rates of high school graduation steadily climbed for both races over these 60 years, with Black children managing to narrow the gap in each 20-year period since 1962. Federal programs, especially Head Start for young children, importantly aided this change. Established in 1965, Head Start became a nationwide program by the 1970s that provided lasting benefits. Darren Walker, the Black president of the Ford Foundation, credits his childhood Head Start training in Lafayette, Louisiana, as the essential beginning of his meteoric career (Ford Foundation, 2015).

76 Anti-Black Racism in America

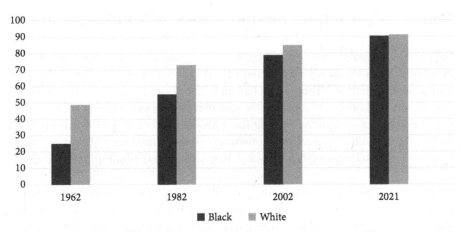

Figure 5.1 Percentage of Americans 25 years or older who graduated from high school, by race
Source: U.S. Census Bureau, 2022b.

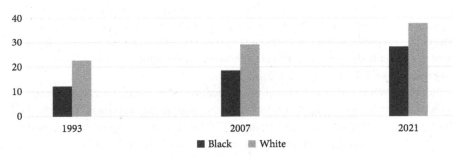

Figure 5.2 Percentage of Americans 25 years or older who completed 4 years of college, by race
Source: Cunningham et al., 2017.

Increased high school completion rates make possible higher rates of college attendance. In Figure 5.2, we see rising levels of college completion for both races, but Black students have yet to close the roughly 10% gap with White students. The 101 HBCUs provide an important part of this increase in Black higher education. Simultaneously, predominantly White institutions have also begun to enroll significantly more Black students.

This improvement in the amount of Black education is vital in many ways. In particular, high school completion is vital for obtaining a job in an economy that demands increasingly higher levels of prior training. Now post–high school training is becoming essential for the new job market. The development of artificial intelligence (AI) makes that clear. Access to junior college is rapidly becoming necessary for expanding technical jobs—a point to which we will return in the final chapter on reparations.

Closing Off Black American Entry into the Pipeline of Privilege

Fierce right-wing opposition to affirmative action in elite universities has risen in recent years. On June 28, 2023, the Supreme Court ended affirmative action for minority students in higher education. Given the 6–3 Republican majority, the decision was expected even though it overturned past High Court decisions as well as an array of lower-court decisions over the previous 45 years. It was widely expected because it was basically a political, not a legal, decision. Similar to its earlier overturning of *Roe v. Wade* on abortion, the reactionary Court's Republican majority threw aside multiple past Court decisions and faithfully followed the right-wing thrust of Donald Trump and the far-right Federalist Society.

We have noted repeatedly that attendance at elite, predominantly White universities is typically the entry ticket into the pipeline of privilege for Black leaders in both politics and business. Not surprisingly, racist attempts to end entry to this path have become numerous in recent years. A combination of dark money, Trump-appointed federal judges, and the tireless efforts of a former stockbroker have now succeeded in essentially closing this one important anti-racism path. Born and raised in Benton Harbor, Michigan,[7] Edward Blum has dedicated his life to ending affirmative action in college admissions and other programs that benefit Black Americans. He set up Students for Fair Admissions, Inc., to which some White billionaires have heavily contributed, and Blum now lives on an estate in South Thomaston, Maine.

Blum's first attempt to end affirmative action in college admissions failed in 2016 by a 4–3 decision of the High Court. He had recruited Abigail Fisher, a White woman who had been turned down for admission to the University of Texas at Austin— Blum's alma mater. He followed the same recruitment procedure for the Harvard and University of North Carolina cases. The Court's racist decision has special meaning for me (see Sidebar 5.3).

A Masterclass of Modern American Racism

Chief Justice John Roberts's decision in the affirmative action college cases accurately reflects current racist contentions among many upper-status White people. First, he completely ignores structural differences between the races as detailed throughout this volume. He keeps his whole discussion at the individual level, as if only some individual Black Americans have been affected by racism. He manages this despite the fact that the High Court in non-racial cases routinely uses the institutional level of analysis. Of course, based on the institutional analyses of this book, no Black

---

[7] This predominantly Black town of 10,000 people in the southwestern corner of Michigan has experienced two severe race riots (1966, 2003), one occurring when Blum was growing up. It is not known if this shaped his racist fervor.

78 Anti-Black Racism in America

American fully escapes American society's institutional restraints - not even former President Barack Obama.

Modern racist elite thought is also careful to appear non-racist. At length, Roberts writes, "Nothing in this opinion should be construed as prohibiting universities from considering an applicant's discussion of how race affected his or her life, be it through discrimination, inspiration or otherwise. A benefit to a student who overcame discrimination, for example, must be tied to that student's courage and determination. Or a benefit to a student whose heritage or culture motivated him or her to assume a leadership role or attain a particular goal must be tied to that student's unique ability to contribute to the university. In other words, the student must be treated based on their experiences as an individual—not on the basis of race." (Supreme Court of the United States, 2023).

Some critics have viewed this statement as unadulterated gibberish. Others view it as an escape clause for universities. I think it is largely an attempt to appear non-racist—a key component of modern racism. It carefully ignores the relevant racial opinions of justices of the past. Former Justice Harry Blackmun (1978) asserted a lasting truth: "In order to go beyond racism, we must first take account of race. There is no other way. And in order to treat some persons equally, we must treat them differently."

Dismayed by this half-century retreat, believers in affirmative action have suggested many ways universities might mitigate at least some of the effects of *Students for Fair Admissions, Inc. v. Harvard*. Some may work, but only at the margins. Even Richard Kahlenberg, an expert testifying for Blum, admitted that no workable race-neutral alternatives would allow Harvard to maintain the racial diversity it had achieved.

It is also important to note who the High Court omits from its reasoning. The military academies are explicitly excluded. So, too, are the many White students who get into the Ivy League because their parents had attended previously (so-called legacy admissions) or their parents had given large gifts to the university. The NAACP Education and Defense Fund soon sued to bar such procedures. George W. Bush boasted that he had proved a "C" student at Yale could become president. Put simply, there has been massive affirmative action for wealthy White Americans at the nation's major universities for years (see Sidebar 5.4).

The elite university route to high governmental positions is also long established. For 10 years (2011–2020), all nine of the Supreme Court's members were graduates of Ivy League schools, until Amy Coney Barrett from Notre Dame joined the Court in 2020. About a tenth of the present U.S. Congress went to Ivy League schools, and nine presidents of the United States were graduates of Harvard.[8] This past history led the three authors of a new study on affirmative action for the rich to suggest turning their

---

[8] They include the two Adamses, the two Roosevelts, Rutherford Hayes, John Kennedy, Barack Obama, and the two Bushes graduated from Harvard's Business School.

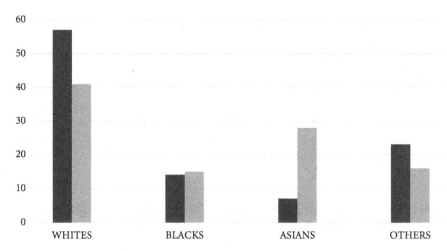

Figure 5.3 Harvard 2026 admissions compared to 2022 American population racial proportions
Source: Pazzanese, 2022.

findings upside down (Chetty, Deming, and Friedman, 2023). That is, change the selection procedures for admission to elite universities, and you would necessarily be significantly changing America's political elite as well.

Let's face the obvious fact: the whole Blum effort was to open up more places for White applicants at prestigious universities. The use of Asian American applicants, and not Whites, was an attempt to make it look otherwise. To their credit, many young Asian Americans repudiated being used in this fashion. And guess which group were the victims: Black Americans, of course. Let's look at the population data for 2022 compared with Harvard's 2022 admissions for the class of 2026 (Figure 5.3).

Asian Americans were over-accepted four times their population percentage. White Americans were under-chosen. Once we remove the "legacy" acceptances and other White "special cases," the loss of non-wealthy Whites is substantial. The other category consists of Latinos and foreign students. The 2026 acceptances appear to constitute a highly diverse student body, but the Court decision will make it far less so. Apart from adding still more Asian American students, the Court's ruling greatly benefits applicants from wealthy families. Blum and his billionaire backers have been allowed to narrow Black entry into the pipeline of privilege that has been so crucial to Black American advancement.

The Second Body Blow to Black Advancement

The previous chapter revealed why Black Americans as a group have not been able to establish a solid capital base. Given their desire for further education, this led to extensive Black student use of government educational loans.[9] It allowed far more Blacks to enter the pipeline of privilege. But by the same 6–3 count the Supreme Court ruled that President Biden's effort to forgive part of these loans was illegal. This effort could have wiped out more than $400 billion in student debt, with Black Americans disproportionately aided. Thus, the Court first ruled against extensive Black entry into elite institutions and then dealt a major setback to Black economic strength. The decisions taken together dealt a sharp blow to the slow, steady progress Black America had been making in many areas—apparently a primary goal of the Federalist Society that packed the High Court.

State Laws That Ban Books and Prohibit Teaching about Race in Public Schools

Following up on the gross misreading (or plain ignorance) of CRT, Republican-controlled states have enacted laws aimed at ending the teaching of racial material in the public schools. Governor Sarah Huckabee Sanders of Arkansas banned the teaching of CRT upon assuming office. In addition, she banned the use of the word "Latinx" for no discernable reason. Iowa passed a law that prohibits any instruction that even suggests America could be "fundamentally racist or sexist." The widespread banning of books on race from school libraries smacks of authoritarian rule and can only lead to more, not less, prejudice and discrimination. Teachers and librarians in Florida and other states can either avoid the subject, simply lie about the nation's racial past, or teach the truth and risk up to a year in jail.

Biased Texts

Part of this problem involves the widespread use of textbooks that advance thoroughly twisted versions of American history (Klein, 2021). Of course, there is a long history of racially flawed textbooks and avoidance of racial matters in American classrooms (Greenlee, 2019). Slavery and racism were *never* mentioned in my 11 years of Richmond schooling in the 1930s and 1940s. Instead, I learned a lot about the "war between the states" and its Virginian generals: John Ewell Brown ("Jeb") Stuart, Thomas ("Stonewall") Jackson, and Robert E. Lee.

Three companies—Abeka, Bob Jones University Press, and Accelerated Christian Education—produce most of these texts and claim to serve about 2,400 schools. One 2017 study found that a third or more of all private schools funded in part by federal vouchers used works from at least one of these three biased sources. Their products reject evolution, teach that the biblical Noah had baby dinosaurs on his ark, and discourage students from doing their own experiments. On race, they typically ignore

[9] Unfortunately, many Black aspirants lost the opportunity by unknowingly applying to fraudulent "colleges," such as the now-banned Corinthian College chain and Trump University.

or downplay the savagery of slavery and the racial discrimination that followed. One 11th-grade history text casually observes that "slaves seemed to be better investments than indentured servants" (Klein, 2021). Another insisted that "most Black and White Southerners had long lived in harmony"—it was "power-hungry individuals stirred up the people" (Ravitch, 2020).

Arguably, parents may have the right to miseducate their children. It becomes problematic, however, when public funds are used to spread racist beliefs. Billions of tax dollars fund these texts and the private schools that use them, both from such states as Florida and Louisiana as well as the federal government through vouchers.

A Final Assessment

Black Americans have long believed in the central importance of education. And recent decades have finally witnessed important gains at both the high school and college levels. While Black-White segregation in education remains widespread throughout the nation, those who have managed to attend interracial secondary schools have formed the rising Black middle class. Although still underrepresented in predominantly White colleges and universities, Black participation in both these schools and in historically Black colleges has increased. The rapid growth of Black studies programs furthered the growth of racial studies. Although there is still a long way to go to attain full educational opportunity, Black Americans have achieved a significant reduction in educational racism. It remains to the seen just how much lasting damage the two 2023 Supreme Court decisions have done to Black American progress.

Highly recommended for further reading on this subject:

Johnson, R. C. (2019). *Children of the dream: Why school integration works.* New York: Basic Books.

Sidebar 5.1 Derrick Bell and His Critical Race Theory

Decades ago, at an academic conference, I debated Derrick Bell, the originator of critical race theory. Current gross mischaracterizations of CRT by the nation's extreme right wing bring back my memories of the event.

The debate concerned the racial desegregation of public schools. As throughout my career as a social psychologist, I argued that such action was necessary for the nation finally to overcome its racist legacy. Bell argued sternly against desegregation. Give Black Americans equal resources (as if this were ever politically possible), he maintained, and let Blacks run their own schools and communities separately. I was dismayed to hear him, because Bell had been an effective and outspoken advocate of desegregation both as a federal official in the Lyndon Johnson administration and as a lawyer for Thurgood Marshall's NAACP Legal and Education Defense Fund.

82 Anti-Black Racism in America

Although we differed in our views, it was still a friendly debate. We were long-standing friends from our time together in Washington during the 1960s. At the close, we hugged each other, and he whispered to me, "You keep up the fight, Tom, but I have given up hope. It just hurts too much to continue to believe America will ever change on race."

What made this occasion especially painful for me was that I knew Bell as an extremely astute lawyer who as a veteran had served his country in Korea. With an open, friendly personality, he was respectful of conservative students in the many law classes he taught. In short, he was the very opposite of the White-hating Black intellectual depicted by critics who never knew or read him.

Bell's primary concern was to understand how American racism had persisted over the centuries despite repeated protests and incremental improvements. CRT, as it later became labeled by others, was his answer. Racist outcomes had been baked into the nation's primary institutions from the beginning and had proven highly influential and resistant to modification. How could it be otherwise when more than 1,800 slave owners have served in the U.S. Congress, and 12 of the first 18 presidents were slaveowners (Weil, Blanco, and Dominguez, 2022)?[10]

Those who reject this central point of CRT have never read the U.S. Constitution. Article 1, section 2, clause 3 reads, "Representatives and direct taxes shall be apportioned among the several states which may be included within this union, according to their respective numbers, which shall be determined by adding to the whole number of free persons, including those bound to service for a term of years, and excluding Indians not taxed, **three-fifths of all other persons**" (boldface added).

Ever wonder why this three-fifths figure was used? This racist provision carefully provided southern states with precisely enough members in the House of Representatives to stave off any future attempts to abolish the institution of slavery. Some would argue that "three-fifths of a person" describes how Black Americans have ever since been treated.

Similarly, the weird electoral college system set up for winning the presidency has its pro-slavery origins (Kelkar, 2016; Vox, 2017). This undemocratic system has recently yielded two disputed presidential elections—in favor of G. W. Bush in 2000 and Trump in 2016 and 2024.

Nor, apparently, have the CRT critics ever read the cold words of Chief Justice Roger Taney in his *Dred Scott* decision in 1857, which held that a slave owner could reclaim an escaped slave living in a free state. When America was founded, Blacks "were considered as a subordinate and inferior class of beings who had been subjugated by the dominant race, and, whether emancipated or not, yet remained subject to their authority, and had no rights or privileges but such as those who held the power and the Government might choose to grant them."

---

[10] The 12 presidents who owned slaves were George Washington, Thomas Jefferson, James Madison, James Monroe, Andrew Jackson, Martin Van Buren, William Henry Harrison, James Tyler, James K. Polk, Zachary Taylor, Andrew Johnson, and Ulysses S. Grant (White House Historical Association, 2022).

Race and Education   83

Bell and those who further advanced CRT stressed the continued effects in American law of this racist beginning and later rulings by the highest court in the land.[11] Now, as we note throughout this volume, social science provides widespread support for this view for many institutions in addition to the law. Institutional racism has proven resistant to change in part because the nation's racist structure contains various social systems that tightly interlock with and strongly support each other. Throughout this book, we note how racial discrimination in one realm of society sturdily influences racial effects in other realms.

Spurred on by Fox "News" and racist blogs, the Republican Party has maligned CRT as yet another means of stirring up the racial fears of a susceptible portion of White America. Apparently without having read a single page of Bell's many books, these biased media commentators claim that CRT theory holds that virtually all White people are racists, that White children are being taught to be ashamed of their race, and even that White people should be exterminated. None of these extravagant claims is remotely true, although they sometimes emanate from surprising sources. Allen Guelzo, a Civil War historian at Princeton University who has written books on Abraham Lincoln and Robert E. Lee, incredibly claims CRT rejects the principles of the Enlightenment and views Whites as oppressors like the Nazis viewed Jews (Thiessen, 2021).

This is calculated nonsense. CRT does not address individuals; it consists of *structural* contentions. Even if many White Americans do not personally favor racial discrimination, we all live within these structures that shape our behaviors and beliefs. Virginia's Republican governor Glenn Youngkin cynically ran on the promise that he would end the teaching of CRT in Virginia's schools "on day one"—an easy task since there were no schools in the state teaching it. What is really being said by these extreme right-wing commentators is that racial issues should not be taught in the public schools. They seem to recognize the nation's dark racial history, so dark that we must be forbidden to teach it.

For many years, southern Democrats were the consistently racist force in the U.S. Congress. But by the mid-1960s, once President Johnson signed the Voting Rights Act, Republicans began to pursue their "southern strategy" and oppose civil rights legislation.

This blatant attempt to obscure the truth about American racism and break from the earlier Republican Party's progressive tradition on race did not begin with Trump. Starting with Richard Nixon in the 1960s, Republicans have long employed "dog-whistle" racism. Nixon opposed school integration indirectly by attacking busing. Reagan vilified a fanciful Black "welfare queen." G. H. W. Bush's presidential campaign produced a fearsome advertisement featuring a Black criminal named Willie Horton. G. W. Bush dwelled on Obama's birth certificate and his Arabic middle name, Hussein. The most grievous example is Reagan's first presidential campaign speech in 1980 supporting "states' rights." He delivered it in Philadelphia, Mississippi, close to where three civil

---

[11] In December 2022, a symbolically important act took place: Taney's statue was finally removed from the Capitol and replaced by a stature of Thurgood Marshall.

84   Anti-Black Racism in America

rights advocates had earlier been lynched by the locals. Finally, Donald Trump has constantly expressed blatant racism, to the delight of many of his followers.

Florida's governor Ronald DeSantis, trying to outdo Trump in anti-Black leadership, blocked an Advanced Placement course for Black American studies in the state's schools. He even advanced the idea that slavery had benefited Blacks—something he did not learn in his Yale history courses. These are pure acts of White supremacy (Rubin, 2023).

Derrick Bell died in 2011 at the age of 80. Were he still alive, he would surely view the misuse of his theory as further reason for his despair of ever achieving a racism-free America. We can understand his despair without embracing it ourselves.

Sidebar 5.2   A Personal Reaction to the High Court's Actions

Having taught graduate and undergraduate students at both Harvard (1956–1980) and the University of North Carolina (1955–1956) for a quarter of a century, the High Court's anti-affirmative action decision involving both schools has special meaning for me. It led me to recall the great students I taught at the two schools, many of whom would not have been attending had Blum won his case earlier. As a rare Southerner on the Harvard faculty teaching race relations at that time, my classes attracted both Black and White southern students.

Blum's contentions would exclude some superb White as well as minority students— a point largely ignored in the debate. Two White students in particular come to mind. One was from the South and wrote a senior honors thesis under my direction. Like all-Black schools, his all-White schools had no special preparation classes for the Scholastic Achievement Test and the American College Test. Nor did his family have the resources to pay for special preparation courses for these tests. Yet Harvard's astute admissions office, which I admired once it abandoned earlier Jewish quotas in the 1950s, had, with the help of Harvard alumni, somehow correctly determined that he was qualified for admission. He went on to become a stalwart leader for school desegregation as the school superintendent of a major city in the Deep South known for its long history of racial violence. Such action took great courage as well as conviction.

The second White student I vividly remember came from rural Idaho. His SAT score, too, was not especially high. Nevertheless, he was an outstanding student at Harvard who went on to become a distinguished lawyer. Apart from the biasing of test scores from special test-taking classes, these tests poorly predict later academic performance save at the extremes. That is, very high scorers do perform well later, and very low scorers do perform poorly later. The fact that the tests do help at the extremes explains why some colleges have reinstated the tests after having abandoned them. Most test-takers, however, score within the large middle range and do not fall within these extremes.

Harvard admissions, unencumbered then by Blum's racist restrictions, also managed to find numerous outstanding Black students who worked with me. I tried to persuade them to become social psychologists, but Thurgood Marshall was their hero at that point, so most of them became civil rights lawyers. One exception, Jewelle Gibbs, went on to become a professor of social work at the University of California at Berkeley.

Recalling these outstanding students adds to my deep regret that the Supreme Court majority has closed down a major avenue for outstanding young Americans, Black and White, to enter the pipeline of privilege from which all nine of the jurists had benefited themselves.

Sidebar 5.3 My Advocacy for Integrated Education and the Objectivity Issue

For two decades (1959–1979), I vigorously advocated for interracial schools. I wrote numerous popular articles and gave dozens of public lectures in support of the effort. The talks were sponsored either by local universities or by the school systems themselves. I always cited the research provided in this book for how these schools benefited Black students. But I realized that White audiences cared most about how their students fared.

After all, who is likely to attend a public lecture by a Harvard professor on desegregated schooling? I suspected my audiences were filled with White parents who had hopes of sending their children to elite universities like Harvard. And the responses during the question periods following the lectures bore out my intuition. I needed to offer them positive outcomes of interracial schools for their children.

I was aided by the generous cooperation of Harvard's Admissions Office. The admission officers kindly allowed me to sit in on their work sessions. Here I learned they were systematically giving a positive point for applicants who had interracial experience. They did so in the hope that those with diversity experience would help strengthen interracial relations on Harvard's campus. It alone could not get you admitted, but it helped. Here was what I was looking for—an incentive for my largely White audiences.

I emphasized this point in all of my public lectures on integrated education, and the White audiences invariably took special notice. I furthered the point by citing the available research on the point. For example, Brewster Smith had found that Peace Corps volunteers with prior diverse experience did much better overseas; those without such experience disproportionately dropped out of the service.

These activities call into question my objectivity (Pettigrew, 2022b). Was it proper for me as a race researcher to be actively advocating desegregation? Did it bias my research? My answer is shaped by Gunnar Myrdal's (1944) insightful position on values in science. He held values to be inherent in social science. Be aware of your values, he urged, struggle against their biasing effects, and alert your readers to them (as I have in this book).

Thus, objectivity becomes a sought-after goal that can never be fully satisfied. Yet this does not exclude social commitment. But such commitment must be combined with an equally strong commitment to competent research. Science and values need not conflict. Donald Campbell (1959) argued that strong motivation can lead to greater

86   Anti-Black Racism in America

investment in tracing an accurate map of reality. Indeed, I have endeavored to employ the most rigorous methods possible in order to understand better what the most effective remedial actions are for combating racism.

A prime example of this view of values in operation is provided by Janet Schofield (1982) in her book *Black and White in School*. A firm supporter of racially desegregated education, Schofield studied a middle school in Pittsburgh for three years as it struggled to establish racial integration. She uncovered the many problems and difficulties involved in the process and recommended ways to improve on how school desegregation can be better achieved.

Her values led her to the subject; her training as a social psychologist led her to conduct a solid ethnographic study and to uncover the problems and needed remedies. Rather than blinding her to the many problems of implementing racial desegregation in schools, Schofield's values impelled her to comprehend the difficult process as fully as possible. Her book deservingly won scientific prizes and was cited by the U.S. Supreme Court.

Sidebar 5.4 Affirmative Action for Rich Whites

There has been an enormous growth in computer capacity over recent decades—doubling about every two years, in accord with Moore's law. This has made it possible for the quantitative social sciences to conduct massively large studies on important topics that were not possible previously.

One such study uncovered the existence of an entrenched affirmative action program for accepting wealthy White applicants to the "elite 12" of the nation's leading private universities—the eight Ivy League schools (Brown, Columbia, Cornell, Dartmouth, Harvard, Pennsylvania, Princeton, and Yale) together with four others (Chicago, Duke, Massachusetts Institute of Technology, and Stanford). Actually, the study did not find the rich being given significantly special privilege at MIT, so the bias is concentrated in the remaining 11 schools. These schools form the "pipeline of privilege" described earlier in this volume.

Chetty, Deming, and Friedman (2023) amassed data from federal records of college attendance and parental income taxes for nearly all college students from 1999 to 2015 for the 12 key schools and four leading public schools for comparison—the Los Angeles and Berkeley campuses of the University of California and the Universities of Michigan and Virginia. In addition, the study secured detailed anonymized internal admissions assessments from three of the private universities that covered a half-million applicants.

Many significant findings flow from this immense study. The favored applicants to the elite universities came disproportionately from parents who earned more than $611,000 annually (the nation's top 1% in 2015). They constituted 16% of the acceptances at the Ivy League schools. Had there been no affirmative action practices for them, they would have been only 10% of the acceptances. For applicants with the same SAT or ACT test scores, these rich applicants were 34% more likely to be chosen. Even wealthier applicants—those from the richest 0.1% of American families—were twice as likely to be chosen as others with the same test scores.

In turn, these students are far more likely to be chosen by elite graduate programs and to obtain high-paying, prestige jobs. Thus, these elite institutions have been actively perpetuating the intergenerational transfer of opportunity and wealth. They have become in effect arbiters of opportunity for the nation. And the increasing split in the population has become the college-educated versus the non-college-educated.

The four public universities (UCLA, UC-Berkeley, Michigan, and Virginia) did not show these trends. And some technical schools—MIT, California Tech, and Cooper Union—have not allowed legacy acceptances.[12]

Chetty and his co-authors estimate that about a third of the over-acceptance of rich Whites can be explained by the fact that they apply to these high-ranking universities in greater numbers than other Whites. The rest of the discrepancy is a result of affirmative action for the wealthy.

How did this affirmative action process operate? The primary way White bias operates is though legacy programs—children of graduates as well as children of people who had made large financial contributions to the school. Stanford and the University of Southern California report that this process involved about one in every seven of their admissions.

Legacy admissions of the rich has financially benefited these schools over the years. However, now that the practice is publicly and widely denounced, its days seem numbered. Many schools have voluntarily ended legacy admissions: Amherst, Wesleyan, Occidental, Virginia Tech, Carnegie Mellon, Johns Hopkins, Maryland, and Pittsburgh. And the four public universities studied by Chetty and his colleagues have not been using legacy admissions.

Aside from legacy admissions, there are other ways this program has operated - for instance, over-accepting star athletes in largely all-White sports emphasized at expensive preparatory schools (e.g., crew, lacrosse, fencing). Moreover, these schools secure ties with the admissions offices of elite universities and learn how to write effective letters of recommendation. And the admissions offices often give the rich White applicants an extra boost in non-academic areas, such as extracurricular activities and personality ratings.

The study's data end in 2015. University officials have countered that since that date they have given greater priority to income diversity. Figure 5.3 suggests that Harvard had already made some changes prior to the High Court's ruling. More lower-income and first-generation applicants have been accepted since 2015 at many of the elite schools. More outright grants rather than loans are now being provided. Harvard and a few other institutions are offering free tuition for families earning under certain low amounts of income. It is too soon to gauge the total effect of these recent changes for minorities and low-income Whites.

---

[12] Rochester Institute of Technology is a notable exception, still accepting legacy applicants.

88 Anti-Black Racism in America

In short, the elite private universities have long carried on a huge affirmative action admissions program for wealthy White Americans that dwarfs the tiny programs established in recent years for Black Americans.

Blum and the High Court apparently saw no problem with this pro–rich White bias. Only affirmative action for non-Whites taking up a minuscule number of spaces from Whites was their focus of concern. Edward Blum, his Federalist Society backers, and six Supreme Court members eliminated the programs for Black students to make still more room for wealthy White students.

Chapter 6
Race, Crime, and Justice

America has one of the highest rates of incarceration in the world.[1] By 1995, Americans constituted only 5% of the world's population but roughly 25% of the world's prisoners (Forman, 2017). And Black Americans comprise a staggeringly large part of this mass incarceration. Figure 6.1 plots by race the thousands of Americans incarcerated over the 40-year period 1980–2020 (USA Facts, 2021b). Note how the numbers of Blacks and Whites in prison are generally close to each other.

But remember that there are more than five White Americans for every Black American. So the number of Black people in prison is proportionately roughly five times higher than that of White people. Political conservatives argue this disparity reflects the fact that Black Americans are committing more crimes. But this claim ignores the racist discrimination deeply embedded in the American legal system.

Figure 6.1 reveals two periods of change in imprisonment. Note the sudden rise in the incarceration of Blacks in the 1990–2000 decade. This is the result of the so-called "war on drugs" (see Sidebars 6.1 and 6.2). Then note the sudden decline in

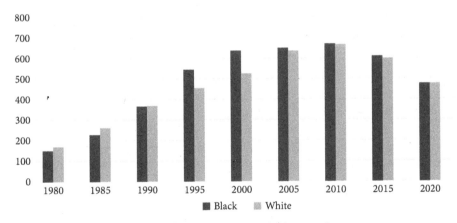

Figure 6.1 U.S. Incarcerations by race 1980-2020 in thousands
Source: USA FACTS, 2020b

---

[1] Some claim that the incarceration rate in the United States is the highest in the world. But this claim assumes that some nations, such as China, are accurately reporting their rates. If you add the imprisoned Uyghur, China's rate would be the highest.

Anti-Black Racism in America. Thomas F. Pettigrew, Oxford University Press. © Oxford University Press (2025).
DOI: 10.1093/9780197803134.003.0007

incarcerations in the 2010–2020 decade. This was largely caused by the COVID-19 pandemic and the resultant need to reduce prison populations.

Criminal Justice Trends

Crime has long had a central place in racist thought. As Harvard's Khalil Muhammad (2019) details at length, the misuse of racial crime statistics has been a standard means of frightening White Americans and convincing them that Black Americans are dangerous and violence-prone. This planted belief is then used to support racial segregation throughout society.

In the 1930s, sociologists, particularly those in the Chicago School, together with Thorsten Sellin (1935), warned that these crime statistics were not to be trusted, that they reflected racist practices at every level of the criminal justice system. But their warnings were generally ignored even after Gunnar Myrdal's (1944) influential *An American Dilemma* further echoed them. As Muhammad (2019, p. xvii) bluntly puts it, "From the beginning, the collection and dissemination of racial crime data was a eugenics project, reflecting the supremacist beliefs of those who created them."

Six decades ago, I wrote in *A Profile of the Negro American*: "Negro rates of apparent crime are high; though just how high in comparison with White apparent crime is difficult to determine by possible racial discrimination at every stage—arrest, conviction, sentencing, and parole" (Pettigrew, 1964b, p. 140). Much the same can be said today. Rampant racial discrimination in criminal justice has in some ways actually become worse since the 1960s.

Arrests

The Bureau of Justice Statistics (Snyder, Cooper, and Mulako-Wangota, 2017b) reports that Black arrest rates for fraud are three or more times higher than those of Whites. These rates have declined sharply since 1980 for both groups, but the ratio differential has remained roughly the same. And arrest rates for aggravated assault have remained three to five times higher for Blacks since 1980 (Snyder, Cooper, and Mulako-Wangota, 2017a).

Blacks are almost four times more likely than White Americans to be arrested for marijuana, even though usage of the drug is similar across the two groups (*American Civil Liberties Union News*, 2016). In Washington, D.C., in 2010, Black arrest rates for marijuana possession was actually eight times that of Whites (Forman, 2017). This explains why President Biden, providing pardons in 2022 for all those federally convicted of simple marijuana possession, was hailed as particularly helping Black offenders.

Medical and criminal problems intersect. Black drug addicts begin to steal to afford their drugs. One such case involved Malcolm X, the Black Muslim leader of the 1960s (see Sidebar 6.1).

In some areas, racial and class discrepancies have been directly built into the law. Once the Black Panthers began to display their guns in the 1960s, Congress finally became interested in some weak gun control legislation. It tried to limit the sale of inexpensive, low-quality handguns known as "Saturday night specials." These were the typical weapons of poor Black (and White) people, but more lethal and expensive weapons were allowed to continue to be sold. As one journalist put it, the law was enacted "not to control guns but to control Blacks" (Sherrill, 1975).

In total, arrest rates for adults for all crimes are two to three times higher for Blacks (Snyder, Cooper, and Mulako-Wangota, 2017c). Back in 1960–1961, the was two and a half times more than for other Americans (Federal Bureau of Investigation, 1960–1961).

Imprisonment

Blacks are presently convicted at about five times the rate of Whites, as shown in Figure 6.1. This marks a definite increase over the past 70 years. Between 1950 and 1960, for both state and federal prisons, the differential was about three times (Pettigrew, 1964b). Many factors contributed to this disparity in both eras, but poverty is especially involved. Accused Black Americans (and Latino Americans) are less able to hire a defense attorney and can make less use of cash fines, appeals, and other legal protections.

As in the 1960s, these elevated Black rates are partly a function of discrimination at every step in the legal process (Alexander 2012; Forman, 2017). (See Sidebars 6.1 and 6.2.) Indeed, the sweeping "war on drugs" in the 1980s and 1990s enhanced these rates of racial discrimination throughout the nation's criminal justice system. By 2010, Black imprisonment rates in both federal and state prisons were seven times higher than White rates.

Part of this rapid expansion was fueled by the Violent Crime Control and Law Enforcement Act of 1994 (Schoenfeld, 2018). This act gave states an incentive to reduce parole availability by providing millions of federal dollars to expand their prison capacity. Once new prisons are built, more people get well-paying jobs they wish to keep and communities become dependent on the new income - all of which enhances political support for mass incarceration. Californian prison officers made about $48 an hour in 2022; that averages out to $95,000 a year—almost twice as much as they could have earned in other employment.

92 Anti-Black Racism in America

By 2020, Black imprisonment rates had declined by 37%, but were still more than four times those of Whites. A major reason for this reduction was changes made necessary by the COVID-19 pandemic (Carson, 2021). In 2015, prior to the pandemic, 2.3 million people, about half of them Black convicts, were housed in the nation's extensive but uncoordinated prison network (Sawyer and Wagner, 2023).[2]

Sentencing

The most glaring racial disparity in sentencing involves the diverse types of cocaine (Justice Reform Resources, 2021). The Anti–Drug Abuse Act of 1986 established a 100-to-1 sentencing discrepancy between crack cocaine (favored by Blacks) and powdered cocaine (favored by Whites). Thus, a mere 5 grams of crack cocaine triggered an automatic five-year jail sentence, but it took 500 grams of powdered cocaine to warrant the same sentence. About 77% of the people sentenced for crack cocaine were Black, while only about 7% were White.

It took 23 years before Congress partially addressed the problem by reducing the disparity from 100 to 1 down to 18 to 1. In 2018, the First Step Act made the ratio reduction retroactive. This released more than 2,000 prisoners and reduced the sentences of more than 3,700 people most of them Black Americans. At this writing, the EQUAL Act has been passed by the House of Representatives but is stalled in the Senate. It would eliminate all differences between the two forms of cocaine. But over these 37 years since the 1985 act, literally thousands of Americans—most of them Black—have had their lives completely disrupted by this discriminatory sentencing. Finally, late in 2022, Attorney General Merrick Garland told federal prosecutors to stop seeking sentencing disparities in cases involving crack and powered cocaine.

Sentencing data on executions also reveal discrimination. Banned in most Western nations, execution rates have declined in the United States, but sharp racial discrepancies remain. During the 1930s, among males over 17 years of age, Black convicts were 17 times more likely to be executed than White convicts (Von Hentig, 1940) - mostly in the South.

The U.S. Supreme Court in 1972 suspended the death penalty. But once the High Court reinstated the death penalty in 1976, racial discrepancies reappeared. As of 2014, 42% of those on death row were Black convicts even though they comprise only 14% of the nation's population (Ford, 2014). Louisiana's percentage of Blacks on death row is more than twice the proportion of the state's Black population. In Georgia, research on 2,000 homicidal trials in Georgia during the 1970s and

---

[2] In 2023, there were 1,566 state prisons, 98 federal prisons, 1,323 juvenile correctional centers, 3,116 local jails, and 80 Native American reservation jails in the United States. The total of more than 6,000 facilities omits military prisons, immigration detention centers, and prisons in the nation's territories (Sawyer and Wagner, 2023).

1980s uncovered vast racial disparities in capital punishment (Baldus, Pulaski, and Woodworth, 1983).

Not all such racial differences occur in the South. Baldus and his colleagues (1998) analyzed 667 homicides that occurred in Philadelphia between 1983 and 1993. They found that Black defendants were almost four times more likely than White defendants to receive a death sentence for the same crime.

American law's lengthy sentences are another way it differs sharply from the legal systems of other Western countries. Six states even add to life sentences the stipulation that no parole is possible. Such sentencing became common in the 1970s and has continued, fueled by so-called "wars" on crime and drugs. It reflects vindictiveness toward the criminal for the crime committed rather than effective policy. No room for redemption is granted.

Now federal and state prisons are piling up with elderly prisoners and their costly medical problems. Yet crime is largely a young person's activity. These thousands of old prisoners, a majority of whom are African Americans, are far beyond committing crimes. "Death by incarceration" is the term used by opponents of such sentencing, some of whom filed a complaint against the practice with the United Nations (Rios, 2022).

Parole and Probation

Racial discrimination is also evident in the granting of parole and probation. While Blacks are convicted of crimes roughly five times more often than Whites, in 2018 they were about four times more likely to be on parole and only 2.6 times more likely to be on probation (Moyd, 2021). These discrepancies are important, because there are about two people who are on probation or parole for every one who is in prison.

A key problem is that parole board members, often comprised of White citizens who are unfamiliar with the penal system, are typically afraid of possible recidivism (Moyd, 2021). Should a convict they freed later commit a crime, they could be blamed. In Alabama, 90% of parole applicants, most of whom are Black, are denied (Chandler, 2023). Racist attitudes, implicit and explicit, lead many White board members to suspect wrongly that Black prisoners are far more likely than Whites to return to crime.

However, this suspicion of parole boards cannot explain some extreme decisions. In 2023, the Alabama Bureau of Pardons and Paroles denied medical parole to Leola Harris, a 71-year-old Black woman who had been a model prisoner for more than 20 years and was dying of renal disease. She also suffered from diabetes and hypertension. Confined to a wheelchair, she was not even allowed to attend her six-minute hearing (Cobb, 2023).

Race shapes such outcomes. Black Americans accused of killing a White American receive the most death penalty convictions. Whites accused of killing another White and Blacks accused of killing another Black tend to receive somewhat lower percentages of the death penalty. Finally, Whites accused of killing a Black - as in the highly publicized police murders of recent years—are the least likely to receive the death penalty. Consequently, since 1976 only 21 White defendants who murdered a Black victim have been executed, compared with 299 Black defendants who killed a White (Death Penalty Information Center, 2022).

In Texas from 1982 to 2020 the scant six cases of Whites executed for killing a Black involved truly horrendous crimes: combined rape and murder of Black women, public dismemberment of a victim's body, and the killing of two minority policemen (R. A. Smith, 2022). That these "White men suffered the ultimate penalty for committing crimes against people of color had more to do with the threat they posed to the stability and 'legitimacy' of the judicial system as an important hierarchy enhancing institution" (R. A. Smith, 2022, p. 250).

Further evidence that racism is involved when the defendant is Black and the victim is White is furnished by the Stanford University research cited in Chapter 1 (Eberhardt et al., 2006). Recall that the likelihood the accused Black in this situation will be sentenced to death is significantly greater if the defendant is perceived to be more stereotypically Black. Meeting White conceptions of what looks like a "Black" defendant can actually shape a life-or-death verdict.

It has long been assumed that joblessness is a primary cause of crime—especially Black property crime. But extensive research reveals that this relationship is actually more complex. Kleck and Jackson (2016) compared nationally representative samples of serious property crime offenders and non-offenders. They found that many categories of unemployed people do *not* commit more property crime—such as the underemployed and those not working for such socially accepted reasons as physical impairment and sickness. Only one unemployed group showed the expected pattern of greater serious property crime: those not in the labor force for socially unacceptable reasons.

Recidivism

Parole board members have reason to be concerned about granting parole to young offenders. Two-thirds of federal crime offenders released in 2005 before they were 21 were rearrested, compared with only one-eighth of prisoners released after they were 64 years old (U.S. Sentencing Commission, 2017).

But parole board fears spill over to older prisoners who are well past their criminal youth. Age is highly and negatively correlated with crime. It increases throughout adolescence, peaks at age 17, and then begins to decrease gradually (Cornelius, Lynch, and Gore, 2017).

The basic recidivism problem with parole programs throughout the nation involves the restricted, often hopeless situation that many parolees find themselves in upon release. Ironically, the odds of constructing a new, crime-free life are reduced by many of the very governmental measures enacted to limit recidivism.

Even when released, ex-convicts face legal discrimination in multiple areas. Many employers specify that those with a criminal record need not apply. Yet research on the topic repeatedly shows that ex-convicts are no more likely to quit or be fired than other hires (Marks, 2022). Some areas, such as Iowa and Philadelphia, offer cash incentives to employers for hiring the formerly incarcerated. The U.S. Department of Labor helps spur such hiring on its CareerOneStop platform. And the federal government offers a substantial tax credit for such hiring: the Work Opportunity Tax Credit (WOTC). If the new hire works 400 hours or more, the full WOTC can be claimed. For ex-offenders, the maximum WOTC per eligible employee is currently $2,400, and there is no limit to the number of qualifying ex-offenders an employer can hire. These programs are premised on research that indicates they can pay for themselves or even save public funds by reducing costly recidivism rates.

As Chapter 8 will note, many states deny voting rights to the previously incarcerated. This is especially the case in states dominated by Republicans, who correctly perceive that Black convicts are highly likely to vote for Democrats. In Florida, the electorate in 2018 voted to restore voting rights to Floridians with felony convictions. The legislature soon thwarted the popular vote by requiring ex-convicts to pay all fees and fines owed before they could vote. Then police began to arrest those who had voted but had not paid all fees, citing them for committing a felony, with a potential $5,000 fine and five years in prison. To enable one-party rule, the public's referendum was simply overpowered.

Jury duty is ruled out for former felons in 31 states and the federal government. This excludes about 6% of the nation's adult population and 30% of Black adult males (Kalt, 2003). Public benefits of many types are denied, while multiple fees and fines are assessed.

Housing is an especially acute problem for ex-convicts. Public housing is generally denied released felons. Housing advertisements often state explicitly that those with criminal records need not apply. Consequently, they often make up a major portion of the homeless. One study estimated that three-fourths of the people living in Oakland, California's homeless encampments had been incarcerated (Levin, 2022a). Alameda County, California, home to both Berkeley and Oakland, found that of its 9,700 unhoused people in 2022, 30% had experienced interactions with the criminal legal system within the past year. So the county, out of special concern for the homeless, banned criminal background checks for housing—employing what are called "Fair Chance Ordinances" (Levin, 2022a).

Similar actions are starting to emerge throughout the nation. Seattle and Portland have passed Fair Chance laws, and California's legislature is considering one. So is New York City, which formerly banned those with a criminal record from public housing. Research found that those with criminal records are overrepresented among the homeless. But when supplied with supportive housing, recidivism drops (Metraux and Culhane, 2004, 2006).

96 Anti-Black Racism in America

Parolees must regularly see supervision officers, but these required visits often interrupt job schedules and act more as a monitoring device rather than providing needed support services. Supervision officers are typically undertrained and overworked. Moyd (2021) concludes, "It is hard to fathom that 15-minute interactions three days a week could have any significant impact on transforming lifestyles."

Considering all these barriers to a new life without crime, it is not surprising that American recidivism rates are high. Yet, if carefully managed, massive release of convicts through parole and probation is not the risky endeavor that many fear (Gill, 2022). During the height of the COVID-19 pandemic, the U.S. Justice Department under the Cares Act released more than 11,000 convicts from federal prisons.[3] Older, sick prisoners in low- and medium-security prisons were especially selected. Those with sex offenses were barred, but otherwise no one was automatically excluded because of their crime, sentence length, or time served.

In the past, recidivism over the first three years after release has been reported for one-third to two-thirds of prisoners. But *only 17* of the mass release of more than 11,000 were later found guilty of new crimes, according to the Federal Sentencing Commission (2017). Only one of these 17 lapses was violent (an aggravated assault), and none involved sex offenses. A recidivism rate well below 1% provides strong evidence against life and mandatory sentencing as well as keeping elderly convicts in jail.

Police Involvement

The police use of deadly force has long been a disturbing component of American crime control. The eruption of White police shooting Blacks has finally received focused attention by the mass media and triggered the Black Lives Matter movement. But it is unclear that these police murders actually represent an upsurge from the past. In past years, fatal force by the police in the Black community was also common, but it was routinely ignored by the White world.

In the 1940s and 1950s, I recall the Richmond, Virginia, newspapers more often than not put such notices of police killings in or near the back section's obituary notices. It was simply considered a routine event, with the police version accepted uncritically. In fact, I cannot recall a police shooting of a Black ever being a frontpage headline story in the city's two newspapers of that time. What is new is not police violence but the mass media's belated and intense attention to it.

The Washington Post took up this issue in 2015 after the shooting in Ferguson, Missouri, of unarmed Michael Brown (Alexander, Rich, and Thacker, 2022). It found that the relevant FBI data undercounted fatal police shootings by more than half. Reporting by police departments is voluntary, and many of the worst perpetrators do

---

[3] Other authorities also released prisoners for the same reason. Denver County, Colorado, and Cuyahoga County, Ohio, reduced their jail populations by 50% and New York City by 42%.

not report their data. The *Post* found during the 2015–2022 period that *more than $1.5 billion* were spent to settle thousands of claims of police misconduct throughout the nation. As just one example, Rochester, New York, paid $12 million to the family of Daniel Prude, who stopped beathing after police put a hood on him and held him down until he died.

Moreover, particular officers are repeatedly involved but allowed to continue on the force. The *Post* found that 25 officers were involved in 20 or more such payments, 239 in 10 or more payments, and 3,522 in 3 or more payments! Routinely, police unions stoutly defend police perpetrators of these recurrent racial crimes regardless of the situation.

One might think that this heightened attention to the problem would alter police procedures and lower the rate of police killings. But this is not the case. Law enforcement set a record high in 2022 of at least 1,176 killings - in which the majority of victims were Black (Levin, 2023a).

Understandably, insurance companies are threatening to cancel coverage if police departments do not impose restrictions on such tactics as car chasing for minor infractions (Kindy, 2022). This pressure may help bring needed change to routine and discriminatory police tactics.

Black-on-Black murders rose to new heights in the 1980s and early 1990s, together with use of crack cocaine. Jesse Jackson claimed that more Blacks had been killed by Blacks in one year than the total of Black victims of lynching (Castaneda and Montgomery, 1994).[4] Particular emphasis was placed on ridding the community of guns, but this "war on guns" led to a host of problematic police procedures that greatly increased the number of Black arrests for minor violations.

The "pretext-stop" strategy became a favorite technique. Using any minor infraction as an excuse, police stop and search cars for guns, drugs, or anything else for which the driver could be detained. We noted in Chapter 1 that this tactic was most rampant in counties where anti-Black prejudice was especially prevalent (Ekstrom, Le Forestier, and Lai, 2022; Stelter et al., 2022). These same high-prejudice counties also more often favored "militarization" of the police, including providing them with semi-automatic weapons and armored vehicles (Jimenez, Heim, and Arndt, 2022).[5]

A massive study of 20 million traffic stops reveals just how biased and widespread this stop-and-search procedure has become throughout the nation (Baumgartner, Epp, and Shoub, 2018). It looked at 14 years of data from North Carolina (2002–2016). Blacks drove 16% less than Whites but were 63% more likely to be stopped. And when the researchers took into account the amount of time the drivers were on the road, Blacks were almost two times more likely to be stopped. Yet contraband was more likely to be found in searches of White drivers. These data are not

---

[4] Jackson's sweeping statement would have been correct had he said "recorded" lynchings. The number of unrecorded lynchings is likely to be substantial. Police failure to report lynchings as lynchings even extends today to central Iowa (J. M. Smith, 2022).

[5] Such military equipment had been made widely available under the Federal Government's "1033 program." It provided more than seven billion dollars of such armament (Jimenez, Heim, and Arndt, 2022).

unique to North Carolina. Later work revealed similar racial trends in both stops and searches in 16 other states—including the northern states of Connecticut, Illinois, Maryland, Ohio, and Vermont (Baumgartner et al., 2017).

The most detailed data on police stops have been compiled by the *American Civil Liberties Union News* (2023) for California in 2021. While Blacks constitute just 6% of the state's population, 15% of the stops were of Black drivers. In addition, Blacks were more likely than Whites to be searched, ordered from their vehicle, handcuffed, detained, and subjected to force.

Although fraught with potential for police overreach, the U.S. Supreme Court found the traffic stop procedure to be constitutional.[6] Forman (2017) stresses that this technique is largely reserved for the poorest of Black neighborhoods. And he describes a poignant case of a middle-aged Black woman who lost her hard-won job with FedEx through the misapplication of this police tactic. The jails were filling up. By 1990 one of every four young Black men were encased in the nation's criminal system once you combine probation, parole, and prison (Forman, 2017).

Black Americans have long sought the hiring of Black police. Forman (2017, pp. 78–115) provides a concise history of these efforts. Given the grim history of clashes with White police, there was the expectation that Black officers would identify with the Black community and treat fellow Blacks more humanely than White officers did. But the effort to give Black police equivalent powers to White police was an uphill struggle.

Many cities, particularly in the South, strongly resisted the hiring of Black police. When they did, strict boundaries were established to limit the authority of the Black officers when dealing with Whites. In 1959, 83% of police forces in the South restricted Black police to segregated Black districts and did not allow them to arrest Whites (Rudwick, 1962). Moreover, a national report found that White officers were rarely punished for abuse of Blacks (Fogelson, 1977). In 2023, Memphis charged five police officers with the murder of a 29-year-old Black man, Tyre Nichols. All five of the officers were Black. While White racism is a major factor in the problem, the Nichols murder demonstrates the significance of police norms.

I remember the first time I saw a Black policeman in the South. It was 1960, and he was directing traffic at a busy intersection in Charleston. When I mentioned this to White interviewees, they insisted I was mistaken. Racial change was often neither accepted nor even perceived at the time.

In the 1960s and 1970s, the primary attempt to improve the racial practices of police centered on their hiring and promoting Blacks. Virtually all major Black organizations made it a primary demand (Forman, 2017). Through the U.S. Department of Justice, I joined with other social scientists in these efforts to increase Black hiring. Looking at just the numbers, these efforts were a success. By 2022, 26 of the nation's 50 largest cities had Black chiefs, and one in every nine police in America was Black.

---

[6] *Whren v. United States*, 517 U.S. 806 (1996), 813.

Race, Crime, and Justice   99

I vividly recall speaking to an audience of police chiefs at the Harvard Business School in the summer of 1971 at a lecture organized by the U.S. Justice Department. I was impressed by the range of racial views in the all-White group, from enlightened chiefs to unabashed racists. Arguments broke out among them over how Blacks should be treated.

My talk centered on hiring Blacks and was informed by the suggestions of one of my students, Thomas Crawford. He had been a White cop on the beat in San Diego before becoming a doctoral student in social psychology at Harvard.[7] Based on his experience, Crawford believed that only a small minority of San Diego police officers committed the lion's share of the racial abuses. He was not invoking the popular "It's just a few bad apples" excuse. The basic problem was how the whole force tolerated these bad apples. The force knew precisely who these officers were but did little or nothing to stop their biased actions. The "thin blue line" ideology of "us versus them" held sway, backed by police unions.

The hope that increasing Black participation in police departments would solve the problem was largely mistaken—as the horrific Memphis killing of a young Black driver by five Black officers painfully reveals. While it surely helped, the major change in police behavior that we had hoped for did not emerge. Forman (2017) stresses a social class explanation for this. The new Black police were middle class, and they looked down on the Black street criminals they dealt with daily. Some reported being "embarrassed" in front of their White colleagues.

But there is a related, more powerful dynamic operating. The new Black recruits had to conform to the established departmental norms to win acceptance and improve their promotional possibilities. Even the Black chiefs often found they lacked the power to achieve what they had hoped to accomplish. There are exceptions, such as the notable reforms instituted in Charleston, South Carolina, by Chief Reuben Greenberg, a Black man. His improvements demonstrate effective change can be accomplished.

Think about the details of the infamous choking death of George Floyd in Minneapolis in 2020. The senior White officer, Derek Chauvin, knelt on Floyd's neck for nine minutes. He had long been known in the force for excessive behavior and had received 18 complaints for his violent actions on his official record. Three years earlier, Chauvin pled guilty to using "unreasonable force" on a 14-year-old boy by placing his knee on the boy's neck.

Three junior officers aided Chauvin by holding back the crowd that gathered around him and Floyd. Two of the officers were Asian Americans—making them vulnerable to internal police censure if they had intervened, stopped their senior officer, and saved Floyd's life. The chief of police in Minneapolis at the time was Medaria

---

[7] Crawford won the Society for the Psychological Study of Social Issues' Allport Intergroup Research Award and became a distinguished professor of social psychology at the University of California, Irvine. I was grateful for his informed help. Teachers especially learn from students who have had quite different life experiences.

100 Anti-Black Racism in America

Arradondo, the city's first Black chief. He had made useful changes but soon found himself overwhelmed by events and retired.

Just as Crawford observed about the potent role of police unions a half-century earlier, the police union of Minneapolis was deeply implicated in the Floyd murder (Nesterak, 2020). The Minneapolis Police Officers Federation had consistently supported Chauvin throughout his two decades on the force and his repeated citations for violent behavior. Bob Kroll, an ardent Trump supporter, was president of the Federation. He denied that racial issues were involved. In a letter sent to his union's members, Kroll initially said he was working with Chauvin's attorney and fighting to keep Chauvin's job. But as the protest became worldwide, he softened his stance and complained that the whole force should not be tarnished by the proverbial "bad apple."

Past data on the behavior of the Minneapolis police cast doubt on Kroll's argument (Nesterak, 2020). While only 20% of the city is Black, 60% of the documented use of excessive force by the police occurred against Blacks, and 63% of police killings were of Black victims. Furthermore, Blacks and Native Americans were eight times more likely than Whites to be arrested for such low-level offenses as trespassing and disorderly conduct. The police union apparently saw no problem with these recurrent practices.

A later U.S. Justice Department (2023) report based on three years of study of the Minneapolis police found it guilty of multiple practices: (1) use of "unjustified deadly force and unreasonable use of tasers"; (2) "unlawful discrimination" against Blacks, Native Americans, and the disabled; (3) "violations of the rights of people to engage in protected speech"; and (4) suppression and punishment of protesters and journalists.

In her valuable book, *America on Fire*, Elizabeth Hinton (2021) emphasizes the growing significance of police violence. She looks at smaller city protests in particular: in Cairo, Illinois; Stockton, California; and York, Pennsylvania, among others. Her chief finding is that *police violence almost invariably leads to community violence generally*. Hinton stresses that White authorities typically react in ways that exacerbate the problem of community violence—expanding policing and prisons—rather than treating the root causes of racist discrimination.

A Final Assessment

Focusing solely on criminal justice, it is not possible to claim that American racism is declining. While there have been improvements in some areas, the overall picture remains bleak. In fact, we have noted definite steps backward in some areas. Given such useful books as those by Alexander, Forman, Hinton, and Muhammad, there is now more attention to the racial injustice that persists. But effective, widescale remedial action has yet to emerge.

Highly recommended additional reading on this subject:

Alexander, M. (2012). *The new Jim Crow: Mass incarceration in the age of colorblindness.* Revised edition. New York: New Press.

Race, Crime, and Justice **101**

Forman, J., Jr. (2017). *Locking up our own: Crime and punishment in Black America.* New York: Farrar, Straus & Giroux.

Hinton, E. (2021). *America on fire: The untold story of police violence and Black rebellion since the 1960s.* New York: Liveright.

Muhammad, K. G. (2019). *The condemnation of blackness: Race, crime and the making of modern urban America.* Cambridge, MA: Harvard University Press.

Sidebar 6.1 Meeting Malcolm X at Harvard

Malcolm X gave three speeches at Harvard in the early 1960s.[8] Showing off their entrepreneurial skills, the Harvard Law School students sold tickets each time to packed audiences. In addition to an honorarium, Malcolm made a further request: prior to his speeches, he wanted to hold a seminar with Harvard faculty. I leaped at the chance to meet him, but only three others joined me. One was Archie Epps, the associate dean of students at Harvard who later edited a book of Malcolm's speeches at Harvard (Epps, 1991).

At the session in a seminar room in Williams James Hall, Malcolm held forth, delighted by the occasion. He was accompanied by Louis Farrakhan, who later became the head of the Nation of Islam. Malcolm was nervously aware of Farrakhan's presence and often looked over his shoulder to see his reactions to the conversation. But Farrakhan remained silent in a corner throughout the afternoon and did not shake our hands as Malcom did.

When it came my turn, I asked Malcolm why he often referred to a "Mrs. Greenberg" as his White prototype in his speeches. Why drag anti-Semitism into the discussion? Why not just say "Mrs. Pettigrew"?

Malcolm responded in seconds: "If I did that, listeners could not be sure I meant a White woman." He had a point. There are many Black Americans named Pettigrew but few named Greenberg. As throughout the discussion, Malcolm showed himself to be very quick and sharp - in many ways, extremely "street smart." He was the best example I have ever met of a very bright person who had not had the benefit of an extensive education.

This directly reflected his hard life. His father, a Garveyite minister, died under suspicious circumstances when Malcolm was six years old. His mother was institutionalized soon after, and he then lived in a series of foster homes. He did well in school and was elected class president in the eighth grade. But, according to Malcolm, he quit school when a Michigan school teacher told him that his ambition to be a lawyer was not fitting for "a nig—."

After moving to the East, Malcolm became addicted to drugs. He was arrested for theft, trying to get the money to pay for the drugs. But once in jail, he made good use of

---

[8] The third of the speeches is available on the web. All three are provided in Epps's volume, *The Speeches of Malcolm X at Harvard* (1991).

102   Anti-Black Racism in America

his time. With help from Black Muslims, he overcame his addictions and began to read voraciously everything he could find in the prison library.

Once released from prison, he rose quickly in the ranks of the Black Muslims. He became known nationally as a spokesman for the Nation of Islam and an advocate for "Black power." The White media viewed him as the fearful opposite of Martin Luther King Jr. But read his speeches, and you will see that such fears reveal as much about the White media as it did about Malcolm.

He broke from the Black Muslim movement in 1964 after going on a hajj to Mecca. This major experience had a profound effect on him. There he witnessed people of all colors interacting as equals. Malcolm wrote, "The true Islam has shown me that blanket indictment of all White people is as wrong as when Whites make blanket indictments against Blacks." He predicted that his change in thinking could lead to his being murdered by the Black Muslim organization. Indeed, soon after his extraordinary change, he was murdered in New York City.

In a celebrated television interview, Ken Clark also had a chance to size up Malcolm X. Neither Clark nor I were surprised by his remarkable conversion after the hajj. We both sensed that the thinking of this self-educated man ran deeper than was initially evident. Using current personality theory, Malcolm X offers a prime example of someone who was "open to new experience."

Sidebar 6.2 The "New Jim Crow" Thesis

Michele Alexander (2012) maintains that the mass imprisonment of Black Americans constitutes "the new Jim Crow." Her thesis is that there have been in American history three different systems to maintain White control. Initially, slavery sustained White dominance. Following the Civil War and the end of legal slavery, the Jim Crow system of White domination by law, segregation, and violence replaced slavery and maintained White control. Now that Jim Crow practices are receding, Alexander argues that mass Black incarceration operates to perpetuate White supremacy.

Even when released, ex-convicts face legalized discrimination in employment, voting, housing, education, public benefits, and jury duty. So, beyond differential incarceration, the nation's racist justice system infiltrates Black life in multiple ways. As Alexander (2012, p. 2) pithily asserts, "We have not ended racial caste in America, we have merely redesigned it."

Alexander's *The New Jim Crow: Mass Incarceration in the Age of Colorblindness* was an immediate success. It won multiple awards and became a *New York Times* best-seller. Even the well-educated segment of White America had paid insufficient attention to how the nation's legal system was contributing to racial problems. So the book and its troubling data were a shock to many White readers.

Given her varied background, Alexander was an ideal person to write this volume. She graduated from Vanderbilt University and Stanford Law School. Following law school, she clerked for Associate Justice Harry Blackmun of the U.S. Supreme Court and for

Chief Judge Abner Mikva of the U.S. Court of Appeals for the District of Columbia Circuit.

Alexander has taught at Stanford Law School, the Moritz College of Law at Ohio State University, and the Union Theological Seminary. She was hired in 2018 by the *New York Times* as a contributing columnist. The best experience for writing her book came when Alexander directed the Racial Justice Project for the American Civil Rights Union of Northern California. In this role, she launched a major effort against racial profiling by police known as the Driving While Black or Brown Campaign.

Alexander focuses heavily on the "war on drugs," in which differential drug law enforcement by race was a contributing factor in the sudden spike in Black imprisonment (as shown in Figure 6.1).

The New Jim Crow is well-written and well-documented and spares no one and no program. She admits her lawyer husband does not completely agree with her thesis, and she points out problems with affirmative action programs from which she herself benefited. Although occasionally her rhetoric may overreach,[9] she often makes striking and telling comparisons, such as pointing out that there are more imprisoned African Americans today than were enslaved in 1850.

The book's combination of dramatic writing, candor, and supporting data makes a forceful case that many readers find both convincing and alarming.

Sidebar 6.3 The Involvement of the Black Community

James Forman Jr., a Yale Law professor and son of a civil rights leader of the 1960s, challenged Alexander's (2012) argument as too simple. A strong critic of mass incarceration himself (Forman, 2017), he nevertheless worried than the analogy with the Jim Crow system obscures the older system's deeper mechanisms and injustices (Forman, 2012). In her revised edition, Alexander (2012) addressed this issue directly and toned down her earlier comparisons with the Jim Crow racist system.

In his Pulitzer Prize–winning book, *Locking Up Our Own: Crime and Punishment in Black America*, Forman (2017) focuses instead on the involvement of the Black community itself. He stresses the enormous differences between educated Blacks and poor Blacks in their stances on crime. The Black middle class wants more police protection from the crime that often surrounds them. And they are far more likely to be directly involved in the fractured criminal system as judges and other officials rather than be among those charged with crimes. By 2020, the lifetime risk of incarceration for Black high school dropouts was *10 times higher* than for Black youths who had the opportunity to attend college (Western, 2006).

---

[9] One overreach example: "[T]he American penal system has emerged as a system of social control unparalleled in world history" (Alexander, 2012, p. 8). Zulus in South Africa, the Uyghur in China, and other groups throughout history could challenge this sweeping claim.

104   Anti-Black Racism in America

Forman's analysis complements Alexander's thesis rather than contradicts it. He, too, clerked at the Supreme Court, working for Associate Justice Sandra Day O'Connor. But his book derives heavily from his six frustrating years as a public defender in the municipal courts of Washington, D.C. - the only large city in the United States that is predominantly Black.

Whereas Alexander looks at White involvement nationally in the mass incarceration thrust, Forman reveals how many leading D.C. Black residents at first supported this thrust out of fear of widespread criminality and drug use. It began in the 1960s with a serious heroin epidemic and sudden rise in crime. Minimum mandatory sentencing became popular as the number of crimes and the fear of crime continued to rise in the 1970s and 1980s as other drug use became widespread—especially crack cocaine. Little thought was initially given to the fact that the Black community was literally "locking up its own."

Forman carefully traces the change in Black opinion by the 1990s. He witnessed up close the destructive operations of a broken, disaggregated legal system. And he raises some intriguing questions. For example, why did the nation conceive of the spikes in heroin and crack cocaine only in criminal terms as opposed to also being a deadly serious public health crisis? We can add another question: Why have the promising studies of universal basic income not been considered as a means of benefiting the poor and reducing crime (Greenwell, 2022)? Some research findings suggest that, properly designed, universal basic income programs have the potential to help the less fortunate while actually saving public funds in both the criminal and medical domains. This book's final chapter will return to this point.

Chapter 7
Race and Health

There are two basic racial issues in the domain of health. First, what are the discrepancies in health between Black and White Americans? Here there is general agreement as to the disheartening facts. Second, the critical issue of *why* there exists these often large racial discrepancies is in dispute. Consider these two issues in turn.

Racial Health Trends

Black death rates in the 19th century were so much higher than those of Whites that a statistician at the Prudential Life Insurance Company in 1896 predicted that, if the death trends continued, a "gradual extinction" of American Blacks was "only a matter of time" (Wezerek, 2020). Fortunately, Frederick Hoffman overstated his case, although he was right in indicating that serious racial disparities in health existed and would continue into the future. However, he offered racist explanations for the differences and provided his employer a reason to deny Black Americans life insurance (Kendi, 2016, p. 281).

White Americans today enjoy notably better health than Black Americans. The data on life expectancy at birth, provided in Figure 7.1, show the broad trends (National Center for Health Statistics, 2021). Note how the racial differential closed markedly in the 1980s (from 12.6 years in 1980 to 7.0 in 1990). The gap continued to close, although more slowly, from 1990 to 2015 (from 7.0 years to 2.0 in 2015). When COVID-19 and drug overdoses hit, the racial difference in lifespan suddenly expanded to 5.8 years. Preliminary data for 2021 indicate this increase continued after 2020. Black Americans suffered proportionately from COVID-19 significantly more than White Americans.

In comparison with that of White Americans, Black American death rates are especially high for homicide, hypertension, septicemia (blood poisoning), kidney disease, diabetes, and stroke. Their rates are lower than those of Whites for suicide, Parkinson's disease, lung disease, phenylketonuria, and melanoma (Williams, 2012, p. 280).

The greater overall death rates of Blacks compared with Whites narrowed considerably between 1999 and 2015 (Cunningham et al., 2017). Yet major discrepancies remained. The Black rates for those 18 to 64 years of age are still about 40% higher than those for Whites. And this difference emerges in spite of the fact that rural

Anti-Black Racism in America. Thomas F. Pettigrew, Oxford University Press. © Oxford University Press (2025).
DOI: 10.1093/9780197803134.003.0008

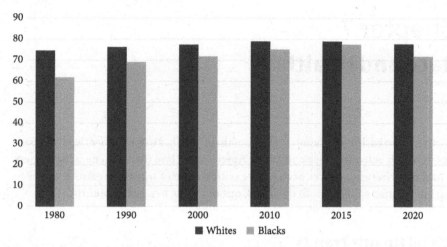

Figure 7.1 Life Expectancy at Birth by Race, 1980–2020
Source: National Center for Health Statistics, 2021.

Americans have consistently higher death rates than urban Americans,[1] and Black Americans are far more urban than White Americans (Lewis, 2022).

Consider infant death rates. While these rates per 1,000 live births have declined sharply since 1960 for all groups, the Black-White ratio remained roughly two to one throughout the half-century from 1960 to 2007. Much of the Black decline since 1995 comes from the pointed drop in births to mothers under 18 years old (Osterman et al., 2022; USA Facts, 2019) (see Figure 7.2). In addition, Black women disproportionately choose to have abortions slightly more often than White women.[2] Despite these changes, the nation's infant mortality rates remain among the world's highest—on a par with those of Slovakia and Poland and twice those of Norway and Portugal (Singh and Van Dyck, 2008).

Heart disease is the leading cause of death in America. The percentage of adults with heart disease is similar for Whites and Blacks, though White rates are slightly higher. Still, as shown in Figure 7.3, deaths due to heart disease are consistently greater among Blacks - exposing the racial disparity in healthcare (Centers for Disease Control and Prevention [CDC], 2019). The rates for both races have declined since 1990, and the racial difference has narrowed. However, by 2018, a significant racial difference in age-adjusted deaths remained.

Black-White differences vary sharply across some diseases. Black American deaths per 100,000 from influenza and pneumonia, for example, were almost twice that of White Americans in 1950 (76.7 to 44.5), yet by 2018 the gap had almost closed (15.8

---

[1] By 2019, the rural death rate was about 18% higher than the urban rate (Lewis, 2022). Within the rural statistics, farm rates are markedly higher than those of small towns.
[2] In 2019, Black women accounted for 38% of legally recorded abortions, White women 33%, and Hispanic women 21% (Kaiser Family Foundation, 2019).

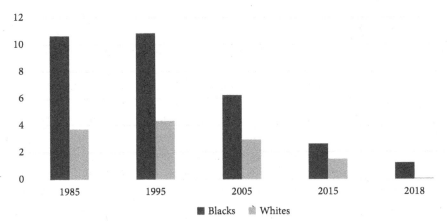

Figure 7.2 Percentage of births to mothers under 18 by race.
Source: Osterman et al., 2022; USA Facts, 2019.

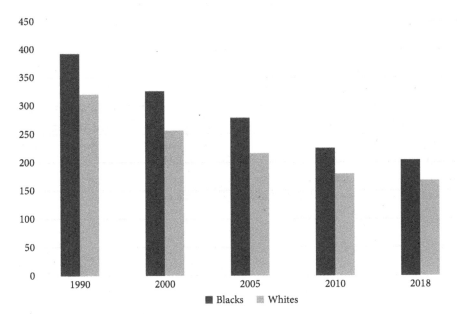

Figure 7.3 Age-adjusted deaths per 100,000 population for heart disease.
Source: Centers for Disease Control and Prevention, 2019.

to 15.0) (CDC, 2019). Black deaths per 100,000 for diabetes mellitus were similar to those of Whites in 1950 (23.5 to 22.9), but by 2018 was double that of Whites (37.6 to 18.8) (CDC, 2019).

According to the National Center for Health Statistics (Hoyert, 2022), Black women giving birth experience almost three times the death rate of White women

(55.3 deaths per 100,000 live births of Black women compared with 19.1 deaths per 100,000 of White women).

Cancer is another major cause of death in America. According to the CDC (2019), Black Americans have higher rates than White Americans for many cancers (e.g., myeloma, stomach, and prostate) and lower rates for a few (urinary, bladder, and thyroid). One particular difference is conspicuous. Protected by darker skin, Black people have a death rate of 1.2 per 100,000 compared to the White rate of 34 for melanoma.

The incidence rate of breast cancer among Black females is lower than that for White females, yet their death rate is higher (Noonan, Velasco-Mondragon and Wagner, 2016). For Black males, the largest racial disparity is for prostate cancer, from which they die at more than twice the rate of White males (Noonan, Velasco-Mondragon and Wagner, 2016).

Five-year total cancer survival rates offer an encouraging trend. From 1975 to 2016, the survival rates rose for White people from 50% to 68%, while the rate for Black people narrowed the gap by rising from 39% to 63% (National Cancer Institute, 2022).

The Core Problem of Drugs

The opioid epidemic has surged among Black Americans. When the most popular addiction-inducing drugs were expensive, the problem was centered among White Americans. When they became cheaper, Black Americans joined the problem in large numbers. Figure 7.4 shows the Black overdose rate catching up with and surpassing the White overdose date rate. Note the steady rise in the White rate compared with the sudden spike between 2015 and 2020 in the Black rate.

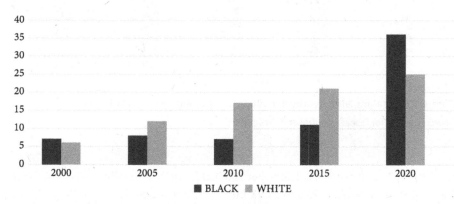

Figure 7.4 Drug overdose deaths per 100,000 people by race.
Source: Newsome, 2022.

Yet data throughout the nation do *not* show that this Black surge is largely a result of Black people taking more drugs. Rather, the rising Black epidemic deaths can be traced directly to unequal access to effective treatment (Newsome and Valentine, 2022). Once again, racial discrimination plays a decisive role. Indeed, White public opinion on the issue can be biased. One study found that it tends to favor medical treatment for White substance abusers, but harsher policies - including incarceration - for Black abusers (De Benedictis-Kessner and Hankinson, 2023).

If they can even get treated, Black addicts typically get only methadone, which requires daily clinic visits and the supervision of a practitioner. This gives addiction a semi-criminalized status as opposed to viewing it for what it is: a public health problem (Newsome and Valentine, 2022). Once the problem spread to White people, the U.S. Congress passed the Drug Addiction Treatment Act of 2000. It offered less stigmatizing treatment options, and it lifted an 86-year ban on treating opioid addiction with narcotic medications. This finally allowed the use of a far better drug - buprenorphine (with such brand names as Subutex and Suboxone).

Yet another problem arose. Most of the doctors who obtain the required special federal licenses to prescribe this much-preferred treatment drug accept only cash or commercial health insurance. Consequently, 95% of buprenorphine patients are White people (Newsome and Valentine, 2022). A further source of racial bias is created in many states by insurance companies requiring only for urban patients prior authorization for addiction treatment as well as for increasingly higher doses of the drug that are more often required by Black patients.

Black death rates are higher for deadly drugs that are relatively inexpensive. Take fentanyl, for instance—a drug said to be as much as 50 times more potent than heroin and much cheaper to produce. In Los Angeles County, California, fentanyl deaths rose dramatically—almost 13% from 2016 to 2021. And 17% of these deaths were of African Americans even though they comprise only 8% of the county's population (Levin, 2022b). Indeed, the whole nation is awash with fentanyl. The U.S. Drug Enforcement Agency (2025) reported that during 2024 it had seized 390 million doses of the deadly drug—enough to kill every American citizen. Hopefully, new and promising vaccines that keep fentanyl from entering the brain will soon be developed for human use (Osborne, 2022).

The criminal justice system, discussed in Chapter 6, is also deeply involved in the addiction issue. Though there are apparently no major Black-White differences in illegal drug use, Black Americans were arrested in 2016 at about five times the rate of White Americans. And the total number of arrests for heroin, used more by Black people, is greater than the arrests for "diverted prescription opioids," used more by White people (Newsome and Valentine, 2022).

Failure to treat addiction effectively in prison results in heavy human and financial costs. It is estimated that two-thirds of those in federal prisons have "a diagnosable substance use disorder." But since few receive treatment, 95% of the addicts relapse once they are released from prison. In the two weeks after release, the overdose risk increases more than 100 times and the chance of death increases 12-fold (Newsome and Valentine, 2022).

The Role of Poverty

In addition to its role in drug addition, poverty has also played a major role in Black deaths from tuberculosis and flu. When the mass movement of Black Southerners to the North occurred, they were often unable to secure adequate housing. The unsanitary living conditions of these poor Black city dwellers in the period 1910 to 1935 caused death rates from tuberculous and flu to be roughly twice that of Whites. Antibiotics eventually reined in tuberculous, but they only became widely available to Black Americans years later (Wezerek, 2020).

Poverty also directly causes lead poisoning rates of Black children to be twice that of White children (Morsy and Rothstein, 2015). Impoverished areas with aging housing stock have lead pipes providing water and lead paint peeling from the walls. Making matters worse, to save money the state of Michigan allowed the water supply of majority-Black Flint to become polluted with lead in 2014–2015.[3] A later review commission wondered if such a reckless, money-saving measure would have been undertaken in a predominantly White city.

Indeed, the nation's next city with a water-quality crisis was Jackson, Mississippi, with an 82% Black population. Combined with the Pearl River flooding from severe storms, Jackson's problem derived from ancient water pipes that had not been replaced for many years, as they had been in other parts of the state. Once again, toxic lead and harmful bacteria put the city's population at great risk. The state government immediately blamed the city and its Black mayor, who in turn blamed the state for its lack of help over the previous decades. In truth, both agencies plus the federal government were all responsible for neglect of the problem.

These water crises were all preventable public health disasters. Maturing brains and kidneys absorb lead that in turn blocks necessary calcium. Symptoms can last a lifetime and include reduced self-control, lowered intelligence, and greater violence in later life. Almost 100 legal cases have been filed against the state of Michigan. Prosecutors in the Flint case were able to obtain only minor misdemeanor convictions against seven defendants using plea bargaining. More serious convictions were thrown out by Michigan's Supreme Court in 2022.

Poverty also leads to less Black health insurance coverage. In 2021, the U.S. Census found that 9.6% of African Americans had no health coverage, compared with 5.7% of White Americans (American Community Survey, 2021).

---

[3] Michigan allowed a similar water catastrophe to occur in Benton Harbor, another predominantly Black city of 9,000. Thus, the three American cities with serious water pollution problems were all among the nation's few predominantly Black cities.

Mental Health

Rigorous data on racial differences in mental health are difficult to ascertain. Psychotic and neurotic rates are greatly influenced by contrasting racial standards used for diagnosis. A study of 294 medical students and psychiatric physicians found that they tended to associate Black faces with psychiatric disorders rather than mood disorders (Tobon et al., 2021). White subjects with *higher* levels of training were the most susceptible to this racial diagnostic bias. Thus, we cannot confidently test for racial trends in such mental disorders as schizophrenia.

There are, however, credible racial data on depression. While Black Americans have recorded lower lifetime and current rates of depression than White Americans, they are more likely to experience more severe symptoms and greater impairment. They are also less likely than White people to receive treatment for their condition (Williams et al., 2007). When they do receive treatment, they are likely to receive fewer antidepressants than White patients (Jung, Lim, and Shi, 2014).

This appears to be a common pattern for numerous conditions. Thus, Black use of both tobacco and alcohol are similar to those of Whites, yet their effects are more serious for Black Americans. Their rates of lung cancer incidence and mortality and for liver damage are markedly higher than for White Americans (Berger, Lund, and Brawley, 2007; Stinson, Nephew, and Dufour, 1996). Indeed, the rate of alcohol-related mortality of Black people is twice that of Whites.

From these and other studies, Noonan, Velasco-Mondragon, and Wagner (2016) conclude that there is a general pattern for African Americans to have similar if not lower incidence rates of mental disorders and substance involvement than whites, but at the same time to suffer higher prevalence of serious mental health and legal problems, with devastating effects.[4]

Suicide rates are consistently higher for Whites, while homicide rates are conspicuously higher for Black Americans. Black homicide rates from 2000 to 2018 have been more than *six times* higher than White rates. Earlier, the racial differential was even greater. In 1990, Black homicide deaths per 100,000 were *nine times* higher than those of Whites (CDC, 2019). Deaths from firearms are the major reason for this situation. In 2014, Blacks constituted almost three out of every five firearm victims. And young Black males were four times more likely to die from a gunshot wound than young Whites (Noonan, Velasco-Mondragon, and Wagner, 2016, p. 5).

Medical Experimentation with Black American Subjects

Black folks' suspicions about American medicine are grounded in history. There is some awareness among White people of the cruel Tuskegee Syphilis Study (1932–1972) in which 399 African Americans who already had syphilis were

---

[4] Prevalence rates include all cases, both new and preexisting. Incidence rates tap only new cases.

intentionally denied treatment so as to study the progression of the disease; 201 others served as controls. The men endured such invasive tests as spinal taps. The study did not end until 1972. Only 74 test subjects were then still alive; 28 had died of syphilis, 100 more from related complications. Forty of the men's wives had been infected, and about 19 of their children were born with congenital syphilis (Mustakeem, 2020). Only after the NAACP Legal and Education Fund in 1974 sued the federal government was compensation of $10 million plus free medical treatment paid to study participants and their descendants.

This event was not a one-time aberration. Harriet Washington (2007), in her well-documented book, *Medical Apartheid*, demonstrates that this study followed in the tradition of American medical experimentation "from colonial times to the present." Among other striking examples, Washington focuses on the South Carolinian physician James Marion Sims (1813–1883), often called "the father of modern gynecology." He repeatedly operated on slave women without anesthetics or their consent. When he operated on White women, Sims was careful to use anesthetics. Sims conveniently accepted the widespread belief that Black people did not feel pain as much as Whites. So, for his slave victims, he felt that his procedures were not painful enough to justify the cost of anesthetics. His fame rests on solving the problem of vesicovaginal fistulas, a fistulous tract extending between the bladder and the vagina. Washington (2007) notes the bitter irony that White women have since benefited from this medical advance that Black women helped to develop, while Black women have typically had less access to the developed treatments and died.

Why the Racial Differences in Health?

White writers, even Thomas Jefferson, have long offered various spurious explanations for racial differences in health (Villarosa, 2022). Black people, in contrast to White people, argued Jefferson (1785) in his famous *Notes on the State of Virginia*, were distinctly different physically, emotionally, and intellectually. Two particular characteristics were often claimed: Black Americans were thought to be better acclimated to heat and to feel pain less intensely than White Americans. You do not have to be a psychologist to surmise that these myths helped to assuage White guilt over their ill treatment of slaves.

These early contentions have persisted in various forms to this day. Differential genetics, poverty, and Black people's risky individual behaviors have been the standard explanations without direct reference to racial discrimination. The *Report of the Secretary's Task Force on Black and Minority Health* (Heckler, 1985), issued by the Reagan administration, is a case in point. It served to bring national attention to racial disparities in an array of medical conditions. Yet the report also emphasized that "money was not the answer." While the report mentions the involvement of social factors, it urged Black Americans to become better informed and change their behavior. The report studiously avoided mentioning racial discrimination as a causal agent. It fundamentally blamed the patient for being sick - yet another example of blaming the victim (Ryan, 1971).

Starting in the 1990s, extensive research finally began to take a rigorous look at the causes of Black health conditions. Racial discrimination began to be looked at as a causal variable with "the weathering hypothesis" advanced by Geronimus (1992) and based on the work of Hans Selye (1907-1982). The famed researcher at McGill Medical School in Montreal made an important observation when he was a young medical student in Prague (Tan and Yip, 2018). He noticed that patients, regardless of their specific diagnosis, reported many of the same symptoms: feeling tired, lack of appetite, weight loss, and dismal mood.

Ten years later this observation led Selye to emphasize the critical role of *stress* - a state of mental or emotional tension resulting from demanding circumstances - underlying these nonspecific signs of illness. He differentiated acute stress from the total response to chronically applied stressors. The latter became known as "Selye's Syndrome" and is the basis for racial theorizing.

In addition to the truly traumatizing racist events a Black American may experience, think of the chronic stressors most Blacks face regularly - the so-called "macro-aggressions" (Pierce, 1970): the empty cab that refuses to stop for you; the store detective who follows you throughout the store; the occasional racial slur you overhear; and the recurrent fear of police misconduct when you or your children are "driving while Black." Also stressful are the ambiguous situations which can be more debilitating than overt discrimination: the gruff, impolite White salesman - was that just his general manner with everyone, or was that racist behavior directed at me? I notice there are no Black diners in the restaurant—does that mean I might not be welcomed (see Sidebar 7.1).

We noted previously that Black people cope with these problems in various ways: leaning on others for social support, concentrating on religious beliefs, confronting the discrimination directly, and avoiding other races (Jacob et al., 2022). All these reactions involve attempts to reduce stress.

Arline Geronimus (1992) combined Selye's work on chronic stress with the everyday experiences of Blacks and devised the valuable hypothesis she termed *weathering*. Villarosa (2022, pp. 17, 80–84, 117, 149–153), in her volume *Under the Skin*, describes the history of this hypothesis and notes the double meaning of the term: "To weather means to wear down, but it also means to withstand, as in weathering a storm."

In broad strokes, the Geronimus hypothesis holds (1) that constant, persistent forms of discrimination lead to the chronic stress that Selye emphasized and (2) that this in turn has numerous detrimental effects on African-American health. While the hypothesis emerged in the area of maternal health and birth outcomes, it has now been applied to a wide variety of physical and mental health conditions, such as depression and feelings of loneliness (Lee and Turney, 2012).

McEwan and Stellar (1993) generalized the idea broadly, named it *allostatic load*,[5] and emphasized its effects on immune and cardiovascular systems. Moreover, the weathering effect appears to hold for "non-dominant groups" throughout much of

---

[5] "Allostatic load" is defined by McEwan and Stellar (1993) as "the cost of chronic exposure to fluctuating or heightened neural or neuroendocrine response resulting from repeated or chronic environmental challenge that an individual reacts to as being particularly stressful."

the race-conscious world: Australia, Brazil, Canada, New Zealand, and South Africa as well as the United States (Bramley et al., 2004; Hamilton et al., 2001; Nazroo and Williams, 2006).

While related to social class, the weathering effect should not be confused with social class. Nor is it limited to Black people. Once social class is controlled, the self-rated health of Jewish Americans is comparable with that of Black Americans and significantly worse than that of other White Americans (Pearson and Geronimus, 2011).

Further evidence for weathering comes from an unexpected phenomenon: the worsening health of immigrant minorities the longer they remain in the United States. One would think, given America's expensive and highly developed medical system, that health status would markedly improve once a group has settled in the country. But David Williams, a Harvard specialist in public health and a West Indian himself from St. Lucia, found just the opposite (Williams et al., 2007). Black Caribbean men systematically evince ever higher psychiatric rates from the first-generation migrants in America to the second generation and then again to the third generation.

Everyone experiences stress. One large study of young adults in Northern California used a natural experiment in 2020 - a contentious year involving the COVID-19 epidemic, wildfires, and George Floyd's publicized murder that culminated in the January 6, 2021 insurrection attempt in Washington, D.C. The researchers found their subjects' psychosocial development was restricted compared with data gathered in 2019 (Buhler et al., 2022). Black and White Americans share such stressors. However, Black people endure yet another set of strong stressors involving racial discrimination (Clark, et al., 1999). Rural southern Black residents who already suffered from chronic, pre-COVID stressors were more likely to contract COVID-19 later (Adesogan, 2021).

The weathering hypothesis does not claim to operate independently of such other life-threatening conditions as poverty, poor medical care, and difficult living conditions. Rather it combines and interacts with these additional causes of poor health (Calabrese et al., 2015).

Poverty's Multiple Negative Effects on Health

As described in Chapter 4, Black people in the United States are significantly poorer than White people. They are more likely to be unemployed, poorly educated, live in a household below the poverty level, and have no health insurance. And they are less likely to own their home (Cunningham et al., 2017). Black American poverty leads directly to impaired health. Williams (2012, p. 283) calls it "part of the causal pathway that links race to health."

Modest income translates into poor diets. Not able to afford a doctor, the poor must rely on crowded and overworked emergency room services. No paid leave and sparse savings mean having to go to work while sick - a practice particularly problematic both for the workers themselves and others during the COVID-19 crisis. It is hardly surprising, then, that both Black and White Americans evince better health as their income rises.

Consider the results of a vast study of 9- and 10-year-old Black (n = 1,786) and White (n = 7,350) children (Dumornay et al., 2023). It focused on the link between racial disparities in adversity exposure and race-related differences in brain structure. The principal finding was that differences in childhood adversity attenuated the magnitude of some race-related differences in gray matter volume. Moreover, poverty proved to be the most predictive of the childhood measures of adversity. The study's researchers believe that these findings may help to explain disparate racial rates of psychiatric diseases.

Poverty also leads directly to poor diet. And adding to the problem of poor diet is the demonstrated fact that major American food companies disproportionately focus their advertising of unhealthy foods and drinks - particularly candy, sodas, snacks, and fast foods - on minority children and adults (Kim, 2022). The Rudd Center for Food and Policy Health at the University of Connecticut found that in 2021 Black adults and youth viewed up to 21% more beverage and food ads than their White peers. The Center also determined that Black children were exposed to 50% more fast-food ads than White children. In addition, fast-food restaurants in heavily Black areas were more likely to have ads that targeted children. These targeted ad campaigns together with the poverty that limits poor Black people to inexpensive food explains why they disproportionately eat more junk food than White people.

Racially segregated housing also contributes to health disparities. In fact, Williams and Collins (2001) maintain that it is "a fundamental cause of racial disparities in health." We have already noted that these segregated ghettoes are more likely to be near a Superfund toxic waste site (Noonan, Velasco-Mondragon, and Wagner, 2016).[6] These sites, not surprisingly, have increased rates of diabetes, childhood cancers, and negative pregnancy outcomes. We will return to the problem of America's massive system of housing segregation in Chapter 10.

The far greater incarceration rates of Blacks compared to Whites (Chapter 6) also have serious medical implications. Jails concentrate individuals with multiple health and social problems, and often do not provide effective healthcare. Since the average prison term is less than three years, large numbers of former inmates are entering the general population annually. When released, many ex-prisoners become homeless and in many states are ineligible for Medicaid benefits. Thus, they spread their health problems to the general population (Freudenberg et al., 2007).

Another medical issue raised by the massive incarceration rates of Black Americans involves the children of prisoners. Stress early in life appears to have the most severe health consequences in later life. High rates of parental incarceration deprive

---

[6] Superfund sites are locations polluted with hazardous waste materials maintained by the U.S. Environmental Protection Agency.

young children of parental care that in itself has negative medical consequences. By 2008, Black children were seven times more likely to have an incarcerated parent than White children. Children of both races in this situation are six times more likely to be incarcerated eventually themselves (Christian, 2009).

Poverty and social class standing, while important, are not the whole story in racial discrepancies in health. American Whites with a high school degree on average live longer than American Blacks with a college degree. At each income level, life expectancy is significantly greater for White than Black Americans (Williams, 2012). And those Black women who answered yes to three racism questions - regarding being treated unfairly at work, in housing, or by the police because they are Black - showed higher levels of obesity, asthma, diabetes, and preterm birth—consistent with the weathering hypothesis (Villarosa, 2022, p. 77).

Also consistent with the weathering hypothesis is premature aging—yet another common trend in racial medical data. The onset of many major diseases is roughly a decade earlier for Blacks than for Whites in the United States. From this accumulating research, we conclude that experiences of racial discrimination are an important type of psychosocial stressor that leads to harmful changes in health status.

Access to Medical Care. Black Americans have less access to medical care. They have less health insurance, although the 2010 passage of Obama's Affordable Care Act (ACA) substantially narrowed this racial gap (Sommers et al., 2015). As noted in Chapter 1, 12 states rejected Medicaid expansion under ACA, eight of them in the South. In addition, far fewer medical facilities exist in both segregated Black rural and urban areas, although neighborhood health centers in some cities, such as Boston, have attempted to address this problem.

An especially egregious example of the effects of restricted medical care occurred in Mississippi (Yang, 2023). The state recorded a 900% increase in newborns with congenital syphilis over the five-year period 1996–2001. Black babies constituted 70% of the 102 newborns treated for the condition in 2020 even though they constituted only 42% of the state's live births that year. The illness occurs when the infection is passed to the fetus while the mother is pregnant. If untreated, there is an 80% chance that it will be passed on. Congenital syphilis can be prevented if the mother receives a series of penicillin shots at least a month before giving birth. Mississippi's Black mothers were disproportionately denied this needed treatment.

Differential Medical Care. Once Black people enter medical care, racist biases still function. We saw how these biases operate in the diagnosis of mental conditions. Yet other biases are also operating. Up until 1968, Black patients routinely received higher doses of radiation than White patients when taking X-rays (Bavli and Jones, 2022). The justification by early radiologists was the old trope from slavery days: Blacks were thought to have thicker skin, denser bones, and heavier musculature; thus, they were thought to require higher doses of radiation. Later research showed that there was no evidence for this procedure, and the practice finally ended.

Another instance of differential care involves a medical formula that measures kidney health. There has been a higher bar for Black patients to register on this measure to receive care. This practice can deny Blacks such needed treatment as transplants that could save their lives (Craven and Snipe, 2022). Biases even emerge for end-of-life treatment. A Dana-Farber Cancer Institute study of Medicare patients found that urban Black patients dying of cancer were the least likely group to receive opioid medications to relieve pain (*Harvard Gazette*, 2023).

While social class affects infant and maternal health, race is more important. A study by the National Bureau of Economic Research revealed that Black families at the *top* of the income distribution have worse health outcomes than White families at the *bottom* of the income distribution (Kennedy-Moulton et al., 2022). While many factors cause this finding, denying women wanted abortions is an important contributor. Research at the University of California at San Francisco included 1,000 women from clinics in 21 states (Turnaway Study, 2022). It found that comparable groups of women who received wanted abortions and women who did not had vastly different outcomes. As you might expect, those turned away included more Black women. The women who failed to obtain wanted abortions had greater economic hardship later, more often stayed in contact with a violent partner, and were more likely to raise the child alone. In addition, giving birth related to more serious health issues than having an abortion. Thus, the U.S. Supreme Court's overturning of *Roe v. Wade* in 2022 had direct and negative racial as well as class implications. Like other recent health decisions of the High Court, it actually killed people.

Problems also arise from the fact that drug companies and other drug testers often have no or too few Black participants in their clinical drug trials (Alsan et al., 2022). "Average" effects of a drug tested on largely White samples may not be accurate for Black patients. Physicians who serve Black patients realize this bias and are more likely to prescribe drugs that have been tested on representative samples.

Black women also receive less prenatal care throughout their pregnancies (CDC, 2005; Martin et al., 2010). Similarly, the implicit racial biases of White oncologists are linked with poorer communication with Black patients and less patient-centered and supportive treatment for Blacks (Penner et al., 2016). In fact, the largest racial disparities in survivorship occur for various cancers. Only 41% of Black patients with rectal cancer receive advanced treatments, compared with 66% of White patients (Miller et al., 2022).[7]

The most remarkable statistic of differential care was stated in a brief filed by the Association of American Medical Colleges to the Supreme Court in the higher education affirmative action case: "For high-risk Black newborns, having a Black physician is tantamount to a miracle drug; it more than doubles the likelihood that the baby will live" (Greenwood et al., 2020). The High Court's Republican majority was apparently unmoved by this striking finding.

---

[7] These treatments—called proctectomy and proctocolectomy—involve removing all or part of the colon and/or rectum when needed in advanced cases.

COVID-19

The precarious position of African Americans in the health sector is made worse when a worldwide emergency occurs. At first, Blacks were hesitant to take the COVID-19 vaccine, but by May 2021 Black vaccination rates equaled those of Whites. Since then, COVID-19 rates for Black Americans have remained consistently higher than those of White Americans (National Urban League, 2022b).

Racial data on COVID was at first scarce, and a fanciful rumor claimed Black skin protected against the virus. Milwaukee County, Wisconsin, with a Black population of about 25%, reported Blacks constituted 45% of cases and 70% of COVID-related deaths. Similarly, Chicago reported that Black residents comprised about 50% of all cases and almost 75% of deaths, although they make up only a third of the city's population. In Louisiana, African Americans are 33% of the state's population but about 70% of the pandemic's deaths (Villarosa, 2022).

One study of the five largest urban counties in Texas offers one explanation for the racial differences (Anderson and Ray-Warren, 2022). It found that ZIP codes with Black and Latino concentrations were less likely to have vaccine distribution sites because they had fewer hospitals and doctors' offices in the area. As had happened earlier with the HIV/AIDS epidemic, the medical vulnerability of African Americans was again laid bare by COVID-19.

By 2022, the racial trends had altered. Black COVID-19 rates continued to decline, and finally fell slightly below those of Whites. A *Washington Post* study uncovered why (Johnson and Keating, 2022). White rates did not continue to decline; instead, misinformed right-wing ideology caused many pro-Trump voters not to wear masks or get booster shots in the name of "freedom."[8] As the *Washington Post* put it, "A lifesaving vaccine and droplet-blocking masks became ideological Rorschach tests."

A Final Assessment

Until COVID-19 hit, American health statistics for Black Americans were generally improving—although Black data continued to lag White data in most categories. The pandemic, however, set these trends moving backward, losing years of previous gains.

For many diseases, Black Americans closed part of the racial disparities that previously existed. Nonetheless, significant racial differences persisted that enhanced the probability of being infected with COVID. One in every six "frontline workers" is

---

[8] This particular misunderstanding of "freedom" is part of the current widespread rejection of the social contract. Its proponents are thinking only of their personal right to do whatever they wish, even if their action may well infect and kill others. Thus, in effect they are claiming the right to harm others. They do not apply the same thinking to having to drive on the right side of the road or not driving while intoxicated—both of which also restrict our "freedom."

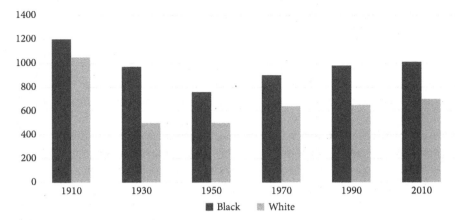

Figure 7.5 Age-Adjusted Mortality rates by race for Ages 0-79
Source: Jackman and Shauman, 2019.

Black and had to work during the crisis. Overcrowded housing adds to the possibility of infection with many kinds of diseases. Black renters are twice as likely to live in a household with more than two people per bedroom (Wezerek, 2020). And Black Americans tend to live closer than White Americans to such environmental hazards as air pollution. Greater poverty remains important, along with restricted access to healthcare and differential racial care when it is received.

No wonder that when we compare White with Black death rates from all causes since 1900, a depressing picture emerges. As Figure 7.5 reveals (modified from Jackman and Shauman, 2019), the racial gap continued through the 20th century into the 21st. Added up over these years, *7.7 million Black Americans would not have died prematurely if there had been no racial discrepancy during the 20th century* (Jackman and Shauman, 2019). This equals 40% of the total Black deaths during the century.

In 2018, Blacks died at higher age-adjusted rates than Whites in 9 of the top 15 causes of death: heart disease, diabetes, cancer, homicide, stroke, kidney disease, hypertension, septicemia, and liver disease. If Black Americans in 2018 had died at the same age-adjusted rates as Whites, it would have avoided 65,000 premature, excess deaths (Jackman and Shauman, 2019).

Taken together, these various processes and trends do not support any sweeping conclusion that American racism in medicine is significantly declining at this time. The Black sociologist W. E. B. DuBois (1906) reached this basic conclusion years ago, writing that health inequities are "not a Negro affair, but an index of social condition."

Highly recommended additional reading on this subject:

Villarosa, L. (2022). *Under the Skin: The Hidden Toll of Racism on American Lives and the Health of the Nation.* New York: Doubleday.

Sidebar 7.1 Stress Can Come from Both Traumatic and Subtle Events

During my almost half-century of university teaching, my Black doctoral students at Harvard University and the University of California, Santa Cruz, have taught me first-hand how constant stress derives from starkly traumatic events to the subtle slights of micro-aggressions.

The worst incident occurred on the 13th floor of Harvard University's William James Hall in the 1970s. A young White woman saw my Black graduate student walking to my office, and then discovered that her pocketbook had been stolen. She at once combined the two events and told Harvard police that a "Black man" had snatched her bag. The two White police officers found my student waiting outside my office for a scheduled appointment. They grabbed and arrested him without any evidence whatsoever. He had no handbag in his possession. He showed them his graduate student card with his photograph on it, but the police falsely claimed that "anyone can obtain one of those." They refused to let him open my nearby office door to get my help. The departmental faculty was furious. Harvard officials later reprimanded the two police officers but refused to fire them. Their principal concern was to keep the sordid incident out of the newspapers.

What made this especially distressing was that the victim came from the Deep South. He had carefully avoided contact with southern police all his life, only to face harassment from Harvard's police. All this happened a half-century ago, but it sticks in my mind as if it occurred last year. The student went on to receive his Harvard doctorate, became a distinguished professor at a New England university, and is now retired.

Even in politically liberal Santa Cruz, California, my Black graduate students have routinely had problems securing suitable housing. As is often the case, they would be repeatedly told that the advertised unit had just been rented. When I would go soon after, I would be immediately offered the apartment. More subtle treatment came from a national chain restaurant. My Black graduate students would invariably be seated at the least desirable table in a half-full room—one near the kitchen and as far from the White customers as possible. They soon stopped going to the establishment.

The worst incident involved pay. There were two pay levels for graduate teaching assistants: the first level paid less to assistants who were relatively new to their studies; the second level paid more to advanced graduate students. The program was administered by a pleasant, middle-aged White woman. One year I had both Black and White teaching assistants, and I noticed a difference in their pay levels. The Black assistant was starting his doctoral thesis but was receiving only the low-level pay, while the relatively new White assistant was receiving the high-level pay. I checked past courses and found that this racial discrepancy had occurred previously. The administrator had been acting out her personal racism quietly and efficiently.

The dean's reaction was similar to that of Harvard's. He reassigned the White woman to another position but refused to fire her. His chief concern was not to have the incident go public. He made his position on race clear years later in a *Wall Street Journal* letter sharply opposing affirmative action programs in higher education. Although this discriminatory event occurred decades ago, it is hard for me to forget how a seemingly pleasant and efficient person could express her racism in such an out-of-sight manner.

Whether blatant or subtle, is it any wonder that such constant reminders of racial discrimination lead to increased stress for Black Americans?

Chapter 8
Race and Politics

Optimists who believe American racism is declining point to Black political gains over recent decades. The 1960s provided the tipping point. President Lyndon Johnson's sweeping Voting Rights Act of 1965 was one of the most effective anti-racism laws ever enacted (see Sidebar 8.1).

This progressive measure set the scene for Black political advances of many types. Of course, reactionary judges at all levels have continuously weakened the act since its passage (Marcus, 2023). Nevertheless, strenuous efforts by Black American voters have made further racial political gains possible. Most Black people agree with W. E. B. DuBois's (1906) sober conclusion that "the power of the ballot we need in sheer defense, else what shall save us from a second slavery."

Just prior to the act, only about 100 Black Americans held elected office in the entire United States; by 2020 more than 9,100 African Americans occupied elected office. African American women have driven recent gains and now comprise more than a third of all Black officeholders. They are often seen by conservative White voters as less threatening than Black male candidates. These newly elected officials are mostly replacing Black male officials who began their careers during the civil rights struggles of the 1950s and 1960s. These newcomers were born after the Civil Rights Acts of the 1960s were enacted, typically attended leading universities, and have been influenced by both the women's rights and civil rights movements (Bositis, 2001, 2003).

Following the 1964 Act's passage, Black Democrats started winning mayoral races throughout the nation: Carl Stokes in Cleveland (1967–1971), Richard Hatcher in Gary, Indiana (1967–1987), Kenneth Gibson in Newark, New Jersey (1970–1986), and Thomas Bradley in Los Angeles (1973–1993). All four of them were the first Black politicians to become mayor of their city. Three of them held their posts for 16 or more years—indicating that their efforts were generally well received by voters. The trend also started in the South, where Harvey Johnson became mayor in predominantly Black Jackson, Mississippi (1997–2005) (see Sidebar 8.2).

Further Problems with the Post-Racism Thesis

We have noted that a major mistake of the post-racism advocates is their assumption that a White vote for a Black candidate for president is proof that the person

Anti-Black Racism in America. Thomas F. Pettigrew, Oxford University Press. © Oxford University Press (2025).
DOI: 10.1093/9780197803134.003.0009

Race and Politics   **123**

is not prejudiced and would not racially discriminate in other situations. However, the racial actions of White Americans are not so consistent—as we noted in Chapter 3 on social norms. Previous to the 2008 presidential election, voters in California, Michigan, and Washington State had passed stern anti-affirmative action referenda; yet all three states provided Obama wide support in both 2008 and 2012.

It is not possible to estimate precisely how many White bigots actually voted for Obama. That said, in the industrial states of Pennsylvania, Ohio, Indiana, and Michigan their numbers, as recorded by exit polls, were substantial. Obama's own campaign surveys traced this phenomenon in detail. Pre-election data measured the racial attitudes of a White sample and found, as expected, considerable prejudice. However, post-election data revealed that a substantial minority of these racially prejudiced Whites had actually supported Obama. Thus, prejudiced attitudes did predict the choices of White voters to some extent, but there were numerous exceptions to the trend.

The post-racism thesis also suffers from two logical and intertwined fallacies: *the ecological fallacy* and *the constant turnout composition fallacy*. The *ecological fallacy* draws conclusions about individuals from macro-level data alone (Pettigrew, 1996). It is a fallacy because macro units are too broad to determine individual data, and individuals have unique properties that cannot be directly inferred from macro data alone. This mistake is often seen in offhand statements made about individual voters from aggregate voting results.

The *constant turnout composition fallacy* involves the assumption that the presidential electorate in 2008 was essentially the same as it was in 2004 - thus, easy comparisons can supposedly be made between the two elections without allowing for changes. But the 2008 electorate was markedly different from the previous election. In 2004, both political parties achieved historically large turnouts. Four years later, the Republican turnout fell, with many of the party's alienated right wing failing to vote. They rejected both candidates.

The Obama campaign orchestrated a record number of Democrats coming to the polls - especially among the young, minorities, political independents, and the left wing of the party. So, rather than representing a massive change in the nation's racial attitudes, the 2008 vote for Obama mostly reflected a shift in the electorate from generally prejudiced right-wingers to generally less prejudiced moderates and left-wingers.

This fallacy is illustrated when the post-racism claimants cite the fact that Obama received only a slightly larger fraction of the total White vote than John Kerry had received in 2004: 43% as opposed to 41%. Given that there was a shift of at least 13% in the composition of voters between the two presidential elections, this 2-percentage-point difference offers negligible support for the post-racism contention. In 2012, Obama garnered 42% of White votes—about the same as Hillary Clinton in 2016.

One might think from reading the post-racism advocates that the 2008 presidential campaign unfolded with scant sign of the nation's traditional racism. This impression

124 Anti-Black Racism in America

is far from the truth. Expressions of racist sentiments in many forms, from violence and campaign tactics to verbal slips, were ever present.

Racial violence escalated and erupted in the North as well as the South. Cross burnings, threats, intimidation, and racist graffiti proliferated across the nation, but typically did not receive nationwide publicity. In New York City, a Black teenager was assaulted by bat-wielding White men shouting, "Obama!" White school children on a bus in Idaho chanted "Assassinate Obama!" And on election night a Black church in Massachusetts was burned in a suspicious fire. The Secret Service reported that there were more threats on Obama's life than for any previous president-elect. Ironically, some leaders of violent White supremacist groups actually advocated voting for Obama. They reasoned that a Black president would ignite their movements and lead to more violence against African Americans. The years since 2016 have at least partly supported their expectations.

One can always shrug off these horrific occurrences as the work of a "lunatic fringe." But unadulterated racism also arose in elite circles in the campaign. Even Hillary Clinton's primary campaign had surrogates repeatedly play the "race card." Two major Clinton staff members accused Obama of having been a drug dealer in Chicago, and her staff leaked a photograph of Obama in Somalian garb to further the fiction that he was a Muslim. Clinton's husband, the former president, implied that Obama was only a marginal Black candidate like Jesse Jackson—who was perceived by many White Southerners as especially threatening. Some Black voters later remembered these incidents and failed to vote for Clinton in the crucial 2016 election four years later.

Geraldine Ferraro, who had been the Democratic vice-presidential candidate in 1984, restated an often-heard anti–affirmation action statement during Obama's first presidential campaign: "If Obama was [sic] a White man," she charged in her 2004 vice-presidential nomination acceptance speech, "he would not be in this position." Clinton professed to see nothing objectionable about the comment, and Ferraro refused to apologize. The crescendo of these efforts came with the revelations about the fiery minister of Obama's Chicago church, the Rev. Jeremiah Wright. Clinton held Obama to be directly associated with Wright's wild rhetoric. She omitted mentioning that she and her husband had invited Rev. Wright to a prayer breakfast at the White House in 1998 which they both attended. Hence, by the same illogic, she was also associated with Wright's rhetoric.

Clinton's primary attacks made it easy for the presidential campaign of John McCain to adopt similar tactics. It repeated and expanded on the elite charge—a thinly veiled return to the old racist accusation against "uppity" Black people who do not know their place and have the audacity to think they are better than White people. Generally, the McCain campaign substituted descriptions of Obama as the strange "other" with the weird background and funny name rather than overtly racial appeals. So it remained for Governor Sarah Palin to forgo all subtlety and declare that "he's not one of *us*" (Trillin, 2008).

Recurrent slips betrayed traditional racist thinking. A Republican club in California issued false ten-dollar bills with Obama's picture accompanied by a watermelon, ribs, and a bucket of fried chicken. The McCain campaign ran an attack advertisement claiming that Obama had been "disrespectful" to Governor Palin—the old southern word recalling sanctions against Black men interacting with White women. A Georgian Republican, Representative Lynn Westmoreland, described both Obama and his wife as "uppity." And a Kentucky Republican, Representative Geoff Davis, remarked about the 47-year-old Obama, "That *boy's* finger does not need to be on the [nuclear] button." The Obama campaign wisely refused to comment on any of these lapses back into "the good old days" of racial segregation when African Americans "knew their place."

Elderly and southern Whites demonstrated that racism is still alive and well in these sizable segments of the American population. By 2020, the elderly—those more than 64 years old—comprised one in every four voters, compared with only one in six back in 1980 (Caplan and Rabe, 2023). Largely overlooked because they do not fit the optimistic post-racism view, many of these older Americans revealed in exit polls that they had voted against Obama largely on racial grounds. In fact, Whites older than 64 were the only age group to vote more often for Republicans in 2008 than in 2004. These data emerge despite four years having passed, with many elderly White voters facing economic problems and many others having died.

In four southern states - Alabama, Arkansas, Louisiana, and Mississippi - fewer Whites voted for Obama than had voted in 2004 for the regionally unpopular John Kerry. In Alabama, Obama received only 10% of the White votes, compared with almost twice that for Kerry.

To hail the end of racism when these large population groups still strongly resisted racial change is clearly premature. Yet change is evident. The oldest cohort of White Americans is dying off, and more tolerant cohorts are replacing them. Likewise, two processes are changing the South: new residents—immigrants, Hispanics, and northern Whites—have moved into the South, and the region's modest school desegregation has produced a slightly more liberal young cohort of White Southerners. Obama surprised many observers by winning in Florida, North Carolina, and Virginia in 2008, and these three states reflect these processes. All three are among the seven states that have received the largest percentages of newcomers in recent years, and they have witnessed somewhat more racial desegregation than other southern states.

Diverging from previous Democratic Party presidential races, the Obama campaign adopted a bold, 50-state strategy. It focused on so-called red states as well as blue states, with particular attention to Colorado, Indiana, Florida, New Mexico, North Carolina, and Virginia - all of which Obama won even though they had cast their votes for Bush in previous elections. This strategy required special attention to increasing both the registration and turnout of African Americans, voters younger than 30, Latinos, and political independents. All of these efforts succeeded. Young,

126 Anti-Black Racism in America

minority, and independent voters all increased their registrations and turnout, while Republicans suffered a decline in turnout. Young voters have been historically difficult to register and convince to vote. Had they voted in earlier elections in their true proportion of the population, both Gore and Kerry would have easily defeated Bush.

Yet the Obama campaign achieved record registration and turnout for both White and Black youth. Two-thirds of those below 30 years of age supported Obama, according to exit polls. This represented a remarkable 12% total and 10% White increase from Kerry's performance four years earlier. However, this did not require a massive change of racial sentiment among the young. Rather it largely reflects the enormous swelling of new voters - previous non-voters as well as those who were too young to vote in 2004.

Not only did young Americans register and vote in record numbers; they also massively volunteered to do the unglamorous grassroots campaigning that characterized Obama's effort - door-to-door interviews, posting signs, making phone calls, driving voters to the polls. These phenomena reveal the importance of Obama's charisma for the young. Fueled in large part by Obama's opposition to the Iraq War - the key issue for many young voters - such a charismatic effect had not been seen since John Kennedy's campaign.

Record minority registration and turnout were also key ingredients of Obama's triumph. Record total turnouts occurred in 37 states and the District of Columbia in spite of lower Republican turnout. African Americans increased their proportion of the total electorate from 11% in 2004 to 13% in 2008, Latinos from 6% to 8%, while the White percentage declined from 80% to 74%—the lowest ever. One in every 6 New York State voters and 1 in 10 California voters was a Black American in 2008. In six southern states, the African American vote rose to a fourth or more of the electorate.

Latinos joined Black voters in these trends. In Colorado, Florida, and New Mexico, sharp increases in Latino registration, turnout, and support were critical for Obama's surprising wins in these previously Republican states. Nationally, exit-poll data indicate that 66% of Latinos cast their ballots for Obama—a record-setting rise of 13% from their 2004 backing of Kerry. And many young Cuban Americans in Florida broke from their group's long attachment to the Republican Party.

Finally, 52% of political independents and 60% of moderates told exit pollsters they had voted for Obama. This represented a 3% shift of independents and 6% shift of moderates from their voting four years earlier. While far-right voters did not favor McCain in the Republican primaries, it was widely believed that the maverick senator from Arizona had special appeal for independents and moderates. Their surprising support was critical for Obama's success, because these middle-of-the-roaders have become an increasingly larger component of the total electorate and disproportionately reside in key "battleground," states where their votes are of strategic electoral college importance.

Obama's special appeal to new, young voters may have long-term benefits for the Democratic Party. Karl Mannheim (1952, p. 301) held that the political events of early life decisively shape each age cohort's political orientation: "[T]he older generation cling[s] to the re-orientation that had been the drama of their youth." Consider the voters who entered the electorate during the 1930s. Their gratitude for President Roosevelt's efforts during the Great Depression led them to be remarkably loyal to the Democratic Party throughout their lives. Their dying off in recent years has been an unnoticed reason for some drop-off in Democratic voting in such areas as Florida, with large numbers of elderly citizens.

Similar, if less dramatic, illustrations of Mannheim's contention occurred for President Kennedy in the 1960s and President Reagan in the 1980s. A comparable phenomenon may take place around the charismatic Obama. His success could have created a cohort of Americans who will favor the Democratic Party for years to come. This trend could be enhanced by the Republican Party's intense opposition to abortion and remedies for climate change and other issues of special concern for the nation's youth.

Post-Obama Black Voting

In the 2020 presidential election, 62.6% of the 32.7 million eligible Black voters cast their votes (USA Facts, 2022a). Thus, one in every nine voters in the 2020 election was an African American - almost equal to their proportion of the nation's population. Their overwhelming support of Biden (87%) made him the easy winner, although 58% of White voters supported Trump. Black support was especially critical in large states with numerous electoral votes such as Michigan and Pennsylvania.

This Black voting surge has led to the further growth of Black officeholders at both the federal and state levels. Note in Figure 8.1 their steady growth in the U.S. Congress. The 118th Congress (2023–2025) boasted three Black senators and 57 Black representatives. All but one in the Senate and two in the House are Democrats.

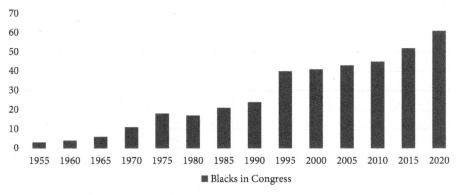

Figure 8.1 Black Americans in the U.S. Congress.
Source: Schaeffer (2023).

Other minorities have also gained representation. In 2001, only 19 Hispanic Americans were members of the U.S. Congress, but there were 54 by 2023. Alaska sent its first Inuit member to the House. All told, 133 senators and representatives identify as minority members. This marks a doubling of representation since 2005. Yet Congress remains predominantly White (75%, while being 59% of the nation's total population). But this dominance is declining as minority membership increases (Schaeffer, 2023).

There have also been four Black governors in recent years: Douglas Wilder, Virginia (1990–1994); Deval Patrick, Massachusetts (2007–2015); David Paterson, New York (2008–2010); and Wes Moore, Maryland (2023–). By 2022, there were 13 Black state attorney generals. More than a third of America's major cities have elected Black mayors—many of them women. In the 1990s, Detroit, Los Angeles, New Orleans, New York, and Washington, D.C., elected Black mayors. Chicago, Dallas, Houston, St. Louis, and San Francisco soon joined them. All these state and city officeholders are Democrats.

Black Voter Suppression. What makes these continued gains remarkable is that they were achieved despite the long history of intense Black voter suppression. The original barrier was the so-called grandfather restriction: if your grandfather was not on the pre-civil war voting rolls (as was true of virtually all Black Southerners), you could not vote. Since Reconstruction (1865–1877), poll taxes and literacy tests have restrained Black voting. In addition, many states disenfranchise all those who have been convicted of felonies—which eliminates 21% of voting-age Black residents in Tennessee and 16% in Mississippi (Fortis, 2022).

Tennessee especially restricts Black voting. Consider the extreme case of Pamela Moses, a Black resident of Memphis (Levine, 2023). She gathered enough signatures to enter the city's race for mayor. But suddenly her voter registration was cancelled although she had been voting for years. Then Moses was arrested at Chicago's O'Hare Airport and given a six-year criminal sentence for voter fraud - thus, ending her voting rights for life. She had made a minor error in her registration for which Whites are rarely charged. This is not an isolated case. Throughout the Deep South, minor mistakes by Black voters, which are largely ignored for White voters, are used to lessen Black political influence. That Moses was a prominent and militant leader in the Black community who was considering a campaign for mayor makes her being selected for such treatment highly suspicious.

Redistricting and other nefarious methods have continued to be used in the South and elsewhere. Ironically, some redistricting simultaneously limits Black political strength while guaranteeing a modicum of Black representation. Bennie Thompson, the chair of the House Select Committee on the January 6 insurrection, is a Black representative from a safe Black district in Mississippi. His seat is safe because carefully drawn district lines restrict Black representation to one seat when the state's Black population fully deserves two seats in the House. This situation is similar to that of Alabama, which the High Court surprisingly overturned in 2023 (*Allen v. Milligan*).

In 2024, all six Republican justices on the High Court ensured the party's narrow majority in the U.S. House of Representatives by rejecting a suit against a wildly drawn House district in South Carolina (Howe, 2024). Their argument defies logic and the political facts. Gerrymandering is permissible, they ruled, if it is strictly for partisan advantage, but is not permissible for racial discrimination. Yet in the Deep South, with 90% or more of Black Southerners voting for Democrats, these two phenomena are virtually one and the same. So, in the name of partisan advantage, the Republican judges allowed to stand a prime example of racially discriminatory gerrymandering. Such gerrymandering throughout Republican-dominated states limits Black political power as well as population-based federal funds to Black communities.

Despite these undeniably positive political gains for Black Americans, there remains a consistently racist side to American politics throughout these same decades since 1970. David Duke, a Ku Klux Klan leader, repeatedly ran as a Republican for high office in Louisiana. The late Senator Jesse Helms of North Carolina made an art form of using racism to win repeated elections. Yet upon his announced retirement, the nation's mass media generally praised him and glossed over his lifelong adherence to and political exploitation of racist beliefs and practices.

Recall, too, the mistreatment of Black voters in the disputed 2000 presidential election. Across the nation, a survey found that 1 of every 10 Blacks sampled reported voting problems—twice that reported by Whites (Dawson and Bobo, 2000). Indeed, this issue was at the core of Florida's hotly disputed voting returns. The U.S. Commission on Civil Rights reports that African American voters in Florida were five times more likely to have their ballots rejected than were other voters (Borger, 2001) - a disparity that drew scant attention from the mass media in its fascination with "pregnant chads." Florida's return to its racist political practices of the past decided the presidential election and changed American history—since 93% of those Black Floridians who did manage to cast their votes supported Vice President Al Gore.

At times, some southern state legislators advance White supremacy legislation that reverts back a century to the 1920s. Trey Lamar provided an example in 2023. He is a Mississippi state representative from the town of Senatobia—8,400 population, 41% of whom are Black Americans. With the capital city of Jackson, Mississippi, in a water impurity crisis similar to that of Flint, Michigan, Lamar advanced the idea that a separate, all-White district be carved out of the city, while the rest of the city, nearly all-Black, be ruled by non-elected officials named by White state officials. In other words, the Republican representative wanted to end Black voting for their own officials in their majority-Black city.

Structural Limitations on Black Political Power. Not all votes are created equal. Along with other Democrats, Black voting power is diminished by the very structure of the American political system—a system that understandably mystifies foreigners when American presidents are elected with a minority of the popular vote. The electoral college system is largely responsible for this inequity. So is the system of

130   Anti-Black Racism in America

granting each state two senators regardless of its size. In 2016, it took 36 votes in blue-state California to equal just one red-state North Dakota vote in senatorial elections. We noted earlier how this unfair system was initially designed to protect slavery (Codrington, 2020; Percival and Dennie, 2022). It now rewards small, rural states that are overwhelmingly White and punishes large, urban states where most Black Americans reside. The effects of slavery still haunt American democracy.

Another major barrier to Black voting involves the massive incarceration of Black Americans - a topic explored in Chapter 6. Here we note how this phenomenon, labeled "the new Jim Crow" by Alexander (2012), seriously weakens Black American political strength. One in every 16 African Americans of voting age is disfranchised because of felony convictions - almost four times the percentage of White Americans who are similarly barred (Uggen et al., 2020). This reduction in the Black voting population is much greater in those states that have explicitly used this method to minimize Black political power. More than one in seven Black citizens are excluded in this manner in Alabama, Florida, Kentucky, Mississippi, Tennessee, and Wyoming— all Republican red states. And the Republican-dominated Federal Fifth Circuit Court of Appeals found Mississippi's 1890 explicitly discriminatory exclusion to be constitutionally acceptable although it bars 10% of the state's Blacks of voting age convicted of a host of even minor crimes. The court majority ruled that the statute had somehow been "cleansed" of its "discriminatory taint."

The most extreme measures passed by Republican-dominated legislatures from Florida to Texas have been aimed at reducing Democratic Party voting generally— such as removing convenient voting drop-boxes and ending voting by mail. Such attempts have a disproportionate effect on Black voters given their overwhelming dedication to the Democratic Party.

These Republican efforts can be quite blatant. In the fall of 2022, Florida governor DeSantis made voting easier in three counties hit hard by the ferocious storm named Ian. These counties had about 5% Black populations. He pointedly failed to make the same move for a fourth county hit equally hard by Ian, Orange County, with its 21% Black population. Perhaps the most radical such legislature was enacted in Georgia in 2021. Along with many other restrictions, the law made it a crime just to pass out water or food to those waiting in line to vote. Critics noted that politicians were now choosing the voters instead of voters choosing the politicians.

To sum up, despite marked gains since the 1964 Voting Rights Act, Black political power is now the target of a frantic attempt to roll back the advances.

Who Are the Black Republican Voters?

The Pew Research Center conducted a special survey in 2022 to learn about the roughly tenth of Black voters who favor Republican candidates (Cox, Muhamed, and Nortey, 2022). It found that Black supporters of the two parties did not differ significantly in income, southern residence, and skepticism about future racial change. However, the Black Republicans were significantly younger. This marks a significant change from the past. Elderly Black people who remembered President Woodrow Wilson's blatant racism and the widespread anti-Black actions of the old southern state Democratic parties were the stalwart Republican voters throughout much of the 20th century. Those Black cohorts have now died and have been replaced by voters who are actually younger than Black Democrats and are less likely to attend church.

Particularly interesting are differences between the two groups in how they view race and racial discrimination. Compared to Black Democrats, Black Republicans report that being Black was a less important part of their personal identity (82% to 58%). They are also less likely than Black Democrats to believe that things that happen to American Blacks in general will affect their own lives (39% to 57%). Thus, Black Republicans racially identify less than Black Democrats.

Black Republicans are also more likely to take an individualistic approach to discrimination. They tend to believe that it consists largely of racist acts from individual bigots (59% to 41%). Black Democrats, however, largely blame structural racism and wish to see major changes in the prison system (57% to 37%), policing (52% to 29%), and the judicial process generally (50% to 35%). By contrast, Black Republicans are less likely to view racial discrimination as the main reason keeping Black Americans from "getting ahead" (44% to 77%). Instead, they are more likely to believe that Black Americans are mostly responsible for their own condition (45% to 21%). Nevertheless, Black Republicans are just as likely as Black Democrats to state that they personally have been racially discriminated against (80% for both groups).

Trends in the 2022 National Election

American democracy dodged a bullet in the 2022 bi-election. What was widely predicted to be a "Red Wave" Republican victory turned out to be a closely fought election that allowed the Democrats to retain narrow control of the U.S. Senate and the Republicans to seize narrow control of the U.S. House of Representatives.[1] There were several reasons media pundits were wrong in their "Red Wave" prediction. Journalists heavily read and influence each other. And they do not have the benefit of two years to write a book, as I do; they must produce their copy on tight deadlines. The prognosticators relied on polls which were in fact fairly accurate. The polls predicted close races throughout the country.

---

[1] The U.S. Supreme Court allowed extreme gerrymandering to remain in place for the election. This action made it possible for just enough Republicans to win and regain a majority in the House of Representatives.

132   Anti-Black Racism in America

But the traditional polls undercounted the young, because these voters are difficult to reach. If you try to sample them via phone, they can simply hang up when they do not recognize the sending number. Campaign advertisements via regular television and news outlets are not seen by most young Americans. To combat this, one Democratic effort engaged youth on social media and even dating apps (Salam, 2022).

Polls have particular difficulty in predicting who will actually vote. Turnout of particular population types has to be calculated on the basis of exit polls, where you can be certain the respondents have indeed just voted. In 2022, unusually heavy voting by White females and especially young voters made a big difference for the Democrats. Exit polls found 72% of young women (18–29 years old) voted Democratic; 70% of young voters supported John Fetterman in the tight and crucial senatorial race in Pennsylvania. Instead of trying to improve their appeal to the young on such issues as combating climate change, the immediate Republican response to these data was to call for raising the legal voting age to 21.

Indeed, the 2022 youth vote was the second highest in almost three decades—topped only by the 2018 bi-election that also went heavily for Democrats (Salam, 2022). In 2022, 27% of voters age 18–29 cast ballots. This may seem like a low percentage, but the youth vote has historically been even lower. This increase occurred despite Texas, North Carolina, and other Republican states making it more difficult to vote on or near college campuses.

Some commentators mistakenly drew the overall conclusion that Black voting had *not* been reduced by the dozens of ways state legislatures in Georgia, Florida, Texas,[2] and other states had contrived to block Black voting. Closer analyses of the data, however, cast doubt on this broad conclusion. Georgia and Texas, in particular, appear to have had smaller Black turnouts than in previous elections. The racial gap between White and Black voting widened in both states. This caused significantly diminished voting for both Stacey Abrams and Beto O'Rourke in their unsuccessful gubernatorial campaigns.

Overall, however, as shown in Figure 8.1, the 2022 election witnessed a continued rise in the political fortunes of Black Americans.[3] Wes Moore became the first Black governor of Maryland. Austin Davis became the first Black lieutenant governor of Pennsylvania. More than 2,000 Blacks ran for some type of office across the country,

---

[2] The three states with the largest number of eligible Black voters—a total of 7.7 million - are also the states that have passed the most restrictive voter suppression laws (Muslimani, 2022). While 7 red states have in recent years passed voter restriction laws, 12 largely blue states have passed 19 laws that expand the suffrage.

[3] Overall, the 2022 election witnessed generally favorable voting for minorities. At least 47 Latinos won election to the House of Representatives - 34 of them Democrats. This marked a new high. Muslim Americans ran for various offices in 25 different states, and 37 (45%) won. Twenty of the winners were incumbents. In addition, Mary Peltola became the first Alaska Native to win a House seat. And Sheng Thao, a second-generation Hmong American who had endured homelessness, was elected mayor of Oakland, California.

Race and Politics   **133**

and roughly half of them won their races. Many of these winners triumphed in predominantly White areas. Increasingly in parts of the nation, Whites are becoming accustomed to voting for competent Black candidates, and this has tempted more Black politicians to run for high office. Moreover, the new Black officeholders have proven at least as competent as their White predecessors - although cynics would say that is hardly a high bar to measure success.

Many Black women have done well politically—often bolstered by White female voters. But three prominent Black women lost their races in 2022 in politically difficult southern states: in Florida, Val Demings running for governor and Aramis Ayala for attorney general; in Georgia, Stacey Abrams for governor.

Elsewhere, however, Black women broke new barriers. Shirley Weber became California's first elected Black secretary of state. Stephanie Thomas became Connecticut's first Black secretary of state. Andrea Campbell was the first Black woman to win the race for attorney general of Massachusetts. And Karen Bass became the first woman and the second Black person to become mayor of Los Angeles. She defeated billionaire Rick Caruso, who spent about $100 million on his losing campaign. Five Black women in 2022 became new members of the U.S. House of Representatives representing districts in California, Texas, North Carolina, Ohio, and Pennsylvania. Eighteen-year-old Jaylen Smith became the nation's youngest mayor when he won election as the Black mayor of tiny (1,800 in 2020), heavily Black (82%) Earle, Arkansas. All these Black winning candidates are Democrats.

Jonathan Jackson won in 2022 a seat in the U.S. House of Representatives. He is the son of Jesse Jackson and, like Michelle Obama, a graduate of Chicago's elite Whitney Young Magnet High School—as well as Northwestern University's Kellogg School of Business. Only two of the new Black representatives are Republicans: John James from Michigan and Wesley Hunt from Texas.

These data are examples of the steady growth in Black representation in the House from 20 to 56 - a 180% rise since 2008. And this growth made it possible for Hakeem Jeffries from New York City to become the first Black Democratic Party leader of the House, replacing Nancy Pelosi after her long reign of 20 years.

Who Are the Most Successful Black Politicians? Given the unrelenting opposition to the growth of Black political power, it is important to check on the characteristics of those Black individuals who have somehow managed to break through the barriers. Here we return to the "pipeline of privilege" theory described previously. Recall that the formally all-White pipeline, once entered, allows early entrance into privileged educational settings that in turn open later opportunities (Pettigrew, 2021). We can check on this contention by reviewing the backgrounds of Barack and Michelle Obama, Vice President Kamala Harris, and the three Black American senators in office in 2022. All but one of them had desegregated educations that placed them firmly and early in the pipeline of cumulative privilege (see Sidebar 8.3).

A Final Assessment

If someone had told you in 2012 that in 10 years Georgia would have a senatorial race between two African American men and at the same time an African American woman would be running for governor, would you have believed them? I suspect not. I certainly did not anticipate any such event. Yet on November 8, 2022, that is exactly what took place. So American racism—even in the Deep South—*has* declined in the political domain. Yet, as with the other social realms, there are efforts underway to subvert these gains. In its nationwide effort to suppress Democratic Party votes, the Republican Party is making strenuous efforts to reduce Black American voting. It thus remains to be seen if these advances can be maintained. We turn in the next chapter to a consideration of interracial contact in the United States.

Sidebar 8.1 The Voting Rights Act and the Southern Vote

When signing the Voting Rights Act, the politically astute Lyndon Johnson remarked sadly, "We've lost the South for a generation." He was speaking of his party, the Democrats, and it has actually been two generations. To his credit, he signed the bill anyway.

Why did Johnson sign the bill? I have a supposition based on my several meetings with him as a member of his White House Task Force on Education (1966–1967). When matters of race were discussed, he typically referred to Mexican Americans. He had close Mexican American friends when he was a boy, and generalized from them to Black Americans.[4] I think that he genuinely believed the nation needed extensive racial change. This belief helped to overcome his political resistance to losing the Democratic Party base in the Deep South.

This was no minor loss for the party. I understood just how tightly the White South had been bound to the Democratic Party from my own experiences growing up in Virginia. The state in the 1940s was tightly controlled by the reactionary "Byrd machine." Led by Senator Harry Byrd, this elite faction ruled Virginia for four decades. The Republican Party was limited largely to the counties of western Virginia, where the White mountain people were also often hurt by the racist legislation passed to control Black Virginians.

Byrd drew national attention when he declared "massive resistance" to the 1954 Supreme Court ruling on school desegregation. His wealth was created by his large apple orchards around Winchester, Virginia. For years, he flew in inexpensive workers from

---

[4] Right after he became president following the assassination of President Kennedy, Johnson called in the heads of the major Black American organizations for one-on-one private discussions. In support of my theory, Whitney Young Jr., then president of the National Urban League, later told me that Johnson had peppered him with questions concerning the similarities and differences between Mexican and Black Americans.

Jamaica to pick his apple crop. Critics observed that Byrd no longer owned slaves, but rented them instead.

So, when I could register to vote in 1949, I had a limited choice. I became a Republican. This infuriated some members of my family. A great-aunt wrote me that she would no longer have anything to do with me. This was no great loss; I never had liked her as she had badly mistreated my father when he was a boy. Born during Reconstruction, she had remained an unreconstructed Confederate all her life. Republicans, to her, were still the invading Yankees, and the Democrats were still the defending Confederates.

Her cohort soon died out, and the Voting Rights Act helped to convert the South from reliably Democratic to reliably Republican. Only now is this breaking up in such states as Virginia and Georgia.

Sidebar 8.2 Black and White Voters for Black Mayoral Candidates

When Black mayoral candidates began winning office in the 1960s, I was fortunate to obtain a major research grant from the Rockefeller Foundation to study this new phenomenon. The University of Chicago's National Opinion Research Center conducted for me repeated probability surveys of White voters in four key cities: Cleveland, Gary, Los Angeles, and Newark (Pettigrew 1972, 1976). Although these cities and their candidates varied sharply, the results were surprisingly consistent. Several uniform trends emerged.

Trend 1: *The first time the Black candidate runs, a large voter turnout routinely occurs.* This is a mixed blessing for Black candidates. They obviously need an expansive Black response, but the high White turnout is likely to include many racially threatened Whites who do not usually vote. This is consistent with the vast research on non-voters. They are repeatedly found to be more apathetic, alienated, authoritarian, and prejudiced than regular voters (Kimball, 1972; Knight Foundation, 2020; Lipset, 1960).

Trend 2: *The second time a successful Black mayor runs for office, the Black voter turnout declines somewhat and the White turnout declines substantially.* The total effect helps the Black candidate. The initially high aspirations of Black voters dampen a bit, while the worst fears of the threatened White voters have subsided considerably during the mayor's first successful term.

Trend 3: *While the racial factor is more important, partisanship does influence White voting even in non-partisan elections.* Jewish and Latino voters tend to favor both the Black candidates and the Democratic Party more than other non-Black voters. Yet even when they are excluded from the analysis and age and education are controlled, the partisanship effect appears in all four cities studied. It is strongest among the college-educated young and weakest among the non-college-educated elderly. The Republican Party is concentrated in small towns and farming areas. The Democratic Party is concentrated in larger cities. So Black mayoral candidates benefit from running as Democrats.

Trend 4: *The Black electorate will consistently provide high turnout and overwhelming support for Black candidates if it is convinced that there is a reasonable chance for the candidate to win.* This means that Black voters calculate how well the candidate can manage with the White electorate.

Many Black communities formed effective get-out-the-vote movements to keep the Black vote high. In Richmond, Virginia, the local Black political organization developed useful techniques that utilized Black churches and social class appeal. Well-dressed college students spoke at Sunday services and asked older, more conservative Blacks to be sure to vote. Arrangements were made for high-status members of the community to drive others to and from the voting places. Having the chance to meet the well-known "Mrs. Johnson" for the first time and ride in her new car proved to be a strong incentive to vote.

Trend 5: *Candidate image is crucial.* The analyses in all four cities showed that the influence of racial prejudice on White voting was mediated by the public image of the Black candidate. Carl Stokes in Cleveland had an open, friendly style that was widely reported in the media. Thomas Bradley in Los Angles presented an efficient, no-nonsense, former police officer appearance that appeased White fears about crime. These images calmed the racial fears of White voters without antagonizing Black voters with "Uncle Tom" obsequiousness to Whites.

Trend 6: *Appealing to hard-core White opposition by addressing non-racial problems can be effective.* The strongest resistance to Black candidates routinely comes from lower-middle-class Whites—not the poorest of the White population.[5] They often feel an intense sense of relative deprivation in comparison with other Americans - including Black American politicians rising in status in their cities. It is this segment of White society that most fears Black advances and leadership. To win them, the Black mayor has to find and address cross-cutting, non-racial issues of general concern.

Both in Gary and Cleveland, surveys found racially prejudiced Whites voting for Black candidates after concrete changes were made that were important to them. White voters in one Gary district voted overwhelmingly against Hatcher in his initial race. He learned that these citizens were especially upset over large, rumbling garbage trucks constantly rolling through their neighborhoods on their way to the city dump. Hatcher simply altered the truck routes, took credit for the change, and gained a third of the area's votes in his re-election.

Likewise, voters in two working-class White precincts in Cleveland provided scant support for Stokes in 1967. Yet they became markedly more pro-Stokes after he opened a needed playground in the area. Thus, many of these White voters valued a new local playground for their children more than their racism. But this does not mean that they

---

[5] This lower-middle-class voting pattern has often emerged throughout the world—in German support for Hitler, in American support for Trump, in Japanese support for Tojo.

had overcome their racism. It is just that racists often value more immediate aspects of their lives than their racial beliefs.

Many of these voting trends at the mayoral level applied later to Obama's 2008 and 2012 presidential elections. See Sidebar 8.3.

It is also encouraging that African American politicians have gained high office in areas where White voters are a large majority, such as governor of Virginia and mayors of Rochester, Minneapolis, and Topeka. Indeed, by 2002 more than half of the nation's 454 Black mayors were elected in cities where African Americans constitute less than half of the population (Bositis, 2003). This trend has encouraged ambitious Black Americans to consider political careers, while White Americans have slowly grown accustomed to having Black leaders.

Forty-four years after the passage of the Voting Rights Act came the ultimate breakthrough for Black politics: the election of a Black American to the presidency of the United States. These four decades of steady, incremental advances made Obama's historic win possible. But even with this essential formation of a political base, it still took a full-fledged "perfect storm" of events for this momentous breakthrough to occur. See Sidebar 8.3.

Sidebar 8.3 It Took a "Perfect Storm" for Obama to Win in 2008

As noted in the introduction, the White American hunger for racial optimism overflowed with self-congratulation when Obama won the presidency in 2008. Many claimed America had entered a new era of "post-racism" (Pettigrew, 2009a), in which race had lost its special significance. To be sure, Obama's election represented a major step forward. But, as later events make clear, racism at all levels continued.

Ever since the 1960s, many White Americans have believed that the nation's race problems were fundamentally solved by the civil rights movement (Chapter 1). We noted how White America in 2004 "celebrated" the 50th anniversary of the *Brown* school desegregation decision, while ignoring the failure to implement the historic ruling. Consequently, African Americans themselves are often held to be responsible for any inequalities that may persist— "blaming the victim" once again (Ryan, 1971).

Obama's victory required a sequence of extremely fortunate events to break serially. When running for the U.S. Senate for Illinois in 2004, Obama trailed in the polls in both the primary and final races. *Break 1:* His major opponent in the Democratic Party primary had to drop out of the race due to a marital scandal. *Break 2:* His major Republican foe also had to drop out of the race due - once again - to a marital scandal.

Break 3: Next, Obama was selected to give the keynote speech at the 2004 Democratic Party Convention. This provided him with a national audience to demonstrate his remarkable speech-making ability. The national buzz about him as a future presidential aspirant began with that memorable address.

Break 4: In the 2008 presidential campaign, he revealed surprising toughness, confidence, and the ability to assemble and manage a dedicated and able staff. His caucus

138   Anti-Black Racism in America

success in Iowa was an essential start to his campaign. This victory in the sixth whitest state in the nation (89% non-Hispanic White in 2007) convinced many voters, especially skeptical Black voters, that he was indeed a serious candidate who, unlike such previous Black presidential candidates as Jesse Jackson, could attract White votes. Surveys showed that from that point on, Black voters throughout the nation overwhelmingly swung their support in the 2008 Democratic primary behind him and away from Hillary Clinton. This translated into crucial primary wins across the South, starting with South Carolina. The significant triumph in Iowa was no accident. Obama had on his staff political operatives who had had previous success in Iowa caucuses, and they planned his campaign with precision.

Break 5: The perfect storm also required that his more experienced and well-financed principal opponent, Clinton, be overly confident and run an inept campaign - problems that she repeated in 2016 against Trump.

Break 6: Republican John McCain ran an equally inept campaign highlighted by the spectacular blunder of choosing Alaska's Governor Sarah Palin as his vice-presidential running mate. To Obama's credit, these bungling campaigns of his opponents were answered with one of the most disciplined presidential campaigns in American history.

Moreover, 2008 offered the Democratic Party a golden opportunity to revive itself after eight long years of George W. Bush's disastrous administration - six years of which the Republican Party controlled all three branches of government. In 2004, exit poll data revealed the two major parties were almost evenly divided in party identification.

Break 7: By 2008, the Democrats had a 10% advantage in party identification—38% to 28%. And at the close of Bush's second term, only 22% of Americans in a *New York Times* poll expressed a favorable view of his eight years in office—a record low for any president since national probability surveys began (Thee-Brenan, 2009). Likewise, a post-election Pew survey found only 13% were "satisfied" with the way things were going in the country compared with 55% who thought so when Bush took office in 2000 (Rosentiel, 2009).

Yet even all these promising elements might well not have been enough for Obama's victory. *Break 8:* The final component of the perfect storm was the sudden and severe turndown in the economy. Indeed, 63% of voters in an exit poll listed the economy as the most important issue facing the nation, compared with only 10% listing the Iraq War (Kuhn, 2008). With McCain widely perceived as incapable of handling the crisis and Obama coolly following the advice of leading economists, the final necessary condition was in place for a victory of the first African-American president. Party affiliation and ideology still played their typically major roles. For example, Obama attracted more votes from independents and moderates. Still, the 2008 election results showed no evidence of a major ideological realignment, although identification with the Democratic Party did rise between 2004 and 2008 (Pew Research Center, 2008).

Frank Rich (2008) summed it up best: "Obama doesn't transcend race. He isn't post-race. He is the latest chapter in the ever-unfurling American racial saga. It is an astonishing chapter. . . . But we are a people as practical as we are dreamy. We'll soon remember

Race and Politics **139**

that the country is in a deep ditch, and we turned to the [B]lack guy not only because we hoped he could lift us up but because he looked like the strongest leader to dig us out."

Sidebar 8.4 The Pipeline of Privilege and Six Leading Black Political Figures

Barack Obama

Growing up in a middle-class White home, Obama was more accustomed to interaction with White than with Black people. According to his memoir, *Dreams from My Father* (Obama, 1995), his breakthrough to the privileged pipeline came when he obtained a scholarship to attend Honolulu's elite private college preparatory school, Punahou. Having had his first four years of education in Indonesia, Obama entered the fifth grade and remained in the posh school until his graduation in 1979. There were only a few other Black students at Punahou, and he reports being uncomfortable except on the basketball court, where he made some close White friends.

With another scholarship, Obama came to the mainland for college at Occidental, a small, mostly White private college in the heart of Los Angeles. Here he became active in the movement advocating for the school's divestment from South Africa and learned he could effectively influence others with his oratory (Obama, 1995, pp. 105–107).

His next step up the privilege ladder was a transfer to Columbia University after two years at Occidental. He majored in political science at Columbia, then spent four years in Chicago as a community organizer before being accepted to Harvard Law School. He excelled and became the first African-American editor-in-chief of the *Harvard Law Review*. Each step—from Hawaii to Los Angeles to New York and finally to Cambridge—marked his gradual entry into the pipeline of privilege.

Michelle Robinson Obama

Growing up in Chicago, Michelle Obama was designated "gifted" by her public school and placed in advanced classes. This led to her being enrolled in a citywide inter-racial magnet school for gifted children. The Whitney Young Magnet School boasted Black students in a slight majority. Her achievements in this special situation won her a scholarship to Princeton University.

Here she, too, felt uncomfortable (Obama, 2021). She worried that the university had accepted her only because her older brother was a Princeton basketball star. (He was later a basketball coach at Oregon State and Brown Universities.) Attendance at Princeton cleared the way for her acceptance in 1985 to Harvard Law School. So her desegregated pipeline consisted of a gifted interracial high school to Princeton to Harvard Law.

Kamala Harris

Harris is a one-person testimony to America's diversity. She has a Tamil-Hindu-Indian mother, a Christian-Jamaican father, a Jewish-American husband and two Jewish

140 Anti-Black Racism in America

step-children. Both she and Barack Obama are among the rapidly growing 3.7 million multiracial members of the Black American population (Tamir et al., 2021).

Her immediate family all became distinguished in their fields: her late mother had a University of California–Berkeley doctorate and was an oncology researcher; her father has a Berkeley doctorate in economics and is a retired Stanford University professor; her sister is a lawyer and former head of the Lincoln Law School in San Jose, California.

When a student in Berkeley's public schools, Harris was bused to the interracial Thousand Oaks Elementary School in 1970 for her kindergarten class—a fact she emphasized in the 2020 presidential debates. Her primary and secondary education took place completely in interracial schools. She attended predominantly Black Howard University (1982–1986), then returned to California to study law at the University of California's interracial Hastings College of Law (1986–1989). Her rise to be the first woman and first non-White vice president of the nation was preceded by her being elected district attorney of San Francisco (2004–2011), attorney general of California (2011–2017), U.S. senator from California (2017–2021), and in 2024 a candidate for president of the United States.

Senator Cory Booker of New Jersey

Booker was one of just three Black American senators in the 117th Congress (2021–2023). He was virtually born into the nation's pipeline of privilege. Both of his parents were executives at IBM, and he grew up in the small, overwhelmingly White, and upper-status borough of Harrington Park, New Jersey. He attended the mostly White Northern Valley Regional High School, which in 1994–1996 was awarded the U.S. Department of Education's Blue Ribbon for Excellence. He played football for the school, and was named to *USA Today*'s all-USA high school team.

Booker attended Stanford University, where he obtained a B.A. in political science and an M.A. in sociology. He also starred as a tight end in football, and was elected senior class president. He won a coveted Rhodes Scholarship to Oxford, where he earned a degree in U.S. history. Booker received his degree from Yale Law School in 1997. These four degrees, all from major universities, make Booker the best formally educated member of the U.S. Senate.

His first two campaigns to become Newark's mayor were unsuccessful, but he persisted and won in 2006. This persistence suggests that Booker will run again in future presidential primaries after losing in 2020. He served seven successful years as mayor, then became the junior U.S. senator from New Jersey in 2013. Booker's remarkable career path, from elementary school to the Senate, has occurred snugly within America's pipeline of privilege.

Senator Timothy Scott of South Carolina

Scott grew up in a one-parent household in North Charleston. His path, too, reveals the pipeline theory of privilege, although from a completely different part of the White world. He went to a Black high school, and then briefly attended mostly White Presbyterian College on a football scholarship before switching to Charleston Southern

University. This largely White institution is a strict Southern Baptist institution that advertises itself as "the best Christian college in South Carolina." It was here that Scott entered the White world of religious fundamentalism.

This important right-wing segment of the state's politics has supported him throughout his steady climb up the political ladder—from Charleston County Council (1995–2009) to South Carolina's General Assembly (2009–2010), and to the U.S. House of Representatives (2010–2011). He was appointed in 2013 to the U.S. Senate by Governor Nikki Haley. Scott won the post in a special election in 2014 and again in 2016. This notable career was undoubtedly aided by the Republican Party insight that the growing Black vote in South Carolina required a response.

Senator Raphael Warnock of Georgia

The 11th of 12 children of 2 Pentecostal ministers, Warnock grew up in poverty in public housing in Savannah, Georgia. He took early courses at Savannah State University before entering Morehouse College in Atlanta, where he earned an honors degree in psychology. Only after attending these two predominantly Black schools did he go on to obtain graduate degrees from New York City's predominantly White Union Theological Seminary.

Warnock is one of the few current Black leaders who did not come up through the White pipeline of privilege. He rose through Black church ranks, and in 2005 became the youngest person ever to become senior pastor of Martin Luther King's famous Ebenezer Baptist Church in Atlanta.

His election to the U.S. Senate in 2020 was made possible by a historically huge Black voter turnout. Warnock is a prime example of a rising Black American who did *not* come through the pipeline of privilege. It was not his White connections but the growing Black voting strength in Georgia, organized by Stacey Abrams, that won him his U.S. Senate seat.

Sidebar 8.5 The Racist Elephant in the Room

Just as this book was going to press, Donald Trump won the presidency for the second time. As in 2016, he lost in the popular vote but won thanks to the undemocratic electoral college system.[6] Many commentators rushed into print to explain the result, but they typically ignored the extensive research on the Trump votes in 2016 and 2020. Had they checked the earlier research, they would have noted the critical role of racism combined with sexism that were basic factors in Trump's vote in all three elections.

The initial explanations centered on education, the popular misperception of inflation and the Democratic Party ignoring its former base with working-class Americans. These contentions were not completely wrong, but they were overly broad. For example, millions of American voters with a college education did in fact vote for Trump, while a

---

[6] As alluded to previously, the electoral college voting system was designed to benefit the slave-holding states (Konagan, 2008).

142 Anti-Black Racism in America

smaller number of non-college voters did vote for Harris. And both racism and sexism explain much of the widely discussed difference between the college and non-college educated.

Consider, too, the fate of Senator Sherrod Brown of Ohio. He has been one of the most consistently pro-labor congressman in Washington for three decades, first in the House of Representatives (1994-2008) and then in the Senate (2008-2024). Yet he lost his bid for re-election. Obviously, factors other than social class were operating.

These initial "theories" largely ignored the elephant in the room – racist and sexual attitudes. Recall that earlier we saw how racism bolstered by an authoritarian view of the world were repeatedly found to be key predictors of Trump's voters in the 2016 and 2020 elections by both political scientists and social psychologists using diverse measures (Pettigrew, 2017; Van Assche et al., 2023). There is every reason to expect similar research findings with the 2024 election results.

Sexist attitudes add to the racist effect – the two are generally positively correlated. Afterall, Trump has won two elections against female candidates and lost to a male candidate. There is a widespread sexist notion that a woman would not be "strong enough" to be an effective president. Voters in Germany, Great Britain, Italy, Mexico and many other nations disagree.

Harris was the complete target for Trump's blatantly racist and sexist attacks – even to the third point of being the daughter of immigrants. Both Trump and his vice-presidential running mate, JD Vance, were explicitly candid about their extreme views on all of these Harris characteristics – from "shithole" Black nations and Haitian immigrants eating pets to immigrant criminals supposedly taking jobs from American citizens. And reactions from his supporters at rallies show that it was these gross violations of modern American norms that especially delighted them. Those followers who were at least a bit bothered by Trump's fanatical positions set them aside as just an unfortunate side of his personality. They often deny supporting Trump to pollsters; This caused the polls to underestimate the Trump vote in all three elections. These voters will learn over his years in office that he was actually being quite honest about his true feelings.

During these four Trump years, we can expect little or no decline in American racism in virtually all of the societal realms discussed in this book.

Chapter 9
Interracial Contact

The eloquent Black American abolitionist Frederick Douglass stated the basic point of this chapter more than 160 years ago:

> A heavy and cruel hand has been laid upon us. As a people, we feel ourselves to be not only deeply injured, but grossly misunderstood. Our White countrymen do not know us. They are strangers to our history and progress, and are misinformed as to the principles and ideas that control and guide us as a people. The great mass of American citizens estimates us as being a characterless and purposeless people; and hence we hold up our heads, if at all, against the withering influence of a nation's scorn and contempt. (Quoted in Alexander, 2012, p. 140.)

True in 1853, and still partly true in the 21st century. Most White Americans today do not know their Black fellow citizens. Precise data on interracial contact are difficult to ascertain. Respondents, especially White Americans, often claim interracial friendships with mere acquaintances. However, we can develop estimates of broad contact trends. Chris Rock, the comedian, was right when he said, "All my Black friends have a bunch of White friends. And all my White friends have *one* Black friend" (quoted in Ingraham, 2014). Indeed, on average, White Americans report just one non-White friend, while Black Americans report a friendship network that includes about eight Whites (Ingraham, 2014). A 2019 national survey found 21% of White respondents reporting that they "seldom or never" interacted with any people of color (Najie and Jones, 2019). About three-quarters of White Americans have no non-White friends at all, and that is probably an underestimate. Of course, some of this difference reflects the fact that there are about four White people for each Black person in the United States. And White Americans who live in such states as Montana and the Dakotas have extremely few Black Americans with whom to interact.

Rarely do White Americans find themselves the only White person in a group of Black people. Growing up in Richmond, Virginia, I had the unusual opportunity of getting to know an all-Black neighborhood through Mildred Adams, the family housekeeper, who became my first "racial tutor." Later, thanks to my close friend Ken Clark, I was often the only White person at numerous Black American meetings.

At first, I felt very conspicuous in such gatherings. I projected on to my associates that they were wondering "Who the hell is this guy? What is this White guy doing here in our space?" In time, however, such anxious concerns eased as I became "one

Anti-Black Racism in America. Thomas F. Pettigrew, Oxford University Press. © Oxford University Press (2025).
DOI: 10.1093/9780197803134.003.0010

144 Anti-Black Racism in America

of the gang." These occasions proved invaluable for my understanding of how Black Americans must feel in the far more frequent occasions in which they find themselves in otherwise all-White settings.

Close ties across racial lines also lend protection against racist accusations. Growing up in Virginia in the 1930s and 1940s, I was subjected to continuous derogative claims about Black folks. But knowing Mildred Adams and her family and neighbors, all I had to do was think of them to realize these ignorant claims were wrong and ridiculous. But if you have no Black friends, you do not have this backstop of knowledge infused with sentiment.

Initiating interracial contact is a "threatening opportunity," in the words of Sanchez, Kalkstein, and Walton (2021). Honest discussion of racial matters is needed to develop genuine cross-group friendship. But this can be threatening. Out of ignorance, you might say "the wrong thing" that offends your acquaintance. Both Black and White Americans told researchers they felt uncomfortable when the Black partner disclosed racial experiences, yet both races felt closer to their friend following such disclosures.

Previous chapters have shown how America's racial patterns systematically restrain equal-status contact between the races. The importance of this restraint is underlined by the extensive findings and theory development in social psychology on intergroup contact.

Intergroup Contact Theory

Intergroup contact theory has become one of the strongest supported theories in social psychology. It boasts a straightforward prediction: if contact occurs under reasonably favorable conditions between members of diverse groups, it will reduce intergroup prejudice (Allport, 1954, 1958; Pettigrew, 1998a, 2016; Pettigrew and Tropp, 2011). The most surprising finding in the vast intergroup contact literature is *the secondary transfer effect of contact* (Pettigrew, 2009b). This effect entails positive contact effects generalizing to non-contacted outgroups. Thus, European reductions in anti-immigrant prejudice spills over to a reduction of anti-Semitism.

Intergroup contact is now social psychology's major theory in the prejudice domain operating at the face-to-face, mesolevel of analysis. Typical of scientific theories, the more we learn, the more interesting questions we open up to test. Recent years have witnessed an enormous extension and elaboration of this basic idea involving thousands of empirical studies.

There have been at least *eight* major meta-analyses conducted to test the theory. First, Pettigrew and Tropp (2006) found that 490 studies revealed a solid −.21 (Cohen's D = −.43) relationship between direct intergroup contact and reduced prejudices of many types. A majority of these studies involve Black-White contact in the United States. A follow-up meta-analysis found that contact studies involving *friends* led to an even stronger relationship between contact and diminished prejudice (Davies et al., 2011).

Interracial Contact **145**

Another meta-analysis showed that structured contact programs fostered positive intergroup attitudes in children and adolescents (Beelmann and Heineman, 2014). Next, Miles and Crisp (2014) analyzed studies of imagined intergroup contact. They uncovered in these studies a significant reduction in both implicit (see Implicit Association Test in Chapter 1) and explicit intergroup prejudice from just thinking about diverse contact.

Studies conducted outside the laboratory using direct and indirect contact interventions also significantly reduce ethnic prejudice (Lemmer and Wagner, 2015). This meta-analysis used only studies of reasonable quality, 85% of which were not included in the original 2006 Pettigrew-Tropp meta-analysis. Yet another meta-analysis validated the extended contact phenomenon when just knowing that in-group members have out-group friends improves attitudes toward the out-group (Zhou et al., 2019).

Finally, two meta-analyses by Jasper Van Assche and an international team of 14 social psychologists (Van Assche et al., 2023) provide the most detailed test of the theory to date. It involved 34 studies with 64,000 respondents across 19 nations. This final meta-analysis sought to test directly criticisms that have been made of contact intergroup research (see Sidebar 9.1).

Together this array of meta-analyses boasts more than 350,000 subjects across more than 850 separate studies in more than 40 nations throughout the globe ranging from Mongolia to South Africa. Their summary statistics were significant for both published and unpublished studies and emerged across a broad range of target out-groups and contexts.

To be sure, more tolerant people are likely to have more intergroup contact and less prejudice—*the two-way causal issue.* We shall return to this point that is now widely recognized and investigated.

Interracial Roommate Studies. The most compelling of this American racial research involves a series of studies of roommate contact conducted on a variety of college campuses. They all had the distinct advantage of a real-life field experimental setting that eliminated the self-selection bias. Although these studies employed somewhat different experimental designs, used different measures, and were conducted by an economist as well as social psychologists, these diverse studies all reached surprisingly similar conclusions.

The largest roommate study conducted to date occurred at UCLA (Sidanius et al., 2008). Its extensive longitudinal design allowed a direct test of the causal link between contact and diminished prejudice. It boasted an experimental design using randomly assigned roommates of four diverse ethnicities: African, Asian, Latino, and White. And it tested affective, cognitive, and behavioral dependent variables. Two major effects emerged: interethnic friendships reduced prejudice, while initial ingroup bias and intergroup anxiety led to fewer intergroup friends. These two effects were of about equal size.

The UCLA research also uncovered secondary transfer effects. Randomly assigned roommates from different ethnicities typically decreased their prejudices even for out-groups not represented in their roommate relationship. White students who

146 Anti-Black Racism in America

had either Black or Latino American roommates displayed less prejudice toward both of these groups. In stark contrast, Sidanius and his colleagues could find no effect - positive or negative - of UCLA's extensive and expensive "multicultural programming."

Black-White roommate research at Ohio State University collaborated many of these positive UCLA results (Shook and Fazio, 2008). This work uncovered an additional point: the students in the racially mixed rooms reported less satisfaction and less involvement with their roommates. Nevertheless, their automatically activated racial attitudes and intergroup anxiety improved over time, while those in same-race rooms show no such changes. Findings from research at Harvard University are consistent with this result. It revealed that two-person and three-person mixed-group rooms without a White majority were no more likely to dissolve in the second year than were all-White rooms (Chakravarti, Menon, and Winship, 2014).

This process fits with the MacInnis and Page-Gould (2015) model, soon to be discussed. Unaccustomed to interracial living, there is some discomfort at first in mixed settings, but the students in mixed-group settings adjust to the situation by the end of the initial year.

Yet another interracial roommate study was conducted at Dartmouth College (Sacerdote, 2001). Among other positive findings, it found that interracial freshmen roommate pairs were significantly more likely to interact with members of different races than were freshmen who roomed with their own race. Bruce Sacerdote, an economist, was so impressed with the anti-racist results of his experiment that he became a strong advocate for educational institutions throughout the nation to adopt random first-year rooming assignments (Zimmerman, 2016).

The Theory's Early History. Contact theory's early history was inauspicious. Without rigorous research to guide them, 19th-century writers largely regarded intergroup contact as dangerous rather than advantageous. Turn-of-the-century racism was involved in these early contentions. These writers were not so subtly defending the South's rigid system of racial segregation.

This pessimistic view of contact was consistent with the writings of William Graham Sumner (1906) and Social Darwinist thought generally. Sumner, a Yale University sociologist and an Episcopal minister, held that cross-group hostility was simply an expected consequence of each ingroup's strong sense of superiority. Consequently, intergroup hostility and conflict were considered natural and inevitable outcomes of intergroup contact. More recent theories make somewhat similar predictions (Jackson, 1993; Levine and Campbell, 1972).

Twentieth-century White writers continued to speculate about intergroup contact without solid empirical evidence. Baker (1934, p. 120) believed that contact between the races, even under conditions of equality, would only breed "suspicion, fear, resentment, disturbance, and at times open conflict." After World War II, however, writers began to shift their views. When groups "are isolated from one another," wrote Brameld (1946, p. 245), "prejudice and conflict grow like a disease."

Interracial Contact **147**

A popular American movement formed to condemn racial and religious prejudice. Called "the human relations movement,"[1] it sought to end prejudice and negative stereotypes. However, this attempt was as naive as it was well intentioned. The movement placed its faith in educating groups about one another and refuting negative stereotypes. It evaded controversy by not seeking the structural changes necessary to enhance intergroup contact and combat discrimination. Instead, the human relations movement celebrated Brotherhood Week each February and hosted dinners for all groups to meet once a year and praise intergroup tolerance.

The movement did counter widespread ignorance about intergroup relations, and ignorance is undeniably a factor in intergroup relations (Stephan and Stephan, 1984; see Sidebar 9.2). Nevertheless, ignorance alone cannot account for the vast institutional barriers that perpetuate racial prejudice and discrimination between racial groups. The movement did not grasp the complexity of intergroup contact. Meeting once a year at dinner is insufficient.

The human relations movement did inspire early research on intergroup contact. Brophy (1945) showed that the more voyages White seamen took with Black seamen in World War II through submarine-infested waters, the more positive their racial attitudes became. Similarly, White police officers in Philadelphia who worked with Black colleagues had more positive racial views than other White police (Kephart, 1957). Gordon Allport contributed to this growing literature by testing the effects of equal-status contact on the anti-Semantic attitudes of non-Jewish undergraduates at Dartmouth College and Harvard University (Allport and Kramer, 1946). He uncovered an almost linear effect: the more equal-status contacts his subjects reported having had with Jewish students, the less anti-Semitic views they expressed.

International probability surveys have also tested the theory with success. The Pew Research Center (Gardner and Evans, 2018) asked probability samples of Western Europeans if they agreed with the statement "In their hearts, Muslims want to impose their religious law on everyone else in this country." If they "personally knew a Muslim," 73% of the respondents disagreed with this anti-Islamic statement, compared with 48% who did not know a Muslim. This contact difference emerged in all 15 countries tested.

All these studies may suffer from the reverse causation problem. Perhaps the seamen, police, students, and survey respondents who were already the least prejudiced were more willing to have outgroup contact. Field studies of public housing using quasi-experimental designs that corrected for this possibility provided the strongest early evidence.

In one of the first large-scale field research studies in North American social psychology, Deutsch and Collins (1951) interviewed White housewives in different public housing projects. Two housing projects in Newark, New Jersey, assigned

---

[1] Not to be confused with the related and larger movement by the same name started by George Mayo. This other movement concentrated on improving employee satisfaction in order to enhance workplace productivity.

148 Anti-Black Racism in America

Black and White residents to apartments in separate buildings. Two comparable public housing projects in New York City desegregated residents by making apartment assignments regardless of race or personal preference. White women in the desegregated projects reported far more positive contact with their Black neighbors, and they expressed greater support for interracial housing and higher esteem for their Black neighbors. Later public housing research replicated and extended these positive findings (Wilner, Walkley, and Cook, 1955). It found that the more intimate the interracial contact, the more favorable the effects.

These contact effects also apply to Black Americans in public housing. Increased equal-status interracial contact in a public housing project in a small midwestern city correlated with more positive feelings and attitudes of the Black residents toward their White neighbors (Works, 1961).

The Rapid Growth of Intergroup Contact Theory. What Allport (1954) originally called a "hypothesis" has now evolved into a full-fledged major theory within social psychology. Although I contributed to this development, I never thought it would advance this extensively so rapidly. The enormous number of replications of contact's positive effect on reducing intergroup prejudices of many types throughout the world, together with the desire of social psychologists to find an effective remedy for intergroup prejudice, helped to spur this rapid growth.

Allport (1954) was especially influenced by Robin Williams's (1947) initial listing of critical contact conditions.[2] Williams astutely predicted that contact's positive effects would be greatest when (1) the two groups shared similar status; (2) the situation fostered personal, intimate intergroup contact; (3) the participants did not fit the stereotype of their group; and (4) the contact activities cut across group lines. Williams's incisive formulation correctly forecast findings of intergroup research decades later.

A second major influence was the work of Allport's Harvard colleague, Samuel Stouffer, and his famous World War II study of unit desegregation during the Battle of the Bulge in Flanders in the harsh winter of 1944–1945. Employing an ingenious quasi-experimental design, Stouffer and his colleagues (1949) demonstrated that fighting side by side with African Americans improved the racial attitudes of the White soldiers. These altered attitudes occurred among White officers and enlisted men as well as White Southerners and Northerners. But the changes were limited to the combat situation and did not initially extend to non-combat situations. A third major influence on Allport's thinking was the public housing field study of Deutsch and Collins (1951), described above.

The Four-Factors Restatement of the Contact Hypothesis. The first edition of *The Nature of Prejudice* appeared in 1954, when I was a third-year doctoral student working with Allport at Harvard. I was immediately engrossed with the book's chapter on intergroup contact. It neatly coincided with my own interracial experiences growing

---

[2] Having served as Allport's assistant when he was drafting *The Nature of Prejudice*, I am aware of the principal influences on his thinking.

up in Virginia. I became so interested in intergroup contact that I chose to take my doctoral special examination on the subject, with the test administered by Allport himself.

Allport's contact chapter is broad and sweeping, and its discursive nature made it difficult to prepare for the examination. I condensed the text down to four key boundary factors that enabled intergroup contact to reduce prejudice: (1) equal status between the groups within the situation, (2) common goals, (3) cooperation between the groups, and (4) authority sanction for the contact. Allport approved of my synthesis, and I used it with his endorsement in later writings (e.g., Pettigrew, 1971). These four factors are now routinely cited as Allport's contact theory, although they are not explicitly listed in his chapter.

But there are serious limitations to this approach. First, it does not do full justice to Allport's rich discussion. Second, it is a "positive factors" approach that later research has found to be too narrow. Allport had assumed that intergroup contact typically *failed* to reduce prejudice. Consequently, he sought to make explicit the positive factors that were *necessary* for contact to diminish prejudice.

This necessary-factors approach created a third problem (Pettigrew, 1986). During the decades following the publication of Allport's volume, writers added further factors they believed were required for intergroup contact to have positive results. As the list of presumed necessary conditions mounted, contact theory was in danger of becoming meaningless. The ever-increasing list of these "necessary" conditions excluded most of the world's intergroup situations and threatened to render the theory trivial. Social psychologists were focusing too much on avoiding Type I errors (false positives) and ignoring Type II errors (false negatives).

A fourth limitation of the necessary-factors approach was uncovered later by my meta-analysis of intergroup contact effects with Linda Tropp (Pettigrew and Tropp, 2006). The four factors thought to be essential for positive intergroup contact effects proved to be highly facilitating but not absolutely necessary.

Further Advances. The 1960s and 1970s witnessed increasing attention to contact theory as its policy implications became more evident. I found it useful as the basis of my expert testimony in support of racial school desegregation in legal cases in Springfield, Massachusetts; Los Angeles; and Norfolk and Richmond, Virginia (Pettigrew, 1979).

The lean four-factor theory of contact is hardly a theory in itself. It says nothing about changes over time and the situational and societal contexts in which the intergroup contact takes place. In 1998, I tried to remedy this by publishing in the *Annual Review of Psychology* a reformulated, more detailed theory of intergroup contact (Pettigrew, 1998a). Figure 9.1 diagrams the article's emphases.

Note that the schematic outline specifies input from all three major levels of analysis: the micro, meso, and macro levels. Drawing on the available contact literature, the article urged that broader, multivariate research approaches be undertaken, especially overtime studies that could follow the temporal development of contact's effects - from initial contact on to established contact and finally to a sense of a unified

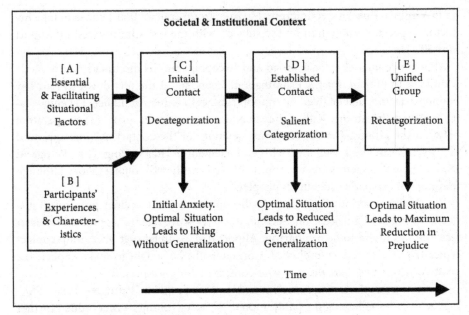

Figure 9.1 The reformulated intergroup contact theory.
Source: Pettigrew (1998a).

single group. This specified time sequence follows the three different categorization processes proposed by various theorists: de-categorization (Brewer and Miller, 1984), salient categorization (Van Oudenhoven, Groenewoud, and Hewstone, 1996), and recategorization (Anastasio et al., 1997; Gaertner et al., 1993, 1994). Although these three were initially seen as rival processes, this time model held all of them to be operating at different times in the contact process.

Unfortunately, most contact studies are not longitudinal. Those that are longitudinal provide the most compelling support for the theory (e.g., Christ et al., 2010; Eller and Abrams, 2004; Levin, Van Laar, and Sidanius, 2003; Binder et al., 2009).

It was not until 2015 that MacInnis and Page-Gould (2015) brought the focus specifically back to the time dimension using longitudinal research. They proposed an over-time model that reconciled an apparent paradox in the intergroup relations literature. Although intergroup contact research routinely reports positive results (Pettigrew and Tropp, 2006, 2008), the largely separate intergroup interaction literature often reports negative outcomes: heightened stress, anxiety, and avoidance (e.g., Shelton et al., 2009; Trawalter, Richeson, and Shelton, 2009).

MacInnis and Page-Gould (2015) advanced a temporal model that brings the two research literatures together as a single process. The model points out that initial intergroup contact is typically stressful and awkward. As this contact continues, however, a threshold is passed wherein the initial stress is alleviated and positive outcomes begin to emerge - consistent with the contentions of Figure 9.1.

Brown and Hewstone (2005) advanced contact theory further by providing an exhaustive review of the many moderating and mediating factors involved in the effects of intergroup contact. Over the past third of a century, their international doctoral students have found intergroup contact diminishing prejudice in their home countries, ranging from Chile, Cyprus, and Italy to Australia, Pakistan, and South Africa. The theory is definitely not limited to the United States.

In the first two decades of the 21st century, the research literature on intergroup contact exploded, from only 30 publications before 1960 to more than 500 from the years 2000 to 2019—almost 100 of them in the journal *Group Processes and Intergroup Relations* alone (Dovidio et al., 2017, p. 607).

Creating Contact. Why are intergroup conflict and prejudice so intense in the world today, when the opportunities for intergroup contact are greater than ever before? The basic answer to this question lies in the massive amount of *intergroup contact avoidance* throughout the world (Paolini et al., 2018). Understanding this process of encouraging people to have intergroup contact is the next task for social psychologists in this area (Kauff et al., 2021).

Slow as it may seem, time seems to be on the side of greater acceptance of diversity. While humans often react negatively in the short term to threats of changes in social diversity, the initial negative effects are typically compensated in the long term by the beneficial effects of intergroup contact (Ramos et al., 2018). Of course, the timing involved can be significantly lengthened by impediments to optimal intergroup contact—such as bigoted modeling by political leaders and intergroup segregation.

Macro-level Contextual Effects

Allport was a specialist in both personality and social psychology, so he naturally thought of intergroup contact in individual terms. In the United States, this focus on the micro level has been dominant—consistent with the nation's strong individualistic culture. European research has consistently had more of a societal-level emphasis, and this work has shown that effective ingroup contact has even greater importance at the macro-societal level of analysis. Social psychology in both Europe and North America is now becoming more contextual by combining the individual and societal levels in its analyses (Pettigrew, 2018a).

Cultural differences emerge as important contexts. Kende et al. (2018) meta-analytically tested intergroup contact theory across 36 cultures. Using the meta-analytic base of Pettigrew and Tropp (2006) and 477 separate studies for a total of 187,025 participants, the authors found that such contact had larger effects in cultures characterized by egalitarian values. Consistent with contact theory's principal contention, each of the 36 cultures revealed a negative relationship between intergroup contact and prejudice. Although the effect still operated in cultures with hierarchical values, it was markedly reduced in these cultures. The cultural context made a difference somewhat greater than the moderator of equal status in the contact situation measured at the individual level.

The immediate social context of the intergroup contact can also shape contact effects. European data involving immigrants suggest that the positive effects of intergroup contact are somewhat stronger when the contact takes place through participation in sports and cultural activities (Herda, 2023a, 2023b).

Another major study of 20 European nations tested the importance of authority support for intergroup contact - the fourth of contact theory's facilitating factors. Green et al. (2020) investigated how official policies governing immigration shaped threat perception and everyday contact with immigrants. These Swiss researchers used multilevel regression with the European Social Survey Round 7's 32,000 participants. At the face-to-face meso level, intergroup contact was once again related to fewer threat perceptions of immigration. But at the macro level of countries, tolerant national policies related to enhanced everyday intergroup contact and reduced symbolic threat perceptions. Further evidence that institutional support enhances the positive effects of intergroup contact, a significant cross-level interaction emerged. The link between contact and reduced threat was stronger in nations with *more tolerant policies* regarding immigrants.

Yet another European study demonstrates how normative structures act as critical contextual variables for intergroup contact effects (Christ et al., 2014). It analyzed with multilevel methods seven large-scale European surveys; five were cross-sectional and two longitudinal. This research specifically tested for macro-level effects of positive intergroup contact reducing prejudice within a variety of macro-level entities: regions, districts, and neighborhoods. It found that these positive macro effects were *larger* than the contact effects at the micro-individual level. In four of the surveys, Christ and his colleagues demonstrated that this significant macro effect was largely mediated by *more tolerant norms*. The authors stressed the importance of this macro-level process, as it can simultaneously impact large numbers of people, most of whom have not themselves had intergroup contact.

Later, a Swiss research group, using different data and methods, confirmed the finding that intergroup contact moderates the effects of social norms involving prejudice (Visintin et al., 2019). They concluded that intergroup contact is a potent tool for reducing conformity to intolerant and anti-egalitarian norms. It is potent because such contact positively improves the *intergroup norms* that in turn enhance both intergroup behavior and attitudes. These findings add a critically significant component to both the theory of and empirical support for intergroup contact theory. Applied to American race relations, these important findings suggest that as Black-White interaction slowly increases, racist norms will recede. There remains the problem of creating intergroup contact. Here there is less research to guide us. We have noted that this is the next big task for social psychological research in this area.

Interracial Contact **153**

Slow and difficult as racial change appears, time nevertheless seems to be on the side of greater acceptance of social diversity. While humans often react negatively in the short term to threats of changes in social diversity, the initial negative effects are overcome in the long term by the beneficial effects of intergroup contact (Ramos et al., 2018; Tropp, 2019). Of course, the timing involved can be significantly lengthened by impediments to intergroup contact, such as bigoted modeling by political leaders and intergroup segregation.

A Final Assessment

Intergroup contact is not by itself a panacea for ending American racism (Hewstone, 2003). But it is an essential component of a wider effort to diminish racism. Its effectiveness at reducing group prejudice is now solidly established by international research. It can also aid the effort to undermine racist norms. But it is still sharply restricted in the United States by racial segregation in education, employment, and especially housing. Until breakthroughs are made in these structural areas, the beneficial effects of interracial contact will remain limited.

The next chapter considers racial segregation in housing.

Recommended for further reading on this subject:

Paolini, S., White, F. A., Tropp. L. R., Rhiannon, N., Turner, N., Page-Gould, E., Barlow, F. K., and Gomez, A. (Eds.). (2021b). Special issue: Transforming society with intergroup contact: Current debates, state of the science, and pathways to engaging with social cohesion practitioners and policy makers. *Journal of Social Issues, 77*(1), 1–274.

Pettigrew, T. F., & Tropp, L. (2011). *When Groups Meet: The Dynamics of Intergroup Contact.* New York: Psychology Press.

Sidebar 9.1 Answering Criticisms of Intergroup Contact Theory

The strongly positive results of intergroup contact research seem almost too good to be true. So numerous cautions and criticisms have been raised. Consider some of the cautions and the answers to them:

1. *The contact phenomenon may be culture bound to Weird (Western, educated, industrialized, rich, and democratic) countries where it has been largely tested.* The Van Assche meta-analysis tested this criticism directly and found no significant difference between the contact effects in Weird and non-Weird countries.

154 Anti-Black Racism in America

2. *Cross-sectional research designs are more likely to show the effect than more rigorous longitudinal designs.* The Van Assche meta-analysis also tested this criticism directly and found it not to be true.
3. *Advantaged respondents will show the contact effects more than disadvantaged respondents.* The Van Assche meta-analysis also tested this criticism directly and failed to validate it.
4. *Those respondents who are high in perceived threat will show the contact effects less than those who are low in perceived threat.* Again, the Van Assche meta-analysis found no difference between high- and low-threat groups.

From these results, the authors conclude that "contact is effective for promoting tolerant societies because it is effective even among subpopulations where achieving that goal might be most challenging" (Van Assche et al., 2023, p. 1).

Sidebar 9.2 A Major Consequence of No Contact

Having no contact with Black Americans need not lead to anti-Black prejudice among White Americans. It can simply lead to a deep ignorance of the Black condition in the United States that is itself harmful. I learned this in a surprising episode at Harvard University in 1955 (Pettigrew, 2022a). As a graduate student, I served as a tutor in Harvard's Dunster House, for which I received my room and board.

Mildred Adams, my family's housekeeper, had a cousin whom I got to know well. She had studied Latin at Virginia Union, Richmond's predominantly Black university; she loved the language and had a genuine talent for it. But Virginia's segregated Black schools did not offer Latin, and the White schools did not hire Black teachers. So she could never obtain a position as a Latin teacher in Virginia's tightly segregated schools. Instead, she, too, worked as a housekeeper and regularly tutored her employer's children in Latin.

Years later, when I told this all-too-true story to friends in the Senior Common Room of Dunster House, my listeners rolled their eyes. They obviously did not believe a word of it. This was *motivated disbelief*: my friends simply did not want to accept that an African-American Latin scholar was working as a housekeeper and teaching Latin only to the children of her employer. They all had generally progressive attitudes on American race relations, but they had had no opportunity for close contact with Black Americans. Without such contact, they were unable to imagine the many obstacles in Black life.

This taught me early how extremely reluctant even well-meaning White Americans are to accept how racism and discrimination severely disrupt individual Black American lives. Denial eases White guilt over racism's effects. This insight led me to begin all 35 of my undergraduate courses on race relations (1956–1998) as well as my 10-part educational television series, *Epitaph for Jim Crow* (Pettigrew, 1964b), with an analysis of the well-documented, if ghastly, phenomenon of racial lynching. This horrible and well-known stain on American history had to be believed, and it established the needed context for the rest of the course.

Chapter 10
Race and Housing

There is massive housing segregation by race in the United States. The statistics to measure this phenomenon are somewhat complex (see Sidebar 10.1), but by any measure, residential separation of the races is intense and widespread. And this particular form of segregation is at the very heart of American racism.

Figure 10.1 shows that it was not always this intense.[1] Drawn from Massey and Denton (1993, p. 21), the chart shows that a great increase in housing segregation occurred between 1910 and 1940 in both northern and southern cities. The index is lower in southern cities because of historic patterns dating back to slavery. In New Orleans, for example, on famed Desire Street, Black servants since slavery typically have retained their residences close to those of their employers.

Figure 10.1 Average Dissimilarity indices average of racial housing segregation, 1860 – 1940
Source: Massey and Denton, 1993.

---

[1] The 1860 data reflect urban separation between free Black people and White people.

Anti-Black Racism in America. Thomas F. Pettigrew, Oxford University Press. © Oxford University Press (2025).
DOI: 10.1093/9780197803134.003.0011

156 Anti-Black Racism in America

A host of factors caused sharp rises in housing segregation in both regions between 1920 and 1940. World War I triggered a stop to European immigration of workers while stimulating the need for workers for the sudden increase in war orders to American industry. At the same time, the boll weevil menace to cotton caused many southern farmers to turn from cotton to other crops that required less labor. These three events, occurring almost simultaneously, triggered a vast Black migration from southern farms to northern industrial cities. This sudden influx of poorly educated African Americans often sparked violent reactions from threatened White residents.

Adding to this tense scene, Black veterans returned from World War I. Having fought for their country, many of these ex-soldiers were no longer willing to accept discrimination in all its forms. Further fuel on the fire was caused by some industries repeatedly using the new Black migrants as strikebreakers. Even now residents of Waterloo, Iowa, tell how this happened in their city's meatpacking industry, where race riots erupted in 1910 and again in 1940 that still adversely shape the city's race relations.

Horrific violence erupted once World War I ended—a starkly dangerous period of American history often omitted from history textbooks. The "Red Summer" of mid-1919 witnessed more than 20 major race riots in large cities, including Chicago, Omaha, and Washington, D.C. One Black veteran, still in his uniform, was lynched in downtown Omaha. There were widespread White fears that the returning Black soldiers would be less willing to accept traditional discrimination. The 1917 Russian Revolution fanned fears of foreign anarchists stirring up trouble, and the Wilson administration encouraged these fears of a "Red Scare."

The worst violence occurred in Tulsa, Oklahoma. Only recently have the full details of the 1921 Tulsa racial massacre of "Black Wall Street" become widely disseminated. A century later, we now know that this prosperous Black section of Tulsa, resented by many White people for its surprising wealth, was largely destroyed. Even airplane bombing added to the destruction. An estimated 300 Black Tulsans lost their lives; 10,000 more were left homeless; millions of dollars of Black-owned property was destroyed. Roughly 600 Black-owned businesses and 1,256 residences were demolished (Perry, 2020).

To its credit, the Oklahoma state legislature has finally recognized the long-suppressed truth of the carnage. It established scholarships for survivors' descendants, encouraged economic development of the area, and made the massacre a required part of the state's school curriculum. Some White Oklahomans, however, resisted even these belated overtures. Local judge Caroline Wall blocked reparations for the three remaining survivors, who were 102, 108, and 109 years old (Jimenez and Riess, 2023). And a newly elected state superintendent of schools, Ryan Walters, ordered teachers to not blame Whites for the massacre. Only individuals - not races - were involved, he claimed. It just happened the violent "individuals" were largely White and the hundreds of victims Black.

Two years after the Tulsa massacre, another racial ordeal occurred in the tiny village of Rosewood, Florida, in which 22 Black and 4 White families lived in peace. Violence flared up on January 1, 1923, when a disturbed White woman falsely claimed that a Black man had attacked her. A drunken White man then killed an innocent Black man. This sparked a rumor among Whites that Blacks were going to retaliate. Soon a White mob formed and mayhem ensued. Two in the White mob were killed, while six Blacks residents - including the sick who could not leave - were shot dead. All save one house in Rosewood was burned to the ground.[2] A *60 Minutes* television program and a movie have been made of the episode. Once exposed, the Florida legislature enacted Rosewood reparations, granting $150,000 to each of the nine survivors who could prove they were in Rosewood in 1923 and scholarships for the descendants of those survivors.

Amid such turmoil, residential segregation solidified. Black people trying to enter all-White neighborhoods were prevented from doing so. Black residents already living in mostly White neighborhoods were often driven out with threats of violence, and some of their homes were burned down. Chicago, in particular, witnessed recurrent bombings of Black-owned residences in predominantly White neighborhoods in the 1920s. When my wife grew up in the 1930s in suburban Chicago, she had no Black neighbors, but Tony "Big Tuna" Accardo lived down the street. White neighbors evidently preferred to live next to this member of Al Capone's infamous crime gang rather than a Black family.

White Rationales for Housing Segregation

The claimed rationale for forced residential segregation was to avoid the assumed loss of value of White-owned homes that would occur if there were any Black neighbors. In large part, this fear was a self-fulfilling result of Federal Housing Administration (FHA) policies.

Surprisingly, racial integration often caused property values to rise. With government policy excluding African Americans from most suburbs, their desire to escape dense urban conditions spurred their demand for homes on the outskirts of urban ghettoes nationwide. Because wealthier Black families "had few other housing alternatives, they were willing to pay prices far above fair market values" (Rothstein, 2017, p. 94).

Other Whites dreaded interracial violence if housing desegregation were to occur—although it was Whites who committed the strife. Some segregationists openly admitted to racist intentions; interracial housing, they feared, would lead to "racial amalgamation" (Rothstein, 2017).

Overcrowding and Blockbusting

Unscrupulous real estate brokers made millions by getting threatened Whites to sell low and charging exorbitant prices to desperate Black families moving into

---

[2] The local area buried the story of Rosewood for decades after the bloody episode. It became widely known only after Gary Moore, a White newspaper reporter, uncovered the story in 1982.

overcrowded quarters. This was a manufactured crisis, and the overcrowding was a direct result of the high prices that forced impoverished Blacks to rent out rooms in their new property.

By 1954, the FHA estimated that Blacks were overcrowded at more than four times the rate of Whites. Among other techniques, brokers would first move large, lower-status Black families into White neighborhoods to frighten middle-class Whites into selling.[3] Such common scaremongering tactics are aptly named "blockbusting" (see Sidebar 10.2). Blockbusting would have been impossible if Black Americans had had available homes to purchase at fair market prices.

Also contributing to blockbusting were the actions of banks and savings and loan associations. Many of them routinely granted mortgages to blockbusters while refusing them in other interracial areas. State regulatory agencies ignored these actions and even allowed real estate boards to expel brokers who had the temerity to sell to Black buyers. For some dealers in Chicago and elsewhere, following the law and helping to start integrated neighborhoods led to their expulsion from the profession.

City Discriminatory Zoning Laws

From 1910 on, southern and border cities began passing zoning ordinances that effectively separated Black from White residential areas. Baltimore was the first. It banned White families from buying homes in predominantly Black areas, and Black families from buying homes in predominantly White areas. Atlanta, Dallas, Miami, Charleston, Richmond, and other cities soon followed.

In 1917, the U.S. Supreme Court in *Buchanan v. Warley* overturned the racial zoning ordinance of Louisville, Kentucky. It did so not on racial grounds, but on a "freedom of contract" principle that property owners should be free to sell to anyone they wished. The decision was simply ignored by most cities using various furtive means. In effect, the 1917 decision changed nothing.

Many cities simply continued to use discriminatory residential zoning past World War II. The damage from redlining and zoning ordinances firmly established separate Black and White residential areas in most American cities that remain segregated to this day. Growing up in Richmond in the 1930s and 1940s, I remember that separate Black and White residential sections were accepted by Whites as "just the way things are." Their recent development was not recognized.

Adding to the racial discrimination, cities learned to locate their schools so as to further both housing and educational segregation. This was especially prevalent in southern cities, where schools were tightly segregated. Richmond engaged in this practice. My high school, Thomas Jefferson, was built in 1929–1930 and located in

[3] Rothstein (2017) describes the techniques used by some real estate dealers. They paid Black women to push baby carriages down all-White streets, Black men to drive by with their car radios blasting loudly, and Black telephone callers asking for someone with a stereotypical Black name.

what was then west of the city, where only Whites were beginning to move and far from Black residential areas. Later, in 1937, Maggie Walker High School was built for Black students. It was carefully placed near Virginia Union University in the heart of the Black residential area. Richmond's White leaders were planning well in advance to maintain racial segregation both residentially and educationally.

Federal Involvement

Reacting to a severe housing shortage in the 1930s,[4] the federal government stepped in and made matters worse. In 1933, the Home Owners Loan Corporation (HOLC) was set up to help homeowners with their mortgages in the midst of the Great Depression. In doing so, the agency drew color-coded maps to evaluate the credit-worthiness of neighborhoods: green was for "best" areas, red for "hazardous" areas. This was the start of "redlining" that was adopted by later agencies, banks, and the real estate industry. Central among the criteria for this color coding was race. The segregationist effects of HOLC actions are still widely present today.

Faber (2020) has shown that cities throughout the nation that had HOLC appraisals were significantly more segregated in 2010 on three different measures than cities that had no HOLC appraisals. The gap between the two types of cities especially widened from 1930 to 1950.

These long-lasting negative effects of redlining can be seen today throughout the nation. Consider Dayton, Ohio, one of the most racially divided cities in the nation. You can view the YouTube presentation on this point, "Redlining: Mapping Inequality in Dayton & Springfield." A similar study for the San Francisco Bay Area is described by Rothstein (2017). This federal housing policy severely limited Black homeownership and business development. Many of the Black areas redlined decades ago remain overwhelmingly Black areas to this day.

Differential Racial Housing Assessments

Redlining also initiated another form of housing discrimination that remains active today: *differential housing assessments.* Homes in White neighborhoods were appraised in 2020 as worth $371,000 more than homes in neighborhoods of color even after the neighborhoods were equated for socioeconomic status and comparable amenities (Howell and Korver-Glenn, 2022). Moreover, this racial gap in assessments is intensifying, with the sharpest rises occurring in fast-selling markets. The COVID-19 pandemic furthered the racial differential (Howell and Korver-Glenn,

---

[4] The housing scarcity lasted through the 1950s and was especially acute for poor White and Black citizens. During World War II, it was even more severe because construction materials were used exclusively for the war effort. The little housing that was built was strictly for the military and its suppliers.

2022). It is estimated that owner-occupied homes in Black neighborhoods are under-valued to a total of $156 billion in cumulative assessment losses (Perry, Rothwell, and Harshbarger, 2018).

In 1934, FHA started insuring home mortgages, but only if the properties were in White-only residential areas. The FHA also favored loans for new construction in the suburbs as opposed to older, inner-city properties. This led to urban decay and the rapid growth of the nation's suburbs. By the time this mortgage inequity was corrected, home prices in the 1970s had risen to where few Blacks could take advantage of the new policy.

This was only the first of many pro-segregation moves of the FHA over the years. The agency's appraisal standards blatantly included a Whites-only requirement. Even if a Black residential district were near a White one, that alone could be grounds for the FHA refusing to grant mortgage insurance. No means of racial separation was too small. In Detroit in 1941, FHA required one builder to construct a tall fence to separate an all-White development from a Black neighborhood (Rothstein, 2017, p. 58).

In 1938, the U.S. Congress established the Federal National Mortgage Association (popularly known as Fannie Mae). It furthered homeownership by making low-cost mortgages available. It did so by purchasing mortgages from local banks and securitizing them. This freed banks to increase their local mortgage lending. And racial discrimination by the banks was rampant. Between 1934 and 1962, only an estimated 2% of the $120 billion in new housing subsidized by the federal government went to non-Whites—and that minuscule percentage includes Asian Americans, Native Americans, and Hispanic Americans as well as African Americans.

The G. I. Bill of 1944, enacted just two weeks after D-Day, was one of the most significant federal laws ever enacted. It dramatically enlarged the White middle class, but it aided Black veterans far less. President Franklin D. Roosevelt was determined to do more for veterans returning from World War II than the government had done for World War I veterans. He began preparing for their return before the war's end.

The G.I. Bill granted World War II servicemen and servicewomen many benefits. The bill provided a $20 weekly unemployment benefit for up to one year for veterans looking for work. Job counseling was available. Those who wished to continue their education in college or vocational school could do so tuition-free up to $500 while also receiving a cost-of-living stipend. This amount may seem small now, but it was fully adequate at the time; my annual University of Virginia tuition at the time as a state resident was $500. As a result, almost half of college admissions in 1947 were veterans.

Veterans who never thought they would be able to afford college saw this as a great opportunity. I went to college with these veterans in 1948–1952, and I can attest to how strenuously they studied. This was their chance for significant advancement, and they were determined not to waste it. They afforded stiff competition in every class I took. The G.I. Bill opened the door of higher education to the White working class in a way never offered before or since in American history. It turned out to be a great investment in raising the educational level of the nation. Now the level needs to be raised again—as discussed in the final chapter.

From 1944 to 1949, nearly 9 million veterans received almost $4 billion from the bill's unemployment compensation program. By 1956, almost 10 million veterans had received G.I. Bill benefits. The education and training provisions of the act existed until 1956, and the Veterans' Administration (VA) offered insured loans until 1962. The Readjustment Benefits Act of 1966 extended these benefits to all veterans of the armed forces, including those who served during peacetime.

Rank racial discrimination marked most of these G.I. Bill programs—especially in the South. The benefits were usually administered by all-White state and local VA offices. In some southern states, tuition applicants were steered to menial jobs or training programs instead of college. Many major all-White colleges routinely rejected qualified Black applicants even in the North. There were no Black students at the University of Virginia while I was there (1949–1952).

Historically Black colleges were unprepared for the deluge of applications they suddenly received when 95% of Black veterans who tried to go to college applied to them.[5] Local southern banks often refused to lend Black applicants money to buy a home even with a loan secured by the federal government. And housing discrimination prevented them from following White veterans who headed to the new suburbs in record numbers.

Thus, the G.I. Bill opened up education and housing for White veterans and vastly improved their post-war American experience. Yet existing discrimination together with the racist practices of the VA greatly reduced the sweeping bill's positive effects for the 1.2 million Black American veterans (*History*, 2019). Some southern postmasters were even accused of not delivering to Black veterans the forms needed to receive unemployment benefits. Funds from VA unemployment insurance were also inequitably distributed by race.

The post-war year 1947 witnessed the first large, mass-produced suburban developments, such as the Levittowns in New Jersey, Pennsylvania, and New York State. The VA and FHA provided the needed support for White buyers while ignoring the widespread use of racially restrictive covenants that governed these sprawling communities. State supreme courts in 13 states upheld the practice of forcing Black buyers from their purchased homes in breach of these covenants. In a 1947 Los Angeles case, a Black man was jailed for refusing to leave the home he had bought in "violation" of a local covenant. A Black homeowner in Oklahoma had his purchase canceled because of a local covenant and was forced to pay all court costs and attorney fees—even the seller's (Rothstein, 2017).

With the federal government disregarding racial discrimination, the various Levittowns excluded virtually all Black applicants. These trends initiated rapid suburban growth that greatly enlarged the scope of housing segregation. Often these new developments advertised in bold, capital letters that they were "EXCLUSIVE." I once went

---

[5] Note once again the Black American hunger for education.

to the Levittown in New Jersey and asked the sales personnel just who was being "excluded"? Was I excluded? A bit embarrassed, a pleasant White saleswoman quicky assured me that I, as a White man, was definitely not among those excluded.

I think she suspected that I might be a tester for the new state and federal anti-discrimination laws. So, she never confessed that non-Whites were the obvious target for exclusion.[6] She did state, "We don't exclude groups, but we do try to exclude undesirables" - a social class reference as much as a racial one. Black Americans as such were not mentioned directly in such restrictive statements. More often such euphemisms as "inharmonious groups," "undesirable neighbors," and "respecting local attitudes" have been routinely employed.

The low-interest loans and mortgages in the G.I. Bill were not directly administered by the VA itself. As with Fannie Mae's mortgage program, this allowed White-run banks and other financial institutions complete freedom to refuse mortgages and loans to Black citizens. And they overwhelmingly did so (Rothstein, 2017). In 1947, only 2 out of more than 3,200 VA-guaranteed home loans in 13 Mississippi cities went to Black borrowers. The same was occurring in the North. Less than 100 of the 67,000 mortgages insured by the VA in New York and northern New Jersey went to non-Whites.

Accusations of racist conduct continue to be made against the VA. In November 2022, the Veterans Legal Services Clinic of Yale Law School sued for Conley Monk, a Black Vietnam War veteran (Horton, 2022). His applications for home loans, healthcare, and educational benefits had been "repeatedly" rejected. The Yale brief demonstrated that from 2002 to 2020 White applicants experienced lower rejection rates than Black applicants for a range of benefits, including disability, home loans, and educational assistance.

In 1948, the U.S. Supreme Court finally addressed the issue of residential segregation (see Sidebar 5.1). Charles Hamilton Houston won his last major legal victory in *Shelley v. Kraemer*. This U.S. Supreme Court case held racially restrictive covenants are unconstitutional and cannot be upheld by the courts. The count was 6 to 0. Indicating how deeply housing segregation was implanted in American society, three of the justices had to recuse themselves from the case because their own homes had exclusionary covenants.

The High Court reasoned that the covenants' power rested on the use of the courts, and that link violated the 14th Amendment to the U.S. Constitution. The FHA, holding tightly to its pro-segregation housing policies, claimed that the decision did not affect their actions. In fact, major resistance to the ruling came from the VA and FHA; the banking and real estate industries also resisted and attempted multiple ways of circumventing the ruling.

---

[6] Earlier, in 1957, a mob of White residents of Levittown, Pennsylvania, harassed the first Black American veteran's family to move into the development (Rothstein, 2017, p. 138). William Levitt was adamantly against allowing Black Americans to be residents of his developments. Although Jewish himself, he even kept Jews out of his upscale development, Strathmore, on Long Island (Lebovic, 2021).

Race and Housing   163

Next, the U.S. Congress enacted the 1949 American Housing Act. This act made the federal government a dominant player in the nation's housing market and was a core component of President Truman's "Fair Deal" program. But it was another step back for aspiring Black homeowners, allowing racially segregated public housing projects as well as racial separation within projects. Proposed integration amendments were flatly voted down by Congress.

Backed by major funding, the program authorized the use of eminent domain to clear "slums" and set up what later was termed "urban renewal." By 1974, 57,000 acres had been "cleared" by the program; in the process, affordable housing was often destroyed. About 300,000 families had to move—more than half of whom were Black citizens. The American Housing Act required that for every new apartment built, another unit had to be demolished or renovated. Many stories tall, in disrepair, and with mostly Black tenants, public housing buildings in America's major cities today stand out as the lasting remains of this controversial program. Urban renewal is in retrospect widely deemed a failure.

Eminent domain destroyed many established Black neighborhoods. Queen City, a large and thriving Black community in Arlington, Virginia, for example, was completely removed to make room for the building of the Pentagon in 1941 (Smith, 2023).

The original G.I. Bill ended in 1956. It had helped 8 million World War II veterans receive higher education, and 4.3 million home loans had been granted to foster homeownership. The lion's share of the bill's benefits went to White veterans and furthered the widening of the White-Black discrepancies in wealth, education, and homeownership (Rothstein, 2017).[7]

Making matters worse, the widespread denial of low-interest loans forced many desperate Black people to obtain *predatory loans*. These loans imposed exorbitant fees and interest rates. They also kept the borrower from acquiring equity. House-seeking Black citizens were desperate for loans, and unscrupulous lenders used deception to entice inexperienced borrowers to acquire loans they could not afford.

The 1950s also witnessed another federal program that furthered overcrowded Black housing and racial segregation. In 1956, President Dwight Eisenhower initiated a nationwide federal program of major highways with the Federal Highway Act. When these new roads crossed through major cities, local leaders saw a chance to obliterate unsightly "slums" while it also provided the most economical alternative for the projects. Consequently, the new roads typically sliced straight through Black housing areas. This disrupted established Black neighborhoods in Buffalo and many other cities. In Detroit alone, the Edsel Ford Expressway (I-94) seized through eminent domain more than 2,800 properties (Perry, 2020, p. 49).

---

[7] As defined by the U.S. Census, the term "homeownership rate" is misleading. It is the percentage of homes that are *occupied* by the owner—not the percentage of adults who *own* their own home. So the term includes households that are owned with a mortgage. If one excludes these households, racial differentials would be even greater.

164   Anti-Black Racism in America

Blocked from moving to White residential areas, displaced residents had to crowd into already impacted Black neighborhoods. The Federal Highway Act also furthered the growth of White suburbs. Worse yet, existing Black homeowners were routinely offered below-market prices for their properties.

My hometown, Richmond, was one of the many cities affected. To make it easy for suburbanites to drive quickly into the central city, the freeway went straight through the city's major Black ghetto. Mildred Adams, my family's housekeeper, found her home directly in the path of the new freeway. As was typical, she was offered a ridiculously low payment for her home. Incensed, my feisty Scottish immigrant mother hired a lawyer and threatened to take Adams's case to court. Knowing they were likely to lose and that the suit might inspire further suits, the highway authority settled immediately. Adams received as compensation a nicer home in North Richmond, although she lost contact with her many old neighborhood friends.

Finally, the Fair Housing Act of 1968 signaled a reversal in federal housing policy. As Title VIII of the broader Civil Rights Act, it attempted to prohibit discrimination concerning the sale, rental, and financing of housing based on race, religion, national origin, sex, and, as later amended, disability and family status. However, it lacked strong enforcement power. Case-by-case implementation is slow at best when faced with an entrenched systemwide phenomenon.

Collusion involving the real estate industry, banks, and federal workers in the Department of Housing and Urban Development (HUD) added to the problems of African Americans seeking housing. Taylor (2019) uncovered examples of such corruption as mortgages being borrowed against dilapidated, worthless properties, appraisers inflating the prices of virtually uninhabitable homes, and Black buyers overpaying for run-down houses they could not afford. The president of the Mortgage Bankers Association personally helped to write HUD's regulatory code.

From these and similar findings, Taylor concluded that the public-private partnership model of affordable housing is doomed to fail. The model's two aims—affordable housing and enhanced profits—have proven incompatible.

Sanctioned Violence as a Defiant Defense. Throughout the 1950–1990 period, some White neighbors turned to violence to maintain racial segregation of housing. They often did so with the support of sympathetic police and other authorities. The rioters were often of lower social status than the Black victims—a further reason for resentment. Major cities throughout the nation experienced continuous incidents of rock-throwing, cross-burning, threatening graffiti, and other means of intimidation designed to force new Black neighbors to leave. This occurred despite the fact that the 1968 Fair Housing Act made violence to hinder residential integration a federal crime.

In Los Angeles in 1945, an entire Black family of four were murdered when their new home in a White district was firebombed. In a White suburb of Louisville, Kentucky, in 1985, a home bought by a Black family was twice firebombed and destroyed. Even as late as 1989, the Southern Poverty Law Center counted 130 cases of violence intended to keep Black American families from moving into all-White neighborhoods (Smothers, 1990; Bell, 2008).

Informal Housing Discrimination in the 1970s and 1980s

Privately refusing to rent to Black applicants remained a widespread practice, especially in large cities. Even a future American president routinely practiced such a policy (Kranish and O'Harrow, 2016). Donald Trump and his father, Fred, owned 14,000 apartments in New York City in the 1960s and 1970s—including a Brooklyn complex managed by the future president.

In July 1972, two testers checked a Trump property. The Black applicant was turned away, while the White tester was immediately offered two available apartments. This result collaborated many similar tests conducted by civil rights groups throughout urban America. The U.S. Justice Department then filed a civil rights case that accused the Trumps of violating the Fair Housing Act of 1968.

The Trumps retained Roy Cohn, the infamous lawyer for Senator Joseph McCarthy, to defend them. Donald called a news conference to claim that "outrageous lies" were being made against him. It took two years before a consent decree was reached. The Trumps finally agreed to stop racially discriminating and to place ads informing minorities that they were now welcome at their properties. Trump later claimed that the settlement was "in no way an admission" of guilt. By contrast, the Justice Department called the settlement "one of the most far-reaching ever negotiated."

Why Racial Housing Segregation Is the Lynchpin of American Racism

The old redlined areas suffer today from reduced homeownership, house values, and rents together with heightened racial segregation (Aaronson et al., 2021). Like mass incarceration, racial housing discrimination is especially critical because it directly enhances racial problems throughout society.

Segregated schools, reduced political power, greater unemployment, diminished wealth, poorer health, more crime, reduced city services, enhanced racial prejudice—these problems for Black Americans can all be traced in large part to racially segregated housing. Consider each of these deleterious effects:

- Segregated schools

Segregated housing leads directly to segregated schools unless unpopular busing is initiated. Chapter 5 discussed the distinct advantages of integrated education.

166   Anti-Black Racism in America

- Reduced political power

Compact Black ghettoes make it easier to limit Black political power by drawing racially gerrymandered districts that dilute Black political strength (see Chapter 8).

- Restricted job opportunities

Being shut out of the suburbs by racial discrimination limits job opportunities for Black workers (see Chapter 4). Increasingly, industry and other employers move to the suburbs, where their long-term Black employees cannot find housing due to continued discrimination. Although valued by their employers, they lose their jobs because of housing discrimination. Zax and Kain (1996) estimated that 11% of Black workers are unable to keep their jobs in the wake of a firm's relocation—far more than among White workers.

- Reduced wealth

Reduced homeownership diminishes Black wealth (see Chapter 4). Data from 2017 reveal that homeowners are about 89 times wealthier than renters: $269,100 total wealth compared to $3,036 (Hays and Sullivan, 2020). Unlike homeownership, renting does not enhance equity. This is one reason the racial disparity in wealth keeps increasing over the years.

- Poorer health

Racially segregated housing also contributes to health disparities (see Chapter 7). In fact, Williams and Collins (2001) maintain that it is "a fundamental cause of racial disparities in health." Overcrowding in ghettoes especially increases the risk of tuberculosis (Acevedo-Garcia, 2001). Lead poisoning in paint in Black homes is all too common and leads to serious medical problems. We noted previously that segregated ghettoes are more likely than other housing to be near a Superfund toxic waste site (Noonan, Velasco-Mondragon, and Wagner, 2016).

We also noted earlier that predominantly Black neighborhoods that were redlined in the 1930s still evince the negative effects of this policy almost a century later. When compared with areas that were highly rated years ago, residents of these lowest-rated areas now experience warmer temperatures, increased air pollution, and shorter life expectancy. They have less green space and fewer trees. They also have 56% higher levels of nitrogen dioxide emitted by vehicles and industrial plants, together with higher asthma rates (Zhong and Popovich, 2022).

Consequently, it is not surprising that numerous studies using a variety of data and methods now find that residents in these old redlined neighborhoods suffer more than others from a range of poor health conditions—especially cardiovascular illnesses (Blakemore, 2023, Motairek et al., 2022; Williamson, 2022). In fact, Blacks and Latinos living in segregated areas were 33% more likely to have heart problems than Whites. Some of these effects reflect the fact that these areas also have less access to medical services (Motairek et al., 2022).

Adding to these problems, the areas in the nation that are most vulnerable to climate change tend to be heavily populated by Black Americans (Cusick, 2023). According to Texas A&M climate change research, areas from Mobile to Corpus Christi are at greatest risk; this includes such heavily Black-populated cities as Birmingham, Memphis, and New Orleans. Moreover, Black residents are overrepresented in the most endangered sections within these areas.

- More crime

Since the average prison term is less than three years, large numbers of former inmates enter the general population annually. When released, most Black ex-prisoners have no choice but to re-enter the ghetto, often to become homeless and likely to slip back into crime (see Chapter 6).

Greater housing segregation, as measured by public housing indices, correlates most strongly with such violent crimes as aggravated assault and robbery, less with property crimes such as burglary and larceny (Bjerk, 2006). Similar results emerge when housing segregation is measured by the spatial isolation of Blacks from Whites (Shihadeh and Flynn, 1996). Severe housing segregation also relates strongly with higher Black homicide rates (Eitle, 2009).

Adding to the critical role of housing segregation in enhanced crime and other negative outcomes is "the neighborhood effect" (Massey, 2001). This occurs when the characteristics of the neighborhood predict individual behavior beyond that of individual variables. It is basically a structural effect that indicates an interaction of both racial and social class effects (Pettigrew, 1981). Neighborhoods shape individual development most deeply during early childhood and late adolescence. And the concentration of male unemployment especially affects social behavior (Massey, 2001).

- Reduced city services

Segregated housing makes it easier to provide fewer city services in concentrated Black areas. For example, streets in Black areas are less often plowed in snowstorms; when a massive storm hits—as in Buffalo in late 2022—inevitably Black residents suffer more. While Black residents make up only 14% of Erie County, New York, they accounted for slightly more than half of the deaths there in early counting (Sacks, 2022). The White county executive blamed the city's Black mayor for the problem. He later apologized.

- Reduced interracial contact

Segregated housing sharply limits optimal interracial contact. Separation invites each group to develop negative myths about the other. And housing segregation prevents interracial contact, which Chapter 9 demonstrates is a major means of prejudice reduction.

Given these housing barriers, it is not surprising that Black citizens have high rates of homelessness (USA Facts, 2023). The U.S. Census found that 48 of 10,000 Blacks in 2021 were recorded as homeless. That is four times that of White Americans, 12 times that of Asian Americans.

In California, the state with the largest unhoused population, Blacks are only 6% of the state yet comprise 26% of the homeless. Most had previously had housing, before high rents drove them out on to the streets (Levin, 2023b).

Little wonder, then, that social scientists have long cited racial segregation of housing to be the "lynchpin" of structural racism in America (Bobo, 1989; Massey, 1995; Massey and Denton, 1993; Myrdal, 1944; Pettigrew, 1971, 1975).

Remedies to End Racial Segregation in Housing

After convincingly demonstrating how the U.S. government is responsible for much of the nation's residential segregation, Rothstein (2017) advances interesting suggestions for possible remedies both big and small. First, he demonstrates that *de facto* housing segregation is a myth obstructing remedies. It was throughout the nation *de jure*; that is, it was established in violation of the law throughout the country. Hence, it can be challenged in the courts as well as in governing bodies.

Rothstein recommends the following remedies. Where constitutionally permitted, ban zoning ordinances that require single-family homes on large lots or that prohibit multifamily units.[8] Amend the tax code to deny the interest deduction to property owners in districts that do not have their "fair share" of African American residents. "Inclusionary zoning" for social class is already established in New Jersey, Massachusetts, and a few municipalities. They have "set-aside" requirements for lower-income families in predominantly middle-class areas.

A Final Assessment

Racial housing segregation across the nation did not emerge naturally. It took years of violence and of malpractice by bankers, real estate brokers, insurance companies, and predatory loan sharks together with governmental polices to create this structural backbone of modern American racism. Indeed, some of the nation's

---

[8] One of Rothstein's suggestions is particularly interesting. In the New York metropolitan area, with its roughly 15% Black population, the federal government could purchase the next 15% of houses that come up for sale in Levittown at today's rates (about $400,000). Then the government could sell the properties to qualified Black buyers for the $75,000 price their grandparents would have paid had they not been barred from doing so. Broader programs could include the federal government offering subsidies for both Black and White home buyers to purchase homes in suburbs that are now overwhelmingly composed of the other race.

leading institutions have contributed to the mass housing separation of Blacks and Whites: Columbia, Chicago, and Texas universities together with Whittier College, the American Federation of Labor, Metropolitan Life Insurance Company, United Auto Workers, and many others (Rothstein, 2017).

Forced racial separation thus feeds racial disparities in other societal realms, from crime and education to economics, politics, and health. Rothstein (2017, p. 191) sums it up succinctly: "Many of our serious national problems either originate with residential segregation or have become intractable because of it." Massey and Denton (1993, p. 16) conclude forcefully that housing "apartheid not only denies [B]lacks their rights as citizens but forces them to bear the social costs of their own victimization."

We conclude that until racial segregation in housing sharply declines, American racism as a whole cannot substantially decline. It is the centerpiece of America's segregationist structure.

Highly recommended for further reading on this subject:

Helper, R. (1969). *Racial Policies and Practices of Real Estate Brokers.* Minneapolis: University of Minnesota Press.

Massey, D. S., and Denton, N. (1993). *American Apartheid: Segregation and the Making of the Underclass.* Cambridge, MA: Harvard University Press.

Rothstein, R. (2017). *The Color of Law: A Forgotten History of How Our Government Segregated America.* New York: Liveright.

Taylor, K.-Y. (2019). *Race for Profit: How Banks and the Real Estate Industry Undermined Black Homeownership.* Chapel Hill: University of North Carolina Press.

Sidebar 10.1 Measuring Housing Segregation

Work on how to measure housing segregation more accurately emerged in the 1960s. The wife-and-husband team of Taeuber and Taeuber (1965) published their influential volume *Negroes in Cities: Residential Segregation and Neighborhood Change* and advanced the *dissimilarity index.* It focuses on *evenness*—the differential distribution of a group's population across a specified geographical area.

The dissimilarity index became the primary way of calculating housing segregation (CensusScope, 2022). This index measures the percentage of a group's population that would have to change residence for each neighborhood to have the same percentage of that group in the entire metropolitan area. In 1960, the index registered .88—near-complete racial segregation of urban housing (Taeuber & Taeuber, 1965, p. 140).

Over the past half-century, this particular national index of residential segregation by race has slowly declined, from a median of .71 in 1980 to .52 in 2020. A median of .52 means that about half of all Blacks in the United States would have to move to all-White neighborhoods before there would be complete racial housing integration. Yet such complete integration is not necessary to foster far more neighborly interracial

170   Anti-Black Racism in America

contact. A median in the .20s or even .30s would be a great advance, similar to that of many interethnic median indices.

The dissimilarity indices vary widely across America's cities. In 2020 they ranged from New York–Jersey City (74.3) and Chicago (73.8) to Charlotte, North Carolina (49.7), and Richmond, Virginia (50.4). Cities with the largest Black populations tend to have higher segregation indices. There are other important dimensions of residential segregation (Massey and Denton, 1988). *Exposure* (or *isolation index*) taps the potential for contact between groups by measuring the probability of Blacks encountering other Blacks. *Concentration* refers to the relative amount of physical space that a minority group occupies. *Centralization* captures how close a group is located to the center of the urban area. And *clustering* measures the extent to which a minority group resides disproportionately in contiguous areas.

Given the multidimensionality of housing segregation, all five of these indices are informative. However, they are not independent dimensions. Eitle (2009) found for 201 metropolitan statistical areas that concentration correlated highly with centralization (+.71), evenness with both clustering (+.75) and exposure (+.66), and exposure with clustering (+.86).

The Geographic Scale Problem

These segregation indices are sensitive to the size of the areas being measured. *The smaller the areas under test, the higher the segregation index is likely to be.*

This statistical issue can actually change substantive conclusions about residential segregation. For example, the dissimilarity indices cited earlier used either census tracts, city wards, or other relatively large areas as their test units. When new data using smaller test units became available, earlier descriptions of the development of urban segregation had to be modified (Logan et al., 2015).

As just described, initial research by Massey and Denton (1993) suggested that racial segregation was slow to develop until "the great migration" out of the South flooded major cities. Recent research using more fine-grained data reveals that this was only part of the story.

Why the difference? Using available data, Massey and Denton (1993) had only relatively large areas as their units of analysis. With newer data using smaller units, Logan and his colleagues (2015) found that there was actually less racial integration than previously believed. Putting the two studies together, we now know that the late 19th- and early 20th-century cities witnessed small aggregates of Black residents living close to each other even before "the great migration." These small Black residential areas do not show up as segregated when large units are employed, while they do show up with more fine-grained analyses.

Sidebar 10.2 The Indefatigable Rose Helper

Rose Helper (1908–1998) was a petite woman who was determined to counter group discrimination wherever she found it. Born in Canada and bilingual in English and

Race and Housing   171

French, she earned her B.A. at the University of Toronto in 1928 and 17 years later her M.A. at Toronto.

She faced down age discrimination twice in her long life. She overcame being initially refused entry into the doctoral program of the University of Chicago's Sociology Department on age grounds alone. Later, she objected to and surmounted the University of Akron's age requirement for forced retirement.

Throughout her career, she had heavy teaching loads and never had the benefit of large research grants with paid assistants. Nonetheless, Helper managed to make a major contribution to the understanding of how racial segregation in housing operates in America's cities. It was a revision of her University of Chicago doctoral thesis, where the noted sociologist Louis Worth was her graduate advisor. Published as *Racial Policies and Practices of Real Estate Brokers* (Helper, 1969), her book received wide attention throughout the social sciences. The book is now available on the internet via JSTOR.

She showed how racial discrimination by the real estate industry, in alliance with banks and the FHA, fashioned and maintained intensive racial discrimination in Chicago's housing. Much of what she wrote still applies today throughout the United States. And her book continues to be cited.

Helper was especially interested in how real estate brokers perceived their own discriminatory actions. Their defensive judgments of Black citizens sound familiar: "they lack certain standards of community life" and "they have no idea of the obligations that go with rights." The Chicago Board of Real Estate branded those few White relators who did sell to Blacks in White areas as "deviants." And the Board opposed the Fair Housing Ordinance issued by the Chicago City Council in 1963.

I was so intrigued by her forceful book that I secured an invitation to present a colloquium in the Sociology Department of the University of Akron just so I could meet her. I was not disappointed. I could easily imagine how this small, friendly, determined woman managed to get Chicago's real estate brokers to reveal their secrets.

Chapter 11
So, Has American Racism Declined?

Race has been the Achilles's heel of American democracy since the first slave ship, the *White Lion*, arrived in Virginia in 1619. Race is at the pivotal core of American history from slavery to the Civil War, Jim Crow and widespread racial segregation in every realm of society, recurrent and bloody lynchings and race riots, massive incarceration of Black citizens, and down to today with its threat to American democracy. The Trump-led insurrection of the 21st century is deeply rooted in the nation's racism. Indeed, every survey of Trump supporters that measures anti-Black prejudice finds it to be a major predictor of their vote—usually the *most* important predictor.[1]

An Admission

Writing this book somewhat altered my view of American race relations. Although I have spent my seven-decade career as a social psychologist specializing in race relations, some of my established opinions on the subject were partially challenged as I dived ever more deeply into the most recent race research and writing. Harsh as I knew American racism was, it now seems to me to be somewhat worse than I had imagined. Over the two years writing this volume, I became a bit more pessimistic about the future of Black-White relations in America. Trumpism and Trump's judicial appointments are setting back much of the hard-won progress of earlier years. And his reelection in 2024 will further this racist trend. This hard right-wing turn has refreshed and further entrenched the nation's long racist tradition.

After intensively analyzing the new data and research, I now realize that racism is even more deeply embedded in America's culture and structure than I had previously dared to surmise. No wonder many political reactionaries do not want critical race theory or the *New York Times* 1619[2] Project taught in the nation's schools. The primary premise of these efforts, that racism is actually "baked" into American society, is all the more disturbing because it is undeniably correct. The previously cited books by Douglas Blackmon (*Slavery by Another Name*), Talitha LeFlouria (*Chained*

[1] This includes literally dozens of studies conducted by researchers from different social science disciplines and using different measures of prejudice. For a summary of these studies, see Van Assche, Dhont, and Pettigrew (2019).

[2] This project, named for the date the first slave ship arrived, attempts to relate the real history of American racism. Not surprisingly, this effort immediately aroused opposition and distain.

Anti-Black Racism in America. Thomas F. Pettigrew, Oxford University Press. © Oxford University Press (2025). DOI: 10.1093/9780197803134.003.0012

So, Has American Racism Declined? **173**

in Silence), and Ibram Kendi (*Stamped from the Beginning*) drive home the fact that slavery's effects continued long after the Civil War and have direct and indirect effects that not only remain but flourish today in American society.

Writing this book also allowed me to see more clearly just how the various realms of American society are so tightly interlocked in perpetrating racism and its varied practices. While in broad strokes racism in attitudes, higher education, and politics has declined, this cannot be claimed for such key areas as wealth and housing. But even where there has been definite improvement, there are strong efforts to turn back the clock. Some wealthy and politically connected White Americans are apparently dedicating their lives to thwart the advancement of Black Americans and return the nation back to the 1950s.

An Interaction Model Fits Current Racial Trends

Four decades ago I advanced a simple model for understanding some of the racial changes that were emerging at the time (Pettigrew, 1981). The model fits loosely what has actually happened in American race relations in the intervening years.

One way to think of the changes is to see them as largely an interaction between race and social class. In statistical terms, an interaction occurs when one cause (race) of an effect (a discriminatory result) is itself influenced by a second cause (social class). In other words, the two causes—race and social class—are not additive in their influence on American race relations. Stated more directly, *the model holds that there have indeed been significant racial advances for upper-status Black Americans. But at the same time, there have been few advances - even some regression - for lower-status Black Americans.*

We have noted repeatedly throughout the book such race and class interactions. Most of the racial gains have been accrued by upper-status Black Americans—in educational attainments, political positions, modestly growing wealth, improved health, far less involvement with the criminal justice system, better housing, and more contact with non-Black Americans.

Lower-status Black people have typically experienced minimal gains and sometimes such actual retrogression as impaired health and heightened incarceration. Obviously, these counter-trends widen the differences in the Black community between the poor and the relatively well-off. As Desmond (2023) emphasizes, this is the racial sub-case of the larger national trend of the American rich getting increasingly richer at the expense of the poor.

Complicating the scene further, contrasting racial trends characterize the different societal realms. While better-off Black Americans typically now own their homes, become well-educated, and can run successfully for political office, they still must be wary of mistreatment from police harassment—the widespread "driving while Black" phenomenon.

174 Anti-Black Racism in America

As a pertinent case in point, think about Jennifer Eberhardt's experiences. As we noted, she won a MacArthur "genius" award, received a Harvard doctorate in social psychology, became a Stanford University professor, and published an important book, *Biased*. Each of these groundbreaking achievements are indications of the decline in American racism.

Yet Eberhardt has also been subjected to the continued dark side of the nation's racism. As she describes in her book (Eberhardt, 2019), she was accosted by a Boston policeman for a minor car registration infraction just the day before she was to receive her Harvard doctorate.[3] She was arrested, handcuffed, and slammed so hard against the car that her sternum was bruised. As soon as Harvard officials intervened, she was released. But her all too common experience underlines how even high-status Black citizens are still at risk for racist encounters. And imagine how she worries whenever one of her sons drives the family car.

Differential Change across Societal Institutions

Throughout the book, we have noted the marked differences in racial change between the various societal realms—from the progress in politics and higher education to the lack of progress in health and criminal justice. Thus, it becomes increasingly problematic to make sweeping statements about racism's effects as a whole - although that is what is generally done in popular assessments. We can make only differentiated judgments. For this, it helps to work from a simple model that organizes how racially discriminatory effects in one area influence the effects in other areas.

From the research reviewed in this book emerges the schematic model shown in Figure 11.1, with housing as the central component.

Two major contentions are advanced in this model. The obvious one is that housing discrimination is the central societal component of racial discrimination in America. As we have noted in the preceding chapters, housing has direct causal links with discrimination in all of the other six domains. It is the key to significant change in the future.

The second contention is more subtle and not fully researched at this point. The model implies that many of the ties between domains are influenced—either moderated or mediated—by housing discrimination. For example, part of the effect of crime's influence on health will be shaped by the overwhelming tendency of Black convicts released from prison to return to the poorest of segregated Black ghettoes. As another example, the effect of Black wealth on intergroup contact depends in part on whether better-off Black Americans use their money to live in intergroup neighborhoods.

---

[3] As further evidence of the complexity of today's race relations, the arresting Boston policeman was a Black officer. He was reflecting the norms of his police department.

So, Has American Racism Declined? 175

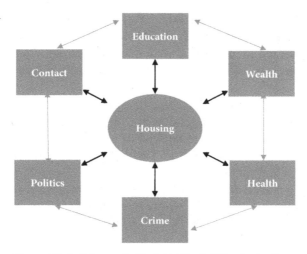

Figure 11.1 Schematic Model of Racial Discrimination

Two Fundamental Obstacles to Progress

Two particularly serious aspects of current American race relations must be addressed: (1) the inability of Black America to overcome the obstacles that prevent the establishment of a sufficient and permanent capital base (Chapter 4) and (2) the widespread lack of interracial contact (Chapter 9). These two acute domains should guide how reparations are designed. Since advances in housing integration respond to both of these needs, they deserve special attention.

Is America Capable of Becoming a Largely Non-racist Country?

After positive events—such as Obama's two election victories—many prematurely came to think that the answer is definitely YES, that *post-racism* time has arrived. At other times—such as the election of a president who often proudly expresses his racism and the Supreme Court's drastic elimination of positive action in higher education—many also may prematurely come to think that the answer is definitely NO, that the strong traces of slavery remain and will continue.

Fortunately, we have data that suggest Americans of many types can, indeed, get along together as equals under the right social circumstances. These data come from the nation's military (Gupta, 2022). Research shows that there are numerous communities that boast emerging non-racist structures—from Killeen, Texas, to Fayetteville, North Carolina. What they have in common is that they are military towns.

Military leaders, following their World War II experience, realized that racial segregation threatened troop morale, cohesion, and efficiency. But many of the military bases were in the South and were following the old racist dictates of the region. Many were even named for Confederate generals: Lee, Jackson, Bragg, and Pickett.[4]

Using their power of command, officers simply began to change the racial norms. And we noted in Chapter 3, powerful norms can shape interracial behavior. For instance, local landlords who were refusing to rent to Black applicants were not allowed to rent to any military personnel. Landlords had to pledge in writing to rent to service members of all races.

In many, but not all, areas of life, the military has gradually become color-blind. And this new policy has produced a series of top Black leaders, including Benjamin Davis Sr., Benjamin Davis Jr., Colin Powell, and Lloyd Austin III. Restricting racial discrimination has allowed Black talent to rise to the top. And 94 Black American servicemen have earned the Medal of Honor. The American military offers a clear example of how strong and enforced norms can bring about lasting change in the nation's race relations.

While hardly perfect, the more open military norms have attracted Blacks into the U.S. Army—especially Black women.[5] Black service members fare substantially better than comparable Blacks on homeownership and household income, although not yet equal to that of White service members. Their children go to integrated schools and attain significantly higher test scores than comparable Black children in non-military schools. Black military families are far more likely to have Whites for friends and know interracial couples.

In short, the military's attempt to alter the nation's racist norms has been the most successful of all sectors of American life. It demonstrates that with enforced integrationist norms, Americans of all types are fully capable of living peacefully together in a largely non-racist nation.

Moreover, norms can change quickly. Racial intermarriage was outlawed in many states until the U.S. Supreme Court struck down those laws in *Loving v. Virginia* in 1967. And now both Black members of the Supreme Court have White spouses.

A Final Assessment

Answering the book's central question—*Is American racism declining?*—we can advance the following points:

---

[4] Changing the names of bases named for generals who had fought *against* the United States did not begin until the 21st century.

[5] Black women comprise roughly twice their population proportion among female active-duty service members (Gupta, 2022).

So, Has American Racism Declined? **177**

1. Yes, American racism is declining. This is true in particular for upper-status Black Americans and in politics. Important gains in higher education were also achieved until six members of the U.S. Supreme Court decided to dial back the clock to the 1950s.
2. But in many areas this decline is minimal at best. In economics, for example, income improvements have raised lower-status Blacks from dire poverty to a paycheck-to-paycheck situation on the brink of poverty. With older Whites tending to leave the labor force disproportionately, however, there may soon finally be positive changes in Black employment. Only minimal improvements for lower-status Blacks characterize medical and housing changes.
3. In criminal justice, it cannot be claimed that there is any improvement - in fact, there has even been some retrogression. Black incarceration rates have declined largely because so many prisoners were released during COVID-19. And police misconduct against Black citizens continues apace, despite enhanced national attention to the ongoing police murders of Black Americans.

This complex situation calls out for racial reparations if a genuine, across-the-board decline in American racism is ever to be achieved—the focus of the final chapter.

Sidebar 11.1 A Return to the Past

Recently I received a kind note from a resident of Omaha, Nebraska. She informed me that she had discovered my old educational television series, optimistically entitled *Epitaph for Jim Crow* (Pettigrew, 1962). I had not known that these 60-year-old shows were still available. My son, Mark, set them up for me on the television, and as I watched this blast from the past, I had a mixed reaction.

On the one hand, it was a pleasant surprise, even if a bit odd. Seeing myself 60 years younger was a nice reminder that I was once far more vigorous than I am now. But on the other hand, I realized what I was saying then is now banned six decades later in many parts of the nation.

No one in 1962 reviewed my scripts before I used them. I rendered abbreviated versions of my quite direct lectures from my Harvard race relations courses at that time. In addition to analyzing the history of racial lynching, I discussed racial discrimination in a variety of areas, similar to the approach of this book. Only several educational stations under threat in the Deep South refused to show the series. Otherwise, it was shown by stations throughout the nation—including Florida, Idaho, Oklahoma, Tennessee, and Iowa.

Yet today if teachers in these five states presented my shows or used the material in their classes, they could be summarily dismissed for defying the racist laws passed in these states in recent years. All five of these states now have placed severe limits on how

178   Anti-Black Racism in America

teachers can discuss American race relations. For example, Tennessee now decrees that teachers cannot teach that "an individual, by virtue of an individual's race or sex, is inherently privileged, racist, sexist, or oppressive, whether consciously or unconsciously" (Aldrich, 2021).

Here is one area in which there has been retrogression during the past six decades.

Chapter 12
The Need for Reparations

"[F]reedom is not enough. You do not wipe away the scars of centuries by saying: Now you go free . . . . You do not take a person who, for years, has been hobbled by chains and bring him to the starting line of a race and then say, 'you are free to compete with all the others,' and still justly believe that you have been completely fair."

This subtle appeal for Black reparations was part of President Lyndon Johnson's commencement address at Howard University on June 4, 1965.[1] More than half a century later, the topic is only now beginning to emerge in the national conversation.

"There is nothing wrong with Black people that ending racism can't solve." This assertion is often repeated in public discourse (Perry, 2020), but it paints an incomplete picture. As President Johnson made clear, if all direct racism suddenly and miraculously vanished, the effects of past racism would still prevail. Indirect discrimination, established by past direct discrimination, would remain. Johnson's analogy is with a track race. He suggests that even if all other aspects of the race were fair, the Black athlete, who had long been hobbled in chains, would have no fair chance of competing. If the race is to be truly fair, means must be taken to equalize the conditions of the two racers. In other words, initial adjustments—reparations—must occur first.

Credit Ta-Nehisi Coates (2014) with reviving discussion about reparations for Black Americans. His article in *The Atlantic* magazine reignited interest in the subject. Coates accurately centered his discussion on housing discrimination and leaned heavily on the social science literature on the topic. The MacArthur "genius" award winner concisely summarized the discriminatory phenomena discussed in Chapter 10: redlining, contract mortgages, discriminatory treatment of Black veterans' benefits, differential housing appraisals, and more. He did not specify how best to design a reparation program. And he spared his readers the depressing information about lynching and the most horrific maltreatments of Black Americans in the 1865–1940 era detailed by Blackmon (2008) in *Slavery by Another Name* and LeFlouria (2016) in *Chained in Silence*.

Instead, Coates humanized the drastic effects of discriminatory housing practices in the current lives of Black individuals in Chicago. His piece had a significant effect in large part because it was published in *The Atlantic*, a major magazine that

---

[1] The first draft of this memorial address was written by the ubiquitous Daniel Patrick Moynihan.

Anti-Black Racism in America. Thomas F. Pettigrew, Oxford University Press. © Oxford University Press (2025).
DOI: 10.1093/9780197803134.003.0013

180 Anti-Black Racism in America

attracts well-educated and influential White readers. The subject had previously been generally limited to commentators who lacked an extensive audience.

Reparations do indeed lie at the heart of the matter. Each of the previous chapters has offered evidence for a serious reconsideration of reparations for African Americans. If anything, when all realms are considered, the case for reparations is even stronger than what Coates advanced. Considerable change in American race relations has occurred over the past century, but it has not been as all-positive nor as all-encompassing as many White Americans would like to believe.

Although reparations have yet to arise as a major issue, they surely will be in the near future. The U.S. Census Bureau agrees; it is contemplating asking Black Americans if they are descendants of slaves (Hackman and Overberg, 2023). Many reactionary White Americans still believe the idea of reparations to be absurd. They conveniently forget that on numerous occasions the United States and individual states have indeed paid reparations to seriously mistreated minorities. We noted earlier that Oklahoma has considered partial reparations for the victims of the Tulsa massacre of 1921; Florida has paid reparations to the victims of the Rosewood massacre of 1923.

At the national level, Bilmes and Brooks (2022, p. 10) remind us that "the federal government in fact has a long history of providing compensation to people who have suffered harms of all kinds through no fault of their own." Their many examples range from those exposed to pesticides or nuclear radiation to those harmed by the loss of agricultural crops or the closure of factories and military bases. The government subsidizes no-fault flood insurance and agricultural insurance. And it insures bank deposits up to $250,000 per account. These varied reparations add up to billions of dollars paid to millions of citizens annually. The authors therefore conclude that "America is skilled in reparations" (p. 12). It is only when Black citizens are involved that critics suddenly rise up in vehement opposition.

The nation has twice paid reparations to minorities for past injustices. First, in 1946, the gross abuse of Native Americans was at least partially recognized. And there was much to be recognized—from routinely violated treaties to the senseless slaughter of hundreds of Lakota tribe members at Wounded Knee in 1890–1891. The program ultimately paid out about $1.3 billion to 176 recognized tribes—about $1,000 to each Native American.

The effects of these reparations were importantly shaped by how the 574 recognized tribes received the funds. Some tribes just let it all be paid out to the individual tribal members. Other tribes shrewdly directed at least some of the funds for structural improvements for the tribe as a whole—such as more land for the reservation, improved roads, and upgraded medical, agricultural, housing, and educational facilities. Numerous junior colleges were established.[2]

---

[2] There are now 35 accredited tribal colleges spread over 76 sites in the United States. Among the best known are Iḷisaġvik College in Barrow, Alaska; Diné College in Tsaile, Arizona; Saginaw Chippewa Tribal College in Mount Pleasant, Michigan; and Keweenaw Bay Ojibwa Community College in Baraga, Michigan.

The Need for Reparations **181**

Eighty years later, it is clear that it was these tribal-wide expenditures that made a lasting difference, not the payments to individual tribal members. Tribes that enhanced indigenous governance, like the Winnebago in northeastern Nebraska, have been particularly successful in their later economic development (Grucza, 2023). These structural reparations provide a valuable model for maximizing the effectiveness of future reparations.

Further payments to the tribes were legislated to facilitate climate relocation. This token follow-up to the 1946 legislation was inserted into the 2021 U.S. Infrastructure Bill. It gave the Bureau of Indian Affairs $216 million for climate resilience (Frank, 2022). This was especially needed by Alaskan tribes to finance voluntary relocation of whole villages threatened by flooding, as Alaska has suffered the greatest rise in average temperature of any American state.

The second major case of national reparations came in 1988, when the gross internment and mistreatment in World War II of loyal Japanese Americans was belatedly recognized. Following the unprovoked Japanese attack on Pearl Harbor on December 7, 1941, fear of sabotage mixed with established racist attitudes provoked the sudden internment of 120,000 people of Japanese heritage. More than half of those interned were children, and two-thirds were American citizens. Although there was *not one conviction* of a Japanese American for spying or committing espionage, citizens as well as non-citizens were herded up on short notice and sent to camps in isolated places throughout the West and Midwest. Many of them lost property that was never returned, or they had to sell what they had at cut-rate prices. It was one of the most serious breaches of the U.S. Constitution by the nation's government in American history.

Ironically, the large Japanese American population on Hawaii was not interned, although one small camp was set up to intern leaders of the local German, Italian, and Japanese communities. But no mass internment was instituted even though this was where the Japanese attack had taken place. Their labor was needed for the Hawaiian economy and the war effort. Once again, *no* convictions for sabotage or espionage by the island's Japanese American residents occurred.

After World War II, there was some publicly expressed guilt over the extreme ill treatment the loyal Japanese Americans had received. But it took years before restitution was granted—just as with Native Americans. The 1988 settlement called for $20,000 to be paid each living Japanese-American who had been in the internment camps (about $51,000 in 2023 dollars). Forty-three years late, this legislation did not cover the many internees who had died.

When the Reparation Act was announced, I had a moving conversation with an elderly Japanese-American friend. As a middle-aged married man with two young children in 1942, he and his family were forced to move to the Manzanar camp in a cold, barren, and isolated part of Southern California. "The most important thing for me was not the money," he said softly, "but that my country, which I have loved and always been loyal to, has finally said it is truly sorry for the wrong it did to my family so many years ago."

182 Anti-Black Racism in America

These cases demonstrate that reparations are neither a new nor a radical idea. I am confident that in the years ahead there will be some type of reparations for Black Americans. And I have a strong plea concerning the form it should take. Learning from the Native American example, Black reparations should not simply involve direct payments to individuals alone. Instead, reparations would be far more effective in the long run if a solid portion also focused on strengthening the structural realms of Black American society—in education, business, health, criminal justice, and housing. The design of such a program would have to be worked out carefully to maximize optimal interracial contact,[3] special aid to the poorest Black citizens, and the future growth of Black America's "piece of the pie."

As emphasized throughout this book, two particularly serious aspects of current American race relations need to be addressed: (1) the many barriers that restrain the ability of Black America to garner a sufficient wealth base and (2) the widespread lack of interracial contact. These acute domains should guide how reparations are designed. And since advances in housing integration respond to both of these needs, they should receive special attention.

Examples of such structural aid include: (1) business grants and loans for new start-up enterprises as well as for expanding current businesses, (2) grants for higher education, and (3) down-payment and "housing revitalization" grants along with property tax caps and settlements for prior predatory lending. For housing, the formerly redlined areas would be the strategic places to start. As Ray and Perry (2020) stress, such efforts will fail if they are not accompanied with effective enforcement of anti-discrimination policies.

Three reasons support the efficacy of structural payments as opposed to entirely individual grants.

1. In the long run, they are likely to be far more effective for future group development than cash payments, as in the Native American case.
2. Structural support aids Black Americans who have no slavery roots in the United States. The large contingent of West Indians in the Black American population, for example, have no history of slavery in the United States, yet they, too, have suffered from racial discrimination while in America. Direct payments would go only to the descendants of former American slaves. But structural payments would also benefit West Indians and recent African immigrants.
3. Structural payments are likely to be more acceptable to resistant Whites than the exclusive outright cash payments to individuals.

[3] Some worry that reparation funds going to predominantly Black institutions would necessarily further racial segregation. But that need not occur. Historically Black institutions already educate roughly twice the percentage of Whites compared to predominantly White universities that educate Black students.

Fox "News" and other far-right political sources have already tried to frighten Whites with forecasts of millions of dollars to go to individual Black Americans. Fox builds on White reluctance to support reparations for Black Americans. Chapter 1 noted that 81% of Whites in 2002 opposed making "cash payments to Black Americans who are descendants of slaves."

But there is a base of support among those people who are aware of the nation's racial history. Even in Detroit, scene of racial strife for a full century, 38% of Whites support reparative policies, according to survey research by the University of Michigan; 74% of Black Detroiters favored such policies, and 30% of Latinos did so (Benson and Simington, 2023; Slagter, 2023).

The same survey also uncovered a strong link between support for reparations and beliefs about Black slavery and poverty. Among respondents who were aware of the historical impacts of slavery and discrimination on Blacks today, members of all three groups were far more likely to support reparations for Black Americans: 73% of Detroiters who agree that the legacy of slavery and discrimination still affects Blacks support reparations, compared with only 30% of those who disagree. Likewise, among those who realize that the average income of Blacks is far below that of Whites, 75% back reparations, compared with only 14% who disagree.

Racists recognize this connection. When they denounce both critical race theory and the *New York Times* 1619 Project and demand they not be taught in schools, they offer clear proof that racists correctly realize the nation's history has a profound effect on how White Americans view the current state of race relations. This is a critical point. As part of what has been called a "collective willful ignorance," most White Americans have no idea about the precarious economic conditions of many Black people and the direct link of these conditions to slavery. Consequently, the idea of economic reparations understandably seems to them unfair and unwarranted. Why should the government give Black people funds when they have almost as much money as I have? Of course, in fact, Black Americans have on average only a small fraction of White income and wealth.

Anti-reparation Arguments

Three interrelated contentions are made in opposition to reparations for Black Americans: (1) it costs too much; (2) my family had nothing to do with slavery; (3) America should not be held liable for something that happened a century and a half ago. There are cogent answers to each of these resistant claims.

1. *It costs too much.* Whatever the final sum of Black reparations turns out to be, it will indeed be a large sum of money. However, this amount should be compared with other federal expenditures. Consider the loss in federal funds rendered by the 2017 tax law hailed by many Republicans as President Trump's greatest achievement. As mentioned earlier, the U.S. Joint Committee on Taxation estimates that the law cost

the federal treasury *$1.9 trillion over 10 years*. According to the nonpartisan Center for Budget and Policy Priorities (2019), its benefits went overwhelmingly to the nation's major corporations and richest individuals, who hardly needed reparations. The heavily minority poorest fifth of Americans received an average tax savings from the bill of $70 compared with $252,300 for the richest 0.1%.

Many of those in Congress who celebrated the 2017 handout to the wealthy were among the leaders of those who opposed reducing student loan debt and other measures that would benefit the poor on the grounds that the federal budget was "out of control"—a situation they themselves had created. They give hypocrisy an even worse name.

Between 2017 and early 2020, President Trump added to the nation's deficit *more than $2 trillion* in unfunded spending program expansions desired by the Republican Party. Like the massive tax cuts, these programs largely benefited large corporations and the wealthy. Later, COVID-19 expenditures added several trillion more to the deficit (Rampell, 2023). Huge federal programs are not new. Right-wing concerns arise when Black people and the poor are the beneficiaries.

In any event, a modest wealth tax can pay for reparations, as discussed below. In the proposed plan, 99.9% of Americans would not be contributing a penny to the reparation funds. Nevertheless, we can be sure that opponents of any reparations will seize on the amount of money involved without comparing it to the routine federal handouts to major corporations and the very rich.

2. *My family had nothing to do with slavery*. "My grandparents did not arrive as immigrants to America until half a century after slavery had been outlawed. So why do I owe anything to Black people?" This complaint suggests that reparations should be for all of the discrimination against Black Americans—not just for slavery.

Two direct counters are relevant here. First, when my six-year-old immigrant mother arrived at Ellis Island in 1904, she had to accept America as it existed—its dark blights as well as its greater opportunities than Scotland offered. Second, she benefited like all other White Americans from the immense, but largely unrewarded, economic contribution that Blacks have made to the nation's overall economy—from cotton and tobacco crops to sports, entertainment, and wartime military service.

3. *America should not be held liable for something that happened a century and a half ago. Afterall, none of us alive today is personally responsible for slavery*. This was explicitly argued in Congress in 2019 by Senate Majority Leader Mitch McConnell of Kentucky. Born in Alabama and raised until 14 in the Deep South, McConnell has apparently maintained the racial views prevalent there in the 1950s when he was growing up.[4]

Soon after the senator made this attack on reparations for Black Americans, Ta-Nehisi Coates answered McConnell with a precise, 800-word reply. Borrowing from his earlier article in *The Atlantic*, Coates tore into McConnell's argument

---

[4] McConnell also made a revealing Freudian slip when he claimed that Black Americans cast votes at rates similar to "Americans."

on both logical and factual grounds (*The New York Times*, 2019). He pointed out that McConnell was arguing that "American accounts are somehow bound by the lifetime of its generations." Should we not continue to honor treaties that were signed 200 years ago despite no one being alive today who signed those treaties?

Factually, the Kentucky senator conveniently overlooks the enormous financial contributions that Black people have made over the years to the national economy—contributions that they were cut out of sharing. Even by 1836, almost half of the American economy derived directly or indirectly from the cotton produced by the more than one million slaves who planted and picked it. Add to that the billions of dollars taken from Black citizens in the years when McConnell was residing in Alabama and Georgia. We have reviewed this throughout the book—from redlining to reduced property assessments.

A Two-Tier Reparations Program

A strong case can be made for a two-tier reparations program: (1) a direct reparations cash program for those whose families experienced slavery in the United States and (2) a larger structural program aimed at shoring up the key institutions of Black America.

To propose such efforts is far easier than actually working out the details of how they should be designed for maximum effectiveness. Fortunately, the Duke University economist William Darity Jr. and his wife, A. Kirsten Mullen (2022), in their book, *From Here to Equality*, provide us with an initial roadmap to consider the multiple issues involved. First, the authors make a spirited case for the necessity of reparations—emphasizing many of the points covered in previous chapters of this book. Then, in their final chapter, they discuss in detail the thorny practical issues of implementation.

They propose the establishment of a reparations supervisory board to manage the program. Payments should be spread over a number of years, making it possible, by their calculations, to pay for the program without raising taxes. Cash payments to the descendants of American slaves would be based on what it would take to close the wealth gap with White Americans.

Different estimates of what was lost in wages while a slave minus their maintenance costs have been proposed. Here different assumptions, as one would suspect, lead to quite diverse estimates. And determining eligibility is made difficult by the fact that the 1850 and 1860 censuses did not list the full names of slaves, only their first name under each slaveowner's name. Nonetheless, the Darity-Mullen estimate is about $267,000 per person for eligible persons.

A direct tax on wealth, similar to that used by other prosperous nations, could cover the cost of an effective reparations program without taxing the middle class or poor. France, Norway, Spain, and Switzerland have such taxes now.

186 Anti-Black Racism in America

According to the Madison Trust Company (2023), there were 759 American billionaires in November 2022 with a combined total wealth of *$4.48 trillion!*[5] Consider a rough, back-of-the-envelope demonstration of how to raise a trillion dollars for reparations. By 2026, it is reasonable to expect there will be about 1,000 American billionaires with a total wealth of at least $5 trillion. Just a 5% wealth tax for one year would yield roughly $250 billion and for each of four years could yield roughly $1 trillion for reparations. Assuming a reasonably strong economy over this decade, the very wealthy could easily acquire more funds than the tax would require. That you can raise a trillion dollars relatively painlessly is made possible by the fact that America is the richest nation on earth, but suffers from an enormous and shameful maldistribution of wealth between rich and poor.

Indeed, many (certainly not all) billionaires have argued that they should be taxed more heavily. Oxfam International (2024) reports that nearly three-quarters of millionaires polled in the G20 countries support higher taxes on wealth, and over half think extreme wealth is a "threat to democracy." In the United States, Warren Buffett and Bill Gates in particular have called for higher taxes on the rich.

Since many of the Black recipients of these payments would make immediate use of the funds—reducing their debt, buying a house, and so on—the reparation funds would help stimulate the national economy for everyone. Unfortunately, however, given the nation's truly humongous imbalance of wealth, these funds would not make a substantial dent in America's disparity between the rich and the poor.

Safeguarding the Reparations

Using the Holocaust Museum's "Never Forget" campaign as a model, Darity and Mullen also urge that their proposed reparations supervisory board offer a financial management curriculum for public schools and other organizations. This effort would help compensation recipients set up their accounts safely and efficiently.

The Structural Component

Just as structural funds were granted to Israel to aid its economic stability after World War II, a second structural leg of compensation is needed. Here are some possibilities for such efforts. (1) Grants to major Black-owned banks could specify that they should make every effort to replace the need to use such predatory loan providers as check-cashing shops. (2) With their financial foundations enhanced, historically

---

[5] A trillion dollars equals 1,000 billion dollars.

Black colleges could be asked to reduce their tuition and other fees. (3) Housing subsidies could begin with those areas that were redlined in the 1930s, where the need is greatest; eventually, reparation efforts must go beyond these especially maligned areas to the broader housing market where racist effects are also prevalent. In short, reparation benefits to structural institutions should include provisions that directly aid the Black individuals that use them.

Black American Attitudes toward Reparations

A national survey of Black Americans conducted by the Pew Research Center in 2022 sought to learn what they thought of reparations (Cox and Edwards, 2022). Most Blacks correctly believe that the legacy of slavery still shapes how they are treated today either a great deal (55%) or a fair amount (30%). And they favor many types of structural payments in the form of educational scholarships and financial aid for starting or expanding a business and for buying or remodeling a home. Poorer Blacks emphasize cash payments to individuals to reduce debt.

While 81% of the Black respondents believed that the federal government had the greatest responsibility for the repayments, many also held culpable other institutions that had benefited from slavery. Among those are businesses and banks (76%), colleges and universities (63%), and descendants of slave-owning families (60%).

But 82% of the respondents think that such reparations to slave descendants is "a little or not at all likely." This is consistent with their general pessimism about other racial changes: 67% believe positive racial changes to the prison system is unlikely; 58% doubt there will be positive reforms of how the police treat Black people; and 44% think equality for Black people in America is unlikely. These Black pessimists are obviously basing their predictions on the slow progress they have witnessed throughout their lives.

In brief, Black Americans understandably believe positive racial change in general and reparations in particular will be difficult to achieve in the future. To be sure, it will be a tough sell given that the far right in American politics is constantly working to restrict Black American rights and opportunities. In Chapter 5, we discussed the well-funded campaign to end affirmative action in the nation's universities, aimed especially at limiting the already small number of Black students at leading American universities.

Moreover, we have recorded the development of similar opposition to even the most modest attempts of the federal government to address past racial discrimination. Chapter 1 on White racial attitudes mentioned that a majority of White Americans still resist governmental action to combat racial inequality. Recall that when asked about government aid for Blacks, 58% of White respondents in both 1975 and 2008 favored "no special treatment." Hence, there was no change on this critical item over a period that otherwise witnessed considerable social change.

The very nadir of these blatantly racist efforts involves the battered and declining group of Black small farmers. Stephen Miller gained notoriety as the anti-immigrant assistant to President Trump and the architect of the heartless immigrant family separation policy at the Mexican border. With "dark money" made possible by Trump appointments and wealthy supporters, Miller founded the America First legal organization. Its often successful tactic is to file lawsuits to block racial progress with a Trump-appointed, far-right judge in Texas (Reinhard and Dawsey, 2022).

One of the group's first actions was to stop a small federal program to support women- and minority-owned restaurants in 2022. Then it turned on Black farmers. These farmers possess only 2% of the nation's agricultural land. They have long been ignored by the U.S. Department of Agriculture for loans and other federal help to support agriculture, the lion's share of which has gone to mammoth agricultural corporations. In the 1920s, Blacks represented about 14% of all farmers, most of them in the South; today they comprise just slightly more than 1% of all farmers.

To help this beleaguered and disappearing group, the Biden administration proposed a small program of aid. In effect, this action was a modest reparation for a group that has been constantly discriminated against for a century and a half. Claiming, perhaps facetiously, to be combating "anti-White bigotry," Miller and his group argued that this small aid program discriminated against White farmers and corporations. Past history played no part in their overtly racist reasoning. We can expect such blatantly racist efforts to continue into the future.

Yet such stout resistance to even the most minimal racial reparation efforts should not be allowed to keep the nation from considering reparations in a larger context. The national consensus on race may continue to change enough for them to be seriously considered in the future. This would be especially possible if the reparations were completely financed by the super-wealthy. If someone had claimed in 2003 that a Black American (much less someone with "Hussein" as his middle name) would win the presidency twice over the next decade, mass-media pundits would not have taken it seriously. Racial matters in the United States can change rapidly—some positive changes and others negative.

The Case for Black Reparations Is Strong

The case for reparations is supported by the data described in the previous chapters covering each major sector of American society. Traditionally segregated, inferior schools have seriously undercut the ability of Black Americans to accumulate wealth across a century and a half (Chapters 2 and 4). So have severe political restrictions that have kept Blacks from electing candidates who could develop helpful legislation (Chapter 8).

Recall, too, in Chapter 4, how Blackmon (2008) and LeFlouria (2016) demonstrated that from 1865 to 1941 the White South found ways essentially to re-enslave

The Need for Reparations **189**

many Blacks—a widespread phenomenon that kept southern Blacks from gaining wealth while enriching even the U.S. Steel Corporation. Continued employment discrimination added to the problem. Poorer health facilities not only lowered the Black lifespan but also restricted the opportunity to amass wealth (Chapter 7). And, finally, residential discrimination has limited Black homeownership—a major source of White wealth (Chapter 10).

On top of all this, we have also noted how even federal programs, such as veterans benefits, have systematically discriminated against Blacks while helping millions of White veterans to enter the middle class.

Perhaps the most blatant and easily remedied example involves the Freedman's Bank fraud (Van Tol, 2024). It was established in 1865 specifically to help liberated ex-slaves as part of Reconstruction efforts. But massive White fraud led to its closure eight years later, with tens of thousands of Blacks losing all they had invested. Van Tol points out that the bank's meticulous records have been "perfectly preserved"; the names, ages, occupations, and family members of the depositors are known. They lost about $3 million, which Van Tol calculates to be about $125 billion today. Here is an easy first step in reparations that the U.S. Congress could make to start the process.

When viewed in full perspective, then, the justification for Black reparations can be forcefully made on social, economic, and moral grounds. Some White Americans have long realized this. Even at the close of the Civil War, Union general William Sherman, after his "march to the sea" through Georgia and South Carolina, confiscated 400,000 acres of valuable coastal land for Black families. He also thought each family should receive a mule from among those animals that survived the war—a promise that became known as "40 acres and a mule." Except for some of South Carolina's Sea Islands, occupied by the Gullah people, Sherman's promise was never fulfilled. Instead, slave owners in some southern states were paid compensation for their lost property: their former slaves.

Not until the resounding 1929 stock market crash leading to the 1932 election of President Franklin Roosevelt did another possibility for Black reparations arise. The FDR administration's policies that intended to alleviate poverty cost about $50 billion—roughly more than $50 trillion in today's dollars (Ray and Perry, 2020). His New Deal did pay off for White Americans, but we saw earlier how most Black veterans failed to get the G.I. Bill's benefits that their White counterparts received, and the Social Security Act rejected domestic and farm workers and thus excluded 60% of Black Americans. This was not corrected until the 1950s.

We have also noted the wealth-restricting effects of convict leasing, redlining in housing discrimination, and restrictive covenants. It is impossible to estimate precisely the enormous losses in wealth that these multiple processes of discrimination caused. The estimates vary widely under different assumptions, but obviously the true amount is enormous. Brookings Institute research suggests that houses in urban Black neighborhoods are on average undervalued by $48,000 each. This amounts to $156 billion that Black homeowners would receive on average if their homes were priced at fair market rates (Ray and Perry, 2020).

The First Glimmers of Genuine Consideration of Racial Reparations

California is the first state to consider reparations for its Black citizens. Admittedly, California is presently the most politically liberal state in the nation, but just a generation ago its voters passed a referendum that ended the use of affirmative action in higher education. And yet in 2020, the state established the California Reparations Task Force, charged with recommending how to make a state reparation program optimally fair and effective.

The Task Force soon found that such a program is difficult to design. It must recommend time frames, payment calculations, and residency requirements. A few flagrantly discriminatory acts have been corrected. For instance, one Black family had owned valuable beach property in Manhattan Beach, California, that was seized without compensation through the use of eminent domain. Once returned, the family soon sold it for $20 million. But many other situations, such as Black losses from homelessness and mass incarceration, are difficult to calculate.[6]

Once the Task Force rendered its report in 2023, the legislature had to act on its recommendations. The Task Force offered extensive historical support for its conclusions, and it stressed structural support for Black housing and businesses and not simply payments to individuals. Opposition immediately arose—some of it from other minorities who felt left out, although they had never endured slavery and its aftereffects.

Beyond California, other reparation efforts have been made in specific circumstances. We noted in Chapter 5 that small compensation programs have, in the past, been established to atone for such specific medical malpractices as the Tuskegee Syphilis study. Other reparation attempts have emerged throughout the nation. Maryland's general assembly passed the Harriet Tubman Community Investment Act, which atones for the ravages of slavery by focusing on homeownership, education, and business ownership (Ray and Perry, 2020). The Virginia state legislature required five of its state universities to compensate Black Virginians for slave labor used in campus construction. The Princeton and Virginia seminaries together with Georgetown University now provide full educational support for the descendants of slaves.

Evanston, Illinois, home to Northwestern University, decided in 2019 to establish a $10 million fund to compensate for the city's long history of housing discrimination (Felton, 2023). The funds were to come from a cannabis sales tax. When this proved insufficient, the town added a real estate transfer tax. But the program has been slow to get off the ground. By 2023, only $400,000 had been disbursed to 16 claimants—$25,000 to each. Paying down mortgages was one of the biggest uses of the funds by the recipients.

---

[6] Not all such situations have been settled. The Burgess family claims their family owns land in California's Marshall Gold Discovery State Park that was also seized by eminent domain, but park authorities dispute the claim (Sanchez and Bennett, 2022).

The Need for Reparations   **191**

Such programs are sharply opposed by such right-wingers as Richard Epstein of the Hoover Institute. They point to poor White families who are also in need, but they do not offer proposals that would help both races. Far-right legal organizations go further. Inspired by the U.S. Supreme Court's striking down affirmative action in college admissions, Judicial Watch has filed a lawsuit claiming that Evanston's modest program discriminates against the town's Whites (Felton, 2024). The counter-argument is that the program is not for Black people per se, but for those whose families earlier suffered from housing discrimination. Had White citizens also suffered housing inequality, they, too, could have been included.

Small programs like Evanston's are also criticized by longtime advocates of reparations, such as Darity. He worries that such small programs act as "detours" that deflect efforts to achieve national reparations. But it is also possible that these initial programs start the ball rolling. They raise the complications involved with reparations and initiate attempts to address them.

Include Poor Whites?

Some observers believe that to win acceptance, reparations for Black Americans must also include needed aid for the nation's White poor. Andrew Delbanco (2022), a Columbia University English professor, advanced this view. The problem with this position is that it would diminish the core point of Black reparations. As my Japanese American friend stressed, a critical component of reparations is that the country is saying unequivocally on the record that it deeply regrets its past maltreatment of the group.

Perhaps a compromise can be managed. When the reparations action is announced, other changes could be simultaneously made that would benefit the poor of all races but not labeled as part of the reparations for Black Americans. An example would be free tuition for all at two-year colleges—a prospect already under consideration in Washington, D.C. About 70% of all college students already have an educational loan. It would create the biggest investment in raising the educational level of Americans since the highly successful 1944 G.I. Bill of Rights from which Blacks were largely excluded.

A major question involves who should receive reparations. Darity believes that only those who have shown over the years *a consistent pattern of Black identification* should be included. Birth and census records, even DNA testing could be employed if needed.

Ray and Perry (2020) note that New Jersey's senator Cory Booker, who introduced the first reparations legislature in the U.S. Senate, discovered through DNA that his lineage stemmed from Sierra Leone. If DNA were taken into consideration, the two Obamas would be treated differently. Michelle Obama would fully qualify for all benefits, as she is descended from a South Carolinian slave family. But Barack, with an African father and White mother, could not claim benefits. You can readily see how

192 Anti-Black Racism in America

such determinations become complex. But the principal target should always be the descendants of the 12.5 million Blacks who were forced against their will to come to America as slaves.

Thinking Bigger Still

Some observers insist we consider more expansive programs, such as universal basic income (Howard, 2023; Boyce, 2020) and Alaska's "universal property."[7] These efforts would meet Delbanco's contention that Whites must be included in any such effort. And both would help Blacks disproportionately.

One innovative possibility involves "baby bonds." Darity, as an economist, focuses on securing a future capital base for Blacks. Darrick Hamilton and Darity (2010) propose that every child born in America be given at birth a trust fund. They suggest an average of $25,000, with poor children receiving far more than the children of the rich. This would begin to close the wealth gap across groups by giving all children a nest egg with which to begin their lives. And we have noted that the wealth gap is extensive. Census data for 2010 shows that 38% of Black households and 35% of Hispanic households have *no* financial assets whatsoever. This compares with 12% of Asian households and 14% of White households.

This program by itself would not close the gaping wealth differentials, but it would offer a promising start. Political conservatives would likely oppose such a program on the suspicion that it would encourage the poor to have more children.

Based on this book's analyses, I urge having a large part of the reparations go for lasting structural changes: racially integrated housing, advanced educational opportunities, improved medical access, and small business development. But the voices of the descendants of slaves must also be heard and considered in drawing up the final legislation.

Universal Basic Income Programs

Basic income programs have received more public attention than Black reparations. Black citizens would disproportionately benefit from such programs, but they are different from Black reparations in their direct effects on racist structures. Basic income efforts would not, for example, directly attack housing discrimination.

In addition to successful tests and programs throughout the world, pilot Basic Universal Income programs have been widely and effectively tested in Atlanta; Baltimore; Columbia, South Carolina; Compton and Stockton, California; Denver;

---

[7] Alaska's universal income fund, paid with mining and oil revenues, provides from $1,000 to $2,000 annually to every woman, man, and child in the state. It began in 1982, and it has had no effect on employment. It is a small version of a universal basic income plan—which has been successfully established in Finland and other nations.

Gainesville; Houston; Los Angeles; New Orleans; New York City; St. Louis; St. Paul; and Shreveport.[8]

Although these pilot tests vary considerably, their results have been largely positive and consistent. For example, the vast majority of recipients do not spend the money on tobacco and drugs—revealing the old reactionary canard to be false. Instead, people overwhelmingly spend guaranteed income to pull themselves out of poverty, to improve their mental and physical health, to extend child care, and to pay down debt. Many use the funds to further their education and enhance their job skills. Nor do they stop working—falsifying another canard.

Early in 2022, an expanded child tax credit was enacted and provided a national test of cash aid to the nation's poor. Up from $2,000 per child annually, parents received as much as $3,600 per child. Moreover, parents received the money even if their tax liability was less than the credit. The positive results of this mini-guaranteed income surprised even its advocates. It alone reduced the child poverty rate by almost 30%. And since income equality leads to reduced crime rates and drug abuse, the public funds spent on such a program are soon repaid handsomely in later reduced costs. The issue here for critics is that the program's cost is paid up front, while the savings occur later.

But *every* Republican senator (including Utah's Mitt Romney), joined by Democratic senator Joe Manchin from the nation's eighth poorest state (West Virginia), refused to extend the program. The child poverty rate increased immediately—41% in the following month. This startling result caused Congress later to reconsider the tax credit, although Republicans continued to oppose it.

A Final Word

If and when substantial national reparations for Black Americans are enacted, that will be the day we can with confidence finally declare that *American anti-Black racism has indeed significantly declined.*

---

[8] For an excellent overview of these various programs, see Greenwell (2022).

Bibliography

Aaronson, R., Fabor, J., Hartley, D., Mazumder, B., and Sharkey, D. (2021). The long-run effects of the 1930s HOLC "redlining" maps on place-based measures of economic opportunity and socioeconomic success. *Regional Science and Urban Economics, 86.* Article 103622.

Aberson, C. L. (2015). Positive intergroup contact, negative intergroup contact, and threat as predictors of cognitive and affective dimensions of prejudice. *Group Processes and Intergroup Relations, 18*(6), 743–760.

Acemoglu, D., and Jackson, M. O. (2017). Social norms and the enforcement of laws. *Journal of the European Economic Association, 15*(2), 245–295.

Acevedo-Garcia, D. (2001). Zip-code level risk factors for tuberculosis: Neighborhood environment and residential segregation in New Jersey. 1985–1992. *American Journal of Public Health, 91*(5), 734–741.

Acs, G. (2013). *The Moynihan report revisited.* Washington, D.C.: The Urban Institute.

Adesogan, O., Zavner, J. A., and Beach, S. R. H. (2021). Covid-19 stress and the health of Black Americans in the rural South. *Clinical Psychological Science, 10*(6), 1111–1128.

Admon, A. J., Iwashina, T. J., Kamphuis, L. A., Gundel, S. J., Sehetya, S. K., and Peltan, I. D. (2023). Assessment of symptom, disability, and financial trajectories in patients hospitalized for Covid-19 at 6 months. *JAMA Network Open, 6*(2), e2255795.

Adorno, T. W., Frenkel-Brunswik, E., Levinson, D. J., and Sanford, N. (1950). *The authoritarian personality.* New York: Harper & Row.

Ager, P., Boustan, L. P., and Eriksson, K. (2019). The intergenerational effects of a large wealth shock: White Southerners after the Civil War. National Bureau of Economic Research. Retrieved February 7, 2023. http://www.nber.org/papers/w25700.

Alba, R., Rumbant, R. G., and Marotz, K. (2005). A distorted nation: Perceptions of racial/ethnic group sizes and attitudes toward immigrants and other minorities. *Social Forces, 84*(2), 901–919.

Aldrich, M. W. (November 19, 2021). Tennessee nails down rules for disciplining teachers, withholding money from schools that teach banned concepts about racism. Retrieved 12.05/2024. https://www.chalkbeat.org/tennessee/2021/11/19/21/2435/crt-tennessee-rules-

Alexander, K. L., Rich, S., and Thacker, H. (March 9, 2022). The hidden billion-dollar cost of repeated police misconduct. *The Washington Post,* Retrieved March 20, 2022. https://www.washingtonpost.com/investigations/interactive/2022/police-misconduct-repeated-settlements/.

Alexander, M. (2012). *The New Jim Crow: Mass incarceration in the age of colorblindness.* Revised edition. New York: New Press.

Allen, T., and Glover, G. (June 17, 2022). Opinion: 101 BCUs get nearly 7 times less money than 1 other school. That must change. *The Washington Post,* Retrieved September 13, 2022.

Allport, G. W. (1954). *The nature of prejudice.* Reading, MA: Addison Wesley.

Allport, G. W. (1958). *The nature of prejudice.* Garden City, NY: Doubleday Anchor.

Allport, G. W., and Kramer, B. M. (1946). Some roots of prejudice. *Journal of Psychology, 22,* 9–39.

Bibliography 195

Alsan, M., Durvasula, M., Gupta, H., Schwartzstein, J., and Williams, H. L. (2022). Representation and extrapolation: Evidence from clinical trials. NBER Working Paper Series.

Ambinder, M. (2009). Race over? *Atlantic Monthly, 303* (1), 62–65.

American Civil Liberties Union News. (2016). Marijuana arrests by the numbers. *80*(1).

American Civil Liberties Union News. (2023). The on-going fight against racial profiling. *87*(1), 1, 3.

American Community Survey. (2021). People without health insurance coverage by race and Hispanic origin. Retrieved December 22, 2022. https://www.census.gov/newsroom/press-releases/2022/health-insurance-by-race.html.

Anastasio, P., Bachman, B., Gaertner, S., and Dovidio, J. (1997). Categorization, recategorization and common ingroup identity. In R. Spears, P. J. Oakes, N. Ellemers, and S. A. Haslam (eds.), *The social psychology of stereotypes and group life.* Oxford: Blackwell, 236–256.

Anderson, K. F., and Ray-Warren, D. (2022). Racial-ethnic residential clustering and early Covid-19 vaccine allocations in five urban Texas counties. *Journal of Health and Social Behavior, 63*(4), 472–490.

Arnadottir, K., Lolliot, S., Brown, R., and Hewstone, M. (2018). Positive and negative intergroup contact: Interaction not symmetry. *European Journal of Social Psychology, 48*(6), 784–800.

Aronson, D., Faber, J., Hartley, D., Mazumder, B., and Sharkey, P. (2021). The long-run effects of the 1930s HOLC "redlining" maps on place-based measures of economic opportunity and socioeconomic success. *Regional Science and Urban Economics.* Retrieved July 12, 2022. https://doi.org/10.1016/regsciurbeco.2020.103622.

Artiga, S., Damico, A., and Garfield, R. (2015). The impact of the coverage gap for adults in states not expanding Medicare by race and ethnicity. The Kaiser Commission on Medicaid and the Uninsured. Retrieved September 25, 2022. http://kff.org/disparities-policy/issue-brief/the-impact-of-the-coverage-gap—in-states-not-expanding-medicaid-by-race-and-ethnicity/.

Awad, G. H., Cokley, K., and Ravitch, J. (2005). Attitudes toward affirmative action: A comparison of color-blind versus modern racist attitudes. *Journal of Applied Social Psychology, 35*(7), 1384–1399.

Bagci, S. C., and Gungor, H. (2019). Associations between perceived positive and negative parental contact and adolescents' intergroup contact experiences. *International Journal of Intercultural Relations, 69,* 76–86.

Bagci, S. C, Husnu, S., Turnuklu, A., and Tercan, M. (2021). Do I really want to engage in contact? Volition as a new dimension of intergroup contact. *European Journal of Social Psychology, 51*(2), 269–284.

Baker, P. E. (1934). *Negro-White adjustment.* New York: Association Press.

Baldus, D., Pulaski, C., and Woodworth, G. (1983). Comparative review of death sentences: An empirical study of the Georgia experience. *Journal of Criminal Law and Criminology, 74*(3), 661–753.

Baldus, D., Woodworth, G., Zuckerman, D., and Weiner, N. A. (1998). Racial discrimination and the death penalty in the post-Furman era: An empirical and legal overview with recent findings from Philadelphia. *Cornell Law Review, 83*(6), 1638–1770.

Barlow, R. K., Paolini, S., Pedersen, A., Hornsey, M. J., Radke, H. R. M., Harwood, J., Rubin, M. and Sibley, C. G. (2012). The contact caveat: Negative contact predicts increased prejudice more than positive contact predicts reduced prejudice. *Personality & Social Psychology Bulletin, 38,* 1629–1643.

Baumgartner, F. R., Christiani, L., Epp, D. A., Roach, K., and Shoub, K. (2017). Racial disparities in traffic stop outcomes. *Duke Forum for Law and Social Change, 9,* 21–53.

196 Anti-Black Racism in America

Baumgartner, F. R., Epp, D. A., and Shoub, K. (2018). *Suspect citizens: What twenty million traffic stops tells us about policing and race.* New York: Cambridge University Press.

Bavli, I., and Jones, D. S. (2022). Race correction and the X-ray machine—the controversy over increased radiation doses for Black Americans in 1968. *New England Journal of Medicine, 10,* 947–952.

BBC News. (2007). First French racism poll released. Retrieved February 20, 2023. https://news.bbc.co.uk/2/hi/europe/6317799/stm.

Becker, J. C., Wright, S. C., Lubensky, M.E., and Zhou, S. (2013). Friend or ally: Whether cross-group contact undermines collective action depends on what advantaged group members say (or don't say). *Personality and Social Psychology Bulletin, 39*(4), 442–455.

Beelmann, A., and Heinemann, K. S. (2014). Preventing prejudice and improving intergroup attitudes: A meta-analysis of child and adolescent training programs. *Journal of Applied Developmental Psychology, 35*(1), 10–24.

Beirich, H., and Potok, M. (2008). Silver lining. *Intelligence Report, 131,* 15–17.

Bell, J. (2008). The Fair Housing Act and extra-legal terror. *Indiana Law Review, 41*(3), 537–553.

Bell, S. B., Farr, R., Ofosu, E., Hehman, E., and DeWall, C. N. (2021). Implicit bias predicts less willingness and less frequent adoption of Black children more than explicit bias. *The Journal of Social Psychology, 163*(4), 554–565.

Benedict, R. (1940). *Race, science and politics.* New York: Viking Press.

Benns, W. (September 2015). American slavery, reinvented. *The Atlantic Magazine.* Retrieved January 12, 2023. https://www.theatlantic.com/business/archieves/2015/09/prison-labor.

Benson, E., and Simington, J. (2023). *Collective remembrance and Detroiters' views toward racial inequity.* Ann Arbor: Center for Racial Justice of the University of Michigan.

Berger, M., Lund, M. J., and Brawley, O. W. (2007). Racial disparities in lung cancer. *Current Problems in Cancer, 31*(3), 202–210.

Biesanz, J., and Smith, L. M. (1951). Race relations of Panama and the Canal Zone. *American Sociological Review, 57,* 7–14.

Bilmes, L., and Brooks, C. W. (2022). The United States pays reparations every day—just not to Black America. Kennedy School, Harvard University. Retrieved February 21, 2023. https://hks.harvard.edu/faculty-research/policycast/us-pays-reparations-every-day - just not to Black America.

Binder, J., Zagefka, H., Brown, R., Funke, F., Kessler, T., Mummendey, A., Maquil, A., Demoulin, S., and Leyens, J.-P. (2009). Does contact reduce prejudice or does prejudice reduce contact? A longitudinal test of the contact hypothesis among majority and minority groups in three different European countries. *Journal of Personality and Social Psychology, 96*(4), 843–856.

Bishop, S. R., Lay, M., Shapiro, S. L., Carlson, L. E., Anderson, N. D., Cadomy, J., Segal, Abbey,S., Michael, S., Velting, D., and Devins, G. M. (2006). Mindfulness: A proposed operational definition. *Clinical Psychology—Science and Practice, 11,* 230–241.

Biskupic, J. (2020). How Ruth Bader Ginsburg is trying to check the conservative majority. CNN News, January 8. American Law and Economics Association Annual Meetings, paper 13. Retrieved December 22, 2021.

Bjerk, D. (2006). The effect of segregation on crime rates. *Semantic Scholar.* Retrieved November 5, 2020. https://www.semanticscholar.org/paper/The-Effect-of-Segregation/on/crime/rates.

Blackmon, D. A. (2008). *Slavery by another name: The re-enslavement of Black Americans from the Civil War to World War II.* New York: Anchor.

Blackmun, H. (1978). Opinion in Regents of the University of California v. Bakke, 438, U.S. 265.

Blakemore, E. (July 16, 2023). Historic redlining linked to worse cardiovascular health for veterans. *The Washington Post*. Retrieved July 20, 2023. https://www.washingtonpost.com/wellness/2023/07/16/redlining-racism-heart-kidney-disease.

Bobo, L. D. (1989). Keeping the lynchpin in place: Testing multiple sources of opposition to residential integration. *Revue Internationale de Psychologie Sociale, 2*(3), 305–323.

Bobo, L. D., Charles, C. Z., Krysan, M., and Simmons, A. D. (2012). The *real* record on racial attitudes. In P. V. Marsden (ed.), *Social trends in American life*. Princeton, NJ: Princeton University Press, 38–83.

Bobo, L. D., Dawson, M. C., and Johnson, D. (2001). Enduring two-ness. *Public Perspective, 11* (May–June), 12–16.

Boin, J., Fuochi, G., and Voci, A. (2020). Deprovincialization as a key correlate of ideology, prejudice, and intergroup contact. *Personality and Individual Differences, 157*, 1–10.

Borger, J. (2001). Jeb Bush blamed for unfair Florida election. *The Guardian*, June 6. Retrieved August 22, 2023. https://www.theguardian.com/world/2001/jun/06/uselections2000.usa.

Bositis, D. A. (2001). Generational shift among Black elected officials. *Focus* (Joint Center for Political and Economic Studies), *29*(7), 5–6.

Bositis, D. A. (2003). Black elected officials reach historic highs: Women drive the increase. *Focus* (Joint Center for Political and Economic Studies), *31*(6), 3–4.

Boyce, J. K. (November 28, 2020). The case for "universal property." *Scientific American*. Retrieved January 4, 2023. https://www.scientifcamerican.com/articles/the-case-for-universal-property.

Braddock, J. H., II. (1980). The perpetuation of segregation across levels of education: A behavioral assessment of the contact hypothesis. *Sociology of Education, 53*(3), 178–186.

Braddock, J. H., II, and Dawkins, M. P. (1984). Long-term effects of school desegregation on southern blacks. *Sociological Spectrum, 4*(4), 365–381.

Brameld, T. (1946). *Minority problems in the public schools*. New York: Harper.

Bramley, D., Herbert, P., Jackson, R., and Chassin, M. (2004). Indigenous disparities in disease-specific mortality, a cross-country comparison: New Zealand, Australia, Canada, and the United States. *New Zealand Medical Journal, 117*(1207), U1215.

Braxton, G. (November 1, 2022). How Hollywood turned a "blind eye" to Emmitt Till: Inside a troubled 67-year history. *Los Angeles Times*. Retrieved February 19, 2023. https://www.losangelestimes.com/entertainment-arts/movies/.

Brewer, J. (February 11, 2023). Long maligned, the Black quarterback emerges as an NFL standard. *The Washington Post*. https://www.washingtonpost.com/sports/2023/02/11/black-quarterback.

Brewer, M. B. (2008*)*. Deprovincialization: Social identity complexity and outgroup acceptance. In U. Wagner, L. Tropp, G. Finchilescu, and C. Tredoux (eds.), *Improving intergroup relations: Building on the legacy of Thomas F. Pettigrew*. Oxford: Blackwell, 160–176.

Brewer, M. B., and Miller, N. (1984). Beyond the contact hypothesis: Theoretical perspectives on desegregation. In N. Miller and M. B. Brewer (eds.), *Groups in contact: The psychology of desegregation*. Orlando, FL: Academic Press, 281–302.

Brophy, I. N. (1945). The luxury of anti-Negro prejudice. *Public Opinion Quarterly, 9*, 456–466.

Brown, R., and Hewstone, M. (2005). An integrative theory of intergroup contact. *Advances in Experimental Social Psychology, 37*, 255–343.

Buchanan, L., Bui, Q., and Patel, J. K. (July 3, 2020). Black Lives Matter may be the largest movement in U.S. history. *The New York Times*, Retrieved March 20, 2022. https://www.nytimes.com/interactive/2020/07/03/us/george-floyd-protests-crowd-size.html.

198 Anti-Black Racism in America

Buhler, J. L., Hopwood, C. J., Nissen, A. T., and Bleidorn, W. (2022). Collective stressors affect the psychosocial development of young adults. *Social Psychological and Personality Science*, *14*(6), 708–726.

Burns, U. (2021). *Where you are is not who you are: A memoir*. New York: HarperCollins.

Buttrick, N., and Mazen, J. (2022). Historical prevalence of slavery predicts contemporary American gun ownership. *National Academy of Science (PNAS Nexus), 1*(03). Retrieved February 23, 2023. https://doi.org/10.1093/pnasnexus/pgac117.

Calabrese, S. K., Meyer, I. H., Overstreet, N. M., Haile, N. M., and Hansen, N. B. (2015). Exploring discrimination and mental health disabilities faced by Black sexual minority women using a minority stress framework. *Psychology of Women Quarterly, 39*(3), 287–304.

Campbell, D. (1959). Systematic errors to be expected of the social scientist on the basis of a general psychology of cognitive basis. Paper presented at American Psychological Association Annual Meeting, Cincinnati, Ohio.

Caplan, Z., and Rabe, M. (2023). *The older population: 2020*. Washington, D.C.: U.S. Census Briefs.

Cardenas, D., and Verkuyten, M. (2021). Foreign language usage and national and European identification. *Journal of Language and Social Psychology, 40*(3), 328–353.

Carson, E. A. (2021). Prisoners in 2020—statistical tables. Retrieved June 15, 2022. https://www.bjs.ojp.gov/content/pub/pdf/p20st.pdf.

Cartright, J. (2021). America's least (and most) segregated metro areas: 2020. Retrieved May 22, 2022. https://cityobservation.org/mostsegregation2020/#:~:text=.

Castaneda, R., and Montgomery, D. (January 17, 1994). In King's name: A mandate. *Washington Post*. Retrieved October 23, 2022. https://www.washingtonpost.com/achieve/local/1994/01/17/in-king's-name-a-mandate/.

Castles, S. (1984). *Here for good: Western Europe's new ethnic minorities*. London: Pluto Press.

CensusScope. (2022). *Segregation: Dissimilarity indices. U. S. Census*. Retrieved May 10, 2022. https://www.censusscope.org/us/rank-dissimilarity-white-black.html.

Center for Budget and Policy Priorities. (2019). Tax law is fundamentally flawed. Retrieved July 22, 2021. https://www.ebpp.org/research/federal-tax/ne.

Centers for Disease Control and Prevention. (2005). Health disparities experienced by Black or African Americans—United States. *Morbidity and Mortality Weekly Report Reports, 54*(1), 1–3.

Centers for Disease Control and Prevention. (2019). *Health, United States, 2019*. Washington, D.C.: CDC.

Centers for Disease Control and Prevention. (2020). *Health, United States, 2020*. Washington, D.C.: CDC.

Chakravarti, A., Menon, T., and Winship, C. (2014). Contact and group structure: A natural experiment of interracial college roommate groups. *Organizational Science, 25*(4), 1216–1233.

Chandler, K. (January 17, 2023). Parole denied for 90% of Alabama inmates, a new low. AP News. Retrieved February 12, 2023. https://apnews.com/article/alabama-state-government.

Charlesworth, T. E. S., and Banaji, M. R. (2019). Patterns of implicit and explicit attitudes: I. Long-term change and stability from 2007 to 2016. *Psychological Science, 30*(2), 174–192.

Charlesworth, T. E. S., and Banaji, M. R. (2021). Patterns of implicit and explicit attitudes: II. Long-term change and stability regardless of group membership. *American Psychologist, 76*(6), 851–869.

Charlesworth, T. E. S., and Banaji, M. R. (2022). Patterns of implicit and explicit attitudes: IV. Long-term change and stability from 2007 to 2016. *Psychological Science, 30*(2), 174–192.

Bibliography   199

Chavda, J. (February 23, 2023). Immigrants and children of immigrants make up at least 15% of the 118th Congress. Pew Research Center. Retrieved March 27, 2023. https://www.pewresearch.org/fact-tank/02/23/23.

Chetty, R., Deming, D. J., and Friedman, J. (2023). Diversifying society's leaders? The determinants and causal effects of admission to highly selective private colleges. *Opportunity Insights*. NBER Working Paper No. 31492. Retrieved September 11, 2023. Opportunityinsights.org/wp-content/2023/07/CollegeAdmissions.

Cha-Jua, S. K. (2010). The new nadir: The contemporary Black racial formation. *The Black Scholar*, 40(1), 38–58.

Christ, O., Hewstone, M., Tausch, N., Wagner, U., Voci, A., Hughes, J., and Cairns, E. (2010). Direct contact as a moderator of extended contact effects: Cross-sectional and longitudinal impact on outgroup attitudes, behavioral intentions, and attitude certainty. *Personality and Social Psychology Bulletin*, 36(12), 1662–1674.

Christ, O., Schmid, K., Lolliot, S., Swart, H., Stolle, D., Tausch, N., Al Ramiah, A., Wagner, U., Vertovec, S., and Hewstone, M. (2014). Contextual effect of positive intergroup contact on outgroup prejudice. *Proceedings of the National Academy of Science*, 111(11), 3996–4000.

Christ, O., Ullrich, J., and Wagner, U. (2008). The joint effects of positive and negative intergroup contact on attitudes and attitude strength. Paper presented at the general meeting of the European Association of Experimental Social Psychology, Opatija, Croatia.

Christian, S. (March, 2009). Children of incarcerated parents. *National Conference of State Legislatures*. Retrieved September 24, 2022.

Clark, R., Anderson, N. B., Clark, V. R., and Williams, D. R. (1999). Racism as a stressor for African Americans: A biopsychosocial model. *American Psychologist*, 54, 805–816.

Clotfelter, C. T. (2004). *After Brown: The rise and retreat of school desegregation*. Princeton, NJ: Princeton University Press.

Coates, T. (June 2014). The case for reparations. *The Atlantic Magazine*. Retrieved December 11, 2015. https://www.theatlantic.com/magazine/archive/2014/06/the-case-for-reparations/361631/.

Cobb, S. B. (June 11, 2023). Executive director's corner: Leola Harris, a dying woman denied parole. Retrieved May 7, 2023. https://:www.redemptionearned.org./executive.

Cohen, R. (2008). Despite Obama victory, strong racial divide remains. *SPLC Report*, 38(4), 2.

Conley, D. (1999). *Being black, living in the red: Race, wealth, and social policy in America*. Berkeley: University of California Press.

Conway, D. A., and Roberts, H. V. (1994). Analysis of employment discrimination through homogeneous job groups. *Journal of Econometrics*, 61, 103–131.

Cornelius, C. V. M., Lynch, C. J., and Gore, R. (April 23, 2017). Aging out of crime: Exploring the relationship between age and crime with agent-based modeling. *Society for Modeling and Simulation International*. Retrieved January 11, 2020. https://dl.acm.org/doi/10.5555/3106078.3106081.

Cox, K. (September 19, 2024). Expanding the Child Tax Credit should be a top protity in 2025 tax debate. Center for Budget and Policy Priorities. Retrieved December 3, 2024. https://www.cbpp.org.cbpp.org.

Cox, K., and Edwards, K. (August 3, 2022). Black Americans have a clear vision for reducing racism but little hope it will happen. Pew Research Center, Retrieved November 15, 2022. https://www.pewresearch.org/race-ethnicity/2022/08/3/black-americans-have-a-clear-vision-for-reducing-racism-but-little-hope-it-will-happen.

Cox, K., Muhamed, B., and Nortey, J. (Novembr 7, 2022). Ten facts about Black Republicans. Pew Research Center. Retrieved March 15, 2023. https://www.pewresearch.org/short-reads/2022/11/07/.

Craig, M. A., and Richeson. J. A. (2014a). More diverse yet less tolerant? How the increasingly diverse racial landscape affects White American racial attitudes. *Personality and Social Psychology Bulletin, 40*(6), 750–761.

Craig, M. A., and Richeson, J. A. (2014b). On the precipice of a "majority-minority" America: Perceived status threat from the racial demographic shift affects White Americans' political ideology. *Psychological Science, 25*(6), 1189–1197.

Craig, M. A., Rucker, J. M. and Richeson, J. A. (2017). The pitfalls and promise of increasing racial diversity: Threat, contact, and race relations in the 21st century. *Current Directions in Psychological Science, 27*(3), 188–193.

Craig, M. A., Rucker, J. M., and Richeson, J. A. (2018). Racial and political dynamics of an approaching "majority-minority" United States. *The Annals of the American Academy of Political and Social Science, 677*(10), 204–241.

Crandall, C. R., Eshleman, A., and O'Brien, L. (2002). Social norms and the expression and suppression of prejudice: The struggle for internalization. *Journal of Personality and Social Psychology, 82*(3), 359–378.

Craven, J., and Snipe, M. (Janusry 4, 2023). The medical system has failed Black Americans for centuries: Could reparations be the answer? *Vox.* Retrieved December 31, 2023. https://medworm.com/106361147/the-medical-system-has-failed-Black-Americans-for-centuries.-Could-reparations-be-the-answer?

Cronbach, L., and Meele, P. (1955). Construct validity in psychological tests. *Psychological Bulletin, 52*(4), 281–302.

Cunningham, T. J., Croft, J. B., Liu, Y., Eke, P. I., and Giles, W. H. (2017). Vital signs: Racial disparities in age-specific mortality among Blacks or African Americans—United States, 1999–2015. *Morbidity and Mortality Weekly Report, 66*(17), 444–456.

Cusick, D. (April 5, 2023). This part of the U.S. will suffer most from climate change. *E & E News.* Retrieved April 12, 2023. https://www.scientificamerican.com/article/this-part-of-the-U.S.-will-suffer-most-from-climate-change.

Darity, W., Jr., Dietrich, J., and Guilkey, D. K. (2001). Persistent advantage or disadvantage? Evidence in support of the intergenerational drag hypothesis. *American Journal of Economics and Sociology, 60*(2), 435–470.

Darity, W., Jr., Hamilton, D., Paul, M., Aja, A., Price, A., Moore, A., and Chiopris, C. (April 1, 2018). What we get wrong about closing the racial wealth gap. S. B. Cook Center for Social Equity. Retrieved December 11, 2022. https://insightcced.org/what-we-get-wrong.

Darity, W., Jr., and Mullen, A. K. (2022). *From here to equality: Reparations for Black Americans in the twenty-first century.* 2nd edition. Chapel Hill: University of North Carolina Press.

Davies, K., Tropp, L., Aron, A., Pettigrew, T. F., and Wright, S. C. (2011). Cross-group friendships and intergroup attitudes: A meta-analytic review. *Personality and Social Psychology Review, 15*(4), 332–551.

Davis, D. W., and Wilson, D. C. (2022). *Racial resentment in the political mind.* Chiacgo: University of Chicgo Press.

Dawson, M. C., and Bobo, L. D. (2000). The racial divide. *The Polling Report, 16*(24), 1, 6–7.

Death Penalty Information Center. (2022). Executions by race and race of victim. Retrieved October 12, 2022. https://deathpenaltyinfo.org/executions/executions-overview/executionsbyraceandraceofvictim.

De Benedictis-Kessner, J., and Hankinson, M. (2023). How the identity of substance users shapes public opinion on opioid policy. *Political Behavior, 46*(1), 1–21.

Delbanco, A. (November 21, 2022). Opinion: Reparations for Black Americans can work if they are reimagined. *The Washington Post.* Retrieved December 5, 2022. https://www.washingtonpost.com/opinions/2022/11/21/.

Bibliography 201

Del Barco, M. (Febuary 26, 2023). Distributor, newspaprs drop 'Dilbert' comic strip after creator's racist rant. *National Public Radio*, 02/27/23. Retrieved February 14, 2023.

DeLuca, L. (February 26, 2021). Black inventor Garrett Morgan saved countless lives with gas mask and improved traffic lights. *Scientific American*. Retrieved February 28, 2021. https://www.scientificamerican.com/article/black-inventor-garrett-morgan-saved-countlesslives.

Denton, N. (1994). Are African Americans still hypersegregated? In R. Bullard, J. Grigsby III, and C. Lee (eds.), *Residential apartheid: The American legacy*. Los Angeles: CAAS Publications, University of California, 49–81.

Derenoncourt, E., Kim, C. H., Kuhn, M., and Schularick, M. (September 18, 2022). *Wealth of two nations: The U.S. racial wealth gap, 1860–2020. National Bureau of Econometric Research*. Working Paper No. 30101. Retrieved January 22, 2023.

Desilver, D. (August 2, 2021). As national eviction ban expires, a look at who rents and who owns in the U.S. Pew Research Center. Retrieved April 12, 2022. https://www//pewresearch.org/evictionscontinuedespitecdc-moratoriam-as-covid-19-ravages-u-s-economy.

Desmond, M. (2023). *Poverty, by America*. New York: Crown.

Deutsch, M., and Collins, M. (1951). *Interracial housing: A psychological evaluation of a social experiment*. Minneapolis: University of Minnesota Press.

De Vries, S., and Pettigrew, T. F. (1994). A comparative perspective on affirmative action: Positieve aktie in the Netherlands. *Basic and Applied Social Psychology*, 15, 179–199.

Dew, C. B. (2016). *The making of a racist*. Charlottesville: University of Virginia Press.

Dixon, T., Jr. (1902). *The leopard's spots: A romance of the White man's burden*. New York: Doubleday, Page.

Dixon, T., Jr. (1905). *The clansman*. New York: Doubleday, Page.

Dodd, V. (October 27, 2020). Black people nine times more likely to face stop and search than White people. *The Guardian*. Retrieved March 15, 2023. htpps://black-people-nine-times-more-likely-to-face-stop-and-search-than-white-people.

Dovidio, J. F., Gaertner, S. L., and Kawakami, K. (2003). Intergroup contact: The past, present, and the future. *Group Processes and Intergroup Relations*, 6, 5–21.

Dovidio, J. F., Love, A., Schellhaas, F. M. H., and Hewstone, M. (2017). Reducing intergroup bias through intergroup contact: Twenty years of progress and future directions. *Group Processes and Intergroup Relations*, 20(5), 606–620.

Dovidio, J. F., Newheiser, A.-K., and Leyens, J. P. (2012). Intergroup relations: A history. In A. W. Kruglanski and W. Strobe (eds.), *Handbook of the history of social psychology*. New York: Psychology Press, 407–430.

DuBois, W. E. B. (1906). The health and physique of the Negro American. In *The Proceedings of the Eleventh Congress for the Study of the Negro Problems*. Pp. 1 - 138. Atlanta, GA: Atlanta University Press.

Duckitt, J., and Sibley, C. G. (2009). A dual-process motivational model of ideology, politics, and prejudice. *Psychological Inquiry*, 20(2–3), 98–109.

Dumornay, N. M., Lebois, L. A. M., Ressler, K. J., and Harnett, N. G. (2023). Racial disparities in adversity during childhood and the false appearance of race-related differences in brain structure. *American Journal of Psychiatry*, 180(2), 127–138.

Earle, M., and Hodson, G. (2022). Dealing with declining dominance: White identification and anti-immigrant hostility in the U. S. *Group Processes and Intergroup Relations* 25, 727–745.

Eberhardt, J. L. (2019). *Biased*. New York: Viking.

Eberhardt, J. L. (December 29, 2021). The magnitude of our mythology. *Observer*. Retrieved April 6, 2022. https://www//psychologicalscience.org/observer/magnitude-mythology.

Eberhardt, J. L., Davies, P. J., Purdie-Vaughns, V. J., and Johnson, S. L. (2006). Looking deathworthy: Perceived stereotypicality of Black defendants predicts capital-sentencing outcomes. *Psychological Science*, 17(5), 383–386.

202 Anti-Black Racism in America

Editorial Board. (September 15, 2022). Opinion: The powder vs. cocaine disparity still exists, and it is still unfair. *The Washington Post.* Retrieved July 7, 2023. https:/www/ washingtonpost.com/opions/2022/09/15/equal-act-crack-power-cocaines-disparity/.

Edwards, K. (February 23, 2022). Most Black Americans say they can meet basic needs financially, but many still experience economic insecurity. Pew Research Center. Retrieved March 10, 2022. www.pewresearch.org/fact-tank/2022/02/23/most-black-americans-say-they-can-meet-basic-needs-financially-but-many-still-experience-economic-insecurity.

Eisner, L., Spini, D., and Sommet, N. (2020). A contingent perspective on pluralistic ignorance: When the attitudinal object matters. *International Journal of Public Opinion Research, 32*(1), 25–45.

Eitle, D. (2009). Dimensions of racial segregation, hypersegregation, and Black homicide rates. *Journal of Criminal Justice, 37*(1), 28–36.

Ekstrom, P. D., Le Forestier, J. M., and Lai, C. K. (2022). Racial demographics explain the link between racial disparities in traffic stops and county-level racial attitudes. *Psychological Science, 33*(4), 497–509.

Eller, A., and Abrams, D. (2004). Come together: Longitudinal comparisons of Pettigrew's reformulated intergroup contact model and the common ingroup identity model in Anglo-French and Mexican-American contexts. *European Journal of Social Psychology, 34,* 229–256.

Ellsworth, P. C. (1991). To tell what we know or wait for Godot? *Law and Human Behavior, 15*(1), 77–90.

Epps, A. (1991). *The speeches of Malcolm X at Harvard.* New York: William Morrow.

Erlanger, S. (November 11, 2008). After U.S. breakthrough, Europe looks in mirror. *The New York Times.* Retrieved November 21, 2008. http://www.nytimes.com/2008/11/08/us/politics/18poll.

European Union Fundamental Rights Agency. (2010). *EU-MIDIS at a glance: Introduction to the FRA's EU-wide discrimination survey.* Strasbourg: Fundamental Rights Agency.

Faber, J. W. (2020). We built this: Consequences of New Deal era intervention in America's racial geography. *American Sociological Review, 85*(5), 739–775.

Farley, R., Richards, T., and Wurdock, C. (1980). School desegregation and White flight: An investigation of competing models and their discrepant findings. *Sociology of Education, 53*(3), 123–139.

Fatherree, D. (2023). *Out of balance: Lack of diversity taints Louisiana criminal justice system.* Montgomery, AL: Southern Poverty Law Center.

Federal Bureau of Investigation. (1960–1961). *Uniform crime reports, 1960–1961.* Washington, D.C.: U.S. Government Printing Office.

Federal Bureau of Prisons. (1954). *National prisoner statistics: Prisoners in state and federal institutions, 1950.* Leavenworth, KS.: Federal Bureau of Prisons.

Feldman, E. (September 23, 2022). Over 16,600 books were banned during the past school year. *Smithsonian Magazine.* Retrieved September 23, 2022. https://www.smithsonianmag.com/smart-news/whus.

Felton, E. (January 9, 2023). A Chicago suburb promised Black residents reparations. Few have been paid. *The Washington Post.* Retrieved January 9, 2023. https://www.msw.com/en-us/news/us/a-chicago-suburb-promised-black-residents.

Felton, E. (June 5, 2024). Evanston sued for reparations to Black residents $25,000 in reparations. *The Washington Post,* June 4. https://www.washingtonpost.com/nation/2024/06/04/Evanston-sued-for-reparatons-to-Black-resident-$25,000-in-reparations.

Fiske, S. T., Cuddy, A. J., Glick, P., and Xu, J. (2002). A model of (often mixed) stereotype content: Competence and warmth respectively follow from perceived status and competition. *Journal of Personality and Social Psychology, 82,* 878–902.

Fogelson, R. M. (1977). *Big city police.* Washington, D.C.: Urban Institute.

Foner, N. (1979). West Indians in New York City and London: A comparative analysis. *International Migration Review, 13*(2), 284–297.

Ford, M. (June, 2014). Racism and the execution chamber. *The Atlantic.* Retrieved October 11, 2022. https://www.theatlantic.com/politics/archieve/2014/06/race-and-the-execution-chamber/.

Ford Foundation (April 1, 2015). Millions of lives transformed: 50 years of Head Start. Retrieved June 10, 2020. https://www.fordfoundation.org. News & Press.

Forman, J., Jr. (2012). Racial critiques of mass incarceration: Beyond the new Jim Crow. *Racial Critiques, 87,* 101–146.

Forman, J., Jr. (2017). *Locking up our own: Crime and punishment in Black America.* New York: Farrar, Straus & Giroux.

Fortis, B. (Novmber 8, 2022). How Tennessee disenfranchised 21% of its Black citizens. *ProPublica.* Retrieved January 22, 2022. https://www.propublica.org/article/tennessee-black-voters-disenfranchised21%ofitsBlackcitizens

Fournier, R., and Tompson, T. (September 20, 2008). Poll: Racial views steer some White Dems away from Obama. WTHR. Retrieved November 1, 2008. http://news.yahoo.com/page/election-2008-political-pulse-obama-race.

Frank, T. (November 8, 2022). Indigenous tribes in U.S. will get $75 million for climate relocation. *E & E News.* Retrieved December 6, 2022. https://www.scientificamerican.com/article/indigenous-tribes.

Freudenberg, N., Mosely, J., Labriola, J., Daniels, J., and Murill, C. (2007). Comparison of health and social characteristics of people leaving New York City jails by age, gender, and race/ethnicity: Implications for public health interventions. *Public Health Reports, 122*(6), 733–743.

Frymer, P., and Grumbach, J. M. (2020). Labor unions and White racial politics. *American Journal of Political Science, 65*(1), 225–240.

Fujioka, Y. (1999). Television portrayals and African-American stereotypes: Examination of television effects when direct contact is lacking. *Journalism & Mass Communication Quarterly, 76*(1), 52–75.

Full Fact. (2017–2018). Stop and search in England and Wales. Retrieved June 26, 2023. https://fullfact.org/crime/stop-and-search-england-and-wales.

Fuochi, G., Boin, J., Lucarini, A., and Voci, A. (2023). A mindful path toward prejudice reduction: Key mindfulness facets and mediators for promoting positive intergroup relations. *Mindfulness, 14,* 2894–2905.

Fuochi, G., Boin, J., Voci, A., and Hewstone, M. (2021). COVID-19 threat and perceptions of common belonging with outgroups: The roles of prejudice-related individual differences and intergroup contact. *Personality and Individual Differences, 175,* 1–8.

Gaertner, S. L., Dovidio, J. F., Anatasio, P. A., Bachman, B. A., and Rust, M. C. (1993). The common ingroup identity model: Recategorization and the reduction of intergroup bias. *European Review of of Social Psychology, 4,* 1–26.

Gaertner, S. L., Rust, M. C., Dovidio, J. F., Bachman, B. A., and Anastasio, P. A. (1994). The contact hypothesis: The role of a common ingroup identity on reducing intergroup bias. *Small Group Research, 25,* 224–249.

Galbiati, R., Henry, E., Jacquemet, N., and Lobeck, M. (2021). How laws affect the perception of norms: Empirical evidence from the lockdown. *PLoS ONE 16*(9): e0256624. Retrieved April 23, 2022. https://doi.org/10.1371/journal.pone.025662.

Gallup Polls. (2021). Race relations. Retrieved March 4, 2021. https://news.Gallup.com/poll/1687/RaceRelations.aspx.

Gamez, A., and Huici, C. (2006). Vicarious intergroup contact and role of authorities in prejudice reduction. *Spanish Journal of Psychology, 11*(1), 103–114.

Garber, M. K. (2001). Many whites misinformed about Blacks. *Focus* (Joint Center for Political and Economic Studies), *29*(7), 4a–4b.

Gardner, S., and Evans, J. (July 24, 2018). In Western Europe, familiarity with Muslims is linked to positive views of Muslims and Islam. Pew Research Center, July 24. Retrieved July 28, 2018. https://www/pewresearch.org/fact-tank/2018/07/24/in-western-Europe/.

Gaubiatz, R., Henry, E., Jacquemet, N., and Lobeck, M. (2021). How laws affect the perception of norms: Empirical evidence from the lockdown. *PLos ONE, 16*(9): e0256624. Retrieved July 22, 2022. https/doi.org/10.1377/journal.pone.8258624.

Gawronski, B. (2019). Six lessons for a cogent science of implicit bias and its criticism. *Perspectives on Psychological Science, 14*, 574–595.

Gelman, A., Park, D., Shor, B., Bafumi, J., and Cortina, J. (2008). *Red state, blue state, rich state, poor state.* Princeton, NJ: Princeton University Press.

Geronimus, A. T. (1992). The weathering hypothesis and the health of African-American women and infants: Evidence and speculations. *Ethnicity and Disease, 2*(3), 207–221.

Gershenson, S., Holt, S. B., and Papageorge, N. W. (2016). Who believes in me? The effect of student-teacher demographic match. *Economics of Education Review, 52*, 209–224.

Gest, J., Reny, T., and Mayer, J. (2018). Roots of the radical right: Nostalgic deprivation in the United States and Britain. *Comparative Political Studies, 51*(13), 1694–1719.

Getachew, Y., Zephyrin, L., Abrams, M. K., Shah. A., Lewis, C., and Doty, M. M. (2020). *Beyond the case count: The wide-ranging disparities of COVID-19 in the United States.* New York: Commonwealth Fund.

Gibbons, F. X., Gerrard, M., Cleveland, M. J., Wills, T. A., and Brody, G. (2004). Perceived discrimination and substance abuse in African-American parents and their children: A panel study. *Journal of Personality and Social Psychology, 86*(4), 517–529.

Gibson, C., Somasundaram, P., Paul, M. L., Salcedo, A., and Rosenzweig-Ziff, D. (2023). Tennessee house expels two Democrats who joined gun-control protests. *The Washington Post,* April 6. Retrieved 05/07/23. https://www.washingtonpost.com/nation/2023/04/06/Tennessee-demo.

Gijsberts, M., and Lubbers, M. (2009). Wederzijdse beeldvorming [Mutual image creation]. In M. Gijsberts and J. Dagevos (eds.), *Jaarrapport Integratie 2009* [Annual report integration 2009]. The Hague: Netherlands Institute for Social Research, 254–290.

Gill, M. (2022). Opinion: Thousands were released from prison during Covid. The results are shocking. *The Washington Post,* September 29. Retrieved October 10, 2022. htpps://www.washingtonpost.com/opinions/2022/09/29.

Gittleman, M., and Wolff, E. (2004). Racial differences in patterns of wealth accumulation. *Journal of Human Resources, 39*(1), 193–227.

Goff, P. A., Eberhardt, J. L., Williams, J. A., and Jackson, M. C. (2008). Not yet human: Implicit knowledge, historical dehumanization, and contemporary consequences. *Journal of Personality and Social Psychology, 94*(2), 292–306.

Goldsmith, P. R. (2016). Perpetuation theory and the racial segregation of young adults. *Social Science Research, 56*, 1–15.

Gollwitzer, A., Okten, I. O., Pizarro, A. O., and Oettingen, G. (2022). Discordant knowing: A social cognitive structure underlying fanaticism. *Journal of Experimental Psychology—General, 151* (11), 2846–2878.

Goodman, L., McCargo, A., and Zhu, J. (February 13, 2018). A closer look at the fifteen-year drop in Black homeownership. *Urban Institute.* Retrieved November 10, 2022. https://www.urban.org/urban-wire/closer-look-at-the-fifteen-year-drop-black-homeownership/.

Gramlich, J., and Edwards, K. (October 10, 2022). Black Lives Matter tops list of groups that Black Americans see as helping them most in recent years. Pew Research Center. Retrieved November 9, 2023. https://www.pewresearch.org/fact-tank/2022.10/10/black-lives-matter.

Graves, S. B. (1999). Television and prejudice reduction: When does television as a vicarious experience make a difference? *Journal of Social Issues, 55*(4), 707–727.

Green, A., Carney, D. R., Pailin, D., Ngo, L, Raymond, K. L., Lezzoni, L. I., and Banaji, M. (2007). Implicit bias among physicians and its prediction of thrombolysis decisions for Black and White patients. *Journal of General Internal Medicine, 22*(9), 1231.

Green, G. T., Visintin, E. P., and Sarrasin, O. (2018). From ethnic boundary demarcation to deprovincialization: The interplay of immigrant presence to ideological climate. *International Journal of Comparative Sociology, 59*(5-6), 383–402.

Green, G. T., Visintin, P., Sarrasin, O., and Hewstone, M. (2020). When integration policies shape the impact of intergroup contact on threat perceptions: A multilevel study across 20 European countries. *Journal of Ethnic and Migration Studies, 46*(3), 631–648.

Greenberg, J. (1959). *Race relations and American law*. New York: Columbia University Press.

Greenhouse, S. (February 26, 2023). Old-school union busting. *The Guardian*, https://www.theguardian.com/us-news/2003/feb/26/.

Greenlee, C. (August 26, 2019). How history textbooks reflect American refusal to reckon with slavery. *Vox*, 6. Retrieved January 8, 2023. https://www.vox.com/www.vox.com/identities/2019/8/26/208297711/slavery-text

Greenwald, A. G., and Banaji, M. R. (1995). Implicit social cognition: Attitudes, self-esteem, and stereotypes. *Psychological Review, 102*, 4–27.

Greenwald, A. G., Dasgupta, N., Dovidio, J., Kang J., Moss-Racusin, C. A., and Teachman, B. A. (2022). Implicit-bias remedies: Treating discriminatory bias as a public health problem. *Psychological Science in the Public Interest, 23*(1), 7–40.

Greenwald, A. G., and Lai, C. K. (2020). Implicit social cognition. *Annual Review of Psychology, 71*, 419–45.

Greenwald, A. G., McGhee, D. E., and Schwartz, J. L. K. (1998). Measuring individual differences in implicit cognition: The Implicit Association Test. *Journal of Personality and Social Psychology, 74*, 1464–1480.

Greenwald, A. G., and Pettigrew, T. F. (2014). With malice toward none and charity for some: Intergroup favoritism enables discrimination. *American Psychologist, 69*(7), 669–684.

Greenwald, A. G., Poehlman, T. A., Uhlmann, E., and Banaji, M. R. (2009). Understanding and using the Implicit Association Test III: Meta-analysis of predictive value. *Journal of Personality and Social Psychology, 97*, 17–41.

Greenwald, A. G., Tucker Smith, C., Sriram, N., Bar-Anan, Y., and Nosek, B. A. (2009). Implicit race attitudes predicted vote in the 2008 U.S. presidential election. *Analysis of Social Issues and Public Policy, 9*(1), 241–253.

Greenwell, M. (10/24/2022). Universal basic income has been tested repeatedly. It works. Will America ever embrace it? Washingtnpost.com/magazine/2022/10/24/universal-basic-income-has-been-tested-repeatedly.

Greenwood, B. N., Hardeman, R. R., Heang, L., and Sojourner, A. (2020). Physician-patient racial concordance and disparities in birthing morbidity for newborns. *Proceedings of the National Academy of Science (PNAS), 117*(35), 21194–21200.

Grid Staff. (2023). Mississippi lawmakers vote to create a separate, all-White-approved court and police system. *Yahoo! News*. Retrieved February 8, 2023. https://newd.yahoo.com/mississippi-lawmakers-vote-to-create.

Grucza, S. (2023). Lending hand as nation-building renaissance grows in Indian country. *The Harvard Gazette*, April. Retrieved June 30, 2023. https://news.havard.edu/gazette/story,2023/04/lending-hand-as-nation-building-renaissance-grows-in-Indian-country.

206 Anti-Black Racism in America

Gupta, S. (February 12, 2022). Why military towns are the most racially integrated places in the U.S. *Science News.* Retrieved June 25, 2023. https://www.sciencenews.org/article/military-towns-integration-segregation-united-states.

Hackman, M., and Overberg, P. (March 30, 2023). U.S. considers asking Black Americans on census if they are slave descendants. *Wall Street Journal.* Retrieved April 21, 2023. https://www.wsj.com/articles/u-s-considers-asking-black-americans-on-census-if-they-are-slave-descendants.

Hamilton, C., and Darity, W., Jr. (2010). Can baby bonds eliminate the racial wealth gap in putative post-racial America? *The Review of Black Political Economy, 37*(3–4), 207–216.

Hamilton, C., and Darity, W., Jr. (2017). The political economy of education, financial literacy, and the racial wealth gap. *Federal Reserve Bank of St. Louis Review, 99*(1), 59–76.

Hamilton, C., Darity, W., Jr., Price, A., Sridharan, V., and Tippett, R. (April 10, 2015). Umbrellas don't make it rain: Why studying and working hard isn't enough for Black Americans. Cook Center, Duke University. Retrieved July 14, 2022. https://socialequity.duke.edu/portfolio-item/umbrellas.

Hamilton, C., Huntley, L., Alexander, N., Guimaraes, A. S. A., and James, W. G. (2001). *Beyond racism: Race and inequality in Brazil, South Africa, and the United States.* Boulder, CO: Lynne Rienner.

Hanson, S. (2020). Here's what the racial wealth gap in America looks like today. *Forbes,* June 6. Retrieved May 10, 2022. https://forbes/2020/06/06/heres-what-the-racial-wealth-gap-looks-like-today.

Harris, B. (February 12, 2023). Mississippi hit by 900% increase in newborns treated for syphilis. NBC News. Retrieved February 14, 2023. https://www.youtube/com/watch?v=supTIOEbgeY

Harris, L. T., and Fiske, S. T. (2006). Dehumanizing the lowest of the low: Neuroimaging responses to extreme outgroups. *Psychological Science, 17*(10), 847–853.

Harvard Gazette. (January 17, 2023). Study shows "startling" inequities in end-of-life opioid treatment. Retrieved January 18, 2023. https://news.harvard.edu/gazette/story/2023/01/study-finds-startling-inequities-in-end-of-life-opioid-treatment.

Haslam, N. (2006). Dehumanization: An integrative review. *Personality and Social Psychological Review, 10*(30), 252–264.

Hassler, T., Ullrich, J., Bernardino, M., Shnabel, N., Larr, C. V., and Ugarte, L. M. (2020). A large-scale test of the link between intergroup contact and support for social change. *Nature Human Behaviour, 4*(4), 380–386.

Hatzipanagos, R., and Bella, T. (2023). A White man was "scared to death" of Ralph Yarl. For Black boys, this isn't new. *The Washington Post.* Retrieved April 22, 2023. https://www.msn.com/en-us/news/us/a-white-man-was-scared-to-death-of-Ralph-Yarl.

Hays, D., and Sullivan, B. (2020). 2017 data show homeowners nearly 89 times wealthier than renters. U.S. Census, November. Retrieved November 6, 2022. https://www.census.gov/library /stories/2020/11/gaps-in-wealth-of-americans-by-household-type/in-2017.

Heckler, M. M. (1985). *Report of the secretary's task force on Black and minority health.* Vol. 1: *Executive summary.* Washington, D.C.: U.S. Dept. of Health and Human Services.

Helper, R. (1969). *Racial policies and practices of real estate brokers.* Minneapolis: University of Minnesota Press.

Herda, D. (2023a). Misperceptions, intergroup prejudice, and the varied encounters between European citizens and non-EU foreigners. *International Journal of Public Opinion Research, 35*(4). Retrieved January 18, 2024. https://doi.org/10.1093/ijpor/edad035.

Herda, D. (2023b). Taking the good with the bad: Examining German citizens' rosters of immigrant contact. *Migration & Diversity, 2*(3), 279–298.

Bibliography 207

Herek, G. M., and Capitanio, J. P. (1997). AIDS stigma and contact with persons with AIDS: Effects of direct and vicarious contact. *Journal of Applied Social Psychology, 27*(1), 1–36.

Hervik, P. (2012). Ending tolerance as a solution to incompatibility: The Danish "crisis of multiculturalism." *European Journal of Cultural Studies, 15*(2), 211–225.

Hewstone, M. (2003). Intergroup contact: Panacea for prejudice? *The Psychologist, 16,* 352–355.

Hewstone, M., Cairns, E., Voci, A., Hamberger, J., and Niens, U. (2006). Intergroup contact, forgiveness, and experience of "the troubles" in Northern Ireland. *Journal of Social Issues, 62*(1), 99–120.

Hinton, E. (2021). *America on fire: The untold story of police violence and Black rebellion since the 1960s.* New York: Liveright.

History. (June 21, 2019). How the GI bill's promise was denied to a million Black WWII veterans. Retrieved July 11, 2022. https://www.history.com/news/gi-bill-black-WWI-veterans-benefits.

Hodson, G., Crisp, R. J., Meleady, R., and Earle, M. (2018). Intergroup contact as an agent of cognitive liberalization. *Perspectives on Psychological Science, 13*(5), 523-548.

Hook, J., Davis, D. J., Owen, J., and Deblalere, C. (2017). *Cultural diversity: Engaging diverse identities in therapy.* Washington, D.C.: APA Press.

Hook, J., Davis, D. J., Owen, J., Worthington, E. L., and Utsey, S. O. (2013). Intellectual humility: Measuring openness to culturally diverse clients. *Journal of Consulting Psychology, 60*(3), 353–366.

Horton, A. (2022). Racial discrimination by Veterans Affairs spans decades, lawsuit says. *The Washington Post,* November 28. https://www.washingtonpost.com/national-security/2022/11/28/veterans-affairs/racial-discrimination-by-veterans-affairs-spans-decades,-lawsuitsays.

Horton, E. (2021). *America on fire: The untold story of police violence and Black rebellion since the 1960s.* New York: Liveright.

Howard, M. W. (January 6, 2023). The U.S. could help solve its poverty problem with a universal basic income. *Scientific American.* Retrieved January 8, 2023. https://www.scientificamerican.com/article/the-us-could-help-solve-itspoverty-problem-with-a-universal-basic-income.

Howe, A. (May 23, 2024). Court rules for South Carolina Republicans in dispute over congressional map. *SCOTUSblog,* May 23. Retrieved June 3, 2024. https://www.scotusblog.com/?s=Court+rules+for+South+Carolina+Republicans+in+dispute+over+congressional+map.

Howell, J., and Korver-Glenn, E. (2022). *Appraised: The persistent evaluation of White neighborhoods as more valuable than communities of color.* St. Louis, MO: Weidenbaum Center on the Economy, Government, and Public Policy.

Hoyert, D. L. (May 2024). Maternal mortality rates in the United States, 2022. National Center for Health Statistics. Retrieved October 2, 2024. https://www.cdc.gov/nchs/data/hestat/maternal-mortality-rates-in-the-United-States./2022/.

Hurst, K. (2022). U.S. teens are more likely than adults to support the Black Lives Matter movement. Pew Research Center, June 15. Retrieved June 20, 2022. https://www.pewresearchorg/fact-tank/2022/06/15/u-s-teens-are-more-likely-than-adults-to-support-the-black-lives-matter-movement.

Ingraham, C. (August 25, 2014). Three-quarters of whites don't have any non-white friends. *The Washington Post.* Retrieved November 3, 2022. https://www.washingtonpost.com/news/wonk/wp/2014/08/25/.

Jackman, M. R., and Shauman, K. A. (2019). The toll of inequality: Excess African American deaths in the United States over the 20th century. *Dubois Review, 16*(K20), 291–340.

Jackson, J. M. (Ed.) (1991). *Life in Black America.* Thousand Oaks, CA: Sage.

208 Anti-Black Racism in America

Jackson, J. W. (1993). Contact theory of intergroup hostility: A review and evaluation of the theoretical and empirical literature. *International Journal of Group Tensions, 23,* 43–65.

Jacob, G., Faber, S. C., Faber, N., Bartlett, A., Ouinoet, A. J., and Williams, M. T. (2022). A systematic review of Black people coping with racism: Applications, analysis, and empowerment. *Perspectives on Psychological Science, 18*(2), 392–441.

Jefferson, T. (1785). *Notes on the State of Virginia.* London: Stockdale.

Jemmott, J. B., Jemmott, L. S., and Fong, G. T. (1998). Abstinence and safe sex HIV risk-reduction interventions for African-American adolescents: A randomized controlled trial. *Journal of the American Medical Association, 19,* 1529–1536.

Jimenez, O., and Riess. R. (2023). Oklahoma judge dismisses Tulsa race massacre reparations case filed by last known survivors. CNN, July 8. Retrieved September 10, 2023. https://www/cnn.com/2023/07/08/us/tulsa-race-massacre-reparations-case-filtf-by-last-known-survivors.

Jimenez, T., Heim, P. J., and Arndt, J. (2022). Racial prejudice predicts police militarization. *Psychological Science, 35*(12), 2009–2026.

Johnson, A., and Keating, D. (October 19, 2022). Whites now more likely to die from Covid than Blacks: Why the pandemic shifted. *The Washington Post.* https://www.washingtonpost.com/health/2022/10/19/covid-deaths.

Johnson, R. C. (January 4, 2011). Long-run impacts of school desegregation and school quality on adult attainments. National Bureau of Economics Research. Working Paper 16664. Retrieved August 12, 2011. https://www.nber.org/system/files/workingpapers/w16664/w16664.

Johnson, R. C. (September 27, 2012). The grandchildren of Brown: The long legacy of school desegregation. Goldman School of Public Policy, University of California, Berkeley. Retrieved September 12, 2022. Berkeley.edu//assets/research.

Johnson, R. C. (2019). *Children of the dream: Why school integration works.* New York: Basic Books.

Jones, J. M. (1972). *Prejudice and racism.* Reading, MA: Addison Wesley.

Jones, J. M. (1997). *Prejudice and racism.* 2nd edition. New York: McGraw Hill.

Jones, J. M., and Pettigrew, T. F. (2005). Kenneth B. Clark (1914–2005)—Obituary. *American Psychologist, 60,* 649–651.

Jost, J. T. (2019). The IAT is dead, long live the IAT: Context-sensitive measures of implicit attitudes are indispensable to social and personality psychology. *Current Directions in Psychological Science, 28,* 10–19.

Jung, K., Lim, D., and Shi, Y. (2014). Racial-ethnic disparities in use of antidepressants in private coverage: Implications for the Affordable Care Act. *Psychiatric Services, 65*(9), 1140–1146.

Justice Reform Resources. (2021). *It's time to end the racist and unjustified sentencing disparity between crack and powder cocaine.* Washington, D.C.: Leadership Conference on Civil and Human Rights.

Kaiser Family Foundation. (2019). Reported legal abortions by race of women who obtained abortion by the state of occurrence. Retrieved January 14, 2020. https://aanhpihealth.org/resource/kaiser-family-foundation-state-health-facts.

Kalt, B. C. (2003). The exclusion of felons from jury service. *American University Law Review, 53*(1), 67–189.

Kaste, M. (2023). DOJ report finds systematic patterns of abuse by the Minneapolis Police Department. NPR, June 16. https://www, npr.org/2023/06/16/1182694978/doi-report-.

Kauff, M., Beneda, M., Paolini S., Bilewicz, B. M. and Christ, O. (2021). How do we get people into contact? Predictors of intergroup contact and drivers of contact seeking. *Journal of Social Issues, 77,* 38–63.

Kelikar, K. (November 6, 2016). Electoral college is "legesse" of slavery, say some constitutional scholars. *PBS News*, Retrieved June 12, 2024.

Kelman, H. (1958). Compliance, identification, and internalization: Three processes of attitude change. *Journal of Conflict Resolution, 2*, 51–60.

Kende, J., Phalet, K., Van den Noortgate, W., Kara, A., and Fischer, R. (2018). Equality revisited: A cultural meta-analysis of intergroup contact and prejudice. *Social Psychological and Personality Science, 9*(8), 887–895.

Kendi, I. X. (2016). *Stamped from the beginning. The definitive history of racist ideas in America*. New York: Bold Type Books.

Kennedy-Moulton, K., Miller, S., Persson, P., Rossin-Slater, M., Wherry, L., and Aldana, G. (November 2022). Maternal and infant health inequality: New evidence from linked administrative data. NBER Working Paper Series 30693. Retrieved February 9, 2023. http://www.nber.org/papers/w30693.

Kephart, W. M. (1957). *Racial factors in urban law enforcement*. Philadelphia: University of Pennsylvania Press.

Khazan, O. (2020). *Weird: The power of being an outsider in an insider world*. New York: Hackette Go Books.

Killian, L. W. (1949). Southern White laborers in Chicago's West Side. Unpublished doctoral dissertation, Department of Sociology, University of Chicago.

Kim, D. (2022). A constant barrage: U.S. companies target junk food ads at people of color. *The Guardian*, November 11, 2022. https://www.theguardian.com/environment/2022/nov/11/junk-food.

Kimball, P. (1972). *The Disconnected*. New York: Columbia University Press.

Kindy, K. (2021). The capital riot ripples through a small Virginia town after a Black Lives Matter activist took on two police officers. *The Washington Post*, March 29. Retrieved June 18, 2022. https://washngton-post.com/politics/2021/03/29/capital-riot-fallout/.

Kindy, K. (2022). Insurers force change on police departments long resistant to it. *The Washington Post*, September 14. Retrieved September 15, 2022. https://washngton-post.com/investigations/2022/09/14/insurers-force-change-on-police-departments-long-resistant-to-it.

King, M. L. (1958). *Stride toward freedom*. New York: Harper.

Kleck, G., and Jackson, D. B. (2016). What kind of joblessness affects crime? A national-case-control study of serious property crime. *Journal of Quantitative Criminology, 32*(4), 489–513.

Klein, R. (2021). The rightwing US textbooks that teach slavery as "Black immigration." *The Guardian*, August 12. Retrieved January 4, 2021. https://www.theguardian.com/education/2021/aug/12/right-wing-textooks-teach-slavery-black-immigration/.

Knight Foundation. (February 19, 2020). New study sheds light on the 100 million Americans who don't vote: Their political views and what they think about 2020. Retrieved August 18, 2022. https://knight-foundation.org/press/releases/new-study-sheds-light-on-the-100-million-Americans-who-don't-vote.

Kohn, M. L., and Williams, R. (1956). Situational patterning in intergroup relations. *American Sociological Review, 21*, 164–174.

Koschate, M., and Van Dick, R. (2011). A multilevel test of Allport's contact conditions. *Group Processes and Intergroup Relations. 14*(6), 769–787.

Kotzur, P. E., Tropp, L., and Wagner, U. (2018). Welcoming the unwelcome: How contact shapes contexts of reception for new immigrants in Germany and the United States. *Journal of Social Issues, 74*(4), 812–832.

Kranish, M., and O'Harrow Jr. (January 23, 2016). Inside the government's racial bias case against Donald Trump's company and how he fought it. *The Washington Post*. Retrieved

February 21, 2021. https://www.washingtonpost.com/politics/inside-the-government's-racial-bias-case-against-donald-trump's-company-and-how-he-fought-it.

Krysan, M., and Moberg, S. (2021). Tracking trends in racial attitudes. Institute of Government and Public Affairs, University of Illinois System. Retrieved March 20, 2022. https://igpa.uillinois.edu/programs/racial-attitudes.

Kuhn, D. P. (November 4, 2008). Exit polls: Economy top issue. *Politico*. Retrieved July 27, 2023. https://poliico.com.exit-polls.

Kurdi, B., Seitchik, A. E., Axt, J. R., Carroll, T. J., and Banaji, M. R. (2019). Relationship between the Implicit Association Test and intergroup behavior: A meta-analysis. *American Psychologist*, 74(5), 569–586.

Langenberg, D. R. (1991). Science, slogans, and civil duty. *Science*, 252(5004), 361–363.

Lebovic, M. (February 16, 2021). America's Jewish "king of the suburbs" kept Blacks out of suburbia. *Times of Israel*. Retrieved February 23, 2022. https://www.times-of-israel.com/how-america's-jewish-king-of-the-suburbs-kept-blacks-out-of-suburbia.

Lee, H. (1960). *To kill a mockingbird*. New York: Lippencott.

Lee, H. (2015). *Go set a watchman*. New York: HarperCollins.

Lee, H., and Turney, K. (2012). Investigating the relationship between perceived discrimination, social status, and mental health. *Society and Mental Health*, 2(1), 1–20.

LeFlouria, T. L. (2016). *Chained in silence: Black women and convict labor in the new South*. Chapel Hill: University of North Carolina Press.

Lemmer, G., and Wagner, U. (2015). Can we really reduce ethnic prejudice outside the lab? A meta-analysis of direct and indirect contact interventions. *European Journal of Social Psychology*, 45, 152–168.

Leung, A. K., Maddux, W. W., Galinsky, D., and Chiu, C. (2008). Multicultural experience enhances creativity: When and how. *American Psychologist*, 63, 169–181.

Levin, S. (December 21, 2022a). California county first in US to pass law banning criminal background checks for housing. *The Guardian*. Retrieved December 24, 2022. https://www.theguardian/us-news/2022/21/us-news/2022/dec/21/california-alameda.

Levin, S. (November 30, 2022b). Fentanyl deaths in Los Angeles County rose 1,280% from 2016 to 2021—report. *The Guardian*. Retrieved December 18, 2022. https://www/.theguardian.com/us-news/2022/nov/30/fentanyl-death.

Levin, S. (January 6, 2023a). "It never stops": Killings by U.S. police reach record high in 2022. *the Guardian*. Retrieved January 7, 2023. https://www.theguardian.com/us-news/2023/jan/06/us.

Levin, S. (June 21, 2023b). Who's unhoused in California? Largest study in decades upends myths. *The Guardian*. Retrieved June 22, 2023. https://www.theguardian.com/us-news/2023/jun/21/us.

Levin, S. (June 1, 2023). The untold story of how a U.S. woman was sentenced to six years for voting. *The Guardian*. Retrieved December 28, 2023. https://www.theguardian.com/us-news/2022/21/dec/27/pamela-moses

Levin, S., Van Laar, C., and Sidanius, J. (2003). The effects of ingroup and outgroup friendships on ethnic attitudes in college. *Group Processes and Intergroup Relations*, 6(1), 76–92.

Levine, R. A., and Campbell, D. (1972). *Ethnocentrism: Theories of conflict, ethnic attitudes and group behavior*. New York: Wiley.

Lewis, O. (1959). *Five families: Mexican case studies in the culture of poverty*. New York: Basic Books.

Lewis, T. (2022). People in rural areas die at higher rates than those in urban areas. *Scientific American*. Retrieved December 14, 2022. https://scientificamerican.com/article/people-in-rural-areas-die-at-higher-rates-than-those-in-urban-areas.

Leyens, J.-P., Paladino, P. M., Rodriguez-Torres, R., Vaes, J., Demoulin, S., Rodriguez-Perez, A., and Gaunt, R. (2000). The emotional side of prejudice: The attribution of secondary emotions to ingroups and outgroups. *Personality and Social Psychology Review*, 4(2), 186–197.

Lieberson, S. (1963). *Ethnic patterns in American cities*. New York: Free Press of Glencoe.

Linder, D. O. (2022). Before *Brown*: Charles H. Houston and the *Gaines* case. Famous Trials. Retrieved July 14, 2022. http://famous-trials.com.brownvtopeka.

Lipset, S. M. (1960). *Political man*. Garden City, NY: Doubleday.

Logan, J. R., Zhang, W., Turner, R., and Shertzer, A. (2015). Creating the Black ghetto: Black residential patterns before and after the great migration. *Annals of the American Political and Social Sciences*, 660(1), 18–35.

Long, H. (July 7, 2023). If we avoid a recession, we can thank Black and Hispanic workers. *The Washington Post*. Retrieved July 14, 2023. https://washingtonpost.com/opinions//employment-black-immigrant-workers.

Lopez, M. H., and Moszimani, M. (October 02, 2023). Key facts about the nation's 47.2 million Black Americans. Pew Research Center. Retrieved December 1, 2023. https://www.pewresearch.org/fact-tank/2023/02/10.

Lucarini, A., Boin, J., Fuochi, G., Voci, A., Verkuyten, M., and Pettigrew, T. F. (2023). The nature of deprovincialization: Assessment, nomological network, and comparison of cultural and group deprovincialization. *Community and Applied Social Psychology*, 33(4), 868–886.

Luscombe, R. (November 11, 2022). Young voters hailed as key to Democratic successes in midterms. *The Guardian*. Retrieved November 14, 2022. https://www.the-guardian.com/us-news/2022/nov/11/young-voters-hailed-as-key-todemocratic-successes-in-midterms/.

Luscombe, R. (2022). Arkansas city elects 18-year-old as youngest mayor in US. *The Guardian*. Retrieved December 8, 2022. https://www.theguardian.com/us-news/2022/dec/08/Arkansas-city-elects-18-year-old-as-youngest-mayor.

MacEwen, M. (1995). *Tackling racism in Europe: An examination of anti-discrimination law in practice*. Washington, D.C.: Berg.

MacInnis, C. C., and Page-Gould, E. (2015). How can intergroup interaction be bad if intergroup contact is good? Exploring and reconciling an apparent paradox in the science of intergroup relations. *Psychological Science*, 10(3), 307–327.

MacKinnon, D. W. (1962). The nature and nurture of creative talent. *American Psychologist*, 17(7), 484–495.

Maddux, W. W., Adam, H., and Galinsky, A. D. (2010). When in Rome . . . learn why the Romans do what they do: How multicultural learning experiences enhance creativity. *Personality and Social Psychology Bulletin*, 36(6), 731–741.

Maddux, W. W., and Galinsky, A. D. (2009). Cultural borders and mental barriers: The relationship between living abroad and creativity. *Journal of Personality and Social Psychology*, 96(5), 1047–1061.

Madison Trust Company. (2023). How many billionaires are in America? Wikipediaj.

Maguire, P. (December 2016). Socially isolated voters more likely to favour Brexit, finds think-tank. *The Guardian*, December 17. Retrieved January 17, 2017. htps://www.theguardian.com/politics/2016/dec/17/socially-isolated-voters-more-likely-to-favour-Brexit-finds-thinktank.

Major, B., Blodorn, A., and Major-Blascovich, G. (2018). The threat of increasing diversity: Why many White Americans supported Trump in the 2016 presidential election. *Group Processes and Intergroup Relations*, 21(6), 931–940.

Mangino, W. (2010). Race to college: "The reverse gap." *Race and Social Problems*, 2(3), 164–178.

Mannheim, K. (1952). The problem of generations. In K. Mannheim (ed.), *Essays in the sociology of knowledge*. London: Routledge & Kegan Paul, pp. 276–320.

Marcus, R. (June 9, 2023). On voting rights, the justices followed the law shouldn't be news, but it is. *The Washinton Post*. Retrieved June 10, 2023. https://www.washingtonpost.com/opinions/2003/06/09/supremecourt.

Marks, G. (Decembr 4, 2022). I have no problem hiring ex-offenders. But they are being let down. *The Guardian*. Retrieved December 8, 2022. https://www.theguardian.com/business/2022/dec/04/small-employer-hire-ex-offender.

Martin, J. A., Hamilton, B. E., Sutton, P. D., Ventura, S. J., and Osterman, M. J. (2010). Births: Final data for 2008. *National Vital Statistics Report, 59*(1), 3–71.

Martinez, A., Prooijen, J.-W., and Van Lange, P. A. M. (2022). The hateful people: Populist attitudes predict interpersonal and intergroup hate. *Social Psychological and Personality Science, 14*(6), 698–707.

Martinovic, B., and Verkuyten, M. (2013). We were here first, so we determine the rules of the game: Autochthony and prejudice toward outgroups. *European Journal of Social Psychology, 43*, 637–647.

Mason, P. L. (1997). Race, culture, and skill: Interracial wage differences among African Americans, Latinos, and Whites. *Review of Black Political Economy, 25*(3), 5–39.

Massey, D. S. (1995). Residential segregation is the lynchpin of racial stratification. *City and Community, 15*(1), 4–7.

Massey, D. S. (2001). Residential segregation and neighborhood conditions in U.S. metropolitan areas. In N. J. Smelser, W. J. Wilson, and F. Mitchell (eds.), *America becoming: Racial trends and their consequences*. Washington, D.C.: National Academic Press, 391–434.

Massey, D. S., and Denton, N. (1988). The dimensions of racial segregation. *Social Forces 67*(20), 281–315.

Massey, D. S., and Denton, N. (1993). *American apartheid: Segregation and the making of the underclass*. Cambridge, MA: Harvard University Press.

Massey, D. S., White, M., and Phua, V. (1996). The dimensions of segregation revisited. *Sociological Methods and Research, 25*, 172–206.

McEwan, B. S., and Stellar, E. (1993). Stress and the individual: Mechanisms leading to disease. *Archives of Internal Medicine, 153*(18), 209–2101.

McFarland, J., Cul, J., Holmes, J., & Wong, X. (2020). Trends in high school dropout and completion rates in the United States: 2019. Washington, D.C.: U.S. Department of Education.

McGhee, H. (2021). *The sum of us*. New York: One World.

McGoogan, C. (January 4, 2023). "You're a slave": Inside Louisiana's forced prison labor and failed overhaul attempt. *The Washington Post*. Retrieved December 12, 2023. https://www.suwed.com/5813522-youre-a-slave-inside-louisiana-s.html.

McKeown, S., and Dixon, J. (2017). The "contact hypothesis": Critical reflections and future directions. *Social and Personality Psychology Compass, 11*, e12295. doi:10.1111/spc3.12295.

McLaughlin, C., and Burnside, T. (May 3, 2017). Bananas, nooses at American University spark protests, demands. CNN News. Retrieved March 9, 2023. https://www.cnn.com/2017/05/03/health/american-university-racially-motivated-incident.

McMullen, T. (February 28, 2019). The heartbreaking decrease in Black homeownership. *The Washington Post*. Retrieved March 8, 2022. httpp://www.washingtonpost.com/news/business/wp/2019/02/28/feature/the-heartbreaking-decrease-in-black-homeownership.

McNutt, M. (2023). Winning a noble race. *Proceedings of the National Academy of Science (PNAS), 52*, 120–130.

Meckler, L., and Rabinowitz, K. (September 9, 2019). The changing face of school integration. *The Washington Post*. Retrieved May 6, 2023. https://www.washigtonpost.com/education/2019.09/12/m

Meleady, R., Seger, C. R., and Vermue, M. (2017). Examining the role of positive and negative intergroup contact and anti-immigrant prejudice in Brexit. *British Journal of Social Psychology, 56*(4), 799–808.

Bibliography   213

Mepham, K. D., and Martinovic, B. (2018). Multilingualism and out-group acceptance: The mediating roles of cognitive flexibility and deprovincialization. *Journal of Language and Social Psychology*, *37*(1), 51–73.

Metraux, S., and Culhane, D. P. (2004). Homeless shelter use and reincarceration following prison release. *Criminology and Public Policy*, *3*(2), 139–160.

Metraux, S., and Culhane, D. P. (2006). Recent incarceration history among a sheltered population. *Crime and Delinquency*, *52*(3), 504–517.

Milbank, D. (2022). Glenn Youngkin didn't mind if some kids got an anti-racist education: His own. *The Washington Post*, January 26. Retrieved February 3, 2022. httpp://www.washingtonpost.com/opinions/2022/01/26/glenn-youngkin-didn't-mind-if-some-kids-got-an-anti-racism-education-his-own.

Miles, E., and Crisp, R. J. (2014). A meta-analytic test of the imagined contact hypothesis. *Group Processes and Intergroup Relations*, *17*(1), 3–26.

Miller, K. D., Noguerira, L., Devasia, T., Mariotto, A. B., Yabroff, K. R., and Siegel, R. L. (2022). Cancer treatment and survivorship statistics, 2022. *CA: A Cancer Journal for Clinicians*, *72*(5), 409–436.

Minard, R. D. (1952). Race relations in the Pocahontas coal field. *Journal of Social Issues*, *8*, 29–44.

Minow, M. (2010). *In Brown's wake: Legacies of America's educational landmark*. New York: Oxford University Press.

Mitchell, G., and Tetlock, P. E. (December 22, 2022). Are progressives in denial about progress? Yes, but so is everyone else. *Clinical Psychological Science*, *11*(4), doi:10.1177/21 677026221114315. Retrieved January 20, 2023.

Moore, A. (April 13, 2015). America's financial divide: The racial breakdown in Black and White. *Huffington Post*. Retrieved July 17, 2022. https://www.huffingtonpost.com/antonia-moore/americas-financial-divide:the-racial-breakdown-in-Black-and-White.

Morial, M. H. (2022). *Pulse of Black American survey*. New York: National Urban League.

Morsell, J. A. (1958). Comment on F. Lee's "changing structure of Negro leadership." *The Crisis*, *65*, 261–265.

Morsy, L., and Rothstein, R. (2015). *Five social disadvantages that depress student performance*. Washington, D.C.: Economic Policy Institute.

Motairek, I., Lee, E. K., Janus, S., Farkouh, M., Freedman, D., and Al-Kindi, S. (2022). Historical neighborhood redlining and contemporary cardio-metabolic risk. *Journal of the American College of Cardiology*, *80*(2), 171–175.

Mourtoupalas, N., and Hawkins, D. (July 20, 2023). The average age of Congress is rising. That's unlikely to change soon. *The Washington Post*. Retrieved July 27, 2023. https://www.washingtonpost.om/poitics/07/20/23/.

Moyd, O. (2021). Racial disparities inherent in America's fragmented parole system. *Criminal Justice*, *36*(1), 6–12.

Moynihan, D. P. (1965). *The Negro Family: The call for national action*. Washington, D.C.: U. S. Government Printing Office.

Muhammad, K. G. (2019). *The condemnation of blackness: Race, crime, and the making of modern urban America*. Cambridge, MA: Harvard University Press.

Muslimani, M. (October 12, 2022). Key facts about Black eligible voters in 2022. Pew Research Center. Retrieved January 22, 2023. https://www.pewresearch.org/fact-tank/2022/10/12/key-facts.

Mustakeem, S. (2020). Myth 3: That Black men were injected with syphilis in the Tuskegee experiment. *Vox*. https://www.vox.com/identities/2020/18/21134644/black-history-month-2020-myths.

214 Anti-Black Racism in America

Myrdal, G. (1944). *An American dilemma*. New York: Harper and Row.

Nacke, L., and Rainer, R. (2023). Two sides of the same coin? On the common etiology of right-wing authoritarianism and social dominance orientation. *Personality and Individual Differences, 207*. https://doi.org/10.1016/j.paid.2023.112169.

Najie, M., and Jones, R. P. (November 15, 2019). American democracy in crisis: The fate of pluralism in a divided country. Public Religion Research Institute. Retrieved January 1, 2024. https://www.prri.org/research/american-democracy-in-crisis:the-fate-of-pluralism-in-a-divided-country.

National Association for the Advancement of Colored People. (April 9, 2016). NAACP history: Charles Hamilton Houston. Retrieved July 13, 2022. https://naacp.org/pages/naacp-history-charles-hamilton-houston.

National Cancer Institute. (January 10, 2022). Seer training modules: Five-year survival cancer rates. Retrieved April 22, 2022. https://training.seer.cancer.gov/lung/intro/survival.html.

National Center for Health Statistics. (2021). Life expectancy at birth, age 65, and age 75, by sex, race, and Hispanic origin: United States, selected years 1900–2019. Retrieved July 22, 2021. https://www.cdc.gov/nchs/data/hus/2020-2021/LExpMort.pdf.

National Urban League. (2022a). *Pulse of Black America survey*. New York: National Urban League.

National Urban League. (2022b). *The state of Black America 2021*. New York: National Urban League.

Nazroo, J. Y., and Williams, D. R. (2006). The social determination of ethnic/racial inequalities in health. In M. G. Marmot and R. G. Wilkinson (eds.), *Social determinants of health*. Pp. 238-266/ New York: Oxford University Press.

Nestereak, M. (June 23, 2020). "I didn't see race in George Floyd": Police union speaks for first time since killing. *Minnesota Reformer*. Retrieved October 18, 2022. https://minnesotareformer.com/2020/06/23/20/I-didn't-see-race-in-george-floyd-police-union-speaks-out-for-the-first-time-sincekilling.

Newsome, M., and Valentine, G. (December 1, 2022). The opioid epidemic is surging among Black people because of unequal access to treatment. *Scientific American*. Retrieved December 2, 2022. https://www.scientificamerican.com/article/the-opioid-epidemic-is-surging-among-Black-people-because-of-unequal-access-to-treatment.

The New York Times. (January 13, 1991). Gravely ill, Atwater offers apology. Retrieved May 14, 2021. https://www:nytimes/1991/01/13/us/gravely-ill-atwater-offers-apology.html.

The New York Times. (2019). Here's what Ta-Nehisi Coates told Congress about reparations. Retrieved October 11, 2020. https://www.new-york-times.com/2019/06/12/us/ta-nehisi.

Nonnan, P. (January 16, 2009). Suspend your disbelief. *Wall Street Journal, 253*(14), A11.

Noonan, A. S., Lindong, I., and Jaitley, V. N. (2013). The role of historically Black colleges and universities in training the health care workforce. *American Journal of Public Health, 103*(3), 412–415.

Noonan, A. S., Velasco-Mondragon, J., and Wagner, F. A. (2016). Improving the health of African-Americans in the USA: An overdue opportunity for social justice. *Public Health Reviews, 37*(12), 1–20.

Norton, M. I., and Summers, S. R. (2011). Whites see racism as a zero-sum game that they are now losing. *Perspectives on Psychological Science, 6*(3), 215–218.

Nosek, B. A., Smyth, F. L., Hansen, J. J., Devos, T., Lindner, N. M., and Banaji, M. R. (2007). Pervasiveness and correlates of implicit attitudes and stereotypes. *European Review of Social Psychology, 18*, 36–88.

Obama, B. (1995). *Dreams from my father*. New York: Three Rivers Press.

Obama, M. (2021). *Becoming*. New York: Crown.

O'Brien, E. (2022). Losing sight of piecemeal progress: People lump and dismiss improvement efforts that fall short of categorial change - despite improving. *Psychological Science*, *33*(8), 1278–1299.

Orfield, G., and Eaton, S. E. (1996). *Dismantling desegregation: The quiet reversal of* Brown v. Board of Education. New York: Norton.

Osborne, M. (December 15, 2022). Scientists create a vaccine against fentanyl. *Smithsonian Magazine*. Retrieved December 26, 2022. htpps://www.smithsonianmag.som/smart-news/scientists-create-a-vaccine-against-fentanyl-a-.

Osterman, M. J. K., Hamilton, B. E., Martin, J. A., Driscoll, A. K., and Valenzuela, C. P. (February 7, 2022). Births: Final data for 2020. National Vital Statistics Reports. Retrieved October 12, 2022. https://www.cdc.goc/nchs/data/nvsr/ncsr70/nvsr70-17.pdf.

Oswald, F. L., Mitchell, G., Blanton, H., Jaccard, J., and Tetlock, P. E. (2013). Predicting ethnic and racial discrimination: A meta-analysis of IAT criterion studies. *Journal of Personality and Social Psychology*, *105*(2), 171–192.

Oswald, F. L., Mitchell, G., Blanton, H., Jaccard, and Tetlock, P. (May 7, 2015). Using the IAT to predict ethnic and racial discrimination: Small effect sizes of unknown societal significance. *Virginia Public Law and Legal Theory Research*, paper 11. Retrieved August 22, 2021. http://dx.doi.org/10.2139/ssrn.2564290.

Oxfam International. (Febuary 27, 2024). Nearly three quarters of millionaires polled in G20 countries support higher taxes on wealth, over half think extreme wealth is a "threat to democracy." https://www.oxfam.org/en/press-release/richest/.

Pacoe, E. A., and Richman, L. S. (2009). Perceived discrimination and health: A meta-analytic review. *Psychology Bulletin*, *135*(4), 531–534.

Pager, D. (2003). The mark of a criminal record. *American Journal of Sociology*, *108*(5), 937–975.

Pager, D., and Shepherd, H. (2008). The sociology of discrimination: Racial discrimination in employment, housing, credit, and consumer markets. *Annual Review of Sociology*, *34*, 181–209.

Paluck, E. L., Green, S. A., and Green, D. P. (2018). The contact hypothesis re-evaluated. *Behavioural Public Policy*, *3*(2), 129–158.

Paolini, S., Harwood, J., Hewstone, M., and Neumann, D. L. (2018). Seeking and avoiding intergroup contact: Future frontiers of research on building social integration. *Social and Personality Psychology Compass*, E12422. https://doi.org/10.1111/spc3.12422.

Paolini, S., and McIntyre, K. (2019). Bad is stronger than good for stigmatized, but not admired groups. *Personality and Social Psychology Review*, *23*(1), 3–47.

Paolini, S., White, F. A., Tropp, L. R., Turner, R. N., Page-Gould, E., Gomez, A. (2021). Intergroup contact research in the 21st century: Lessons learned and forward progress if we remain open. *Journal of Social Issues*, *77*, 11–37.

Parsons, C. A., Sulaeman, J., Yates, M. C., and Hamermesh, D. S. (2011). Strike three: Discrimination, incentives, and evaluation. *American Economic Review*, *101*(4), 1410–1435.

Patriotic Millionaires (2022). Our priorities. Retrieved 12/22/24. https://www.patrioticmillionares.org.

Payne, B. K., Cheng, C. M., Govorun, O., and Stewart, B. D. (2005). Affect Misattribution Procedure (AMP). APA Psychology Tests. Retrieved November 19, 2009. https://doi.org/10.1037/t04568-000.

Payne, B. K., and Hannay, J. W. (2021). Implicit bias reflects systemic racism. *Trends in Cognitive Sciences*, *25*(11), 927–936.

Payne, B. K., Vuletich, H. A., and Brown-Iannuzzi, J. L. (2019). Historical roots of implicit bias in slavery. *National Academy of Sciences*, *116*(24), 11693–11698.

Payne, H., Vuletich, K., and Lundberg, K. B. (2017). Implicit bias reflects systemic racism. *Trends in Cognitive Sciences, 25*(11), 927–936.

Pazzanese, C. (October 28, 2022). What to know about Harvard's case in the Supreme Court. *Harvard Gazette.*

Pearson, J. A., and Geroninos, R. T. (2010). Race/ethnicity, socioeconometric characteristics, co-ethnic social ties and health: Evidence from the National Jewish Population Survey. *American Journal of Public Health, 101*(7), 1314-1321.

Penner, L. A., Dovidio, J., Gonzalez, R., Albrecht, T. L., Chapman, R., and Eggly, S. (2016). The effects of oncologist implicit racial bias in racially discordant oncology interactions. *Journal of Clinical Oncology, 24,* 2874–2880.

Percival, K., and Dennie, M. (2022). *How to fix the census.* Washington, D.C.: Brennan Center for Justice.

Perry, A. M. (2020). *Know your price: Valuing Black lives and property in America's Black cities.* Washington, D.C.: Brookings Institution Press.

Perry, A. M., Rothwell, J., and Harshbarger, D. (November 27, 2018). The devaluation of assets in Black neighborhoods: The case of residential property. Brookings Institute Report. Retrieved March 26, 2019. https://www.brookings.edu/research/the-devaluation-of-assets-in-Black-neighborhoods:the-case-of-residetial-property.

Pettigrew, T. F. (1958). Personality and sociocultural factors in intergroup attitudes: A cross-national comparison. *Conflict Resolution, 2,* 29–42.

Pettigrew, T. F. (1959). Regional differences in anti-Negro prejudice. *Journal of Abnormal and Social Psychology, 59*(1), 28–36.

Pettigrew, T. F. (1961). Social psychology and desegregation research. *American Psychologist, 16,* 105–112.

Pettigrew, T. F. (1962). *Epitaph for Jim Crow: The dynamics of desegregation.* Boston: WGBH-TV.

Pettigrew, T. F. (1964a). *Epitaph for Jim Crow.* New York: Anti-Defamation League. https://www.thirteen.org/programs/dynamics-of-desegregation/.

Pettigrew, T. F. (1964b). *Profile of the Negro American.* Princeton, NJ: Van Nostrand.

Pettigrew, T. F. (1971). *Racially separate or together?* New York: McGraw-Hill.

Pettigrew, T. F. (1972). When a Black candidate runs for mayor: Race and voting behavior. In H. Hahn (ed.), *Urban affairs annual review.* Pp. 95-118. Beverly Hills, CA: Sage.

Pettigrew, T. F. (Ed.) (1975). *Racial discrimination in the United States.* New York: Harper & Row.

Pettigrew, T. F. (1976). Black mayoral campaigns. In H. Brice (ed.), *Urban governance and minorities.* New York: Praeger, 1976, 14–29.

Pettigrew, T. F. (1979). Tensions between the law and social science: An expert witness view. In *Schools and the courts: Desegregation.* Eugene: ERIC Clearinghouse for Educational Management, University of Oregon, vol. 1:23–44.

Pettigrew T. F. (1981). Race and class in the 1980s: An interactive view. *Daedalus, 110*(2), 233–255.

Pettigrew, T. F. (1985). New Black-White patterns: How best to conceptualize them? *Annual Review of Sociology, 11,* 329–346.

Pettigrew, T. F. (1986). The contact hypothesis revisited. In M. Hewstone and R. Brown (eds.), *Contact and conflict in intergroup encounters.* Oxford: Blackwell, 169–195.

Pettigrew, T. F. (1988). Influencing policy with social psychology. *Journal of Social Issues, 44*(2), 205–219.

Pettigrew, T. F. (1989). The nature of modern racism in the United States. *Revue Internationale de Psychologie Sociale, 2*(3), 291–303.

Bibliography 217

Pettigrew, T. F. (1991). Normative theory in intergroup relations: Explaining both harmony and conflict. *Psychology and Developing Societies, 3*(1), 1–16.

Pettigrew, T. F. (1996). *How to think like a social scientist.* New York: Harper Collins.

Pettigrew, T. F. (1997). Generalized intergroup contact effects on prejudice. *Personality and Social Psychology Bulletin, 23,* 173–185.

Pettigrew, T. F. (1998a). Intergroup contact theory. *Annual Review of Psychology, 49,* 65–85.

Pettigrew, T. F. (1998b). Reactions toward the new minorities of Western Europe. *Annual Review of Sociology, 24,* 77–103.

Pettigrew, T. F. (2004). Justice deferred: A half-century after *Brown. American Psychologist, 59*(6), 521–529.

Pettigrew, T. F. (2007). Still a long way to go: American Black-White relations today. In G. Adams, M. Biernat, N. R. Branscombe, C. S. Crandall, and L. S. Wrightsman (eds.), *Commemorating* Brown: *The social psychology of racism and discrimination.* Pp. 45-61. Washington, D.C.: American Psychological Association Press

Pettigrew, T. F. (2008). Future directions for intergroup contact theory and research. *International Journal of Intercultural Relations, 32*(3), 187–199.

Pettigrew, T. F. (2009a). Post-racism? Putting President Obama's victory in perspective. *Du Bois Review, 6*(2), 279–292.

Pettigrew, T. F. (2009b). Secondary transfer effect of contact: Do intergroup contact effects generalize to non-contacted outgroups? *Social Psychology, 40*(2), 55–65.

Pettigrew, T. F. (2010). Deprovincialization. In D. J. Christie (ed.), *Encyclopedia of peace psychology.* Hoboken, NJ: Wiley-Blackwell.

Pettigrew, T. F. (2011). Did *Brown* fail? *Du Bois Review, 8*(2), 511–516.

Pettigrew, T. F. (2015a). Prejudice and discrimination. In J. Wright (ed.), *International encyclopedia for the social and behavioral sciences.* 2nd edition. AmsterdamElsevier.

Pettigrew, T. F. (2015b). Samuel Stouffer and relative deprivation. *Social Psychology Quarterly, 30,* 1–18.

Pettigrew, T. F. (2016). In pursuit of three theories: Authoritarianism, relative deprivation, and intergroup contact. *Annual Review of Psychology, 67,* 1–21.

Pettigrew, T. F. (2017). Social psychological perspectives on Trump supporters. *Journal of Social and Political Psychology, 5*(1), 107–116.

Pettigrew, T. F. (2018a). The emergence of contextual social psychology. *Personality and Social Psychology Bulletin, 44*(7), 963–971.

Pettigrew, T. F. (2018b). Summing up: Did SPSSI answer Dr. King's call? *Journal of Social Issues, 74*(2), 377–385.

Pettigrew, T. F. (2020). *Racism.* In L. Spillman (ed.), *Oxford bibliographies in sociology.* Oxford: Oxford University Press

Pettigrew, T. F. (2021). School desegregation and the pipeline of privilege. *DuBois Review, 18*(1), 1–13.

Pettigrew, T. F. (2022a). *Contextual social psychology: Reanalyzing prejudice, voting and intergroup contact.* Washington, D.C.: American Psychological Association Press.

Pettigrew, T. F. (2022b). Seven decades in social psychology. In S. Kassin (ed.), *Pillars of social psychology: Stories and retrospectives.* Pp. 6-14. New York: Cambridge University Press.

Pettigrew, T. F., Christ, O., Wagner, U., and Stellmacher, J. (2007). Direct and indirect intergroup contact effects on prejudice: A normative interpretation. *International Journal of Intercultural Relations, 31*(4), 411–425.

Pettigrew, T. F., and Hewstone, M. (2017). The single factor fallacy: Implications of missing critical variables from an analysis of intergroup contact theory. *Social Issues and Policy Review, 11*(1), 8–37.

Pettigrew, T. F., and Meertens, R. (1995). Subtle and blatant prejudice in Western Europe. *European Journal of Social Psychology 25*, 57–75.

Pettigrew, T. F., and Taylor, M. C. (1992). Discrimination. In E. F. Borgatta and M. L. Borgatta (eds.), *The encyclopedia of sociology*. New York: Macmillan, vol. 1: 498–503.

Pettigrew, T. F., and Tropp, L. (2006). A meta-analytic test of intergroup contact theory. *Journal of Personality and Social Psychology, 90*, 1–33.

Pettigrew, T. F., and Tropp, L. (2008). How does intergroup contact reduce prejudice? Meta-analytic tests of three mediators. *European Journal of Social Psychology, 38*, 922–934.

Pettigrew, T. F., and Tropp, L. (2011). *When groups meet: The dynamics of intergroup contact*. New York: Psychology Press.

Pettigrew, T. F., Tropp, L., Wagner, U., and Christ, O. (2011). Recent advances in intergroup contact theory. *International Journal of Intercultural Relations, 35*(3), 271–280.

Pew Research Center. (November 5, 2008a). Inside Obama's sweeping victory. Retrieved January 19, 2009. http://pewresearch.org/pubs/1023/exit-poll-analysis/2008.

Pew Research Center (November 13, 2008c). Post-election perspectives. Retrieved January 19, 2009. http://pewresearch.org/pubs/1039/post-electionperspectives.

Pew Research Center. (August 12, 2021). Deep divisions in Americans' views of nation's racial history—and how to address it. Retrieved May 12, 2022. https://www.pewresearch.org/politics/2021/08/12.

Pew Research Center. (August 25, 2023). Americans are divided on whether society overlooks racial discrimination or sees it where it doesn't exist. Retrieved October 12, 2024. https://www.pewresearch.org/shortreads/2023/08/25/.

Pew Research Center. (August 22, 2008). A closer look at the parties in 2008. Retrieved October 12, 2024. https://www.assets.pewresearch.org.

Pew Research Center. (August 25, 2023). Americans are divided on whether society overlooks racial discrimination or sees it where it doesn't exist. Retrieved October 12, 2024. https://www.pewresearch.org/shortreads/2023/08/25/

Pierce, C. (1970). Offensive mechanisms. In F. Barbour (ed.), *In the Black seventies*. Boston: Porter Sargent, 265–282.

Pilkington, E. (Janusry 27, 2023). Texas death row inmates sue state over "brutal" solitary confinement conditions. *The Guardian*. https://www.theguardian.com/us-news/2023/jan/27/

Poinsett, A. (1960). The troubles of bus boycott's forgotten woman. *Jet, 18*, 12–15.

Prentice, D. A., and Miller, D. T. (1993). Plural ignorance and alcohol use on campus: Some consequences of misperceiving the social norm. *Journal of Personality and Social Psychology, 64*(2), 343–356.

Quillian, L., Pager, D., Hexel, O., and Midtbosen, A. H. (2017). Meta-analysis of field experiments shows no change in racial discrimination in hiring over time. *Proceedings of the National Academy of Science (PNAS), 114*(41), 10870–10875. https://www.pnas.org/cgi/doi/10.1073/pnas.1706255114.

Quiocho, A., and Rios, F. (2000). The power of their presence: Minority teachers and schooling. *Review of Educational Research, 70*(4), 485–528.

Ramos, M. R., Bennett, M., Massey, D., and Hewstone, M. (2018). Humans adapt to social diversity over time. *Proceedings of the National Academy of Science (PNAS), 116*(25), 12244–12269.

Rampell, C. (January 17, 2023). Opinion: New species discovered: Republicans who (sometimes) care about deficits. *The Washington Post*. Retrieved January 18, 2023. https://washingtonpost.com/opinions/2023/01/17/.

Bibliography 219

Rank, M. R. (2009). Measuring the economic racial divide across the course of American lives. *Race and Social Problems, 1*(2), 57–66.

Rasmussen, R., Levari, D. E., Akhtar, M., Crittle, C. S., Gately, M., and Urry, H. L. (2022). White (but not Black) Americans continue to see racism as a zero-sum game: White conservatives (but not moderates or liberals) see themselves as losing. *Perspectives on Psychological Science, 17*(6), 1800–1810.

Rattan, A., and Eberhardt, J. L. (2010). The role of social meaning in intentional blindness: When the gorillas in our midst do not go unseen. *Journal of Experimental Social Psychology, 46*(6), 1085–1088.

Ravitch, D. (February 2, 2020). Those Christian textbooks adopted in schools that receive taxpayer funding. [Blog.] Retrieved April 12, 2023.

Ray, R., and Perry, A. M. (April 15, 2020). Why we need reparations for Black Americans. Brookings Institute. Retrieved March 28, 2022. https://www.brookings.edu/policy2020/big-ideas/why-we-need-reparations-for-black-americans.

Reardon, S. F., Grewal, E., Kalogrides, D., and Greenberg, E. (2012). *Brown* fades: The end of court-ordered school desegregation and the resegregation of American public schools. *Journal of Policy Analysis and Management, 32*(4), 876–904.

Reinhard, B., and Dawsey, J. (December 12, 2022). How a Trump-allied group fighting "anti-White bigotry" beats Biden in court. *The Washington Post.* Retrieved December 13, 2022. http://www.msn.com/en-us/news/politics/how-a-trump-allied-group-fighting-"anti-White-bigotry"-beats-Biden-in-court.

Reitzes, D. C. (1953). The role of organizational structures: Union versus neighborhood in a tension situation. *Journal of Social Issues, 9,* 37–44.

Reskin, B. F. (1998). *The realities of affirmative action in employment.* Washington, D.C.: American Sociological Association.

Rich, F. (November 2, 2008). Guess who is coming to dinner? *The New York Times,* 11/2. Retrieved November 10, 2008. http://www.nytimes.com/2008/11/02/opinion/02rich.

Richeson, J. (September, 2020). Americans are determined to believe in Black progress. *The Atlantic Magazine.* Retrieved November 25, 2020. https://www.theatlantic.com/author/jennifer-richeson.

Riley, E., and Peterson, C. (2020). Black Lives Matter: Assessing the role of racial resentment in feelings towards BLM. *National Review of Black Politics 1*(4), 496–515.

Riley R. T., and Pettigrew, T. F. (1976). Dramatic events and attitude change. *Journal of Personality and Social Psychology, 34,* 1004–1015.

Rios, E. (2022). U.S. civil rights groups file complaint against "death by incarceration" to UN. *The Guardian,* September 15. https://www.theguardian.com/us-news/2022/15/civil-rights-us-news/2022/sep/15/civil-rights-us-death-incarceration/.

Ritter, S. M., Damian, R. I., Simonton, D. K., Van Baaren, R. B., Strick, M., and Dijksterhuis, A. (2012). Diversifying experiences enhance cognitive flexibility. *Journal of Experimental Social Psychology, 48,* 961–964.

Rooth, D. O. (2010). Automatic associations and discrimination in hiring: Real world evidence. *Labour Economics, 17*(3), 523–534.

Rosenblum, M., Jacoby-Senghor, D. S, and Brown, N. D. (2022). Detecting prejudice from egalitarianism: Why Black Americans don't trust White egalitarians' claims. *Psychological Science, 33*(6), 889–905.

Rosentiel, T. (January 9, 2009). States of the union before and after Bush. *Pew Research Center,* Retrieved May 14, 2023. https://pewresearch.org/2009/01/09/states-of-the-union-before-and-after-Bush.org.

220   Anti-Black Racism in America

Rothstein, R. (2017). *The color of law: A forgotten history of how our government segregated America*. New York: Liveright.

Rothwell, J. T., and Diego-Rosell, P. (2016). Explaining nationalist political views: The case of Donald Trump. Gallup Research Center. Unpublished Gallup Working Paper. Retrieved July 3, 2022. https://ssrn.com/abstract=2822059.

Rubin, J. (January 23, 2023). Opinion: In blocking an AP Black studies course, DeSantis tells us who he is. *The Washington Press*. Retrieved January 25, 2023. https://washingtonpost.com/opinions/2023/01/23/desantis-doc.

Rudwick, E. M. (1962). *The unequal badge: Negro policemen in the South*. Atlanta, GA: Southern Regional Council.

Ryan, W. (1971). *Blaming the victim*. New York: Pantheon Books.

Sacerdote, B. (2001). Peer effects with random assignment for Dartmouth roommates. *The Quarterly Journal of Economics, 116*(2), 681–704.

Sacks, B. (2022). Buffalo blizzard fuels racial and class divides in polarized city. *The Washington Post*. Retrieved December 30, 2022. https://www.msn.com/en-us/news/us/buffalo-blizzard-fuels-racial-and-class-divides-in-polarized-city.

Salam, E. (2022). Young voters hailed as key to Democratic successes in midterms. *The Guardian*, November 11. Retrieved November 14, 2022. https://www.the-guardian.com/us-news/2022/nov/11/young-voters-hailed-as-key-todemocratic-successes-in-midterms/.

Sanchez, K. L., Kalkstein, D. A., and Walton, G. M. (2021). A threatening opportunity: The prospect of conversations about race-related experiences between Black and White friends. *Journal of Personality and Social Psychology, 122*(5), 853–872.

Sanchez, Z., and Bennett, C. (2022). This family lost their land to a California state park. *National Geographic*. Retrieved June 23, 2023. https://d1j1j8nhhzd/cloufront.not/trending/caifornia-state-park.

Saraiva, C. (2022). Black businesses saw outsize Covid hit to earnings, study shows. *The Washington Post*. Retrieved October 18, 2022. https://www.msn.con/en-us/money/other/black-businesses-saw-covid-hit-to-earnings.

Sawyer, W., and Wagner, P. (March 14, 2023). Mass incarceration: The whole pie 2023. *Prison Policy Initiative*. Retrieved December 26, 2023. http://www.prisonpolicy.org/reports/pie2023.html.

Schaeffer, K. (December 10, 2021). America's public-school teachers are far less racially and ethnically diverse than their students. Pew Research Center. Retrieved November 15, 2022. https://www.pewresearch.org/fact-tank/2021/12/10/America'spublic-school-teachers-are-far-less-racially-and-ethnically-diverse-than-their-students.

Schaeffer, K. (December 9, 2023). U.S. Congress continues to grow in racial, ethnic diversity. Pew Research Center. Retrieved January 16, 2024. https://pewresearch.org/fact-tank/2023/01/09/u-s-congress-continues.

Schäfer, S. J., Kauff, M., Prati, F., Kros, M., and Christ, O. (2021). Does negative contact undermine attempts to improve intergroup relations? Deepening the understanding of negative contact and its consequences for intergroup contact research and interventions. *Journal of Social Issues, 77*(1), 197–216.

Schneider, G. S. (April 17, 2021). A Black high school baseball team won a championship in 1969. Their hometown waited 50 years to celebrate. *The Washington Post*. Retrieved April 19, 2021. htpps:www.washingtonpost.com/local/a-black-baseball-team-won-a-championship-in-1969/their-hometown-waited-50-years-to-celebrate.

Schoenfeld, H. (2018). *Building the prison state: Race and the politics of mass incarceration*. Chicago: University of Chicago Press.

Schofield, J. W. (1982). *Black and White in school: Trust, tension, or tolerance.* New York: Praeger.

Schofield, J. W. (1997). School desegregation forty years after *Brown v. Board of Education*: Looking forward and looking back. In D. Johnson (ed.), *Minorities and girls in school: Effects on achievement and performance.* Thousand Oakes, CA: Sage, 1–36.

Schuman, H., Bobo, L., Steeh, C., and Krysan, M. (1996). *Racial attitudes in America: Trends and interpretations.* Cambridge, MA: Harvard University Press.

Schuman, H. C., Steeh, C., and Bobo, L. (1985). *Racial attitudes in America: Trends and interpretations.* Cambridge, MA: Harvard University Press.

Schwartz, S. H., Cieciuch, J., Vecchione, M., Davidov, E., Fischer, R., Beierlein, C., and Dirilen-Gumus, O. (2012). Refining the theory of basic individual values. *Journal of Personality and Social Psychology, 103,* 663–688.

Sellin, T. (1935). Race prejudice in the administration of justice. *American Journal of Sociology, 41,* 212-217.

Shapiro, T. M. (2004). *The hidden cost of being African American: How wealth perpetuates inequality.* New York: Oxford University Press.

Shapiro, T. M., Meschede, T., and Sullivan, L. (2010). The racial gap increases fourfold. *Institute on Assets and Social Policy Research and Policy Brief,* 1–2.

Shelton, J. M., Dovidio, J. F., Hebl, M., and Richeson, J. A. (2009). Prejudice and intergroup interaction. In S. Demoulin, J.-P. Leyens and J. F. Dovidio (eds.), *Intergroup misunderstandings: Impact of divergent social realities.* New York: Psychology Press, 21–38.

Sherrill, R. (1975). *The Saturday night special.* New York: Penguin Books.

Shihadeh, E. S., and Flynn, N. (1996). The effect of social isolation on the rates of Black urban violence. *Social Forces, 74*(4), 1325–1352.

Shook, N. J., and Fazio, R. H. (2008). Interracial roommate relationships: An experimental field test of the contact hypothesis. *Psychological Science, 19*(7), 717–723.

Shrider, E. A., and Creamer, J. (2023). Poverty in the United States, 2022. U.S. Census. Retrieved December 17, 2023. https://www.census.gov/library/public ations/2023/demo/p60-280.

Shujing, Y., Khir, A. M., Ma'rof, A. A., and Jaafar, W. M. W. (2022). Development and trends of intergroup contact studies. *International Journal of Academic Research in Business and Social Sciences, 12*(10), 376–388.

Sidanius, J., Levin, S., Van Laar, C., and Sears, D. O. (2008). *The diversity challenge: Social identity and intergroup relations on the college aampus.* New York: Russell Sage Foundation.

Sidanius, J., and Pratto, F. (1999). *Social dominance: An intergroup theory of social hierarchy and oppression.* Cambridge: Cambridge University Press.

Sigelman, L., Bledsoe, T., Welch, S., and Combs, M. W. (1996). Making contact? Black-White interaction in an urban setting. *American Journal of Sociology, 101*(5), 1306–1332.

Simmel, G. (1955). *Conflict and the web of group affiliations.* New York: Wiley.

Simonton, D. K. (1997). Foreign influence and national achievement: The impact of open milieus on Japanese civilization. *Journal of Personality and Social Psychology, 72,* 86–94.

Singh, G. K., and Van Dyck, P. C. (2008). *Infant mortality in the United States, 1935–2007.* Washington, D.C.: U.S. Dept. of Health and Human Services Administration.

Slagter, L. (2023). Detroiters' views on reparations connected to perceptions of racial wealth gap, other inequality. *University of Michigan News.* Retrieved April 11, 2023. https://news.umichigan.edu/detroiters-views-on-reparations-connected-to-perceptions-of-racial-wealth-gap,-other-inequality.

Smedley, B. D., Butler, A. S., and Bristow, L. R. (Eds.) (2004). *In the nation's compelling interest: Insuring diversity in the health-care system.* Washington, D.C.: National Academy of Sciences.

222   Anti-Black Racism in America

Smith, D. (June 21, 2023). Queen City: Remembering the Black neighborhood erased for the Pentagon. *The Guardian*. Retrieved June 22, 2023. https://theguardian.com/artanddesign/2023/jun/.

Smith, J. M. (October 26, 2022). When is a lynching a lynching? *The Guardian*. Retrieved October 26, 2022. https://www.theguardian.com/us-news/2022/oct/25/when-is-a-lynching-a-lynching?

Smith, R. A. (2022). The executions of Whites for crimes against ethnoracial minorities: A case study analysis of the exceptions that prove the rule. *Du Bois Review, 39*, 233–255.

Smothers, R. (April 28, 1990). Hate crimes found aimed at Blacks in White areas. *The New York Times*. Retrieved November 24, 2022. hptts://www.nytimes.com/1990/04/28/us/hate-crimes-found-aimed-at-blacks-in-white-areas/.

Snyder, H. N., Cooper, A. D., and Mulako-Wangota, J. (April, 2017a). Arrest rates for aggravated assault. U.S. Bureau of Justice Statistics. Retrieved May 11, 2022. https://www.bis.gov/index.cfm?ty=datool&surl=/arrests/index.cfm#.

Snyder, H. N., Cooper, A. D., and Mulako-Wangota, J. (April, 2017b). Arrest rates for fraud. U.S. Bureau of Justice Statistics. Retrieved May 11, 2022. https://www.bis.gov/index.cfm?ty/datool&surl=/arrests/index.cfm#).

Snyder, H. N., Cooper, A. D., and Mulako-Wangota, J. (April, 2017c). Percent of adult arrests for all offenses. U.S. Bureau of Justice Statistics. Retrieved May 11, 2022. https://www.bis.gov/index.cfm?ty=datool&surl=/arrests/index.cfm#).

Sommers, B. D., Gunja, M. Z., Finegold, K., and Musco, T. (2015). Changes in self-reported insurance coverage, access to care, and health under the Affordable Care Act. *Journal of the American Medical Association, 314*(4), 366–374.

Southern Poverty Law Center. (2021). *Impact report*. Montgomery, AL: SPLC.

Sparkman, D. J., Eidelman, S., and Blanchar, J. C. (2017). Multicultultural experiences reduce prejudice through personality shifts in openness to experience. *European Journal of Social Psychology, 46*(7), 840–853.

Staiger, M. (2022). The intergenerational transmission of employers and the earnings of young workers. Opportunity Insights, Harvard University. Retrieved August 12, 2023. htpps://matthewstaiger.github.io/mathewstaiger.com/The%20intergenerational.

Stearns, E. (2010). Long-term correlates of high school racial composition: Perpetuation theory examined. *Teachers College Record, 112*(6), 1654–1678.

Steele, C. (1997). A threat in the air: How stereotypes shape the intellectual identities and performance of women and African Americans. *American Psychologist, 52*, 613–629.

Steele, C. (2010). *Whistling Vivaldi*. New York: Norton.

Stelter, M., Essien, I., Sander, C., and Degner, J. (2022). Racial bias in traffic stops: White residents' county-level prejudice and stereotypes are related to disproportionate stopping of Black drivers. *Psychological Science, 33*(4), 483–496.

Stephan, W. G., and Stephan, C. W. (1984). The role of ignorance in intergroup prejudice. In N. Miller and M. B. Brewer (eds.), *Groups in contact: The psychology of intergroup relations*. Orlando, FL: Academic Press, 229–255.

Stephan, W. G., and Stephan, C. W. (1985). Intergroup anxiety. *Journal of Social Issues, 41*, 157–175.

Stinson, F. S., Nephew, T. M., and Dufour, M. C. (1996). *U.S. alcohol epidemiologic data reference manual*. Bethesda, MD: National Institute on Alcohol Abuse and Alcoholism.

Stone, J., and Fernandez, N. C. (2008). How behavior shapes attitudes: Cognitive dissonance processes. In W. D. Crano and R. Prislin (eds.), *Attitudes and attitude change*. New York: Psychology Press, 313–334.

Bibliography 223

Stouffer, S. A., Suchman, E. A., DeVinney, L. C., Starr, S. A., and Williams, R. M. (1949). *The American soldier*. Vol. 1. Princeton, NJ: Princeton University Press.

Sumner, W. G. (1906). *Folkways*. New York: Ginn.

Supreme Court of the United States (2023). *Students for Fair Admissions, Inc. v. President and Fellows of Harvard College*. Supremecourt.gov. Retrieved October 11, 2024.

Tadmore, C. T., Hong, Y. Y., Chao, M. M., Wiruchnipawan, F., and Wang, W. (2012). Multicultural experiences reduce intergroup bias through epistemic unfreezing. *Journal of Personality and Social Psychology*, 103, 750–772.

Taeuber, K. E., and Taeuber, A. F. (1965). *Negroes in cities: Residential segregation and neighborhood change*. Chicago: Aldine.

Tamir, C., Budiman, A., Noe-Bustamante, L., and Mora, L. (March 25, 2021). Facts about the U.S. Black population. Pew Research Center. Retrieved May 14, 2022. https://www.powerresearch.org/social-trends/fact-sheet/facts-about-the-U.S.-Black-population.

Tan, S. Y., and Yip, A. (2018). Hans Selye (1907–1982): Founder of the stress theory. *Singapore Medical Journal*, 59(4), 170–171.

Tankard, M., and Paluck, E. L. (2016). Norm perception as a vehicle for social change. *Social Issues and Policy Review*, 10(1), 181–211.

Taylor, K.-Y. (2019). *Race for profit: How banks and the real estate industry undermined Black homeownership*. Chapel Hill: University of North Carolina Press.

Taylor, S. (2006). The political influence of African American ministers: A legacy of West African culture. *Journal of Black Studies*, 37(1), 5–19.

Thee-Brenan, M. (January 16, 2009). Poll finds disapproval of Bush unwavering. *The New York Times*. Retrieved August 22, 2024). https://www.thenewyorktimes.com/poll-finds-disapproval-of-Bush-unwavering.

Thiessen, M. A. (November 11, 2021). The danger of critical race theory. *The Washington Post*. Retrieved July 3, 2022. https://www.washingtonpost.com/opinions/2021/11/11/thedangerofcriticalracetheory.

Thompson, M. V. (2019). *The only unavoidable subject of regret: George Washington, slavery, and the enslaved community at Mount Vernon*. Charlottesville: University of Virginia Press.

Tien, Z., and Ruiz, N. G. (March 27. 2024). Key facts about Asian Americans living in poverty. Pew Research Center. Retrieved March 30, 2024. https://www.pewresearch.org/short-reads/2024/03/27/key-facts-about-Asian-Americans-living-in-poverty.

Tierney, J. (November 7, 2008). Where have all the bigots gone? *The New York Times*. Retrieved November 30, 2008. https://tierneylab.blog.nytimes.com/2008/11/7/wherehaveallthebigotsgone.

Tobon, A. L., Flores, J. M., Taylor, J. I., Johnson, I., Landerus-Weisenberger, A. O., and Bloch, M. H., 2021. Racial implicit associations in psychiatric diagnosis, treatment and compliance expectations. *Academic Psychiatry* 45(1), 23–33.

Tomaskovic-Devey, D., and Stainback, K. (2007). Discrimination and desegregation: Equal opportunity progress in U.S. private sector workplaces since the Civil Rights Act. *The Annals of the American Academy of Political and Social Science*, 609, 49–84.

Traub, A., Sullivan, L., Meschede, T., and Shapiro, T. (February 6, 2017). The asset value of whiteness: Understanding the racial wealth gap. *Demos*. Retrieved January 5, 2023. https://www.demos.org/research/asset-value-whiteness:-understanding-the-racial-wealth-gap.

Trawalter, S., Richeson, J. A., and Shelton, J. N. (2009). Predicting behavior during interracial interactions: A stress and coping approach. *Personality and Social Psychology Review*, 13(4), 243–268.

Trillin, C. (October 15, 2008). He's not one of us: The wisdom of the the crowd. *The New Republic*. Retrieved October 13, 2024.

Tropp, L. R. (2019). Adaptation to diversity: Individual and societal processes. *Proceedings of the National Academy of Science (PNAS)*, *116*(28), 12131–12133.

Tropp, L. R., Smith, A. E., and Crosby, F. J. (2007). The use of research in the Seattle and Jefferson County desegregation cases: Connecting social science and the law. *Analyses of Social Issues and Public Policy*, *7*(1), 93–120.

Tumulty, K. (2008). 2008 voter turnout: Lots and lots more Democrats. *The Washington Post*, December 17. Retrieved January 25, 2009. http://swampland. blogs.time.com/2008/12/17/2008-voter-turnout-lots-and-lots-more-Democrats.

Turnaway Study. (December 1, 2022). The harms of denying a woman a wanted abortion: Findings from the Turnaway Study. Retrieved February 14, 2023. https://www.ansirh.org/research/sheet/harms-denying.

Uggen, C., Larson, R., Shannon, S., and Pulido-Nava, A. (2020). *Locked out 2020: Estimates of people denied voting rights due to a felony conviction*. Washington, D.C.: Sentencing Project.

USA Facts. (2019). Percent of births to mothers under 18 by race and ethnicity. Retrieved October 26, 2022. https://www.usafacts.com/data/topics/people-society/health/maternal-early-childhood-health-percent-of-births-to-mothersunder-18-by-race-and-ethnicity/.

USA Facts. (2021a). Life expectancy in years by race. Retrieved October 14, 2022. https://www.usafacts.org/data/topics/people-society/health/longevity/life-expectancy/.

USA Facts. (2021b). U.S. incarceration rates by race. Retrieved October 22, 2022. https://usafacts.org/data/topics/security-safety/crime-and-justice/.

USA Facts. (2022a). 10 facts for Black History Month. Retrieved May 22, 2022. https://usafacts.org/articles/10-facts-for-black-history-month/.

USA Facts. (2022b). Three charts on diversity in the government's workforce. Retrieved April 30, 2023. https://usafacts.org/articles/three-charts-on-diversity-in-the-government's-workforce/.

USA Facts. (2023). Native Hawaiians and Pacific Islanders have the highest rate of homelessness in the U.S. Retrieved April 2, 2023. https://usafacts.org/articles/how-many-homeless-people-are-in-the-us?

U.S. Drug Enforcement Agency (2025). DEA fentanyl seizures in 2024. Retrieved February 19, 2025. https://dea.gov/dea-fentanyl-seizures-in-2024.

U.S. Bureau of Labor Statistics. (2023). Union members summary. Retrieved December 22, 2023. https://www.bls.gov/news.release/pdf/union2.pdf.

U.S. Census (2020). Annual business survey. Retrieved December 22, 2023. https://www.census.gov/library.stories.

U.S. Census. (2021). Homeownership rates by race and ethnicity: Blacks alone in the United States. Retrieved May 11, 2022. https://fred.stlouisfed.org/series/BOAAAHORUSQ156N, 09.28.2021.

U.S. Census. (2022a). CPS historical time series tables A–Z. Retrieved July 22, 2022. https://www.census.gov/data/tables/time-series/demo/education/.

U.S. Census. (2022b). The moms and pops who own their own businesses. Retrieved May 11, 2022. https://www.census.gov/programs-surveys/abs.html.

U.S. Census. (2022c). Income, poverty and health insurance. Retrieved September 13, 2022. https://www.census.gov/newsroom/press-releases/2022/income.

U.S. Census. (2023). Black individuals had record low poverty rates in 2022. Retrieved December 4, 2023. https://www.census.gov/library/stories/2023/09/black-poverty-rates-in-2022.

U.S. Department of Justice Office of Public Affairs. (June 16, 2023). Justice Department finds civil rights violations by the Minneapolis Police Department and the city of Minneapolis. Retrieved June 25, 2023. https://www.justice.gov/opa/pr/justice-department.

Bibliography 225

U.S. Sentencing Commission. (December 7, 2017). The effects of aging on recidivism among federal offenders. Retrieved February 12, 2018. https://www.ussc.gov/sites/default/files/pdf/research-and-publications/.

U.S. Supreme Court Reports. (1873). The Washington, Alexandria & Georgetown Railroad Company *v.* Catherine Brown. *21,* 675–678.

Van Assche, J., Dhont, K., and Pettigrew, T. F. (2019). The social psychological bases of far-right support in Europe and the United States. *Journal of Community and Applied Social Psychology, 29*(5), 385–401.

Van Assche, J., Swart, H., Schmid, K., Dhont, K., Al Ramiah, A., and Hewstone, M. (2023). Intergroup contact is reliably associated with reduced prejudice, even in the face of group threat and discrimination. *American Psychologist, 78*(6), 761–774.

Van Oudenhoven, J. P., Groenewoud, J. T., and Hewstone, M. (1996). Cooperation, ethnic salience and generalization of interethnic attitudes. *European Journal of Social Psychology, 26,* 649–661.

Van Tol, J. (December 11, 2024). Congress could solve a 150-year-old mistake with these reparations. *The Washington Post.* Retrieved June 30, 2024. htpps://www.washingtonpost/2024/02/22/pay.

Veenman, J., and Roelandt, T. (1990). Allochtonen: Achterstand en achterstelling [Minorities: Disadvantage and subordination]. In J. Schippers (ed.), *Arbeidsmarkt en Maatschappelijke Ongelickheid* [The labor market and societal inequality]. Groningen: Wolters-Noordhoff.

Velasco Gonzalez, K., Verkuyten, M., Wessie, J., and Poppe, E. (2008). Prejudice towards Muslims in the Netherlands: Testing integrated threat theory. *British Journal of Social Psychology, 47,* 667–685.

Velthuis, E., Verkuyten, M., and Smeekes, A. (2020). Supporting immigrant cultural rights: The roles of deprovincialization and identity continuity. *Journal of Applied Social Psychology, 50*(12), 733–743.

Verkuyten, M. (2011). Assimilation ideology and outgroup attitudes among ethnic majority members. *Group Processes & Intergroup Relations, 14,* 789–806.

Verkuyten, M., and Brug, P. (2004). Multiculturalism and group status: The role of ethnic identification, group essentialism and Protestant ethic. *European Journal of Social Psychology, 34,* 647–661.

Verkuyten, M., Martinovic, B., Smeekes, A., and Kros, M. (2016). The endorsement of unity in diversity: The role of political orientation, education and justifying beliefs. *European Journal of Social Psychology, 46,* 866–870.

Verkuyten, M., Thijs, J., and Bekhuis, H. (2010). Ingroup contact and ingroup reappraisal: Examining the deprovincialization thesis. *Social Psychology Quarterly, 73*(4), 398–416.

Verkuyten, M., Voci, A., and Pettigrew, T. F. (2022). Deprovincialization: Its importance in plural societies. *Social Issues and Policy Review, 16*(1), 289–309.

Villarosa, L. (2022). *Under the skin: The hidden toll of racism on American lives and the health of the nation.* New York: Doubleday.

Visintin, E. P., Berent, J., Green, E. G. T., and Falomir-Pichastor, J. M. (2019). Intergroup contact moderates the influence of social norms on prejudice. *Group Processes and Intergroup Relations, 23*(3), 418–440.

Von Hentig, H. (1940). Criminality of the Negro. *Journal of Criminal Law and Criminology, 30,* 662–680.

Vuletich, H. A., Sommet, N., and Payne, B. K. (2023). The great migration and implicit prejudice in the northern United States. *Social Psychological and Personality Science, 15*(5), 498–508.

226 Anti-Black Racism in America

Waldman, M. (March 1, 2023). Voting rights are expanding in blue states, contracting in red. Brennan Center for Justice. Retrieved January 4, 2024. https://www.brennancenter.org/our-work/analsis-opinion.

Ward, C., and Masgoret, A. (2006). An integrative model of attitudes toward immigrants. *International Journal of Intercultural Relations, 30,* 671–682.

Washington, H. A. (2007). *Medical apartheid: The dark history of medical experimentation on Black Americans from colonial times to the present.* New York: Doubleday.

Weil, J. Z., Blanco, A., and Dominguez, L. (2022). More than 1,800 congressmen once enslaved Black people. This is who they were, and how they shaped the nation. *The Washington Post,* August 24. Retrieved September 9, 2022. https://washngton-post.com/2022/08/24/more-than-1,800-congressmen-once-enslaved-Black-people.

Weiner, R. (2022). Dark money in politics an even darker place now, judges warn. *The Washington Post.* Retrieved December 14, 2022. https://washingtonpost.com/dc-md-va/2022/12/15/feg-change-dark-money-in-politics-an-even-darker-place-now-judges-warn.

Wells, A. S., Holme, J. J., Revilla, T. T., and Atanda, A. K. (2009). *Both sides now: The study of desegregation's graduates.* Berkeley: University of California Press.

West, K., Greenland, K., Van Laar, C., and Barnoth, D. (2021). Implicit racism, colour blindness, and narrow definitions of discrimination: Why some White people prefer "All Lives Matter" to "Black Lives Matter." *British Journal of Social Psychology, 60,* 1136–1153.

Western, B. (2006). *Punishment and inequality in America.* New York: Russell Sage Foundation.

Wezerek, C. (August 11, 2020). Racism's hidden toll. In America, how long you live depends on the color of your skin. *The New York Times.* Retrieved December 30, 2022. https://www.newyorktimes.com/interactive/2020.08.11/opinion/us-coron.

White House Historical Association. (March 5, 2022). Slavery in the president's neighborhood FAQ. Retrieved September 12, 2022. https://www.whitehousehistory.org/spn/introduction.

Wikipedia. (2022). The Social Security Act. Retrieved May 28, 2022.

Wikipedia. (2023). Racism in France. Retrieved December 1, 2023.

Wikipedia (2024). General Equal treatment Act. Retrieved December 15, 2024.

Williams, D. R. (2012). Miles to go before we sleep. *Journal of Health and Social Behavior,* 53(3), 279–295.

Williams, D. R., and Collins, C. (2001). Racial residential segregation: A fundamental cause of racial disparities in health. *Public Health Reports, 116*(5), 404–416.

Williams, D. R., Gonzalez, H. M., Neighbors, H., Nesse, R., and Jackson, J. S. (2007). Prevalence and distribution of major depressive disorder in African Americans, Caribbean Blacks, and Non-Hispanic Whites: Results from the National Survey of American Life. *Archives of General Psychiatry, 64.* Retrieved July 7, 2022. http://archpsyc.jamanetwork.com/prevalence-and-distribution-of-major-depressive-disorderin-African-Americans-Caribbean-blacks-and-non-hispanic-Whites-results-from-the-National-survey-of-American-life.

Williams, D. R., John, D., Oyserman, D., Sonnega, J., Muhammed, S. A., and Jackson, J. S. (2012). The mental health of Black Caribbean immigrants: Results from the National Survey of American Life. *American Journal of Public Health, 97*(1), 52–59.

Williams, R. M., Jr. (1947). *The reduction of intergroup tensions.* New York: Social Science Research Council.

Williamson, L. (January 20, 2022). Residential segregation may increase risk for high blood pressure. *American Heart Association News.* Retrieved February 19, 2023. https://www.heart.org/en/news/2022/01/20/residential-segregation.

Wilner, D. M., Walkley, R. P., and Cook, S. W. (1955). *Human relations in interracial housing: A study of the contact hypothesis.* Minneapolis: University of Minnesota Press.

Wilson, W. J. (1978). *The declining significance of race: Blacks and changing American institutions.* Chicago: University of Chicago Press.

Wilson, W. J. (2011a). The declining significance of race: Revisited and revised. *Daedalus, 140*(2), 55–69.

Wilson, W. J. (2011b). *More than just race: Being Black and poor in the inner city.* New York: Norton.

Wyatt, B. (ed.) (2012). *Japanse Americans in World War II.* Washington, D.C.: U.S. Department of the interior.

Works, E. (1961). The prejudice-interaction hypothesis from the point of view of the Negro minority group. *American Journal of Sociology, 67,* 47–52.

Yan, H., Russell, L., and Milanover, B. (March 28, 2013). Bananas thrown at Italy's first Black minister, Cecile Kyenge. CNN News. Retrieved March 3, 2023. https://www.cnn.com/2013/07/28/world/europe/italy

Yang, M. (February 12, 2023). Mississippi sees 90% rise in number of infants born with congenital syphilis. *The Guardian.* Retrieved March 14, 2023. https://www.-the-guardian.com/us-ews/2023/feb/12/mississippi.

Zax, J. S., and Kain, J. F. (1996). Moving to the suburbs: Do relocating companies leave their Black employees behind? *Journal of Labor Economics, 14*(3), 472–504.

Zhong, R., and Popovich, N. (March 9, 2022). How air pollution across America reflects racist policy from the 1930s. *The New York Times.* Retrieved October 29, 2022. https://www.nytimes.com/2022/03/09/climate/redlining-racism-air. How-air-pollution-across-america-reflects-racist-policy-from=the=1930.

Zhou, S., Page-Gould, E., Aron, A., Moyer, A., and Hewstone, M. (2019). The extended contact hypothesis: A meta-analysis on 20 years of research. *Personality and Social Psychology Review, 23*(2), 132–160.

Zimmerman, J. (July 07, 2016). Want greater diversity on college campuses? Increase the number of interracial roommates. *The Washington Post.* Retrieved April 19, 2023. https://washingtonpost.com/opinions/want-greater-diversity-on-college-campuses-increase the number of interracial roommates.

Index

For the benefit of digital users, indexed terms that span two pages (e.g., 52–53) may, on occasion, appear on only one of those pages.

A & P grocers, 38
Abeka, 80–81
Abernathy, Ralph, 27
abortion, 48, 106, 117, 127
Abrams, Stacey, 132–133, 141
Accardo, Tony "Big Tuna," 157
Accelerated Christian Education, 80–81. *See also* textbooks
Adams, Mildred, 143–144, 154, 164
Adams, Scott, 23
addiction, 108–110. *See also* drugs, drug use
affect misattribution, 12–13
affirmative action, 11–12, 18, 32, 39–41, 48, 70, 77–78, 84*b*, 86*b*, 103, 117, 121–124, 175, 187, 190–191. *See also* education
Affordable Care Act (ACA), 19, 116
Africans, 6, 38
age, aging, 116
  attitudes about, 15
  crime and, 93–94
  discrimination, 171
  race and, 3–6, 17
  voting trends by, 125–127, 130–132
aggravated assault, 90, 96, 167. *See also* violence
Alabama, 53–54, 93, 125, 128, 130
Alaska, 181
  universal income fund, 192
alcohol, 111
Alexander, Michele, 100, 102*b*, 103–104
"All Lives Matter," 21
allostatic load, 113–114
Allport, Gordon, 147–149, 151
Amazon, 37
America First, 188
American Civil Liberties Union News, 98
American Civil Rights Union, 103
American Express, 66–67
American Federation of Labor (AFL), 36–37, 168–169
American Housing Act, 163
American Psychological Association, 8*b*
Angola Prison (Louisiana), 52
Annual Review of Psychology, 149
Anti-Drug Abuse Act, U.S., 92

anti-Semitism, 4, 40, 101, 144, 147
Arkansas, 80, 125, 133
Arlington, Virginia, 163
Arradondo, Medaria, 99–100
arrests, 1–2, 8, 51–52, 55, 90–91, 95, 97–98, 100–102, 109, 120, 128, 174. *See also* police
artificial intelligence (AI), 76
Ashe, Arthur, 3
Asian Americans, 7
  affirmative action and, 79
  employment and, 58–59
  housing segregation and, 160, 168
  police officers, 99–100
  wealth and, 58, 63, 192
Association of American Medical Colleges, 117
asthma, 116, 166
Atlanta, Georgia, 158, 192–193
The Atlantic, 179–180
attitudes, 5, 12–15, 20–22, 28, 173
  explicit, 15–21
  implicit, 15, 28, 93
Austin, Lloyd, III, 176
Australia, 113–114, 151
authoritarianism, 22, 31, 42, 80, 142
Ayala, Aramis, 133

baby bonds, 192
Baker, Paul E., 146
Baltimore, Maryland, 158, 192–193
Banaji, Mahzarin R., 15
banks, 180, 187
  Black-owned, 62, 186–187, 189
  discrimination and, 19, 38, 50, 60–61, 158–162, 164, 168–169, 171
Barr, Roseanne, 24
Barrett, Amy Coney, 78–79
Bass, Karen, 133
behavior, 47–48
Bell, Derrick, 81*b*
Bezos, Jeff, 62–63
bias, 22
  in healthcare, 116–117
  implicit, 12–15, 64–65

Index

229

social desirability, 13, 15
  in textbooks, 80–81
Biden, Joseph, 57, 79–80, 90, 127, 188
Bilmes, Linda, 180
BioN-Tech, 41
birth. *See also* infant health; maternal health
  outcomes, 113, 116–117
  preterm, 116
Black Americans
  accomplishments, 28*b*
  age and, 3, 6
  attitudes about, 15–20
  businesses owned by, 62–63, 66*b*, 182, 190, 192
  class and, 3, 5, 73, 103, 116–117, 162, 167, 173, 176
  convict leasing and, 51–54, 55, 65, 189, 193
  coping mechanisms, 26–27
  COVID-19 pandemic and, 56, 58, 105, 118–119, 176
  crime and, 90–96, 167
  criminal justice system and, 28, 90–96, 103*b*, 109, 173, 176
  death rates, 105–109, 110–111, 118–119
  dehumanization of, 24–26
  diversity of, 5–6
  drug use and, 108–110
  economics and, 19, 28, 56–58, 60–66
  education and, 28, 59–60, 65, 66–68, 72–74, 75–77, 79–88, 103, 116, 133, 139*b*, 161, 163, 173, 176, 182, 187, 190
  in elected office, 122, 127–128, 132–133, 135*b*, 137*b*, 139*b*
  employment and, 56–57, 58–60, 63, 94, 166–167, 176, 188–189
  family and, 63–64
  farming and, 179–188
  geography of, 6
  health and, 11–12, 14, 19, 28, 105–110, 112–121, 120*b*, 166–167, 173, 176, 188–189
  homelessness and, 190
  housing and, 173, 176, 182, 190
  housing discrimination and, 120, 155–171, 169*b*, 170*b*, 174, 179–180, 188–192
  interracial contact and, 143–144, 145–148, 152, 154*b*, 167–168, 170, 173–176, 182
  labor unions and, 36–37, 41–42, 44
  lynchings and, 54–55, 83–84, 154, 156, 172, 177, 179
  mass incarceration of, 89–90, 91–92, 98, 102*b*, 103–104, 109, 115–116, 130, 167, 172, 173–174, 176, 187, 190
  medical experimentation on, 111–112
  mental health and, 20, 111, 113, 115
  misperceptions of, 20–22, 28*b*
  norms and, 43–47
  pipeline of privilege and, 59–60, 77, 79–80, 85, 133, 139*b*
  police and, 3–4, 12, 20, 22, 37, 96–100, 103, 120, 173, 174, 176, 187
  political power of, 129–130, 133, 166, 173, 176, 188
  poverty and, 110, 114–117, 118–119, 176, 183
  prejudice toward, 32
  religion and, 6, 26–27, 101–102
  reparations for, 179–180, 182–193
  in social psychology, 27–28
  stereotype threat and, 39
  voting trends, 126–132, 134*b*, 135*b*, 137–138, 141
  wealth and, 49–52, 53–54, 57–58, 60–64, 65–66, 79–80, 163, 166, 173, 174–176, 182–183, 185, 188–189, 192
Black Codes, 51, 54
Black Lives Matter movement, 4, 17, 21, 24, 26, 37, 96
Blackmon, Douglas, 51–55, 172–173, 179, 188–189
Blackmun, Harry, 78, 102–103
Black studies, 73, 81
Black women, 51–52, 54, 57, 66–67, 106–108, 112, 116–117, 122, 128, 133, 176. *See also* gender
blockbusting, 157–158
Blum, Edward, 77–79, 84–85, 88
Bob Jones University Press, 80–81
Bobo, Larry, 15, 27
body weight, attitudes about, 15
Booker, Cory, 140, 191–192
boycott, 2
Braddock, Jomills, 59
Bradley, Thomas, 122, 136
Bragg, Alvin, 25, 176
Brameld, Theodore, 146
Brazil, 113–114
Brewer, Rosalind "Roz," 66–67
Brookings Institute, 189
Brooks, Cornell William, 180
Brophy, Ira N., 147
Brown, Katherine, 1
Brown, Michael, 3–4, 96–97
Brown, Oliver and Linda, 69
Brown, Rupert, 151
Brown, Sherrod, 142
Brown v. Board of Education, 20, 27, 69–72, 137
Bryant, Carolyn, 55
Buchanan v. Warley, 158
Buffalo, New York, 163, 167
Buffett, Warren, 186
buprenorphine, 109
Bureau of Indian Affairs, 181
Bureau of Justice Statistics, 90

230 Index

burglary, 167
Burns, Ursula, 66
Bush, George H. W., 83–84
Bush, George W., 32, 78, 82, 83–84, 125–126, 138
buses, busing, 1–2, 16, 70, 83–84, 165
Byrd, Harry, 134–135

Caddo Parish, Louisiana, 54
California, 95, 98, 114, 126, 129–130, 133, 168
  Reparations Task Force, 190
Campbell, Andrea, 133
Campbell, Donald, 85–86
Canada, 39–40, 113–114
cancer, 108, 111, 115–117, 119
capital gains, 51
capitalism, Black, 62–63
Capone, Al, 157
CareerOneStop, 95
Cares Act, 96
Caruso, Rick, 133
Castles, Stephen, 39
censorship, 75
Census Bureau, U.S., 5, 57, 58–59, 62–63, 75, 180, 185
Center for Budget and Policy Priorities, 183–184
Charleston, South Carolina, 158
Charlesworth, Tessa E. S., 15
Charlotte, North Carolina, 170
Chauvin, Derek, 99–100
check cashing, 62, 186–187
Chestnut, Kenneth, 66–67
Chetty, Raj, 86–87
Chicago, Illinois, 118, 156–158, 170–171, 179–180
Chicago School of sociology, 90
Chicago Tribune, 28–29
childcare, 193
child tax credit, 193
Chile, 151
China, 36
Christ, Oliver, 152
citizenship, 39–40, 53
city services, 165, 167
Civil Rights Act, 28, 122, 164
civil rights movement, 4, 45, 122, 137
Civil Rights Project, 75
Civil War, 172–173, 189
Clark, Kenneth, 8, 23–24, 27, 102, 143
class action suits, 39–41
class, 3, 5, 19, 21, 36, 57, 65, 73, 91, 99, 103,
    136–137, 160–162, 167, 173, 176, 191–192
  education and, 71, 86b
  health and, 114, 116–117
  housing and, 168
  immigration and, 63
  politics and, 141–142

privilege and, 59–60
wealth and, 173
climate change, 127, 132, 167, 181
Clinton, Bill, 124
Clinton, Hillary, 123–124, 137–138
Coates, Ta-Nehisi, 179–180, 184–185
cocaine. *See* drugs, drug use
cognitive closure, 31
Cohn, Roy, 165
Coleman, James, 70–71
Collins, Chiquita, 115, 166
Collins, Mary Evans, 147–148
color blindness, 21, 26, 38, 72–73, 176
Colorado, 125–126
Columbia, South Carolina, 192–193
Commission on Civil Rights, U.S., 129
Communism, 9
Compton, California, 192–193
Confederacy, 3, 176
conflict, 146
Congress, U.S., 57, 78–79, 91–92, 109, 127–129,
    131, 133, 140, 141–142, 160, 163, 184
Congress of Industrial Organizations (CIO),
    36–37
Connecticut, 133
conservativism, 4–5, 15, 18, 34, 36, 64, 70, 89, 122,
    192
constant turnout composition fallacy, 123
Constitution, U.S.
  8th Amendment, 52
  Equal Protection Clause, 71
  14th Amendment, 2, 53, 71, 162
  15th Amendment, 53
  three-fifths compromise, 82
contact, 153, 173, 176
  avoidance of, 151, 154b
  housing and, 167–168, 169–170, 174
  intergroup, 31–32, 47, 153b, 174
  interracial, 5, 20, 143–144, 154b, 167–168,
    169–170, 175, 182
  segregation and, 146
contact theory, 42
  criticisms of, 153b
  history of, 146–151
  intergroup, 20–21, 144–151
  macro-level contextual effects, 151–153
  temporal model of, 149–150
convict leasing, 51–55, 65, 189, 193
coping mechanisms, 26–27
Court of Appeals, U.S., 102–103
courts, 1–2, 4, 25, 38, 70–71, 104, 161–162, 168.
    See also Supreme Court
COVID-19 pandemic, 41, 56, 58, 89–90, 92, 96,
    105, 114–115, 118, 159–160, 176, 184
Crawford, Thomas, 99–100

crime, criminal justice system, 5, 28, 89–104, 102*b*, 103*b*, 109, 131, 173–174, 176
   housing and, 165, 167, 174
Crisp, Richard J., 145
critical race theory (CRT), 75, 80, 81*b*, 172–173, 183
Cultural Deprovincialization Scale, 31
Cyprus, 151
Czech Republic, 72

Dallas, Texas, 158
Dana-Farber Cancer Institute, 116–117
Darity, William, Jr., 60, 63, 185–186, 191–192
Davis, Austin, 132–133
Davis, Benjamin, Jr., 176
Davis, Benjamin, Sr., 176
Davis, Geoff, 125
Dayton, Ohio, 159
death penalty, 92–94
dehumanization, 24–26
Delbanco, Andrew, 191
Deming, David J., 86–87
Demings, Val, 133
democracy, 71, 129–131, 172, 186
Democratic Party, 21, 83, 95, 122, 123, 125–128, 129–133, 134–135, 137–138, 141–142
Denton, Nancy A., 155, 169–170
Denver, Colorado, 192–193
Department of Housing and Urban Development (HUD), U.S., 164
Department of Agriculture, U.S., 188
Department of Justice, U.S., 96, 98–100, 165
Department of Labor, U.S., 95
depression, 111, 113
deprovincialization, 30–32
DeSantis, Ronald, 84, 130
Desmond, Matthew, 173
Detroit, Michigan, 71, 160, 163, 183
Deutsch, Morton, 147–148
Dew, Charles, 25
diabetes, 105–107, 115–116, 119
diet, 115
Dietrich, Jason, 63
disability
   attitudes about, 15
   education and, 71–72
discrimination, 5, 15–16, 20–21. *See also under* banks; housing
   age, 171
   defining, 33–34
   direct, 33, 34–35, 37–39, 50, 179
   employment, 14, 38–39, 41–42, 42*b*, 56
   health disparities and, 112–117
   housing, 4, 38–39, 50, 60–61, 65, 102, 120, 174, 179

   indirect, 33–35, 38–39, 50, 179
   labor unions and, 36–41
   as normative, 33–35, 42–43
   prejudice and, 33, 43, 50
   psychological effects of, 39
   remedies for, 39–41
   in United States, 37–38, 39–40, 41–42, 51–55
   wage, 35
   in Western Europe, 38–39, 40–41
disparate impact, 35
disparate treatment, 35
Disraeli, Benjamin, 4
dissonance, 21–22
diversity, 5–6, 30, 66–67, 74, 78–79, 85, 87, 139–140, 145, 151, 153
DNA testing, 191–192
Douglass, Frederick, 143
Dred Scott v. Sandford, 82
Drug Addiction Treatment Act, 109
Drug Enforcement Agency, U.S., 109
drugs, drug use, 39, 90–92, 97, 101–103, 104–105, 108–110
   in prison, 109–110
Du Bois, W. E. B., 68, 119, 122
Duckett, Thasunda Brown, 67
Duckitt, John, 22
Duke, David, 129

Eberhardt, Jennifer, 22, 24–25, 27–28, 174
ecological fallacy, 123
economics, 5, 19, 28, 35, 49–68, 66*b*, 176
   politics and, 138, 141–142
education, 5, 19, 39, 56, 60, 65, 84*b*, 102–103, 141–142, 160–161, 163, 173, 174–175, 176–178, 182, 190–191, 192–193
   content of, 75, 80–81
   desegregation and, 20, 27, 59, 70–71, 72–74, 81*b*, 84, 85*b*, 134–135, 137, 149
   housing and, 165
   legacy admissions, 78–79, 86*b*
   pipeline of privilege and, 66–68, 85–86, 133, 139*b*
   religion and, 80–81
   school funding, 72
   segregation and, 28, 69–70, 81, 153–154, 158–159, 165
   trends in, 73–74, 75–76
   wealth and, 50, 60, 79–80
Eisenhower, Dwight D., 163
Eitle, David, 170
electoral college, 82, 129–130, 141
Eliot, T. S., 30
Ellison, Marvin, 68
Embiid, Joel, 6
eminent domain, 163, 190

232 Index

emotion, 20, 24, 26
employment, 39, 48, 50, 58–60, 102, 165–166, 176,
    188–189, 193
    discrimination, 14, 38–39, 41–42, 42b, 56
    formerly incarcerated and, 95
    gender and, 57
    hiring and promotion, 18, 20, 41–42, 56, 98
    housing and, 165–167
    nepotism baby effect, 63
    segregation in, 153
    unemployment, 56, 94, 161
England. *See* United Kingdom
Epitaph for Jim Crow, 55, 154, 177b
Epps, Archie, 101
Epstein, Richard, 191
EQUAL Act, 92
Equal Employment Opportunity Commission,
    U.S., 38
equality, 4, 16, 32, 45, 146, 175–176, 187. *See also*
    inequality
ethnography, 86
European Social Survey, 152
Evanston, Illinois, 190–191

Faber, Jacob W., 159
Fair Housing Act, 164–165
family, 63–64
fanaticism, 24
Farrakhan, Louis, 101
Federal Bureau of Investigation (FBI), 96–97
Federal Highway Act, 163–164
Federal Housing Administration (FHA), 157–158,
    160–162, 171
Federalist Society, 77, 79–80, 88
Federal National Mortgage Association (Fannie
    Mae), 67, 160, 162
Federal Reserve, 57, 67
Federal Sentencing Commission, 96
FedEx, 98
fentanyl, 109. *See also* drugs, drug use
Ferguson, Missouri, 96–97
Ferguson, Roger, Jr., 67
Ferraro, Geraldine, 124
Fetterman, John, 132
First Step Act, 92
Fisher, Abigail, 77
Fiske, Susan T., 26
Flint, Michigan, 110
Florida, 75, 80–81, 95, 125–127, 129–130,
    132–133, 177–178, 180
Floyd, George, 3–4, 99–100, 114
Ford Foundation, 75
Forman, James, Jr., 98–100, 103–104
Fox "News," 23, 47, 83, 183
France, 40, 185

Frank, Leo, 55
Frazier, Kenneth, 67
Freedman's Bank, 189
freedom of contract, 158
Freedom Riders, 2, 53
Friedman, John N., 86–87
Frymer, Paul, 37

Gainesville, Florida, 192–193
Garland, Merrick, 92
Garner, Eric, 3–4
Garvey, Marcus, 62
Gates, Bill, 186
Gawronski, Bertram, 13
gender, 3–4. *See also* Black women
    discrimination and, 37–38, 40–41
    education and, 71–72, 74
    employment and, 57
    health and, 106–108, 112, 116–117
    implicit bias and, 13
    politics and, 122, 128, 132–133, 141b
    pipeline of privilege and, 59
    race and, 25, 51–52, 54, 57, 66, 67, 74, 106–108,
        112, 116–117, 122, 133, 167, 176
    stereotype threat and, 39
Gendron, Payton, 23
generational replacement, 17
genetics, 112. *See also* DNA testing
geography, 6
Georgia, 51–52, 54–55, 75, 92–93, 130, 132–133,
    134–135, 141
Germany, 40–41, 142
    General Equal Treatment Act (Allgemeines
        Gleichbehandlungsgesetz - AGG), 40
Geronimus, Arline, 113
gerrymandering, 129, 166
ghetto, 21–22, 115, 157, 164, 166–167, 174
Gibbs, Jewelle, 84–85
G. I. Bill, 160–163, 189, 191
Gibson, Kenneth, 122
Ginsburg, Ruth Bader, 30–31
Gore, Al, 125–126, 129
Great Britain. *See* United Kingdom
Great Depression, 53, 126–127, 159
Great Migration, 65, 170
Green, Eva G. T., 152
*Green v. County School Board of New Kenty
    County, Virginia*, 70
Greenberg, Reuben, 99
Groppi, James, 8
Group Deprovincialization Scale, 31
Group Processes and Intergroup Relations, 151
groups. *See also* contact; contact theory
    contact and, 47, 144–153, 174
    deprovincialism and, 31

Index   233

in *versus* out, 24–26, 30–31, 33, 39, 145
  norms and, 43–48, 152
Grumbach, Jacob M., 37
Guelzo, Allen, 83
Guilkey, David K., 63
guns, gun control, 91, 97, 111
gynecology, 112

Haiti, 6
Haley, Nikki, 141
Hamilton, Darrick, 192
Handel, George Frideric, 30
Harris, Kamala, 133, 139–140, 141–142
Harris, Lasana T., 26
Harris, Leola, 93
Haslam, Nick, 25–26
Hatcher, Richard, 122, 136
hatred, 23–24
Hayes, Rutherford B., 54
Head Start, 75
health, 4–5, 11–12, 14, 19, 28, 105, 165, 166–167,
    173–174, 176, 188–189, 192–193
  discrimination and, 112–117
  housing and, 110, 114–115, 118–119, 165–167,
    174
  medical experimentation, 111–112
  mental health, 111, 113–115
  poverty and, 110, 114–117, 118–119
  trends in, 105–110
healthcare, 106, 114–115
  access to, 116, 166–167
  differential, 116–117
heart disease, 106, 119, 166–167
Heisman Trophy, 29
Helms, Jesse, 129
Helper, Rose, 170*b*
heroin, 104, 109. *See also* drugs, drug use
Hewstone, Miles, 151
highways, 163–164
Hinton, Elizabeth, 100
hiring. *See under* employment
Hispanic Americans, 5–7, 134
  COVID-19 pandemic and, 56, 118
  education and, 79
  in elected office, 128
  employment and, 58–59
  health and, 11
  hiring discrimination and, 56
  housing segregation and, 160, 166–167
  interracial contact and, 145–146
  reparations and, 183
  voting trends, 126, 135
  wealth and, 50, 192
historically Black colleges and universities
    (HBCUs), 73, 76, 186–187

HIV/AIDS, 27, 118
Hoffman, Frederick, 105
Holder, Eric, 6
Holocaust, 55
Holocaust Museum, 186
homelessness, 95, 115, 156, 167, 168, 190
Home Owners Loan Corporation (HOLC), 159
homeownership, 159–161, 163–165, 176, 190
  wealth and, 50–51, 60–61, 166, 188–189
homicide, 105, 111, 119, 167
homosexuality, 48
Hoover Institute, 191
Horton, Willie, 83–84
hostility, 146
housing, 5, 51, 173, 176, 192
  city services and, 167
  class and, 168
  contact and, 167–168, 169–170, 174
  crime and, 165, 167, 174
  differential assessments, 159–165
  discrimination and, 4, 38–39, 50, 60–61, 65,
    102, 120, 165, 174, 179
  dissimilarity index, 169–170
  education and, 165
  employment and, 165–166
  Fair Chance Ordinances, 95
  federal involvement in, 159, 163–164, 168–169
  formerly incarcerated and, 95
  health and, 110, 114–115, 118–119, 165–167,
    174
  military and, 176
  political power and, 165–166
  public, 147–148, 163
  segregation and, 16, 19, 28, 50, 65, 115, 153,
    155–171, 169*b*, 170*b*, 174, 179–180, 186–187,
    188–189, 190–192
  violence and, 164–165
  wealth and, 50–51, 60–61, 65, 165–166,
    174–175, 182, 188–189
  zoning laws and, 158–159
Houston, Charles Hamilton, 162
human relations movement, 147
Hunt, Wesley, 133
Hurts, Jalen, 29
hypertension, 105, 119. *See also* health

Idaho, 124, 177–178
immigration, 22, 31–32, 38–42, 48, 142, 144, 156,
    184
  class and, 63
  contact and, 152
  education and, 72
  employment and, 58–59
  health and, 114
Implicit Association Test (IAT), 13–15

234 Index

incarceration, 28, 51–53, 89–92, 98, 102b, 103–104, 109–110, 115–116, 130–131, 167, 172–174, 176, 187, 190
Indiana, 125–126
indifference, 23, 32
inequality, 15–16, 26, 187
   discrimination and, 33–35, 191
   government intervention in, 18, 187
   wealth, 50, 62–63, 193
infant health, 106, 113, 116–117
influenza, 106–107, 110
Infrastructure Bill, U.S., 181
insurance, 19, 38, 97, 105, 109–110, 116, 160–161, 168–169
insurrection, 114, 128, 172
intentionality, 34
interaction model, 173–175
intersectionality, 7
Iowa, 80, 95, 137–138, 156
Iraq War, 126, 138
Italy, 142, 151

Jackson, Dylan B., 94
Jackson, James, 27
Jackson, Jesse, 27, 124, 133, 137–138
Jackson, Jonathan, 133
Jackson, Ketanji Brown, 67
Jackson, Mississippi, 110, 129
Jackson National Life Insurance Company, 38
Jackson, Thomas ("Stonewall"), 80, 97, 176
James, John, 133
James, Will, 54
Japanese Americans, reparations for, 181, 191
Jarrett, Valerie, 24
Jefferson, Thomas, 112
Jefferson County, Kentucky, 71
Jeffries, Hakeem, 133
Jemmott, John, III, 27
Jewish Americans
   health and, 114
   intergroup contact and, 147
   voting trends, 135
Jim Crow, 1, 28, 54, 102, 103, 172
   "new Jim Crow," 102b, 103, 130
Johnson, Harvey, 122
Johnson, Lyndon B., 64, 81, 83, 122, 134, 179
Joint Committee on Taxation, U.S., 183–184
Jones, James, 27
Jones, René, 68
Jost, John T., 13
J. P. Morgan Chase Bank, 62, 67
Judicial Watch, 191
jury duty, 95, 102

Kahlenberg, Richard, 78

Kain, John F., 166
Kalkstein, David A., 144
Kende, Judit, 151–152
Kendi, Ibram, 33, 54, 172–173
Kennedy, John F., 126–127
Kentucky, 130
Kerry, John, 123, 125–126
Keyes v. School District No. 1, Denver, Colorado, 70
kidney disease, 105, 116–117, 119. *See also* health
Kimberly-Clark, 66
King Kong, 25
King, Martin Luther, Jr., 2, 8b, 23–24, 27, 32, 62, 102, 141
Kleck, Gary, 94
Korean War, 48
Kroll, Bob, 100
Ku Klux Klan (KKK), 53, 129
Kuminga, Jonathan, 6
Kyenge, Cécile, 25

labor unions, 36–42, 44
Lamar, Trey, 129
language, 6, 21–22
larceny, 167
Latinos, Latino Americans. *See* Hispanic Americans
law, 83
   discrimination and, 34–35, 39–42
   racial norms and, 46–47
lead poisoning, 110, 166. *See also* health
Lee, Harper, 75
Lee, Robert E., 3, 80, 83, 176
Lee Academy (Clarksdale, Mississippi), 70
LeFlouria, Talitha, 51–52, 53–54, 172–173, 179, 188–189
Lehman Brothers, 53–54
Lester, Andrew, 25
Levittowns, 161–162
Lewis, John, 27
Lewis, Oscar, 63–64
Lexington, Kentucky, 71
Leyens, Jacques-Philippe, 24
liberalism, 4, 15, 18–19, 34, 37, 42, 52, 120, 125, 190
life expectancy, 105, 116
life sentences, 93
Lincoln, Abraham, 83
literacy, financial, 62
liver disease, 119. *See also* health
Lockheed Martin, 38
Logan, John R., 170
Los Angeles, California, 133, 161, 164–165, 192–193
Louisiana, 52, 54, 81, 92–93, 118, 125
Louisville, Kentucky, 158, 164–165

Index   235

Loving v. Virginia, 176
Lowe's Home Improvement, 68
Lucarini, Alice, 31
lung disease, 105. *See also* health
lynching, 54–55, 83–84, 154, 156, 172, 177, 179.
   See also violence

MacArthur Awards, 27–28, 174, 179
MacInnis, Cara C., 146, 150
MacKinnon, Donald W., 30
macro-aggressions, 113
Madison Trust Company, 186
MAGA (Make America Great Again), 23, 47–48
Mahomes, Patrick, 29
Major League Baseball, 22
Malcolm X, 91, 101*b*
Manchin, Joe, 193
Mannheim, Karl, 126–127
March on Washington, 17
marijuana, 90, 190. *See also* drugs, drug use
marriage, interracial, 16, 19, 47, 176
Marshall, Thurgood, 72, 81, 84–85
Martin, Trayvon, 3–4
Maryland, 132–133
   Harriet Tubman Community Investment Act,
      190
Massachusetts, 124, 133, 168
Massey, Douglas S., 155, 169–170
maternal health, 107–108, 113, 117
McCain, John, 124–126, 138
McCarthy, Joseph, 165
McConnell, Mitch, 184–185
McEwan, Bruce S., 113–114
McGhee, Heather, 19, 37
McKay, Claude, 6
McNutt, Marcia, 41
Medicaid, Medicare, 19, 116–117
melanoma, 105, 108
Merck Pharmaceuticals, 67
methadone, 109. *See also* addiction
Metropolitan Life Insurance Company, 168–169
Mexico, 63, 142
Miami, Florida, 158
Michigan, 127, 133
micro-aggressions, 120
Mikva, Abner, 102–103
Miles, Eleanor, 145
military, 48*b*, 148, 175–176
Miller, Stephen, 188
Milliken v. Bradley, 71
Minard, Ralph D., 44–45
mindfulness, 22, 31–32
mindlessness, 22, 29–30
Minneapolis Police Officers Federation, 100
Minow, Martha, 72

Mississippi, 53, 55, 116, 125, 128–130, 162
Mitchell, Gregory, 5
Monk, Conley, 162
Moore, Wes, 128, 132–133
Morgan, Garrett, 28–29
Mortgage Bankers Association, 164
mortgages, 160–162, 164, 179, 190
Moses, Pamela, 128
motivated disbelief, 154
Moyd, Olinda, 96
Moynihan, Daniel Patrick, 64
Muhammad, Khalil, 90, 100
Mullen, A. Kirsten, 185–186
multiculturalism, 31
Muslims, 147
Mutombo, Dikembe, 6
Myrdal, Gunnar, 85, 90

NAACP, 17
   Legal Defense and Education Fund, 69, 81,
      111–112
National Academy of Science, 41
National Basketball Association, 29
National Bureau of Economic Research, 52, 74,
   78, 117
National Center for Health Statistics, 107–108
National Football League, 29
National Labor Relations Board, 37
National Memorial for Peace and Justice, 55
National Opinion Research Center (NORC), 135
   General Social Survey, 15–16
National Urban League, 17, 32
nationalism, 31
Nation of Islam, 101–102
Native Americans, 7
   in elected office, 128
   health and, 11
   housing segregation and, 160
   police and, 100
   reparations for, 180–181
neighborhood effect, 167
Netherlands, 38–39, 40–41
New Deal, 189
New Jersey, 140, 162, 168
New Mexico, 125–126
New Orleans, Louisiana, 155, 192–193
New York City, 95, 124, 170, 192–193
New York state, 126, 162
New York Times, 4, 17, 28–29, 103, 138
   1619 Project, 172–173, 183
New Zealand, 113–114
Nichols, Tyre, 3–4, 98
Nixon, Richard, 62, 64, 70, 83–84
Nobel Prize, 41
Noonan, Allan S., 111

236 Index

norms, normativity, 33–35, 42–46, 176
  behavior and, 47–48
  formal, 43
  informal, 43
  intergroup, 152
  law and, 46–47
  in military, 48*b*
  personality and, 46
North Carolina, 97–98, 125–126, 132–133
  Agricultural and Technical College, 9
North Dakota, 129–130
Norway, 106, 185
nostalgia, 48

Obama, Barack, 3–4, 14, 19, 21, 68, 77–78, 83–84,
    116, 122–123, 124–127, 133, 137, 137*b*, 139,
    175, 188, 191–192
Obama, Michelle, 66, 68, 125, 133, 139, 191–192
obesity, 13, 116
objectivity, 85–86
O'Connor, Sandra Day, 104
Ohio, 75, 133
Oklahoma, 161, 177–178, 180
Olajuwon, Hakeem, 6
Omaha, Nebraska, 156
openness, 31
opioid epidemic, 108
optimism, 4
O'Rourke, Beto, 132
overcrowding, 157–158, 166
Oxfam International, 186

Page-Gould, Elizabeth, 146, 150
Pakistan, 151
Palin, Sarah, 124–125, 138
Panama, 44
Parchman Prison (Mississippi), 53
Parkinson's disease, 105
Parks, Rosa, 1–2
parole and probation, 93–95. *See also*
    incarceration
Paterson, David, 128
Patrick, Deval, 128
payday loans, 62
Peace Corps, 85
Pelosi, Nancy, 133
Pennsylvania, 127, 132–133
people of color, 21–22, 94, 143
perpetuation theory, 59
Perry, Andre M., 182
personality, 46
Pettigrew, Ann Hallman, 9–10
Pettigrew, Thomas F., 144–145, 151–152
Pew Research Center, 17, 21, 130–131, 147, 187
Pfizer Pharmaceutical Corporation, 41

Phagan, Mary, 55
phenylketonuria, 105
Philadelphia, Pennsylvania, 93, 95
Picasso, Pablo, 30
Pickett, George, 176
pipeline of privilege, 59–60, 66*b*, 74, 77, 79–80,
    85–86, 133, 139*b*
Plessy v. Ferguson, 69, 71
pluralistic ignorance, 46–47
pneumonia, 106–107
Poitier, Sidney, 6
Poland, 106
polarization, 28
police, 9–10, 20, 103, 120, 131, 147, 149, 164, 187
  Asian American police officers, 99–100
  Black police officers, 98–100
  murders of Black Americans, 3–4, 22, 93–94,
      96–100, 176
  racial profiling, 12, 38, 103, 113, 116, 173, 174
  stop-and-search procedures, 97–98
  violence and, 37, 96–100, 131
politics, 3–5, 13, 21, 122, 134, 137*b*, 139*b*, 141*b*,
    173–174, 176, 188
  class and, 141–142, 173
  discrimination and, 34
  economics and, 138, 141–142
  gender and, 128, 132–133, 141*b*
  government intervention in racial
      discrimination, 18, 21
  housing and, 165–166
  nostalgic, 48, 56
  power and, 34, 129–130, 133, 165–166
  voting trends, 122–133, 135*b*
polls, polling, 16–18, 21, 123, 125–126, 131–132,
    137–138, 186
pollution, 110, 118–119, 166
Portugal, 106
post-racism, 4, 122–127, 137, 175
poverty, 28, 56, 58–59, 65–66, 110, 112, 114–117,
    118–119, 174, 176, 183, 189, 193
  culture of, 63–64
Powell, Adam Clayton, Jr., 27
Powell, Colin, 6, 176
Pratto, Felicia, 27
predatory loans, 163, 168–169, 186–187
prejudice, 22–26, 29*b*, 32, 39, 43, 50, 165
  contact and, 144–153, 154*b*, 167–168
  discrimination and, 33
  norms and, 44–45
prescription medications, 109, 117
progress, 2–3, 5, 26–28, 175
Project Implicit, 15
promotion. *See under* employment
protest, 2, 9–10, 17
provincialism, 22, 29–31

Prude, Daniel, 3–4, 96–97
Prudential Life Insurance Company, 105
psychiatric disorders, 111, 115
psychology, social, 8*b*, 12–13, 14–15, 20–22,
    26–28, 34, 39, 45, 46–47, 86, 99, 142,
    144–145, 147–149, 151–152. *See also* contact
    theory
public accommodation, 38
public benefits, 102
Public Broadcasting System, 55

race
  age and, 3–6, 17
  attitudes about, 15–22
  changes in, 3–4
  city services and, 167
  class and, 3, 5, 19, 21, 36, 57, 65, 73, 91, 99, 103,
    114, 116–117, 136–137, 160–162, 167, 173,
    176, 191–192
  contact and, 5, 20–22, 42, 47, 143–153, 154*b*,
    167–168, 173, 176, 182
  crime and criminal justice system and, 28,
    89–104, 102*b*, 103*b*, 165, 167, 173–174, 176,
    187
  discrimination and, 33–42, 42*b*, 43, 50–55
  economics and, 28, 49–68, 66*b*, 176
  education and, 28, 59–60, 65, 66–69, 70–88,
    81*b*, 84*b*, 85*b*, 86*b*, 103, 133, 139*b*, 160–161,
    163, 165, 173, 174, 176, 177–178, 182, 187,
    190, 191–192
  employment and, 14, 15, 18, 20, 38–39, 41–42,
    42*b*, 48, 50, 56–60, 94, 165–167, 176, 188–189
  gender and, 25, 51–52, 54, 57, 66, 67, 74,
    106–108, 112, 116–117, 122, 133, 167, 176
  geography and, 6
  health and, 4–5, 11–12, 14, 19, 28, 105–119,
    120*b*, 165–167, 173–174, 176, 188–189, 192
  housing and, 5, 16, 19, 28, 38–39, 50–51, 60–61,
    65, 95, 102, 110, 114, 115, 118–120, 147–148,
    153, 155–171, 169*b*, 170*b*, 173–174, 176,
    179–180, 182, 192
  implicit bias and, 12–13, 14–15
  norms and, 43–48, 48*b*, 176
  politics and, 3–5, 13, 18, 21, 34, 48, 56, 122–134,
    135*b*, 137*b*, 139*b*, 141*b*, 165–166, 173–174,
    176, 188
  progress and, 2–3, 5, 26–28
  religion and, 6, 17, 26–27, 101–102
  stereotype threat and, 39
  wealth and, 21, 49–52, 53–54, 57–58, 60–64,
    79–80, 163, 165–166, 173–176, 182–183,
    185–186, 188–189, 192
Racial Justice Project, 103
racism, 2–5, 7–9, 28, 172–175, 176–178
  biological, 15–16

  conformity and, 42
  coping with, 26–27
  "costs everyone," 19, 37, 84, 134
  defining, 7
  individual, 7
  interpersonal, 7
  progress and, 175
  across societal institutions, 174
  structural, 7
railroad, 1
Rasmussen Reports, 23
Ray, Rashawn, 182
Readjustment Benefits Act, 161
Reagan, Ronald, 83–84, 112, 127
real estate, 19, 60–61, 157–159, 162, 164, 168–169,
    171, 190. *See also* banks; housing
recidivism, 94–96
Red Scare, 156
Red Summer, 156
redlining, 158–159, 165–167, 179, 186–187, 189
religion, 6, 17, 26–27, 71–72, 80–81, 101–102
reparations, 18, 62–63, 65–66, 156–157, 175, 177,
    179–183, 185–193
  arguments against, 183–185
Reparations Act, 181
Republican Party, 15, 21, 52, 54, 71, 75, 77, 80,
    83–84, 95, 123, 125–127, 129–135, 138, 141,
    183–184, 193
resentment, 23
restrictive covenants, 161–162, 189
Reuther, Walter, 36
Reynolds Metal Company, 42
Rich, Frank, 138–139
Richeson, Jennifer, 26–28
Richmond, Virginia, 71, 158–159, 164, 170
riots, 156, 164–165, 172
Rittenhouse, Kyle, 18
robbery, 167
Roberts, John, 77–78
Rochester, New York, 96–97
Rock, Chris, 143
Rockefeller Foundation, 135
Roe v. Wade, 77, 117
Roelandt, Truus, 38–39
Romas, 38
Romney, Mitt, 193
roommate studies, 145–146
Roosevelt, Franklin D., 57, 126–127, 160, 189
Rosewood, Florida, massacre in, 12, 180
Rothstein, Richard, 159, 168–169
Rudd Center for Food and Policy Health
    (University of Connecticut), 115
Russia, 40, 156

Sacerdote, Bruce, 146

238 Index

Sahin, Ugur, 41
Sam's Club, 66
Sanchez, Kiara L., 144
Sanders, Deion, 29
Sanders, Sarah Huckabee, 80
San Francisco, California, 159
savings, 62
Schofield, Janet, 86
Schuman, Howard, 15
Scott, Timothy, 140–141
Seattle, Washington, 71
segregation, 1–2, 9–10, 21–22, 29–30, 43–44,
    85–86, 90, 98, 102, 125
  contact and, 20, 146–149, 151, 153
  education and, 12, 16, 20, 27, 28, 45, 59, 65,
    67–68, 69–74, 81, 84, 133, 134–135, 137, 139,
    154, 158–159, 165
  healthcare and, 116
  housing and, 16, 28, 50, 59, 65, 115, 147–148,
    153, 155–171, 169b, 170b, 179–180, 186–187,
    188–189, 190–192
  military and, 148, 176
Sellin, Thorsten, 90
Selma, Alabama, 8
Selye, Hans, 113
sentencing. *See* crime, criminal justice system
septicemia, 105, 119
Service Employees International Unions (SEIU),
  37
sexism, 4, 57
sexuality, attitudes about, 15
Shakespeare, William, 24
Shelley v. Kraemer, 162
Sherman, William, 189
Shreveport, Louisiana, 192–193
Sibley, Chris G., 22
Sidanius, Jim, 27, 145–146
Sims, James Marion, 112
sit-in, 2, 9–10. *See also* protest
60 Minutes, 156–157
skin tone, attitudes about, 15
slavery, 25–28, 33, 51–52, 53–54, 64–65, 75,
    80–82, 84, 102, 112, 116, 129–130, 155,
    172–173, 175, 180, 182–183, 184–185, 187,
    189–190, 191–192
Slovakia, 106
Smith, Brewster, 85
Smith, Jaylen, 133
social constructs, 13
Social Darwinism, 146
social domain, 3, 5
social dominance orientation (SDO), 22, 27, 31
social sciences, 4, 7, 12, 21–22, 34, 64, 71, 83, 179
  quantitative, 86
  value and, 85–86

Social Security Act, 57, 189
social work, 84–85
Society for the Psychological Study of Social
  Issues, 8
sociology, 7, 35
South Africa, 2, 46, 72, 113–114, 151
South Carolina, 9–10, 129, 137–138, 140–141, 189
Southern Poverty Law Center, 164–165
Spain, 185
St. Louis, Missouri, 192–193
St. Paul, Minnesota, 192–193
Stalin, Joseph, 52
Starbucks, 37, 66
states' rights, 83–84
Steeh, Charlotte, 15
Steele, Claude, 27
Stellar, Eliot, 113–114
stereotype, 22, 28–29
stereotype content model, 26
stereotype threat, 27, 39
stigma, 39, 109
stock market, 62, 189
Stockton, California, 192–193
Stokes, Carl, 122, 136–137
Stouffer, Samuel, 9, 148
stress, 39, 113–114, 115–116, 120b. *See also*
  health; weathering
stroke, 105, 119
Stuart, John Ewell Brown ("Jeb"), 80
student loans, 57, 79–80, 184, 191
student movement, 9–10
Students for Fair Admissions, Inc. v. Harvard,
  77–78
subprime mortgages, 19
suburbs, 161–162, 164, 166
suicide, 13, 105, 111
Sumner, William Graham, 146
Sunak, Rishi, 4
Superfund toxic waste sites, 115, 166
Supreme Court, U.S., 57, 67, 71, 77–81, 84–88,
  92–93, 98, 102–104, 117, 128–129, 158, 162,
  175, 176, 191
*Swann v. Charlotte-Mecklenburg Board of
  Education*, 70
Sweden, 40–41
swimming pools, 19
Switzerland, 185
syphilis, 111–112, 116

Taeuber, Karl E. and Alma F., 169
Taney, Roger, 82
Tarzan, 25
taxes, 72, 168, 183–184, 185–186
Taylor, Breonna, 3–4
Taylor, Keeanga-Yamattha, 164

Index 239

Taylor, Steven, 27
Teachers Insurance and Annuity Association of
America, 67
Teamsters Union, 36–37
Tennessee, 75, 128, 130, 177–178
Tetlock, Philip E., 5
Texas, 52, 94, 118, 130, 132–133
textbooks, 80–81
Thatcher, Margaret, 4
Thomas, Stephanie, 133
Thompson, Bennie, 128
Tierney, John, 4
Till, Emmett, 55
tobacco, 111
tolerance, 43, 152
Toyota, 38
Treasury, U.S., 57, 183–184
Tropp, Linda, 144–145, 149, 151–152
Truman, Harry S., 48, 163
Trump, Donald, 4, 15, 21, 23, 25, 47–48, 57,
59–60, 77, 82–84, 127, 138, 141*b*, 165, 172,
183–184, 188
tuberculosis, 110, 166
Tulsa, Oklahoma, massacre, 156, 180
Tureci, Ozlem, 41
Turkey, 41
Tuskegee Syphilis Study, 111–112, 190
Twain, Mark, 30
Tyson, Cicely, 6

U.S. Steel Corporation, 53–54, 188–189
Ukraine, 40
United Auto Workers, 37, 168–169
United Kingdom, 38, 142
Commission for Racial Equality, 40–41
universal basic income, 104, 192–193
Urban Institute, 64

values, 85–86
Van Assche, Jasper, 145, 153*b*
Vance, JD, 142
Van Tol, Jesse, 189
Veenman, J., 38–39
Velasco-Mondragon, Hector Eduardo, 111
Veterans' Administration (VA), 161–162, 189. *See
also* military
Veterans Legal Services Clinic, 162
victim blaming, 20, 23, 112, 137
Villarosa, Linda, 113
violence, 24–25, 53, 84, 90, 96, 102, 123–124,
156–157, 167–169
non-violence, 2, 18
police and, 37, 96, 99–100
by White racists, 18, 23, 124, 156–157, 164–165

Violent Crime Control and Law Enforcement Act,
91
Virginia, 69, 83, 125–126, 134–135, 190
voting, 28, 95, 102, 122–124, 125–130, 134*b*, 188
age and, 125, 127, 130–132
suppression of, 128–130, 134
Voting Rights Act, 83, 122, 130, 134*b*, 137

Wagner, Fernando A., 111
Wales, 38
Walker, Darren, 75
Wall Street Journal, 4, 121
Walmart, 62, 66
Walters, Ryan, 156
Walton, Gregory M., 144
Ward, Charlie, 29
war on drugs, 89–91, 93, 103–104
Warnock, Ralph, 141
Washington, Harriet, 112
Washington Post, 96–97, 118, 156
wealth, 21, 49–52, 53–54, 57–58, 60–64, 163,
165–166, 173, 175–176, 182–183, 185,
188–189, 192
class and, 173
education and, 79–80
housing and, 50–51, 60–61, 65, 165–166,
174–175, 182, 188–189
taxes on, 185–186
weathering, 113–114, 116. *See also* health
Weber, Shirley, 133
welfare queen, 83–84
Well, Caroline, 156
West Indies, 6, 63, 114, 182
Westmoreland, Lynn, 125
West Virginia, 59
White Americans
class and, 116–117, 136–137, 160–161, 191
COVID-19 pandemic and, 56, 118–119
criminal justice system and, 90, 93–94, 97–98,
109, 115–116
desegregation and, 70–71, 72–75
drug use and, 108–109
education and, 73–74, 79, 84–85, 86*b*, 116,
158–159, 160–161, 163
employment and, 63
explicit racial attitudes, 15–20
family and, 64
health and, 105–108, 110–111, 114–116,
117–119
housing segregation and, 157–158, 159–160,
161–163, 164–165, 168–169
interracial contact and, 143–144, 145–148, 152,
154*b*
misperceptions of Black Americans, 20–22, 28*b*
norms and, 43–46

240 Index

White Americans (*Continued*)
  pipeline of privilege and, 59–60, 85–86
  police and, 100
  prejudice and, 22–23, 24–26, 32
  racism and, 4, 19, 37, 84, 134
  reparations and, 182–184, 189, 191–192
  violence and, 18, 23, 124, 156–157, 164–165
  voting trends, 122–123, 125–127, 132–133,
    135*b*, 137–138
  wealth and, 49–52, 57, 60–61, 62–63, 163, 192
White Citizens' Councils, 70
White flight, 70–71
White House Task Force on Education, 134
White Lion, 172
White supremacy, 3, 28, 54–55, 59–60, 70, 72, 84,
  102, 124, 129
Wilder, Douglas, 128
Wildfires, 114
Williams, David R., 114–115, 166
Williams, Robin, 148
Wilmington, Delaware, 71

Wilson, William Julius, 56
Wilson, Woodrow, 56–57, 130–131, 156
Wisconsin, 118
women's rights, 122
Woolworth, 10
Work Opportunity Tax Credit (WOTC), 95
Worth, Louis, 171
Wright, Daunte, 3–4
Wright, Jeremiah, 124
Wyoming, 130

Xerox, 66

Yarl, Ralph, 25
Young, Whitney, Jr., 32
Youngkin, Glenn, 75, 83

Zax, Jeffrey S., 166
Zeitlin, Jide, 68
zero-sum thinking, 18–19, 23, 36
zoning ordinances, 158–159, 168
Zuckerberg, Mark, 62–63